Obeah, Orisa, and Religious Identity in Trinidad

Volume I

Religious Cultures of African
and African Diaspora People

SERIES EDITORS

Jacob K. Olupona, *Harvard University*
Dianne M. Stewart, *Emory University*
& Terrence L. Johnson, *Georgetown University*

The book series examines the religious, cultural, and political expressions of African,
African American, and African Caribbean
traditions. Through transnational, cross-
cultural, and multidisciplinary approaches to
the study of religion, the series investigates
the epistemic boundaries of continental and
diasporic religious practices and thought
and explores the diverse and distinct ways
African-derived religions inform culture and
politics. The series aims to establish a forum
for imagining the centrality of Black religions
in the formation of the "New World."

TRACEY E. HUCKS

Obeah,

VOLUME I
OBEAH

Orisa

&

Religious Identity in Trinidad

Africans in the White Colonial Imagination

DUKE UNIVERSITY PRESS—DURHAM AND LONDON—2022

Printed in the United States of America on acid-free paper ∞
Designed by Aimee C. Harrison
Typeset in Quadraat Pro and Avenir LT Std
by Westchester Publishing Services

Library of Congress Cataloging-in-Publication Data
Names: Hucks, Tracey E., [date] author.
Title: Obeah, Orisa, and religious identity in Trinidad. Volume I,
Obeah : Africans in the white colonial imagination / Tracey E. Hucks.
Other titles: Obeah : Africans in the white colonial imagination |
Religious cultures of African and African diaspora people.
Description: Durham : Duke University Press, 2022. | Series:
Religious cultures of African and African diaspora people | Includes
bibliographical references and index.
Identifiers: LCCN 2022020342 (print) | LCCN 2022020343 (ebook)
ISBN 9781478013914 (hardcover)
ISBN 9781478014850 (paperback)
ISBN 9781478022145 (ebook)
Subjects: LCSH: Obeah (Cult)—Trinidad and Tobago—Trinidad—
History. | Religion and sociology—Trinidad and Tobago—Trinidad—
History. | Religions—African influences. | Black people—Trinidad
and Tobago—Trinidad—Religion—History. | Cults—Law and
legislation—Trinidad and Tobago—Trinidad—History. | Religion and
law—Trinidad and Tobago—Trinidad—History. | Postcolonialism—
Trinidad and Tobago—Trinidad. | BISAC: RELIGION / General |
SOCIAL SCIENCE / Black Studies (Global)
Classification: LCC BL2532.O23 H835 2022 (print) | LCC BL2532.O23
(ebook) | DDC 299.6/70972983—dc23/eng/20220729
LC record available at https://lccn.loc.gov/2022020342
LC ebook record available at https://lccn.loc.gov/2022020343

ISBN 9781478092780 (ebook other)

Cover art: Page from a Trinidad colonial slave register reprinted
by permission from National Archives (of the United Kingdom).
Photograph of procession reprinted by permission from the
Adefundara Foundation.

To Perla A. Holder, who taught me from the best of Trinidad's tradition of excellence.

To Kestor Loney, my classmate and friend who left the world too soon. I will always remember your dream of someday becoming the prime minister of Trinidad and Tobago.

&

Always to my parents, Doretha Leary Hucks and Joseph Richard Hucks, who walked this earth with dignity, integrity, and the love of family.

Contents

Preface

Obeah, Orisa, and Religious Identity in Trinidad is a collaborative study, the fruition of an idea that germinated in the plush accommodations of the Hotel Nacional de Cuba in Havana, Cuba, during the spring of 1994. Dianne Stewart and I were attending El Segundo Encuentro Internacional Yoruba, an international conference on Yoruba religion, and among the panelists was Iyalorisa Dr. Molly Ahye, an Orisa priestess from Trinidad and Tobago. We had read about Trinidad's Yoruba tradition of "Shango" in books by George Simpson and his mentor Melville Herskovits, who received a grant of $3,250 from the Carnegie Corporation to conduct research in Trinidad in 1939, but we had much to learn about the richness of Trinidad's Yoruba diaspora. We were determined to do so after meeting Molly Ahye.

Iya Molly lectured on the Yoruba-Orisa religion in Trinidad and Tobago. In addition to describing the ritual and ceremonial life of the Orisa community, she discussed Orisa devotees' struggle for religious freedom, a struggle they seemed to be winning—at least to a much greater degree than their counterparts in other regions of the African diaspora. By the end of our trip, we began to envision a womanist approach of "harmonizing and coordinating" our scholarly efforts to co-produce a volume on the Orisa religion in Trinidad and the role of women in the tradition's transformation during the latter decades of the twentieth century.[1] We were graduate students at the time and knew this book idea would be a future project for both of us.

We made our first research trip to Trinidad in December 1998 and over two decades conducted archival and field research that resulted in not one but two volumes, which we both expected and did not expect. Our two-volume project, as the title suggests, expanded beyond a focus on Orisa to incorporate a study of Obeah, an opaque repertoire of African spiritual systems that has been practiced throughout the Caribbean and regions of the Americas. In our first monographs, I wrote about Orisa and Dianne about Obeah; in this case, we switched subjects, because I was better suited to address the historical framing of Obeah in early colonial Trinidad. We determined, too, that Dianne was better suited to explore how Orisa devotees intellectualize and make meaning out of their beliefs and spirituality. In this endeavor, Dianne addresses our original aim for this project by engaging womanist and feminist discourses to examine institutional developments within the Orisa tradition and shifts in both internal and external narratives of Orisa presence and practice in post-1980s Trinidad. During this period Molly Ahye and other contemporary Orisa mothers held prominence as local and global leaders in this rapidly changing religious culture, and we discovered that a proper treatment of their contributions required Dianne to flesh out other pertinent themes. Thus, volume II expanded into a study of the religious imagination and sacred poetics of African descendants—"Yaraba" *nation-builders*, Black Power sacred scientists, and women-mothers—in Trinidad who over a century and a half have held together "a moving continuity" they have called "Ebo," "the Yaraba Dance," "Yaraba Work," "African Work," "Orisa Work," "Shango," "Ifa," and "Orisa."[2]

While the project unfolded, we developed new perspectives as a result of our wider scholarly activities. We also offered direction to the field of black religious studies, especially through our 2013 article, "Africana Religious Studies: Toward a Transdisciplinary Agenda in an Emerging Field," which appeared in the inaugural issue of the *Journal of Africana Religions*. In that article we revisited the Herskovits/Frazier debate, its cultural and ideological context, and its impact on theoretical and methodological norms in the scholarship of academics trained in black religious studies/theology. We specifically explored roughly seventy-five years of knowledge production that, with few exceptions, had reduced black religion to black church studies and black Christian theology. Far too many works had missed opportunities to conceptualize black people's African religious heritage. The scholarship gave little attention to the "image of Africa" in the black religious imagination, limiting our understanding of the polyreligious and polycultural realities that indeed characterized the spiritual lives of enslaved Africans in the United States and elsewhere.[3] We concluded our article by providing some of the conceptual architecture and theoretical justifications for transdisciplinary Africana religious studies research as a way forward in twenty-first-century scholarship on African-descended peoples—their religions and cultures—in the Americas and the Caribbean.

While seeking to enrich Caribbean and Africana studies, we imagine this project as a contribution to a developing body of research in religious studies on the methodology we began to formulate in our 2013 article. I approached the archives with the intention of examining Obeah as an assemblage of Africana sacred practices and cosmologies.[4] Instead, what I unearthed in the archives on Trinidad was a colonial cult of obeah fixation operating as a lived religion.[5] Our most salient definition of religion in this project rests within the tradition of Charles H. Long. For Longians, religion is "orientation in the ultimate sense, that is, how one comes to terms with the ultimate significance of one's place in the world."[6] The colonial cult of obeah fixation "comes to terms" with its "place in the world" through imaginations and persecutions of Obeah/African religions. In the colonial imagination, obeah functions as *cultus* (derived from the Latin words "to inhabit," "habitation," "toiling over something"; variant stem of *colere*, meaning "till"—the Old English word for station, fixed point).

With this etymology in mind, *cultus* encompasses the concept of inhabiting a fixed point. I discovered a singular and fixed approach to Obeah in the colonial archives that reduced it to an imaginary terrorizing supernatural blackness. African Obeah was virtually eclipsed by colonial obeah, a set of beliefs, rites, practices, and meanings mapped onto an imaginary enfleshed terror—the black body. Within this fixed orientation, ridding colonial Trinidad of obeah became of vital (and violent) significance to its civic, social, and public tapestry. Such devotion is what bound members of the colonial cult of obeah fixation one to another. Volume I courageously interprets the cult's lived religion by taking up the topic of obeah and African religious repression. Thus, refracted through a chronological account of African religious repression (volume I, authored by Tracey E. Hucks) and struggles for religious freedom (volume II, authored by Dianne M. Stewart), our study of Trinidad attends to the problem of religious identity as an outgrowth of colonial "racecraft":[7] it excavates the authentic religious identity of colonial whites and offers a textured theoretical interpretation of Africana religion as a healing modality that has provided blacks with authenticating narratives, identities, and modes of belonging. Bridging phenomenology of religion, indigenous hermeneutics,[8] and black affect theory, our interpretation pioneers an affective turn in Africana Religious Studies and underscores haunting insights of Afropessimist and black nihilist conversations that never lose sight of the black "death-bound-subject."[9]

Equally significant, our volumes contribute to the wider fields of religion and Africana/black studies in several respects: First, through explorations of colonial obeah, African Obeah, and Orisa, they excavate the phenomenon of relationality to expand the definitional and theoretical terrain for conceptualizing religion as sites of black care *and* black harm. An analytic of relationality has considerable implications for the broader study of religion.[10] It provides a lens for investigating contacts, interactions, and exchanges among and across seen and unseen persons/entities. Whether within the context of religious traditions or within social structures broadly speaking, relationality is an indispensable guiding category for assessing intimacies that reveal and conceal individuals' and groups' authentic religion. Our collaborative study demonstrates that although orientation is the first step in the creation of a religious ethos, it is relationality that sustains a religious ethos and actually gives rise to religion, whether that religion is established through intimate care, intimate terrorism, or something else. Orientation determines positionings and suggests locative awareness while relationality operationalizes the perceptions and affects that substantiate them. Considering the singularity of whites' collective soul-life, we take seriously William James's designation of religion as "the feelings, acts and experiences of individual[s] . . . so far as they apprehend themselves to stand *in relation to* what-ever they may consider divine."[11] This understanding of religion accords with our privileging of affect and its mobilizing power in the making of religion. Interpreting colonial affects, however, led us to conclude that what white colonists considered divine was the image of themselves tethered to the mutilated black body; and the black body was a divine mirror of the white soul—the sacred fetish whites needed and created to live, breathe, and have their being. Sadly, as innovative as James was in theorizing religion, he was terribly shortsighted in his impoverished understanding of African religions. Our study both invalidates James's shortsightedness and embraces his privileging of affects, experiences, and relationality which help us to interrogate dimensions of religiosity that James himself could not perceive, namely *white racecraft as lived religion.*[12]

Second, and relatedly, in its investigation of the white colonial imagination our study offers a new theoretical interpretation of lived religion. Third, using indigenous hermeneutics, it theorizes *nationhood* in the Americas and the Caribbean as an autonomous Africana index of identity. Fourth, it contributes to Africana Religious Studies a foundational methodological imperative and method of applying indigenous hermeneutics within comparative assessments of African and African diasporic cultures/religions. Fifth, it elevates the Africana concept of *work* as a religious studies category for ritual practice and spiritual intervention. Sixth, it advances a mode of theological reflection that privileges religious imagination and cultural values rather than systematic approaches to doctrine. Seventh, its analysis of white colonial responses to African heritage religions and its interrogation of the religious nature of antiblackness establish a new point of departure for theorizing white libidinal power. Eighth, it connects threads of continuity among African and African diasporic womanisms and feminisms through the non-gendered Africana concept of *motherness* and establishes an arena within Africana/black studies for further comparisons of womanist and feminist intellectual lineages.

Book-length studies on Trinidadian Obeah and Orisa are still quite sparse, but to our knowledge, anthropologists and other social scientists have produced them. To help balance the growing number of important ethnographies that focus on Orisa ceremonies and rituals, and to expose the religious dimensions of white colonial power, we emphasize what religious studies scholars are trained to examine: the symbols, originary narratives (myths), performances, practices, rituals, and experiences that orient religious persons as they confront limits and shape possibilities for themselves. As scholars in the humanities—a trained historian of religion and a theologian—we treat interiority perhaps as much as we do the exterior worlds of the figures and personalities the reader will meet throughout each volume. Privileging their sacred poetics and self-narrations whenever possible, we offer what we believe is a new way to think about black religion, black religious imagination, black love, and religious belonging in the African diaspora.

Bringing this project to completion involved numerous field trips to Trinidad between 1998 and 2013 and one continuous year of ethnographic fieldwork (2000–2001), during which we visited Orisa shrines across the nation; frequented rituals, ceremonies, and educational workshops; and conducted more than forty interviews and two oral histories. Our research also involved combing through disparate sets of archives in Trinidad, Nigeria, Cuba, Jamaica, France, England, and the United States. Most of these trips were undertaken to conduct archival research at the National Archives of Trinidad and Tobago; Heritage Library of Trinidad and Tobago; University of the West Indies, Mona, Jamaica; University of the West Indies, St. Augustine, Trinidad; Bibliothèque Nationale de France; Bibliothèque du Saulchoir; British Library; National Archives in Kew Gardens; Lambeth Palace Library; School of Oriental and African Studies, University of London; Northwestern University Archives; and Schomburg Center for Research in Black Culture. We also gained access to Hansard Reports, bills, and acts of Parliament from the Parliament of the Republic of Trinidad and Tobago, as well as unpublished correspondence, minutes, devotional literature, and educational materials at various Orisa shrines in Trinidad. Nonetheless, although we believe both volumes reflect our careful historical and ethnographic work on Obeah and Orisa, they are not intended to be comprehensive histories or ethnographies of these traditions. Rather, they bear witness to the dynamic endurance of African heritage religions among Trinidad's pluralistic black diasporas, identifying Africa as the epistemic source of an enduring spiritual legacy and potent religious orientation across three centuries. This theoretical move propitiously anticipates productive scholarly frameworks in the future of Obeah and Orisa studies. But it also demands a sea change in how scholars analyze global antiblackness and account for the foundational pillars of religions in the Americas and the Caribbean.

Tracey E. Hucks and Dianne M. Stewart

Acknowledgments

Throughout my journey with this project, several colleagues have asked me how I was able to navigate the terror, violence, and torture that emerged from the colonial annals of Trinidad. The terror of the archives was indeed palpable, yet beneath the terror were real persons, now ancestors, whose lives had been imperiled under Euro-colonial assault, whose spiritual gifts to cure, heal, and divine were suppressed, whose eyes and spirits had to bear witness to the vileness and violence of white colonists, whose innocence had been negated, and whose stories lay stifled amidst imperial scripts. They helped me to rescue and to uncover their names, their voiced and voiceless fates, their attempts at resistance, their dignity in the face of colonial subjugation, all while permitting me spaces of reverence and compassion to shed tears in their honor and for the barbarity of their fates. For this, I acknowledge first and foremost: Polydore, Pierre, Bouqui, Leonard, Thisbe/Kitsimba, Felix, Jean Louis, La Rose, Noel, Antoine, La Fortune, Aubinot, Yala, Youba, Teotis, Robineau, Dosou, Joseph Faustin, Michael Gordon, Goliah, Manuel, Salveste, Andres, Fara, Cattherina, Louison, Pedro, Ginny, Hou Quervee (John Cooper), and Abojevi Zahwenu (Mah Nannie) for speaking through the archives, for defying the silence, for persevering against historical erasure.

In the Yoruba-Orisa tradition—Ibeji, the Twins—are sacred and a sign of good fortune to come. The Ibeji share one soul but enter the world as two separate entities. Such is the case of this two-volume study on Trinidad: volume I is *Taiwo*, sent into the world to see if it is safe. Volume II is *Kehendi*, the next to arrive in the *creactive* birthing sequence. In an academic discipline that privileges solitude of the scholar and the singularity of contributions to knowledge, I want to thank Dianne Marie Stewart for daring to trust in the power of womanist collaboration. Dianne's late teacher and mentor, Dr. James Cone once urged in a speech to black scholars, "Don't let it be said that you did not do your best intellectual work"—Together we do our best intellectual work and gift our intellectual offerings to Africana Religious Studies.

I give special acknowledgment to Iya Sangowumni (Patricia McCloud) who professed, "You both would have laid in my womb at some incarnation. That is why you are such good sisters one to another. Whenever children are returned to you, gather them, help elevate them, and love them, so that I can be blessed and so can you, for us finding each other again." I am honored to call her spiritual mother.

On behalf of both of us, Dianne has in volume II graciously undertaken the obligation of thanking in detail the many Trinidadian colleagues, comrades, and omorisa who supported us in the great endeavors of this research project over the course of our many visits. To this list, I add my own recognition of Rawle Gibbons and Funso Aiyejina who, like Dianne and me, value intellectual collaboration. I am especially indebted to the Walker family who opened their hearts to me as daughter, sister, "Mumzy," "Aunty," "Queen." Furthermore, this volume would not be possible were in not for Iya Dr. Molly Ahye, a great ancestor and priestess whose power and dignity illumined in our first meeting in Havana, Cuba, and inspired this collaborative scholarly pursuit.

A research project of this scope and magnitude necessarily benefits from the generosity of many funding sources. Volume I was supported by grants and fellowships from the following: the Christian and Mary F. Lindback Foundation, the National Endowment for the Humanities, the American Academy of Religion Collaborative Research Grant, Mellon Tri-Co Faculty Forum Seed Grant, Haverford College Center for Peace and Global Citizenship, Haverford College Louis Green Research and Travel Fund, Colgate University Publication Subvention and Expense Grant, and the Women and Religion in the African Diaspora Project. Moreover, I am thankful to President Brian W. Casey and the esteemed faculty of Colgate University who supported my research sabbatical in order to complete this project while I was Provost and Dean of the Faculty.

I want to thank the anonymous reviewers whose close examinations and critical engagements helped to enrich the volume in insightful and valuable ways. Dianne and I profited tremendously from an all-day manuscript symposium funded by Davidson College and the Emory College of Arts and Sciences Departments of African American Studies and Religion. Carol Anderson, chair of African American Studies at Emory University, specifically hosted the symposium where J. Lorand Matory, Roseanne Adderley, and Kenneth Bilby provided us with extensive and invaluable feedback and suggestions for consideration; both volumes are strengthened because of their input. In addition, I thank Jerome Handler for his generosity and sharing of many primary sources on Obeah. Ras Michael Brown deserves a special commendation and debt of gratitude for reading the entire manuscript and offering his superb commentary. I also extend my deepest appreciation to Miriam Angress and her team at Duke University Press who ushered this work along in firm and supportive ways; any author would be fortunate to have Miriam as an editor. I commend The Religious Cultures of African and African Diaspora People Series co-edited by Jacob K. Olupona, Dianne M. Stewart, and Terrence L. Johnson for its steadfast commitment to producing new knowledge in the field of Africana Religious Studies; this Series is an ideal home for our two volumes.

There are several ancestors, elders, and teachers/mentors whose wisdom speaks through this text. First and foremost, the brilliant intellectual spirit of Dr. Charles H. Long continues to live on in this and all of my scholarly endeavors. Chapter 3 of this volume is especially shaped by my tutelage under my advisor Dr. David D. Hall. Volume I also benefitted greatly from courageous teachers, mentors, and role models such as Josiah U. Young, Harvey and Gertrude Sindima, J. Lorand Matory, Jacob K. Olupona, Evelyn Brooks Higginbotham, Valerie Smith, and Farrah Griffin. At times, I could almost hear the resolute, unapologetic, and uncompromising voices of James H. Cone, Katie Geneva Cannon, and Manning Marable as I boldly penned these pages.

I have been blessed with a community of colleagues throughout my career who have supported and encouraged my scholarly pursuits of the religious image and symbol of Africa. They include Yvonne Chireau, Margarita Guillory, Lee H. Butler Jr., Raymond Carr, Rachel Harding, Kamari Clarke, Kola Abimbola, Evelyne Laurent-Perrault, Stephen Finley, Claudine Michel, Devyn Spence Benson, Jualynne Dodson, David Carrasco, and Linda Thomas.

To the students who offered their time and effort to this project, I thank you: Benesha Walker and Abayomi Walker who were my research assistants in Trinidad; Elaine Penagos, Emory University, who tirelessly and meticulously gathered images and permissions; and Amina DeBurst Banks who was present with me in my office at Haverford College when the very first line of this book was written: The revolt was set for Christmas Day.

On my way to speak at Dr. Charles Long's memorial service in North Carolina, I was given the gift of time and space to write at the African American owned Raleigh Taproom in Terminal 2 of the RDU airport. Feeding me a soulful meal of crab cakes, cheesy grits, and good music, I sat for several hours composing the Afterword of this volume. Thank you.

To my sisters in the C.A.L.M. Collective—Sunni, Alexandria, Laurie, Ada, and Myrtle (in Spirit)—you have my profound gratitude. Cynthia, Nia, Marcella, Karen, Garfield, Teresa, Pascal, Veronica, Susan, Tonya, Emma, Sarah W., Stephanie, Lamine, Claude, Tracy—I cherish your friendship.

Finally, I am nourished and sustained in this life by ancestors and family. To my parents, Joseph and Doretha Hucks, and those in the Hucks, Dozier, Bond, Leary lineage, I thank you for your presence at my humble altar. I recognize my Aunts Liza, Gloria, and Lugenia who are powerful woman elders in my family. Blessed with many cousins, I want to acknowledge their gifts of love and support in my life, especially: Charlene, Darrell, Valerie, Delsenia, Debbie, Robin, Monique, Janique, Carlton, Garry, Nicole, Booker T., Dennis, Doris, Patricia, Sandra, Kurt, Al, Larry, Andre, Nairah, Zahir, Jacob, and Brenda.

I close with a heartfelt acknowledgment of my sister Terri Hucks Mims, my nieces Kareemah S. Mims, Iysus Kareemah Mims, Sinai Mims, and Amina Tyson and my nephews Omar Kasim Mims and Kasim Joseph Tyson. My love for each of you is unconditional and unwavering and you bring joy to my life across your many generations. The foundation for all of my achievements and accomplishments in life stems from my family Village.

Introduction
to Volume I

In the thirties, a feast was a strange thing. We built a bamboo tent; covered it with coconut leaves; bar round the sides of the coconut leaves because it could not have been anything that was permanent. The police would always make a raid. And in that time, we had no electricity and all of these things. We would get flambeaus; we would put kerosene in a bottle; and we would put a wick. And that supplied the light, plus what candles you could get to put on the ground. And so, from these humble beginnings came the Orisa people.

We had a man that was a very good Yoruba man that you don't hear the Yoruba people speaking about him; they whisper—a fellow they call Mr. Francis. The name of Mr. Francis is known in Yoruba as Mojunta, the dead one, because Mojunta Francis would have done anything.[1] Some of the people believe that he was what you call a true Obeah man. Anything that was done . . . that might have been along the supernatural was considered Obeah. If a person came by and they prayed for a sick and that sick even recovered, that was Obeah. If they prayed for a person to break their hand or foot that was deserving of it—that was Obeah. So, anything that was out of the norm of the society in which we live is Obeah.[2]

During our final 2001 interview with Orisa elder Babalorisa Sam Phills (1924–2007), we never anticipated that his remarks about the two most salient repertoires of African religion in Trinidad—Obeah and Orisa—would foreshadow the eventual framing of our two-volume study. Through a focus on Obeah (volume I) and Orisa (volume II) in Trinidad, Dianne M. Stewart and I explore the problem of religious identity that ensues from obscene violations of black bodies and psyches and antiblack colonial state violence, and we address the affective and political dimensions of the black religious imagination in confronting the afterlives of slavery and colonialism. Because religion/theology scholars wrestle with interiority, attempt to apprehend and empathize with how religious subjects orient themselves in the world, and interpret the religious imagination of devotional communities, we conceive *Obeah, Orisa, and Religious Identity in Trinidad* as an aperture to new knowledge about black/African religious formation in an understudied Caribbean context with implications for future research on black religion in the broader African diaspora.

Volume I situates the beginnings of African religious expressions in Trinidad within repertoires of Obeah, an Africana nomenclature whose complexity as an umbrella term for African spirituality and thought systems remains eclipsed in the colonial record. With an emphasis on what we term Africana *nationhood* and *religious nationalism*, volume II explores Orisa, the second-most-pronounced religious system to have touched the lives of African descendants in Trinidad since liberated Yorubas were transported to this southernmost British Caribbean colony in the mid-nineteenth century.[3]

In Baba Sam's concise narrative of Orisa beginnings in Trinidad, the violence and persecution associated with the historical circumstances in which custodians of the Orisa religious culture operated are carryovers from a colonial era of Obeah's brutal repression.

One thing I claim with certainty in volume I is that ubiquitous colonial terror visited upon Obeah practitioners invited an Africana response that foregrounded defensive *and* offensive spiritual-medicinal technologies, including curative and poisonous remedies for personal and social afflictions. Thus, we learn more about Obeah as a repository of lethal potions, weaponry, and warfare than we do about Obeah as a source of priestly authority, divine revelation, and expertise in midwifery. When I commenced my research, I aspired to balance the discursive script on Obeah by underscoring the lesser-known narratives of Obeah's welcomed presence in the lives of Afro-Trinidadians across the centuries. I slowly discovered, however, that this goal would need to be postponed, for sources privileging the intentions and actions of Africans allegedly or actually involved with Obeah were anything but forthcoming. My search for eighteenth- and nineteenth-century parallels to Baba Sam's nuanced description of Obeah failed to produce tangible results. Instead, the sources rendered a portrait of white colonial anxieties and race-making rituals that deserved interrogation and theorization.

The attention given, then, to the obeah phenomenon among the white ruling class in this volume in no way diminishes my commitment to the larger project of understanding Obeah's many valences and dynamic iterations across varied historical periods in Afro-Trinidad.[4] Indeed, when possible, Africana perspectives are privileged throughout both volumes in theorizing Obeah as African religious culture in Trinidad. Baba Sam's account, for example, prepares readers to traverse a central meeting place where Obeah and Orisa are collapsed in the colonial criminal record and in Trinidad's popular imagination. He introduces us to a Yoruba man, Mr. Francis, aka Mojunta, whom some dubbed "a true Obeah man." As Yoruba (and indeed other liberated African *nations*) populated postemancipation waves of indentured laborers, those who became custodians of their inherited African religions—leaders, healers, and practitioners—were considered purveyors of obeah, a nomenclature that many liberated Africans would have found alien. John Cooper, Mah Nannie, and Ebenezer Elliott are three such personalities from the nineteenth and twentieth centuries whom readers will encounter in each volume. They bore official priestly titles in the Rada (Dahomean) and Yoruba traditions, respectively, yet across two centuries, none could escape the ascriptive power of the colonial obeah appellative.

In Search of Polydore: The Challenge of Colonial Archives

While researching comparative perspectives on Obeah in the wider British Caribbean, for volume I, I came across Old Polydore in the UK colonial archives. He stood trial in Jamaica in an 1831 case designated "The King Against Polydore 'for Obeah.'" Polydore "pleaded Not Guilty" in the case. What I gleaned from the colonial transcript was that a woman named Jane Henry had a brother, Reid Baylor, who was "very sick" and "could neither walk nor ride," and "what the Doctor could do was no use." Because her brother's condition was "getting worse," Jane chose to consult Old Polydore, who was known to "give Baths to persons when taken sick." In diagnosing Jane's brother, Polydore revealed the moral neutrality of Obeah and admitted that his previous assistance to another man had resulted in "her [Jane's] Brother's shadow in the [silk] Cotton tree and his hand nailed to it." Requesting "2 Dollars, a Cock and pint of Rum" to now assist Jane, Polydore "took out the gut of the cock and left it at the Cotton tree" and "threw the rum at the Cotton tree," or, in another witness's account, Polydore "threw part of the Rum on the Cotton tree and . . . held the live cock in his hand by the two legs and beat his head on the Cotton tree until he killed it" and "the blood gushed out onto the tree." It was then advised to "hire Negroes to cut down [the] Cotton tree as it had killed too many people"; so the "Cotton tree was chopped up." In the closing ritual, Polydore "made them stand at the door and he poured some rum in each of their hands and mixed chalk with it until it became like soap suds and then rubbed it on the dead cock." Polydore informed those who gathered at the ritual "that he pulled [Jane's] Brother out of the Cotton tree" along with "two babies" and "that nothing would hurt her brother and he would get better."[5]

I was introduced to Polydore through colonial lenses as "a slave belonging to Alexander McCrae, Esquire, of Clarendon," being prosecuted on behalf of "The King" for the criminal charge of "Obeah." Although his not-guilty plea is registered, Polydore's official referent is "the Prisoner," and his associates are "cautioned to speak the truth" against him even if they are "not Christened." Polydore was said to have "extorted from [Jane] some money, and some articles of food, performing in her presence . . . certain foolish ceremonies," and feigning "his preternatural powers." In the end, Polydore's religious rituals were deemed unlawful and felonious, and it was further commanded "that the said slave Polydore be transported from this Island for life." When Polydore emerges later in the 1836 British colonial record (still imprisoned but not transported), his crime is deemed less severe and "in short it appears to have been a mere case of quackery, with the substitution of conjuration for drugs," thus resulting in the commuting of his sentence.[6]

As a contributor to the burgeoning field that Dianne Stewart and I have conceptualized as Africana religious studies, I was compelled to reflect on what it means to encounter Africana religions largely entrenched in prosecutorial archives and mediated through colonial tongues.[7] My major conundrum was how to distill the substance of Africana religions through the archival filters of an "imperial imagination."[8] How might I reconcile my ambivalent gratitude at finding the truncated and illicit life of Polydore in the colonial records of Jamaica and those of Yala, Youba, La Fortune, and others in the colonial records of Trinidad with the frustration of being burdened by archives that fixed Africana religions within a moral terrain of malevolence and evil?[9]

Scholars of black performance studies and race theory interrogate phenomena (e.g., lynchings, policing blackness with lethal force) that foster the "epidermalization of blackness"—"the inscription of meaning onto skin color."[10] My challenge in the archives has been what I term the epidermalization of religion—a theology of "racecraft" violently mapped onto black bodies and religious performances in Trinidad.[11] Consequently, approximating historically and contemporarily the reach and range of Obeah traditions in the lives of African descendants in Trinidad and the wider Caribbean requires interpreting with hermeneutical ingenuity the archived silences and marginalia in available colonial materials as well as the un/remembered details of oral data wherever they (dis)appear across the centuries. The conditions of erasure that contextualize African religions in Trinidad require a peculiar scholarly discernment, an extension of Saidiya Hartman's method of critical fabulation: to do this work well, indeed thoroughly, I had to utilize the analytical "gift" of second sight and double vision—the methodological precision of seeing what is actually invisible and decoding the theological griffonage so characteristic of the colonial pens that have scripted the most enduring and damaging religious narratives about African-descended peoples.[12]

Still, my archival challenges went beyond those of representation and the historical muting of African-descended voices. Trinidad's evolving pan-colonial history entailed Spanish occupation for its first three centuries, French economic and cultural domination during the slave period, and British colonial rule from 1797 to 1962. Thus, I had to negotiate three sets of colonial archives and three colonial languages, in addition to indigenous African languages virtually absent in the archives. Unlike older slave colonies, such as Spain's Cuba, France's Haiti, and Britain's Barbados and Jamaica, Trinidad's colonial records, newspapers, court reports, parliamentary acts, travel accounts, and missionary archives convey scant early observations of Africana religions. In addition, the African presence and vocal imprint are rare across the centuries, and studies in popular culture on calypso and carnival extensively outnumber comprehensive secular histories. Collectively, these impediments have made me more cautious about reaching premature conclusions, more attuned to the complexities and diversities of diaspora, and more steadfast in deploying transdisciplinary approaches to this Africana religious studies project.

Geocontextual Considerations: "Caribbeaning" Diaspora

The Caribbean is the first, the original, and the purest diaspora.

In "Caribbeaning" diaspora, I chart a theoretical landscape in diaspora studies that takes seriously the intellectual legacy of the late Stuart Hall, the esteemed cultural theorist and sociologist of the Caribbean.[13] I propose a discourse on diaspora that not only positions Africa as the central locus of dispersal, movement, and migration but also advances a nuanced engagement with the Caribbean as a porous geography for diaspora formations. I carefully consider the intra-Caribbean and wider intradiaspora movements of African populations formed by Atlantic repopulations and exchange. Yet, even as it hosts this African diffusion, the Caribbean is also the terminus of concurrent non-African diasporas.

Caribbean geographies and their historical inhabitants have been multiply "diasporized," observed Hall: "everybody there comes from somewhere else."[14] More specifically, Trinidad has been host to the diasporas of Spain, France, England, Ireland, Africa, neighboring Caribbean regions, and the United States. Even the indigeneity of the Lokono (or Arawak) and Kalina (or Carib) is disputed: these people-groups find their roots in South American dispersion. Thus, when Caribbeaning diaspora, I accept that entire populations' "true culture, the places they really come from, the traditions that really formed them, are somewhere else," leaving me to conclude that "retention characterized the *colonizing cultures* as well as the *colonized*."[15] For example, with reference to cultural reproduction in the Caribbean, Hall argues:

> If you look at the Little Englands, the Little Spains and the Little Frances that were created by the colonizers, if you consider this kind of fossilized replica, with the usual colonial cultural lag . . . they were keeping alive the memory of their own homes and homelands and traditions and customs. This very important double aspect of retention [among colonizing cultures and colonized] has marked Caribbean culture from the earliest colonial encounters.[16]

Leveling notions of Caribbean diaspora, Hall extends to Europeans the analytical nomenclature of "survival," "assimilation," "retention," and "syncretism" often mapped exclusively onto African-descended diasporas. Ultimately, I offer Caribbeaning diaspora to advance a useful framework of analysis, for it provides a typology of diaspora applicable to translocal regions of the Caribbean. Diaspora is then recast as "both a process and a condition . . . constantly remade through movement, migration, and travel, as well as imagined through thought, cultural production, and political struggle," as historians Tiffany Ruby Patterson and Robin D. G. Kelley posit in "Unfinished Migrations: Reflections on the African Diaspora and the Making of the Modern World."[17] In the specific case of Trinidad, most helpful in examining its African heritage religious cultures has been an approach that considers Patterson's and Kelley's concept of "unfinished migrations" alongside historian Kim Butler's "phases of diasporization" over time.[18]

"Phases of Diasporization" in Trinidad

African presence in Trinidad was facilitated by a host of European handlers over an extensive period. An initial 470 Africans were transported to the Spanish colony in 1606 in fulfillment of an order for 500 enslaved Africans placed with Dutch merchants. As Catholic planters were incentivized to resettle in Trinidad by the first *cédula de población* in September 1776, those numbers grew: the 1779 statistics on new immigrants into Trinidad reveal an increase of 1,500 enslaved Africans. A second *cédula*, the "Royal Cedula on Colonization of 1783," transformed the number of enslaved Africans in the colony: Trinidad's enslaved population increased to 20,464 in 1803 and 25,696 in 1813. Most notable about this population was that 94 percent, or 24,154 of the total 25,696, were African-born captives who had originally been settled in French colonies such as Haiti and Martinique.[19]

Because Trinidad's rate of African captive increase was not as exponential as that in Britain's lucrative slave colony of Jamaica, with the close of the transatlantic slave trade in 1808, Trinidad resorted to an "intercolonial slave trade" that imported close to 4,000 enslaved persons from Dominica and Grenada.[20] By 1813, severe restrictions were placed upon importations into Trinidad as a result of growing agitation and abolitionism in England. Smuggling ensued as an illegal alternative; however, the colonial government responded with heavy penalties and a mandated "registry of plantation slaves" that meticulously recorded an array of data including country of origin.[21] Regarding its inhabitants of African descent, enslaved and emancipated/liberated Africans from Atlantic and intradiaspora transport and trade populated the colony. Following a small group of black loyalists that trickled into Trinidad after the American Revolutionary War, approximately 1,000 more African Americans from the United States were relocated to Trinidad between 1815 and 1816 as compensation for their loyalty to the British crown in the War of 1812. Other militia populations included those of African descent from Britain's West India Regiment posted within the Caribbean. Trinidad was likewise home to a diaspora of free and mixed-race people who would own close to 40 percent of the enslaved population by 1813.[22] Finally, after emancipation in 1834, Trinidad continued to experience phases of African diaspora in that the British-established Liberated African Department facilitated a movement of close to 32,000 "liberated" Africans confiscated from illegal Spanish and Portuguese slave vessels into Britain's Caribbean territories. Trinidad absorbed nearly 9,000 of this total number, many bearing "recognizable Yoruba or Central African cultures."[23]

Why are these phases of diaspora important to the study of Africana religions in Trinidad? Our knowledge of African diasporas in Trinidad has been deduced largely through statistics derived from population censuses, immigration documents, and colonial port disembarkation data, with several records indicating African *nation-al* and/or cultural origins. Historical periodization of Trinidad's phases of diaspora remains crucial in plotting the trajectories of its Africana religions. For example, analyzing obeah trials during the slave period differs significantly from examining Company Villages of African American Baptists that missionaries in the 1840s stated "perpetuate[d] Africanism in their worship" and were skilled in the "special art of 'bush medicine,'" which differs again from the study of the Mandingoes in Trinidad in the 1830s, who were deemed "Mohametans," or the Rada and Yaraba (Yoruba) of Trinidad's postemancipation liberated African communities. Such a chronological charting disrupts any notion of a static or monolithic African population in Trinidad and precludes facile assumptions and broad theorizations of creolization, syncretism, and cultural reconstruction. Therefore, the conclusions I reach regarding the nature of Africana religions in the region must necessarily be in close correspondence with Trinidad's changing diasporas.

Returning to Stuart Hall, the current study of Africana religions in Trinidad derives from a story of what he calls "the other Caribbean; the Caribbean that was not recognized, that could not speak, that had no official records of its own transportation, no official historians." As a religious historian, I adopt a chrono-thematic approach to Obeah through the late nineteenth century; I sift colonial documents through a sieve in order to filter Africana narratives from the colonial mire. Chapter 1 situates the reader in the colonial mapping and emerging of a slave colony of Trinidad (see figure I.1).

Not officially joined with Tobago until 1889, Trinidad stood singly as a Spanish, then British, yet sizably French, slave colony. This opening chapter examines the competing negotiations of imperial nation (Spanish, British, French), indigenous nation (Carib and Arawak), diasporaed[24] *nation* (African, free colored), and migrating nation (East Indian and Chinese). In other words, how might readers reimagine the colonial landscape of Trinidad as a constant navigation of geopolitical conflicts and religio-cultural contacts

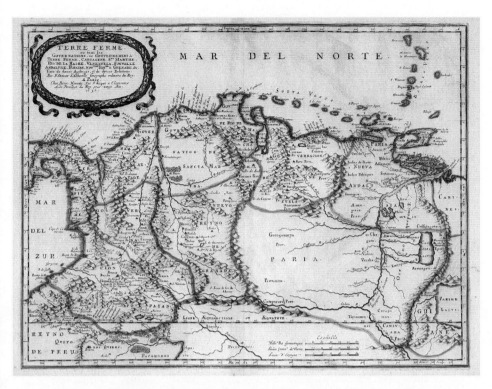

FIGURE I.1 Trinidad, 1656. S. Luscombe, "Map of Trinidad, 1656" [online], https://www.britishempire.co.uk/images2/1656trinidadandtobagomap.jpg.

among indigenous societies; Spanish, British, and French settlers; Asian immigrants; and persons of African descent both captive and free who constituted the majority of Trinidad's populace?

Chapter 1 intentionally disaggregates this last group of inhabitants into distinct identifiable social categories of African-descended communities and examines each community's social status. Africa was not a national consensus symbol of unified racial solidarity but emerged as a complicated identity canvas for figuring, *nation-al*, geographical, linguistic, and racially hybrid identities. In the eighteenth and nineteenth centuries, Trinidad did not possess a homogenous African population or collective religion. Its diversity encompassed enslaved persons of *multi-nation-al* origins on trial for obeah, black Baptist militia and their families resettled from the United States, stationed soldiers serving in the West India Regiment, free coloreds or mixed-race populations who looked to Catholicism and to the British Crown in order to legitimate their Trinidadian citizenship, and liberated Africans who maintained strong ritual ties to their immediate pasts. Thus chapter 1 seeks both to canvass and to complicate the diversity of these African-descended communities amidst a broader plural society.

Chapter 2 furnishes a documentary analysis of religious repression in Trinidad under Governor Sir Thomas Picton during the early nineteenth century. The perceived religious practices of Africa became unsympathetically symbolized and criminalized as obeah, resulting in colonial legislation, religious fear and trembling, and social panic. Obeah was the inspiration for a preponderance of colonial laws across the Caribbean, as well as a unique body of legal cases brought before the colonial commission in Trinidad. Each case disclosed angst and alarm related to the presence of enslaved Africans, the perceived risk Obeah posed to slavery and Christian domination, and Obeah's reputed similarity to the bedlam of European occultism. This chapter most explicitly interrogates the European imaginary regarding Obeah and the consequential Euro-colonial lived religion of violent somatic practices. In so doing, it reveals how public rituals performed upon the enslaved black body symbolized exertions of colonial power and socioracial consumption.

The conversation about Obeah as it was constructed in the nineteenth-century white racial and literary imagination continues in chapter 3. The chapter offers a comparative reading of nineteenth-century Trinidadian and North American fiction produced by female authors who disseminated portraitures of Obeah and/or black religiosity to a wider white readership in the Atlantic world. Looking specifically at *The Slave Son* (1854), written by Marcella Fanny Noy Wilkins, and Harriet Beecher Stowe's *Uncle Tom's Cabin; or, Life among the Lowly* (1852), the chapter explores the influence of North American nineteenth-century literature upon the British Caribbean and scrutinizes how slavery, religion, and gender overlap in two hemispheric slave economies. Its main focus is to make sense of representations of black/ African spirituality, especially the obeah representations found in colonial literature. North America and the Caribbean are engaged in this chapter not as mutually exclusive territories but as interpenetrating geographic regions of the Atlantic world that seek to wrestle with African presence, religious traditions, and women's positionalities.

Chapter 4 concludes the discussion of nineteenth-century Obeah with a close examination of two obeah court cases levied against liberated Africans in 1870s and 1880s British Trinidad (see figure I.2), the first of which was the most extensively documented case in the colonial record, "No. 5518, Case of John Cooper, Convicted of Obeah."

FIGURE I.2 Trinidad, 1872. S. Luscombe, "Map of Trinidad, 1872" [online], https://
www.britishempire.co.uk/images2/1872maptrinidad.jpg.

The landmark legal case of John Cooper (1871–1872) and that of his brother
Mah Nannie (1886) are situated within five important historical contours:
the liberated African presence in Trinidad; the reinscription of obeah laws
in 1860s Trinidadian legislation; the shifting colonial responses to Obeah in
postslavery society; competing notions of healthcare among Africans and
colonists; and the reconstitution of cultural ties and nations that diasporaed
liberated Africans forged as distinguishing markers of identity. The Afterword recapitulates central connections between both volumes of this collaborative study on Obeah and Orisa in Trinidad: nationhood; inter-nation-al
exchanges and cooperation among Africans; African religious repression
and the law; colonial and decolonial mythmaking; and comparisons of the
antiblack violence that governed colonial Trinidad with contemporary manifestations of the same atemporal gratuitous violence in the diasporic space
of the United States.

The narratives constructed across this volume and volume II are woven
together by a conceptual focus on the image, imaginaries, and heritages of
Africa as a central preoccupation of varied publics in colonial Trinidad. Both
volumes address the themes of repression and nationalism, the memory and
disfigurement of Africa, and the sustained appearance of nation-al African

religious cultures in Trinidadian history. In many respects, violence and persecution, be they physical, cultural, psychological, or discursive, are some of the thickest threads lacing together the two volumes. As a result, one of the principal questions addressed is how the factor of omnipresent terror conceals and reveals legacies of African heritage religious cultures in Trinidad and, by extension, the wider Caribbean and Americas.

The Formation
of a Slave Colony

RACE, NATION, AND IDENTITY

The revolt was set for Christmas Day. Trinidad's Spanish, British, and French colonial settlers were thrown into a state of hysteria, alarm, and panic. Beginning in 1797 with the island's first full-term transition governor, Sir Thomas Picton, who succeeded Sir Ralph Abercromby, British colonial rulers feared the emerging plantation frontier was in great peril from imminent revolt. The early years of British governance were rife with anxious apprehensions and forebodings unfolding within the ethos of French Saint-Domingue's slave insurrections. As a result, Governor Picton's torturous civil repressions increased in Trinidad at the turn of the nineteenth century due to the assembling of enslaved populations and their perceived threats of African sorcery. At the core of the 1805 conspiracy were "French and African Negroes" as well as enslaved and free members of the West India Regiment residing in the areas of Diego Martin, Maraval, and Carenage who organized themselves into "Bands" thought previously to be "harmless social organizations that gathered on plantations for the 'practice of native African dancing.'"[1] Now fueling insurrection, "Band" leaders had plotted to wait until the high festivities of Christmas Day, 1805, to launch a widespread slave rebellion that would begin in the Cuesa Valley and eventually extend to the entire island of Trinidad. In the end, "the object of the plot was the elimination of all the whites and free coloured peoples in the island."[2] Rumors spread rapidly of the impending plot, and martial law was declared by Picton's successor, Governor Thomas Hislop. Hislop proclaimed that all "Negro or other slaves who may be found to have offended any of the ordinances now in existence will be immediately punished with death," and those "attempting to escape from the patrols will be immediately shot."[3] The Minutes of Council reveal the confession of a prisoner in custody who "was invited to join with his regiment those of the Carenage on Christmas-day for the purpose of rising against the whites; that having effected their purpose there, they were to proceed to town to set it on fire, after which a general massacre of the whites and free coloured people, and those blacks who refused to join the insurgents."[4] The "chief instigators of the intended insurrection" were eventually arrested and found guilty by the Supreme Tribunal of what the colonial regime ruled a "diabolical plot."[5] The accused leaders were sentenced to death by hanging and, according to the official legal record, "their heads to be exposed after death on poles erected for the purpose, and their bodies to be hanged in chains on the sea side near the district where they resided."[6] Nearly forty accomplices—inclusive of a half dozen women, both free and enslaved, some from the Shand Plantation in Carenage—who prepared to poison their masters were arrested and differentially sentenced "to have both ears cut off," "to have the tip of the ears cut off," "to be flogged under the gallows and then banished from the Colony forever," to "receive 100 lashes," "to be returned to their owners, first having an iron ring of ten pounds weight affixed to one . . . leg to remain thereon for the space of two years," "to work in chains for life," and for "free men—to be returned into slavery, and sold for the benefit of the Colony."[7] In the slave colony of Trinidad, "the Governor's swift action in stamping out the slave revolt had the desired effect in re-establishing internal peace."[8]

The early formation of the imperial colony of Trinidad and its rise to a slave colony were riddled with competing racial, social, and national conflicts. "Internal peace," as proclaimed by Governor Hislop, was in actuality an imaginary, murky, and messy configuration under settler colonialism. Given the historical "interimperial rivalry, warfare, and competition," colonial Trinidad from Spanish to British rule was rarely, if at all, peaceful.[9] Tensions derived in large part from the diverse array of European and African communities that converged, often through coercive and violent forces, in imbricated layers over multiple generations. It was well known by the white inhabitants of the time, as recorded in one letter, that "we had nearly experienced a rebellion of the negroes here and a general massacre of the whites, which, had it taken place, would have involved all the Windward Islands in general devastation. The explosion of such a volcano here as well as St. Domingo would have completely overwhelmed not only the British but all the other Colonies."[10]

Trinidad's exceptionally diverse inhabitants collectively engineered an "inter-society pluralism" that traversed cultural, phenotypical, and social distinctions.[11] The mechanisms for this pluralism often relied on cultural processes steeped in ambiguity and antipathy. "Obeah" stood out as particularly notable in its role as both an interior process of connection, healing, and resolution within African-descended communities (Obeah) and an exterior process of European colonial authorities who confined and criminalized those communities (obeah).[12] Both facets of Obeah/obeah operated simultaneously and, in some instances though not all, in a dialectic fed by the intentional manipulation of mutual misapprehensions. Obeah/obeah thus reveals, in a way unlike any other, the architecture of Trinidad's inter-society pluralism in its many ambivalent and contested manifestations. For Trinidad, however, a direct view of Obeah as an indigenous process does not appear in the conventional contemporary archival source material. At best, we see the colonial process of obeah in the historical legislative and judicial record, which nevertheless affords some indication of the shadows of the otherwise unseen domain of Obeah. Further, the realm of Obeah in Trinidad can be imagined through our deeper and broader knowledge of Obeah in the Americas, all of which was connected through the shared cultural and biological ties of those Africans dispersed throughout the Atlantic world.

A reconceptualization of Obeah begins with a triangulated analysis of material from seemingly disparate colonial and contemporary diasporas such as Jamaica, Barbados, Grenada, Trinidad, Suriname, and the United States. This transatlantic/diasporic understanding of Obeah raises questions about why Obeah has an institutional and structural legacy that contravenes the colonial Caribbean construction of obeah. The earliest African understandings of Obeah in eighteenth-century Jamaica and Barbados unveil a complex system of spiritual doctoring mastered by priests whose principal role in their communities was healing physical, mental, spiritual, social, and cosmic dis/ease. Moreover, Obeah priests/doctors in Suriname (the African diasporic region that Melville Herskovits characterized as having the most "African retentions") have long been revered and consulted as expert healers rather than considered to be criminal and malevolent sorcerers.[13]

Colonial historians, missionaries, magistrates, travelers, and settlers regularly wrote about Africans' spiritual expressions, and in the process they gave birth to a new genealogy of obeah. Underneath their fantasies of "obeah sorcery" lurk useable details that in fact corroborate an early documentation, though often missed by many scholars, of *Obeah as an Africana spiritual system of holistic healing and healthcare* influential across the Americas and the Caribbean. It is important to remember that for death-bound-subjects attuned to the life-giving powers of the dead, healing and healthcare practices had to involve slave strikes and revolts, such as Trinidad's aborted 1805 conspiracy.[14]

Thus, Obeah operationalizes the axiom that one person's medicine is another person's poison. The potential for harm and aggression is no less apparent in any other system of healing, including modern Western medical systems where certified medical practitioners take the Hippocratic Oath to do no intentional harm to their patients.

Similar oaths were part of Obeah's moral system. However, especially within the chaotic climate of racial slavery, violations were numerous, and suspicions of violations were even more abundant. Obeah accounted for ethical transgressions and might be viewed from another angle as a commentary on and regulator of power in its distribution in all facets of life and social experience. What we generally see in the colonial records, even when Africans are commenting on Obeah within their own communities, is a lopsided emphasis on bad medicine. Fears and anxieties surrounding its deployment and harmful effects are most pronounced, while there is minimal information about how African communities navigated the tensions, gaps, and overlaps between ethical and corrupt Obeah practitioners and antisocial impostures whom colonial authorities also perceived to be dealing in obeah. Volume II will return to this theme with more theoretical precision. Moving toward that discussion, the reader is cautioned to consider the healthcare needs of death-bound-subjects and the creative modalities they inspired. Africana spiritual care modalities were unintelligible to the whites who owned, policed, and tortured African persons for practicing Obeah and other pluralized African (or Africana) religious traditions. Colonial authorities had no epistemological access to African religions. Planters and governors could hardly distinguish African spirituality from the obeahic ideations they circulated locally and within their European metropoles. In fact, unlike in many other Caribbean colonies, in Trinidad several centuries would pass between the Spanish colonization of the island and its peopling by multiple African *nations* that would contribute to the birth of an Obeah assemblage and orientation that neither torture nor death could obliterate.

Spanish Colonial Rule and
the Making of a Multinational Slave Society

As a Spanish territory beginning in 1498, Trinidad struggled to establish a colonial nation that could neatly assuage its multiple, and often violent, ethno-tensions. Trinidad's advent as a colony followed, with little exception, the strategic peopling patterns of European empires as they sought to secure Atlantic territories by subduing and decimating the indigenous populations, establishing European colonial and religious rule of the conquered territory, commencing the eventual importation of enslaved Africans, and instituting the colonial and global economy of slavery. In the fissures of this history reside much violence, bloodshed, resistance, and warfare as aboriginal, European imperial powers, and African (and later Asian) populations uneasily cohabited within Trinidad's island boundaries. This introductory chapter will provide an overview of the early colonial history of Trinidad and its emergence as one of the later slave colonies in the Atlantic world.

Although short-lived when compared to the Spanish Crown's colonies, slavery in Trinidad, from aboriginal to African, was nonetheless driven by harsh labor demands, excessive physical brutality, and high mortality rates. The Spanish arrived in Trinidad in 1498 and enslaved the indigenous Arawak and Carib inhabitants as the island's first laborers by the following century. They relied heavily on the indigenous populations for their primary labor supply and often cited indigenous bellicosity and cannibalism as justification for enslavement.[15] As early as 1511, the king in Burgos issued a "cedula to all persons giving permission to wage war upon and enslave the Caribs of Trinidad and other places" and proclaimed that "these Carib Indians may be captured and taken to such ports and Islands wheresoever and that these Indians may be sold for profit without any punishment or penalty for doing so and without paying any duty provided they are not taken nor sold outside of the Indies."[16] The reason provided for such a mandate was that Caribs "refuse to listen nor will allow any to settle but defend their lands by arms and prevent any from landing in the Islands . . . and in such resistance have killed several Christians . . . and also have made war on the Indians of many other Islands nearby and have taken these Indians for eating and have eaten them."[17] They were represented in the documents repeatedly over centuries as cannibals, savages, and murderers of Catholic clergy, and as in need of salvation from the Devil via submission to the Christian faith. Spanish colonists were subsequently asked to "exercise all zeal to reduce these Caribs to our Holy Catholic Faith . . . and bring them to our obedience so that they may live peacefully and trade with our settlers of the said Island."[18] Historian Linda Newson documents that their enslavement could be justified in Trinidad because the "Carib are people who eat human flesh and have other rites and evil customs and are very warlike."[19] Despite efforts by Dominican missionaries in the Spanish Americas to protect these populations from further enslavement, by the mid-1530s indigenous persons in Trinidad were well into being forced to work on sugar estates and thousands were sold as enslaved laborers to settlers on other islands, wreaking devastation upon these early indigenous populations.[20]

Alongside the persistent slave raids of the Spanish, indigenous populations suffered the ravaging effects of infectious disease, massive dislocation, famine, and depressed fertility.[21] At the time of the initial Spanish encounter, the indigenous population of Trinidad may have numbered as high as 40,000.[22] Reduced to some 5,000 people by 1680, indigenous communities diminished to just over 1,000 inhabitants during the next century, due in no small part to a smallpox epidemic in 1739.[23]

Sixteenth-century aboriginal communities did not, however, bear the onslaught of Spanish rule and violence unanswered. Compulsory enslavement by the Spanish ignited early nationalist coalitions across aboriginal subgroups as strategies of defense against their common European adversary. Defining this nationalism was a transcendence of local cultural differences and a tactical commitment to indigenous collaboration. According to Newson:

> The weakened nature of the socio-political organisation of the Indians and the declining status of civil leaders in Trinidad in the sixteenth century was in part compensated for by the development of links between villages and the emergence of military leaders based on the common interest of defence rather than kinship. During the sixteenth century energies that had formerly been expended in intervillage warfare were channelled into a form of "nationalism" and the defence of the island.[24]

Newson points out that this incipient nationalism did not completely replace "intervillage rivalries," but it caused them to move toward alliance "as the need for a united opposition against the Spanish grew and military organization that cut across village loyalties developed to co-ordinate defence activities."[25] For example, aboriginal communities selected military leaders who worked cooperatively on combat strategy and recruited skilled men from numerous villages. One aboriginal leader, Baucunar, emphatically declared in 1553 that "we go to war not for amusement or pleasure, but to die for our land, defending our sons and wives."[26] Moreover, in summarizing the motives of the Spanish *conquistadores* Baucunar surmised "truthfully they wish to make us their slaves and subjects so that we should sow their lands, and those to whom we should not be acceptable take us from our fertile banks, carrying us off in fetters and chains by sea to get to know foreign lands. In their estates and farms you will die of inhuman work, separated fathers from sons, brothers from beloved brothers."[27]

In the face of deteriorating numbers and defensive efforts, the indigenous population registered one of the last recorded instances of collective resistance waged against Spanish imperialism and its religious institutions in the late seventeenth century. Capuchins organized Catholic mission settlements for indigenous populations following their arrival in Trinidad in 1687. Residing within these settlements, "the Indians worked for about two days a week on the mission estate, and under the *mita* system of forced labour they were obliged to work outside the mission for Spanish land-owners for sixteen days in the year. . . . The authority of the missionaries over the Indians was complete, and their judicial and police powers were extensive."[28] One such mission, San Francisco de los Arenales, became the target of aboriginal insurgency. In December 1699, the aboriginals burned the mission to the ground, murdered its Capuchin friars, and rained their arrows on Spanish soldiers and the area governor in a lethal attack. Following these deeds,

> the Amerindian rebels buried the bodies of the priests hurriedly, threw the Governor's body into the river, and immediately headed for the sea coast in anticipation of retaliation. . . . Surrounded by water and by their enemies on land, many of them preferred to die rather than to submit to capture. Women pulled their children from their breasts, threw them and their older children into the sea, and then themselves followed with many of the menfolk.[29]

The Spanish Crown heavily scrutinized the treatment of indigenous communities as a way of avoiding such future catastrophes and subsequently issued a royal decree commanding that "any settler who ill-treated his Amerindian workers, who had in any way tolerated or committed excessive wrongs against these workers, should be deprived of them," and forbidding settlers to force indigenous workers to labor on estates against their will.[30] By the end of the eighteenth century, indigenous labor supplies had been virtually depleted and the Spanish Crown's intentional protection of its remaining members made it difficult to sustain Trinidad's growing agricultural demands. The challenges of a dwindling supply of workers amidst an emerging cash crop economy prompted the Spanish to launch an aggressive campaign of filling their labor void with captive Africans.

African presence in fifteenth- and sixteenth-century early Trinidad was minimal. Colonial Spaniards found it far more lucrative to engage in the selling of slaves for wealth building than to use them in the cultivation of land. They preferred "quick profits from trading to uncertain profits from agricultural development."[31] Emphasizing this point, Newson corroborates it:

> Although there was a shortage of labour in Trinidad the Spanish settlers preferred to make short-term profits by buying negroes from foreigners and settling them in other parts of the Indies rather than employing them

on their estates. In 1605 Dutch merchants are known to have accepted an order from Trinidad colonists for 500 slaves to be delivered the following year. In the fulfillment of the contract 470 negroes were landed in Trinidad by Isaac Duverne in 1606. However, in 1613 the Governor Sancho de Alquiza reported that the colonists had bought some negroes from foreigners but had resold them at 150 *pesos* each.[32]

Because of the high profit margin yielded by trafficking Africans, the Spanish saw very little benefit in retaining Africans on its mostly uncultivated and uninhabited island. Instead they continued to rely on the limited aboriginal labor pool to produce tobacco and cocoa, Trinidad's chief exports in the late seventeenth and early eighteenth centuries.

The first initiative on the part of the Spanish Crown to turn its efforts inward toward the development of Trinidad as a large-scale residential slave colony and estate system was on September 3, 1776, when a *cédula de población* was issued in Spain encouraging Catholic planters from nearby colonies to resettle in Trinidad. Under the cedula, new settlers would be issued large acres of fertile land while being "exempted from import duties on any goods, including slaves, that they brought to the island."[33] French planters in possession of their own slave labor from islands such as Dominica, St. Vincent, St. Lucia, Martinique, Guadeloupe, Grenada, and Tobago were especially invited to partake in furthering Trinidad's agricultural experiment. Census data taken in the year 1777 revealed a population breakdown (exclusive of aboriginals) of 340 Europeans, 870 free mulattoes, and 200 enslaved Africans in Trinidad.[34] In 1779, some 2,000 new immigrants entered Trinidad, out of which an overwhelming 1,500, or 75 percent, were enslaved Africans as well as fugitive slaves.[35]

In 1783, a second *cédula de población* radically transformed Trinidad's population and cash crop economy. Issued in a letter signed by the king of Spain, the Royal Cedula on Colonization of 1783 contained twenty-eight articles outlining the stipulations for foreign immigration and economic development in Trinidad.[36] The articles served as guidelines to "establish regulations, and to grant various privileges for the population and commerce of the said Island."[37] Because of the cedula's critical importance to the social, cultural, and economic evolution of Trinidad into a lucrative slave society, Articles I–XXVIII are worth summarizing in brief as illustrations of Trinidad's potential attractiveness to global Catholic prospects:

1   All foreigners wishing to settle in Trinidad must be of "the Roman Catholic persuasion" and subjects of nations in alliance with Spain.

II   All foreigners must take "the oath of fealty and submission" by which they shall promise to obey the laws and general ordinances to which Spaniards are subject.

III   White foreigners shall receive approximately 30 acres of land for each family member and approximately 15 acres for each accompanying slave.

IV   Free blacks and people of color, "as planters and heads of families," shall receive half of the land grant given to whites and an additional half for each accompanying slave.

V   After five years' residency, foreign settlers shall "receive all the rights and privileges of naturalization" and be eligible for civil and military service.

VI   No head tax or personal tribute shall be imposed upon foreign settlers at any time. The exception shall be that after ten years there will be an "annual sum" of one dollar for each "Negro or coloured slave."

VII   If within the first five years of residency foreign settlers choose to return to their former places, they may do so without paying any export duty on goods and property in their possession.

VIII   "Former and recent settlers" may have the power of "bequeathing their estate to their relations or friends wherever they may be."

IX   Property may be inherited by widows and multiple children.

X   Any foreign settler wishing to travel to Spain, any Spanish province, or "an enemy's country" must receive permission from the governor.

XI   "Spanish and foreign settlers" shall not be required to pay tithes for ten years and thereafter will only have to pay half tithes, or 5 percent.

XII   For the first ten years, there will be no royal duty on "the sale of produce and merchantable effects."

XIII   All "inhabitants should be armed even in time of peace, to keep the slaves in subjection, and resist any invasion or the incursion of pirates."

XIV   All vessels belonging to settlers shall be registered in Trinidad and "be accounted as Spanish vessels."

XV   The African slave trade shall be free of all duty for a period of ten years, after which time there will be a 5 percent fee on the "current value" of slave cargo.

XVI Using Spanish ships, enslaved Africans may be procured from other islands in alliance with Spain after obtaining "a licence from the Government."

XVII "The intercourse of Spain with the inhabitants of Trinidad, and the exportation of licenced produce from the said Island to American islands and dominions [of the Crown] shall be entirely free from all duties for the space of ten years."

XVIII "All Spanish and foreign merchandise," including wine, oil, and "spirituous liquors," shall be exported to Trinidad "free of all duty" for ten years.

XIX As a means to increase the growth of trade and population, for the "space of ten years . . . the vessels belonging to the inhabitants" of Trinidad and the "subjects of Spain" may "sail directly with their cargoes from the ports in France," where Spanish consuls reside . . . and "shall take an exact inventory of everything that is shipped . . . paying five per centum on the entry of the goods and merchandize." The import of monetary currency through this means is prohibited.

XX "Accurate invoices" of all cargo must be kept for duty purposes.

XXI So that "recent inhabitants may be furnished with the most necessary supplies for their maintenance, their industry, and agriculture," livestock such as "horned cattle, mules, and horses" shall be available at prime cost until "such time as they have sufficient stock to supply themselves."

XXII Flour and meal shall be supplied for a period of ten years.

XXIII All supplies "required by the settlers for their agricultural pursuits shall be imported into Trinidad and sold at prime cost for a period of ten years."

XXIV Two parish priests, "skilled and versed in foreign languages," shall be appointed to Trinidad and serve as priests to the new settlers.

XXV Slaveholding settlers may propose ordinances to the governor that "shall be most proper" for regulating the "treatment of their slaves and preventing their flight."

XXVI All "equipage and effects of the settlers" shall be thoroughly examined to prevent vermin and so as to "prevent the introduction of ants into the island."

XXVII Settlers shall establish sugar refineries in Spain free from all duty.

XXVIII   Settlers shall direct any questions they deem worthy of "Royal consideration" to the governor and the chief secretary of states for the Indies.[38]

One historical interpretation of the cedula could be that its invitation to foreign immigrants symbolized a decline of Spanish colonial rule in Trinidad.[39] An alternative reading might examine the nuanced and surreptitious means by which Spain attempted to *expand* its colonial empire at the expense of foreign settlers. Embedded in the letter from the Crown were deliberate strategies for promoting foreign development without relinquishing total Spanish authority. In other words, the cedula's prescriptions solicited immigration on the one hand while at the same time it attempted to consolidate and solidify Spanish control in the region.

In circumscribing rigid boundaries around religion and political allegiance, the Crown was able to subsume national diversity under an umbrella of Catholicism and an axiom of Spanish nationalism. The cedula strategically sought to assimilate vast groups of sundry immigrants in four vital senses. First, it compelled ecclesiastical homogeneity by establishing Catholicism as the official faith of Trinidad. This policy subsequently alleviated Spanish fears of Protestantism as well as minimized potential religious dissent. Second, the cedula fortified the Crown's colonial authority by obliging solemn "oaths" of allegiance to Spanish civil rule and by commanding the bearing of arms in order to maintain Spanish civic order, deter pirate invasion, and fortify slave subjection. Third, the cedula quickly naturalized foreign immigrants into Spanish colonial citizenry, thus subsuming former national and colonial allegiances. Related to this was an attempt to expand Spanish regional domination by extending eligibility for colonial military service to foreign settlers. Finally, Spain sought to secure its economic hegemony by declaring ownership of all foreign shipping vessels and by controlling all modes of import, export, and trade in Trinidad. However, in spite of the Crown's detailed measures to ensure Spanish sovereignty, the bevy of foreign subjects within colonial boundaries inevitably bred uncertainty. Trinidad's Spanish governor, Don Jose Maria Chácon, was indeed ruling what historian Bridget Brereton labeled "a restless, international colony."[40]

Trinidad as a Slave Colony 1783–1838

The 1783 *Cédula* radically reconfigured and reconstituted Trinidadian society because it "marked Trinidad's beginning as a viable slave economy," according to historian A. Meredith John.[41] By the late eighteenth century, Trinidad was rapidly becoming an island where close to two-thirds of its population would be enslaved Africans; its first sugar factory would be built by 1787.[42] Trinidad's demand for development and slave labor can be understood best as the rise of the colonial "frontier." Arthur L. Stinchcombe in his *Sugar Island Slavery in the Age of Enlightenment: The Political Economy of the Caribbean World* asserts that "plantation development created a frontier (defined here as the invasion of a mode of land use that was much more labor and capital intensive and more productive than the land use previously there) and so created pressure to move people there, the more fertile the land was, the more intense that frontier pressure."[43]

Six years prior to the second cedula, the 1777 census recorded that the colony housed only 200 Negro slaves. Twenty years after the issuance of the 1783 cedula, the "frontier pressure" of Trinidad had yielded a slave population with an increase of over a hundredfold: a recorded 20,464 in 1803, and 25,696 in 1813; "by 1815 enslaved Africans comprised about 67% of the population," according to Bridget Brereton.[44] Within a wider Caribbean perspective, six years after the cedula, there were 50,000 white inhabitants, 10,000 free people of color, and 500,000 enslaved Africans in the British colonies.[45] The primary source of Trinidad's slave increase was not direct importation from Africa but planters on nearby islands seeking financial stability after the Haitian Revolution or planters relocating from Martinique, Dominica, and Grenada.[46] The demand for slave labor to cultivate the island was so great that "many free Negroes and mulattoes were kidnapped and brought to Trinidad, where to their horror, they heard themselves declared slaves," resulting in a corresponding trade of "kidnapped freemen."[47] Of the slaves that entered Trinidad, an overwhelming 94 percent were native Africans. In 1813, nonracially mixed Africans constituted 24,154 of a total slave population of 25,696.[48] Unlike islands such as Jamaica and Cuba that had developed a sizeable mixed-race group among its enslaved population over centuries, Trinidad's late entry into slavocracy precluded this. According to John:

> There were few colored slaves—slaves with white ancestry—in Trinidad in 1813. In a well-established slave colony such as Jamaica, many color gradations had evolved over the generations: mulatto, quadroon, sambo, mustee, mustaphino. In Trinidad, however, slaves had been present in the island for only thirty years at the time of the initial [slave] registration: there had not yet been the opportunity for a large colored population to develop. Overall, only 6% of the Trinidadian slaves were colored . . . among the plantation slaves, only 4%, or 699 slaves, were colored.[49]

Trinidad's majority mixed-raced population would be found not among the enslaved but among a class of free colored immigrant inhabitants and slave-holders. Given their distinct status vis-à-vis enslaved Africans, the threat of alliances forming across racial/caste boundaries between enslaved and mixed colored communities was highly unlikely in Trinidad. The plantation slave system, with its accompanying legal reinforcements, ensured that social roles in Trinidad remained clearly demarcated between the free colored and enslaved. Trinidad was reflective of what Elsa Goveia identifies as a wider "three-tier socio-racial pattern prevailing in the Caribbean" consisting of European planters and settlers, free coloreds, and enslaved Africans.[50]

When the British assumed control of Trinidad from the Spanish in 1797, it was with a vision of establishing Trinidad as a thriving slave colony akin to Jamaica and Barbados. Debates in the British House of Commons ensued on how best to supplement Trinidad's demand for slave labor in cotton, coffee, and sugar cultivation, and one suggestion within these deliberations was to extend the African slave trade in order to procure further captives. In 1802, abolitionist-leaning member of Parliament George Canning announced in the House of Commons that in order to replicate the slave economy of its profitable Jamaican colony, Trinidad would have to increase its slave population by at least 250,000, and such a number could only be achieved through direct African importation. According to Canning, Jamaica had been nearly a half-century in the making of its present state of cultivation. Trinidad, in the nineteenth century, was in about the same state as Jamaica had been in 1763: "If there was a question of suddenly cultivating such an Island as Trinidad, we must make up our minds to the destruction of about a million of the human species."[51]

Growing abolitionist sentiments in Britain swayed the tide against the further enslavement of new Africans throughout its colonies. *Voyages: The Trans-atlantic Slave Trade Database* indicates that sixty-eight ships transported African captives from West and West-Central Africa—most from the Bight of Biafra and unspecified regions—to Trinidad between 1802 and 1808, an average of one ship per month over the six-year period.[52] Despite these importations, and especially after Britain's abolition of the international slave trade, effective in 1808, Trinidad increased its labor supply by establishing an "inter-colonial slave trade" among neighboring Caribbean islands. According to historian Eric Williams, this alternative slave trade involved "the transfer of slaves from the less productive and less profitable older islands to the newer and virgin soils of Trinidad and British Guiana. Between 1813 and 1821, Trinidad received over 3,800 such slaves, of whom nearly 1,100 came from Dominica and nearly 1,200 from Grenada."[53] Prior to this time, an overwhelming 4,000 had been imported from the island of Martinique.[54]

Documentary evidence yields some insight into the content of *lived slavery* and the inner slavescape of nineteenth-century British Trinidad. First, the vast majority of Trinidad's slaves were African born. After the close of the slave trade, colonial authorities required slave owners to deliver specific data concerning each enslaved African to the British Registrar's Office. The slave registries that spanned 1813–1834 in Trinidad recorded information on enslaved populations as to whether they were "African" or "creole" and, if "African," "the name of the country or district in Africa from which he or she was brought" along with noting any "tribal marks" or "country marks" that were visibly identifiable.[55] Moreover, 82 percent of Trinidad's slave population worked on agricultural plantations. In the late eighteenth and early nineteenth centuries, they were bound to one of close to 650 agricultural estates in Trinidad devoted to the production of cotton, cocoa, coffee, or sugar. Each plantation had on average between twenty-six and fifty-six slaves. More than half of all enslaved Africans were between the ages of twenty and thirty-five. They labored in various capacities such as field workers, hired hands, skilled laborers, domestic servants, or drivers and overseers. In addition, cash crop plantation labor such as that for sugar estates required sundry tasks related to the engine mill, boiling house, cane carting, cane weeding, and field work.[56] Enslaved Africans subsisted on a weekly ration of either four pounds of salt fish or three pounds of salt meat along with sixty plantains or six quarts of cassava. A small plot of land was allotted for vegetable cultivation on some plantations. Each year, the enslaved population was issued only two sets of clothing, one in May and one in December.[57]

Enslaved persons on Trinidad's plantation estates could expect to work under harsh conditions, be punished if they disobeyed, and die prematurely. Those residing on plantation estates were more likely to suffer from dysentery, yaws, leprosy, fevers, diphtheria, whooping cough, ulcerated sores, consumption, parasitic diseases such as worms, and malnutrition.[58] Published in 1820, *A Review of the Colonial Slave Registrations Acts in a Report of a Committee of the Board of Directors of the African Institution* specified that "the advocates of the Colonial slaves have always alleged the causes of the decline in the Slave population to be chiefly two—the excess of forced labour and the insufficiency of food; to both of which abuses there are far the strongest temptations on the sugar estates."[59] Given these conditions, the average enslaved African man lived until age thirty-nine and the average woman until forty-five. Alongside these figures were extremely high infant mortality rates. A third of all babies died before age one and a little less than half of all children born on Trinidad plantations never reached the age of five.[60] It is also important to keep in mind that there were multiple factors influencing mortality rates, such as the type of labor and even the nationality of the estate owner, with British-owned slaves dying at a faster rate than those of the Spanish and French.[61]

Slaves labored a minimum of thirteen hours each day, but if assigned to a sugar mill, they might be required to work through the night for as long as thirty hours.[62] Sundays were given off in some instances in addition to a few annual holidays such as Christmas Day, New Year's Day, Good Friday, and Corpus Christi. Several plantations experimented with giving Saturdays off in order to allow the slaves to work small plots of land, in lieu of providing weekly food rations. However, African-born slaves proved quite defiant in their refusal to work the plots—for which they were mistaken as "lazy"—making it necessary to abandon the idea.

> In gangs composed of new Africans, those who adopt it have had reason to repent of the experiment, a new Negro being naturally lazy and inactive, that he would rather suffer hunger and enjoy his repose than procure himself his subsistence by industry. The increasing opulence of the inhabitants having literally enabled them to augment their force by considerable purchases of this description of Negro, the custom of giving Saturday becomes highly imprudent and would occasion great losses to the Colony: Whereby it is hereby abolished and prohibited, under penalty of fifty dollars for every delinquent.[63]

Historical data citing recalcitrant and insubordinate behavior among African-born slaves was also coupled with reports of gendered forms of insurgency. Although the records are often silent on the question of women, colonial officials do reveal that enslaved women in Trinidad verbally castigated masters and stewards and outwardly defied commands. In 1825, Governor Woodford reported that "cases of insolence and insubordination frequently occur among the female slaves."[64] Throughout British colonial records were public debates "regarding the flogging of female slaves" given their tendency to assume an "Amazonian cast of character," leaving colonists asking the question in 1823, "What controul are we to have over [them]?"[65] In a confidential correspondence dated July 3, 1826, Governor Ralph James Woodford commented on the state-of-the-nation update on Trinidad's slave plantations: "I found the negroes generally conducting themselves well; the exceptions were among the females. . . . The women are every where complained of as having become much more refractory and licentious than they were wont to be."[66] Finally, a British commandant stationed in the Chaguanas region of Trinidad wrote to Governor Woodford in 1823 regarding the acts of verbal resistance visited upon colonial planters by female slaves. Advocating the use of the whip, the letter stated, "It is notorious that female slaves more frequently merit punishment than males, that powerful instrument of attack and defence, their tongue, is exerted in insufferable insult, the propensity to which is only checked by the dreaded whip."[67]

Concerning women, the records also indicate that colonial officials considered the reproductive rates of female slaves to be relatively low in Trinidad. With the close of the slave trade, stringent laws against slave smuggling, and the dire need for labor to operate plantations, colonial masters hoped that enslaved women would reproduce at a more rapid rate to supply their labor needs. In the 1820s, enslaved births were greatly impacted due "to inattention to the health of pregnant women, to insufficient food, and to extreme and murderous agricultural labor."[68] Colonial records also confirmed that female slaves commonly practiced abortion as a form of resistance against forced breeding.[69] Moreover, affecting slave fertility were also factors such as "chronic malnutrition" among female slaves and sterility as a result of widespread venereal disease among enslaved populations.[70] Contrary to the colonial perception of "low" fertility, on average an enslaved woman in Trinidad bore five children over the course of her life.[71] However, collectively these slave births were in no way able to sustain the increasing colonial requirements for labor.[72]

Slavery and Colonial Law

The social treatment of the enslaved in Trinidad was heavily regulated by colonial law. Governor Chácon, the last Spanish governor before transition to British rule, declared in the late 1780s that "the first and princip[al] occupation of slaves must be agricultural and not those labours that require a sedentary life."[73] Chácon was preoccupied with creating a major slave economy based on the exportation of agricultural goods. Therefore, the efficient supervision of plantation labor was the colony's first priority. Spanish laws covered a comprehensive range of subjects related to slave welfare, such as provisions, accommodations, illness, religious education, slave marriages, and punishments. More specifically, reminiscent of the early Spanish Siete Partidas,

> it included a prescription for compulsory religious education and observance of the numerous religious holidays, seventeen in all. . . . There

were also humane provisions with regard to food, clothing and lodging. It forbade all slaves under 17 and over 60 to be forced to work. . . . The law allowed the owner or the manager to punish a slave, but the punishment was not to exceed 25 lashes.[74]

Masters were instructed to report major slave offenses to the justice, where appropriate "corporal punishment" would be determined "according to the importance of the crime" and "the delinquent shall suffer, after having been approved of by the Audience of the District, whether it be death or mutilation of members."[75] Under these laws, disobedient slaves were to "be punished, either by the master of the Estate or by his Steward, according to the offence, with prison, chains or lashes, which must not exceed the number of twenty five, and those must be given in such a manner as not to cause any contusion or effusion of blood."[76] The Spanish slave codes appeared "benign" by British standards, as seen in a late eighteenth-century observation: "Whatever guilt Spain may incur by perseverance in a barbarous traffic, it must be admitted that her code of slave laws . . . deserves to be mentioned with the highest praise. Its mildness and equity are honorable to the feelings of the framers."[77]

Spanish slave codes would soon be replaced by the British Slave Code of 1800, fashioned by Lieutenant-General Sir Thomas Picton, who ruled from 1797 to 1804. This new code bespoke severity in its meta-legal enactment. Published as an "Ordinance of the Governor" on June 30, 1800, the document opened with a direct acknowledgment of Trinidad's diverse national identity and the challenges that lie therein in creating a unified slave colony:

> Whereas, in a West Indian Colony settled by different nations, varying in customs and opinions, it is important to incite the inhabitants of every class to mitigate the situation of their slaves, by rendering their servitude as limited and easy as possible and promoting their natural increase, so as that in course of time the importation of slaves from Africa may be considerably diminished, if not totally dispensed with; and whereas, those desirable ends cannot be more effectually attained, than by compelling owners of slaves to lodge, clothe, and maintain them sufficiently . . . by prescribing reasonable grounds to the power of masters and others, having charge of slaves, and by instructing them in the principles of Christianity, to inspire them with some degree of morality.[78]

Geared toward the treatment of slaves as a way of maximizing their labor efficiency and economic productivity, Governor Picton's code communicated a language of duty to the master class and a language of subjugation to the enslaved. Masters were to provide their slaves with "good and comfortable houses, well wattled and thatched so as to be perfectly wind and watertight"; a portion of land in order to produce "a sufficiency of ground provisions for himself and his family"; "half an hour in the morning for breakfast and two hours at noon for dinner" during the workday; and a hospital on each plantation for "the Negro who from sickness is incapable of doing his duty."

Specific punishments for slaves were also stipulated. Masters could now inflict up to thirty-nine lashes of the whip (as opposed to the maximum of twenty-five lashes under Spanish law) upon their slaves without regard to the severity of wounds inflicted in a single beating. The slave who suffered these lashes "could not be flogged again on the same day" until after "he be recovered from the effects of that punishment." Additionally, masters could not "inhumanely" strike a slave with "an edged weapon, such as a cutlass, axe, sword, or with a bludgeon or loaded beaustick."[79] As the boundaries of Trinidad's legal codes expanded and contracted in concert with the profitability and productivity of its enslaved labor force, these laws served as the arbiters and regulators of an organized and highly efficient method of securing, maintaining, subjecting, disciplining, and governing the victims of colonial slavery.

In regulating the importation of Africans into the colony, a British Order in Council dated March 26, 1812, sought to "provide more effectually for the prevention of the illegal and clandestine importation of Slaves into the island of Trinidad" by establishing a public registry. The registry would serve as an official record of "the registration and enrolment of the names and descriptions of all Negroes, Mulattoes, and Mustees, who now are, or at any time hereafter shall be held in a state of slavery within the said island, and of the births and deaths of all such Slaves."[80] After the British legally closed the slave trade in 1807, prohibiting all direct importations from Africa into its colonies, the increasing demand for labor in Trinidad encouraged the illegal smuggling of Africans into the colony in direct violation of the statute. According to John, the Slave Trade Abolition Act of 1807 (which became effective the following year) ended the transatlantic slave trade but also regulated the intercolonial slave trade:

> Slaves could be moved from one colony to another only under license from the governor or customs house of the exporting colony. If the slaves were destined for a recently acquired colony, such as Trinidad, a license was also required from the governor or customs house of the importing

colony. Furthermore, a quota was imposed on the number of slaves that could be imported into a colony, of not more than 3% of the extant slave population of that colony.[81]

To offset the illegal smuggling of slaves into Trinidad, which increased to nearly 5,000 in a single year, the order provided meticulous instructions for the "Registry of Plantation Slaves" and the "Registry of Personal Slaves."[82] Slave owners had to register slaves within one month of establishing residency and provide specific information, such as name, marital status, number of children, age, color, country or colony of origin, employment, physical description, and baptismal status. Owners were then required to take an oath attesting to the fact that the information provided was "without fraud, deceit, or evasion."[83] They also needed to provide an annual account of any deductions or additions to their slave pool, any "bodily defect or deformity" on their slaves, or any slave now categorized as dead, born, sold, manumitted, or deserted. The order further stipulated severe penalties for anyone "falsely" and "willfully" providing fraudulent information concerning slaves in their possession:

> And it is hereby further ordered, That if any person or persons shall, by means of any false or fraudulent return . . . keep or hold, or attempt to keep or hold, in Slavery, any African or other Negro or Mulatto, or other Coloured Person, which shall have been illegally imported or brought into the said island, and shall be thereof lawfully convicted . . . or they shall forfeit and pay for every offence, the sum of Three Hundred Pounds Sterling Money . . . and shall moreover, after any such conviction, be for ever after incapable of owning, holding, or possessing any Slave or Slaves within the said island.[84]

The order closed with an admonishment to all British colonial officials to ensure that these civil codes were being "effectually observed, obeyed, and executed, by all persons within the said island," and were duly warned that "they shall answer the contrary at their peril."[85]

Looking at it from a hemispheric perspective, slavery in Trinidad lasted for five short decades before its full abolishment in all British colonies on August 1, 1838, so Trinidad never reached the magnitude and enormity of Britain's earlier slave colonies in Jamaica and Barbados, and it functioned at a level several centuries behind its counterparts. At the time of emancipation, there were some 22,359 slaves manumitted in Trinidad, compared to Jamaica's over 300,000, demonstrating that Trinidad had never been able to fully overcome its labor shortage nor escape the challenges surrounding its pan-colonial diversity.[86]

From the eighteenth century, when Spanish governor Chácon attributed "the disunity" in Trinidad "to the mixture of nationalities and races and colours," to the years just before emancipation, when British Lord Goderich in his capacity as Secretary of State for War and the Colonies wrote that "society in Trinidad is divided into castes as strongly marked as those of Hindustan," the challenges of ethno-nationalism and diverse inhabitants prevailed.[87] The vast presence of free mixed-race coloreds of African descent, covered next, further complicated this social conundrum.

Racial Ambiguity, Nationalism, and *Les Gens de Colour* of Trinidad

Spain's eighteenth-century invitation to inhabit the island of Trinidad received an overwhelming response from Catholic planters. Thousands of French planters entered Trinidad eager to take full advantage of the island's economic prospects and came equipped with their own labor pool of enslaved Africans. Outnumbering the European French settlers in large quantities, surprisingly, were "free coloureds," who attempted to either transfer or improve upon the liminal social status they experienced in their former colonies. After the Spanish Crown issued the cedula of 1783, "many free coloureds [came] to Trinidad in the 1780s and 1790s . . . attracted by the promises of free land grants, citizenship and access to public posts" that were being advertised.[88] More specifically, they would have arrived from Martinique, Saint-Domingue, Guadeloupe, Dominica, St. Lucia, St. Vincent, and Grenada.[89]

Unlike Trinidad's enslaved population, free coloreds enjoyed a social standing that enabled them to become landed "small estate owners" and slaveholders. Historian Bridget Brereton points out the racial inequity in distribution and indicates that "although coloured immigrants were to receive half as much land as their white counterparts, they were nevertheless formally given land by the Spanish government as planters and slave-owners, with all the status which that implied in a plantation society."[90] Trinidad's population a year before the cedula totaled 2,813, including a small class of 295 free coloreds. Less than fifteen years after the issuance of that cedula, Trinidad had some 4,476 free non-whites in its midst, consisting primarily of what the Spanish identified as *pardocracia* or "racially 'mixed' people."[91]

Lisa Clayton Robinson asserts, quite remarkably, that "Trinidad had the largest free Afro-Creole population in the Caribbean."[92] Adhering to the terms of the cedula, free coloreds had "to swear allegiance to the Spanish king" in return for sixteen acres of land for themselves and for each slave accompanying them (versus thirty-two acres for whites and sixteen acres for each accompanying slave), the legal right to property, and "after five years' residence . . . all the privileges of a Spanish citizen."[93] According to Brereton, after the 1783 cedula, the "whites were outnumbered, not only by the slaves, but also by the free coloureds."[94] Therefore, it was on the strength of both foreign white settlers who arrived after the cedula and on the substantial efforts of free colored planters that Spain's once barren colony of Trinidad was propelled into the global agricultural market.

> After 1783 the island's plantation economy was controlled largely by the French settlers, white and coloured, who brought with them slaves, capital and long experience in the cultivation of cotton, coffee, sugar and other tropical export crops. . . . Late in the day, Trinidad stepped into line as a major producer of West Indian staples and as a creator of wealth for planters and merchants. . . . In the south nearly all the settlers were French, white and coloured, and here flourishing plantations were established.[95]

Trinidad soon developed into a profitable cash crop colony.[96] In less than fifteen years after the cedula, 468 new plantations, with an area of approximately 85,000 acres, were developed in Trinidad by white and free colored French planters.[97] Free people of color, in particular, carefully navigated the social terrain of Trinidad in an effort to maintain their precarious privileged status. By the late eighteenth and early nineteenth centuries, Trinidad had become a colony described as "Spanish in name, French in fact, African at its base."[98]

After Britain wrested Trinidad from the Spanish in the late 1790s, free people of color had to fight incessantly to acquire rights proportionate to their wealth. Undercurrents of nationalist tendencies emerged among free coloreds in subtle yet challenging increments during the first quarter of the nineteenth century. They certainly did not want to jeopardize their economic standing as planters, slave owners, and artisans in Trinidadian society, even as they pushed to elevate their social status above British colonial restrictions. To varying degrees throughout the colonial Caribbean, "free people of colour," Eric Williams maintains, "suffered from various disabilities, social in nature, such as segregation, obstacles in the way of their professional advancement and exclusion from civil offices. They demanded . . . admission to the civil service and full equality with the whites, to whom they made overtures for a common front based on identity of economic interests."[99]

After the cedula, free coloreds entered Trinidad at such high rates that by the mid-1790s, they outnumbered white settlers two to one. By 1813, they owned 37.3 percent of the agricultural estates and 31.5 percent of enslaved

Africans in southern Trinidad. They then grew to constitute an overwhelming 58.5 percent of Trinidad's urban population by emancipation in the 1830s.[100] Their numerical predominance worked to their disadvantage, however, as it made colonial authorities view them as a potential social threat.

Free coloreds occupied a social space wrought with ambiguity and incertitude. Under Spanish rule, they existed within a de facto social order that glossed the margins of equality. However, beginning with the reign of Governor Picton and particularly underscored with Governor Woodford who assumed office in 1813, British officials disregarded the intermediary social status of free coloreds and systematically dismantled the "hierarchy of prestige" that afforded them privilege.[101] Consciously aware of themselves as a national civic group, they organized various petitions requesting full political participation. Their collective dissent signaled to British authorities that "they were well aware that the grant of an assembly and British laws would seriously undermine their legal and political position. They were letting the government know that the free coloured leadership was justifiably afraid of government by an assembly in which they would have no representation," thus they supported a system of Crown Colony governance, dissimilar to most Euro-Atlantic colonial settlers who sought greater representation and autonomy.[102] The sheer magnitude of the free colored presence in Trinidadian society meant their influence and concerns could not be easily ignored. Politically, the government of Trinidad had, in part, mobilized in response to the sizeable presence of free colored landowners.

Following the conquest of the island in 1797, the British established Trinidad as an "experimental colony" and "the first territory under English rule to have the Crown Colony form of government."[103] According to Scott MacDonald, "the Crown Colony system had been established to eliminate the hazy power of Spanish institutions, to silence the vocal English merchants . . . who demanded representative government, and to keep power out of the hands of those of African and mixed African-European descent."[104] British officials wrestled with the question of self-governance for Trinidad, which would inadvertently empower propertied free coloreds and politically dislocate the white minority. In a letter addressed to the secretary of state, Governor Picton argued the following:

> One of the objects, first and most important to determine, will be the right of voting, and it may be thought expedient, as in the old Islands, to exclude the Free People of Colour; here by far the most numerous class in the Colony and of whom many possess considerable property. The distinction

will render them at all times dissatisfied with the situation and liable to be affected in their loyalty by every prospect of change or amelioration. Of two things one will necessarily happen, they must be either formally rejected, or openly acknowledged.

The establishment of the Crown Colony, which relied on appointments from the local governor and prohibited an elected assembly, was the concession. It circumvented the voting question for free people of color and blocked them from having any potential political power. The British found themselves facing obstacles similar to those the Spanish had confronted as they navigated the knotty social challenges of a diverse society.

In eighteenth- and nineteenth-century Trinidad, contending national and racial identities bespoke political instability and social uncertainty. Governor Picton characterized Trinidad in 1802 as "a country composed of such combustible material."[105] In a colony where the white population consisted of former Spanish rulers, British colonial officials, and French planters while the non-white population was composed of an enslaved labor class and a free colored majority, social unrest was perceived as imminent. The presence of free coloreds elicited a shared ambivalence on the part of both Spanish and British officials. Although welcomed as "extremely profitable subjects," free coloreds stirred fears as potential insurrectionists, as many had migrated into Trinidad from the revolutionary hotbeds of Martinique, Guadeloupe, St. Lucia, and Saint-Domingue (Haiti).[106]

The island's last Spanish governor, José María Chacón, expressed his growing uneasiness regarding the free colored population and its disruptive capacity as social agitators along with that of enslaved Africans: "The contact which our people of colour and our Negro slaves have had with the French and Republicans have made them think of liberty and equality and the first spark will light the whole Colony in a blaze."[107] More pointedly, Chacón added:

> The English are attacking the French islands and as many . . . as can escape fly to the shores of Trinidad where there is no force to prevent them settling. The greater part are Mulattoes and Negroes which increases in consequence our numbers, and infuses them with the same ideas and desires and make the danger of a rising more imminent each day.[108]

Colonial fears and anxieties were high, particularly in the wake of the Haitian Revolution, where free coloreds assisted in toppling France's lucrative slave colony with its estimated 300 million dollar net worth and its position as supplier of "three-fourths of the world's sugar."[109] Free coloreds were marked as social hazards because, according to Brereton, "in Saint-Domingue (Haiti) the civil war had begun when free coloureds asserted their rights, and in Trinidad they were feared as a possible source of subversion and danger. The whites claimed to see the spectre of slave revolt behind every attempt by a coloured man to assert his freedom."[110] They were deemed revolutionary sympathizers, "a possible source of subversion and danger," and a potential class of "dangerous revolutionaries."[111] One colonial inhabitant character-ized the free coloreds as a population "mostly composed of refugees and desperate characters, who had been implicated in all the rebellions and massacres in the neighbouring islands."[112] He concluded that "their princi-ples are incompatible with regular government."[113] These contemptuous views culminated in one white planter's summation of free coloreds as "a vile and infamous race."[114]

Britain's Governor Picton was consumed with fears of slave revolt and was equally as emphatic in his disdain for free coloreds. Saint-Domingue, Marti-nique, Guadeloupe, St. Lucia, Grenada, and St. Vincent were all experiencing varying degrees of unrest when Picton assumed his charge in 1797.[115] Hints of their feared seditious tendencies were apparent in Picton's remarks label-ing free coloreds "a dangerous class which must gradually be got rid of."[116] Regardless of the governor's trepidations, free coloreds and free blacks in Trinidad could not readily be ignored, as they wielded power through their numbers, their involvement in politics, and their substantial land owner-ship.[117] Thus, Picton chose the route of social restrictions, heavily imposing them upon free communities of African descent while apprehensively seek-ing to lead and fortify a majority non-white, foreign-born colony. Among other historians, James Millette attributes to Picton an intolerance to socially accommodate an interstitial space for mixed-race populations in colonial territories. Picton possessed the "invaluable merit of guile for maintaining and perpetuating the inequalities of colour."[118] According to Millette, "the existence of a class of free coloured and black persons greatly outnumber-ing the white population of various nationalities gave the problem of colour and race a sharpness not to be found elsewhere in the contemporary West Indies."[119] In March 1803, the colonial commissioners wrote to the secretary of state to express the fear that Governor Picton, having "conducted himself in so extraordinary a manner with respect to the Free People of Colour and Slaves," had incited a "dangerous spirit," causing an increase in "dangerous persons" being "deported from the Colony, for conspiring against His Maj-esty's Government," much "to the great satisfaction of everyone desirous of the tranquility of the Colony."[120] In response, Colonel William Fullarton, appointed first commissioner for the government of Trinidad, followed up with an additional letter to the secretary of state, again critiquing Picton's "most outrageous violence in order to intimidate all persons capable of giving evidence or information" as well as the "violent proceedings" of his commission.[121]

Subsequent governors such as Sir Thomas Hislop (1804–1811) would uphold these racial and social distinctions and actively thwart the efforts of free coloreds to plead their case before the British Crown. A petition in 1810 signed by 236 free colored residents implored Governor Hislop to sanction their "Petition to the Throne" seeking "a secure and equitable mode of existence," asking relief from "unnecessary regulations" and "unexpected disadvantages," as well as protection "from the establishment of any future law which . . . might possibly be calculated solely to vex and personally to degrade us in our individual capacities."[122] In his reply, the governor was "of the opinion that an address from the people of colour to the Throne would be premature." It also "would lead to a suspicion that they [free coloreds]were apprehensive, that in the proposals which may be suggested for the security, welfare, and happiness of His Majesty's subjects generally, their interests should be overlooked—a conclusion which no circumstance hitherto affecting them can justify."[123] Similar to his predecessor, Governor Hislop was a soldier faced with a colony containing 6,264 free colored inhabitants and a white population of 2,495. He undoubtedly framed the larger issue driving his concerns as "one of revolution and its suppression, not of political accommodation."[124]

Ruling from 1813 to 1828, a decade after Picton, Governor Ralph James Woodford designated this free colored body "the worst enemy" and "encouraged or directly instituted new forms of discrimination and social degradation against them; he insulted them by his own strongly prejudiced attitudes towards them and by the example he set to officials and whites in general in their interactions with them."[125] From 1820–1823, Governor Woodford's incarceration rates reflected this discrimination as he jailed 2,517 enslaved and free people of color versus 386 colonial whites.[126] Under Woodford's rule, there was a surge in free coloreds' declaration of their rights, having established themselves as a class of prominent proprietors on the island (see figure 1.1).

Despite Woodford's efforts at restriction, landed free coloreds mobilized against these colonial constraints and petitioned the British Crown. With the support of several white planters, a "Memorial of the Free People of Colour" was put forth on November 19, 1823, demanding "admission without respect of colour to the full enjoyment of those rights" that had been enjoyed prior to British rule.[127] The memorial also insisted upon the "removal of all

AN ADDRESS

to the

RIGHT HON. EARL BATHURST

His Majesty's Principal Secretary of State for the Colonies
relative to the claims
which the

coloured population of Trinidad have to the
same civil and political privileges with
their white fellow-subjects.

BY A FREE MULATTO
OF THE ISLAND

"And if not equal all, yet free,
Equally free; for orders and degrees
Jar not with liberty, but well consist."
Paradise Lost, B. V v. 79.

LONDON
Printed in the year 1824

FIGURE 1.1 Free coloreds in Trinidad invested considerable effort in acquiring rights equal to their white colonial counterparts, often making direct entreaties to the British officials on their own behalf. From Anthony de Verteuil, *A History of Diego Martin 1784–1884* (Port of Spain: Paria Publishing, 1987). Reprinted by permission of Paria Publishing.

restrictions at present imposed upon assemblage for purposes of amusement, information, benevolence, or for any other purposes not inconsistent with the law administered to our white fellow subjects" and the "removal of all impediments in the way of marriage between white and free coloured."[128] An important voice representing the free coloreds was Dr. Jean Baptiste Philippe, from an elite free colored family, educated at Edinburgh, and author of *Free Mulatto* cataloging the grievances of free coloreds in Trinidad. *Free Mulatto* was published in 1824 after Philippe and another free colored representative traveled to England arguing on behalf of "free colored" and "mulatto" civil rights.[129] Governor Woodford, skeptical of the granting of rights to free coloreds, communicated his impressions to the Crown: "It is no doubt harsh to the minds of Englishmen to make these distinctions in a British territory, and not allow to owners of property the right which that property carries with it in England, but if the whites are to maintain their ascendancy, and Great Britain is to preserve her West India as colonies, this distinction must, as it appears to me, be maintained."[130] Woodford concluded with an admonishing reminder of "the example of St. Domingo," as though prophesying the fate of Trinidad should Britain consider conferring rights to free coloreds. Despite his efforts, colored nationalism triumphed, and a year after the cessation of Woodford's rule, the strictures were lifted by an Order of the King in Council in July 1829:[131]

> Whereas by certain Laws and Ordinances heretofore made . . . His Majesty's subjects of Free Condition, but of African Birth or Descent, are subjects to various Civil or Military disabilities in the said Island to which His Majesty's Subjects of European Birth or Descent are not subject; and it is expedient that all such distinctions Should be abolished and annulled. His Majesty is therefore pleased by and with the advice of the Privy Council, and it is hereby Ordered that every Law, Ordinance and Proclamation, or pretended Law, Ordinance or Proclamation in force within His Majesty's said Island of Trinidad, whereby His Majesty's Subjects of African Birth Or Descent, being of Free Condition, are subjected to any disability, Civil or Military, to which His Majesty's Subjects of European Birth and Descent are not subject, shall be, and the same and each of them are and is forever repealed, abolished, and annulled.[132]

Free people of African descent struggled to gain a sense of social security in a colony where racial slavery still formed the basis of its economy. Although the racial composition of free people of color often overlapped that of the enslaved, the two groups did not customarily partake of the same social and legal status in Trinidad. Perhaps departing from prevailing perspectives, one scholarly interpretation of the politics of free coloreds is that "the reluctance of the free people of color collectively to call for immediate emancipation for the masses of slaves is not proof that free people of color entirely rejected the idea that slaves were connected to them in some way."[133] Rather, their status as "economically privileged actors" complicated their "revolutionary inclinations," and instead they opted to work "within the limits of the strategic actions available to them" in order to maintain their fragile social stability.[134]

Although free coloreds were made to inhabit a tenuous social space in Trinidad, they fought hard for self-preservation and social mobility to minimize any cultural, educational, or religious distance between them and their white counterparts. They aspired to attend the same European schools of higher learning, to enter into the same respectable professions, and to adhere to similar Catholic piety and values. In analyzing the mixed-race population, it is suggested that "because of the preferential treatment they received, the mulattos classed themselves apart from the dark Negroes, and maintained living patterns more like those of the whites."[135] According to Clement "many of the educated colored colonials acquired the air, manner, and accents of cultivated British gentlemen," and "prestige accrued to those who adhered to the patterns of the white elite, especially in marriage, occupation, education, and standard of living."[136]

Throughout the Caribbean, free coloreds were often seen as what former North American slave Adeline Marshall called "no nation" people.[137] Marshall commented, "I call dem 'no nation' cause dat what dey is, ain't all black or all white, but mix."[138] Thus, free coloreds occupied a liminal social space in Trinidad society as on many adjacent islands. They were often viewed as a "buffer" group, or what Governor Beckwith of Barbados called "a barrier between the whites and the slaves."[139] British secretary of state Lord Liverpool described them as "reconciled to the middle situation which they occupy between the whites and the slaves."[140] Historian Scott MacDonald argues that in Trinidad "it should be emphasized that the majority of those involved in the movement for equality were light-skinned Afro-Creoles and that the struggle was for the rights of the free colored, not the rights of the enslaved black population."[141] He adds, "To many of the free colored, there was a fear of 'slipping back' and being associated with the black slaves who, it was perceived . . . symbolized the uncivilized and barbaric traditions of Africa."[142] They therefore viewed themselves as enormously distinct from the masses of Trinidad's enslaved population, whom many of them owned. As a result, enslaved blacks did not exempt free coloreds from the contempt they held for the larger white planter class, and as a class, free coloreds were equally targeted, as in the 1805 attempted rebellion (described in this chapter's opening passage). Therefore, their middling status, ideologically thematized as "no nation," made their national allegiance suspect to both white colonists and enslaved Africans while situated at the racial crossroads of both bloodlines.

"Inter-Society Pluralism" from Slavery to Emancipation

The population of slaves and free coloreds constituted the overwhelming majority of African-descended presence in Trinidad. Under the British governors who ruled from slavery through emancipation—Abercromby, Picton, Fullarton, Hislop, Munro, Woodford, Smith, Grant, and Hill—Trinidad defied neat Euro/African racial binaries, instead constituting what George Eaton Simpson identified as an "inter-society pluralism."[143] For Simpson, this pluralism was a distinguishing component of much of the wider Caribbean, with its mixture of colonial co-inhabitants generating a strained multinationalism and multi-racialism.

Although Governor Picton was certain of Trinidad's profitability as a slave colony, others such as abolitionist, George Canning in England, mentioned previously, resisted the expansion of slavery into new British territories and instead argued in the House of Commons for land cultivation through free labor and settlement.[144] In April 1803, the Colonial Department advised that in order to "prevent the spirit of Insurrection arising amongst the Negroes," the "best manner" was to "introduce a race of free cultivators, kept distinct from the Negroes and by their interests attached to the White Planters."[145] Thus, in the same year, 1806, when "Parliament prohibited the slave trade to the new conquered or ceded colonies, including Trinidad," the island experienced its first wave of Asian immigrants as free laborers.[146] The Chinese, with their agricultural background, were deemed suitable and industrious laborers for the colony, with one British proponent of this initiative stating, "Two Chinese labourers with a light plough and a buffalo would do as much as 40 stout Negroes."[147] Driven by romantic racialism, the British sought to vigorously recruit Chinese laborers to Trinidad and gave careful thought to devising a recruitment strategy. In 1803 correspondence from Kenneth MacQueen to the Right Honorable John Sullivan, Under Secretary of State, proposed:

> The Chinese being naturally a cautious and jealous people the prospect about to be held forth to them should be highly encouraging and at the time specified in explicit and unequivocal terms. They should be told,

for instance, that Trinidad is a large fertile island ceded to [Great] Britain[;] . . . that it is the wish of British Government to have it inhabited not by slaves but by a free people; that the Chinese are preferred to all others, as being natives of a warm climate, and still more as being industrious, sober, orderly people and that they may assure themselves of receiving every encouragement and protection under the mild influence of the English laws.[148]

As a result, a few hundred Chinese immigrants entered Trinidad on October 12, 1806. Explaining to existing proprietors the meaning of the Chinese arrival in the colony, Governor Hislop proclaimed, "His Majesty, for reasons connected with the safety, and prosperity of his West Indian possession, has thought it expedient to introduce a race of free cultivators, who, from habits and feelings, will keep themselves distinct from the Negroes, and who from interest will be inseparably attached to the European proprietors." Guided by racialized reasoning, the Crown anticipated that Chinese immigrants would form "a barrier between us, and the negroes; with whom they (the Chinese) do not associate; & consequently to whom they will always offer a formidable opposition."[149] Disappointingly, the hopes and expectations placed on this new free labor class were short-lived. Forty Chinese immigrants opted to leave Trinidad in the first year, while another dozen perished due to disease; by 1810 approximately thirty remained on the island, choosing instead to be shopkeepers rather than agriculturalists.[150] Not until the early 1850s, following the emancipation of slaves in the British Caribbean, would Chinese labor in particular, and Asian labor more broadly, be successfully recruited to Trinidad.

Following the abolition of slavery, formerly enslaved Africans who resided on the island were reluctant to continue meeting the labor demands of Trinidad's plantation estates. Therefore, Asian immigrants such as the Chinese entered the Caribbean in much larger numbers after emancipation (along with sizeable numbers of new populations of liberated Africans, discussed later). Historian Fiona Rajkumar estimates that between the 1850s and 1860s, some 18,000 Chinese entered the Caribbean as indentured laborers. Their contracts of indentureship were on average three to five years in tenure and did not have the repatriation stipulations as would be the case for later Asian immigrants. Over time, according to Rajkumar, Chinese indentured laborers in Trinidad "abandoned the plantation, many even before their contract ended[,] by redeeming or purchasing the remaining years."[151] Even in this second wave, Chinese immigrants were again not a sustainable labor force for the agricultural expectations of Trinidad.

Increased success among Asian indentured populations would eventually come with workers from the British colony of India. According to O. Nigel Bolland, "By the mid-1840s, West Indian planters had persuaded the British government to support Indian immigration (a loan of half a million pounds helped to finance the scheme) and by 1851 it was well under way. British Guiana received 238,909 East Indians, Trinidad received 143,939, Jamaica imported 36,412, St. Lucia 4,354, Grenada 3,200, and St. Vincent 2,472."[152] Unlike the Chinese, of the nearly 150,000 East Indians who arrived in Trinidad starting in 1845, about 90 percent decided to become permanent inhabitants after their period of indenture ended, according to historian Sherry-Ann Singh.[153] Moreover, Asian populations imported the religious traditions of Hinduism, Islam, Confucianism, and Buddhism to nineteenth century Trinidad.

In line with the rapid increase and continued diversification of its residential population, less than a decade after the arrival of the first Chinese immigrants in 1806 the British government also opened acres of land to an additional free community of African descent: "Merikans," or black North American populations from the US South.[154] Their systematic arrival, beginning in 1815, further added to the plurality of African-descended communities. The North American blacks entering Trinidad were primarily former slaves, exposed to Baptist and southern US Africana traditions, who joined the British Corps of Colonial Marines fighting against their American masters in the War of 1812. In exchange for their military service, the British offered them land and resettlement opportunities in British-dominated territories.

Populations of African Americans, primarily Baptists, from South Carolina and Virginia arrived in Trinidad incrementally between May 1815 and August 1816.[155] Their distinct form of Baptist worship reflected their southern American background and "a knowledge of herbs and its [sic] preparations, which they applied as cure for almost every medical disorder."[156] They joined a much smaller population of enslaved African Americans who arrived more than a decade earlier, in 1803, following the "War of American Independence": "as a reward the slaves received their freedom as well as land in the crown colony of Trinidad."[157]

The arrival of close to one thousand Black North American ex-soldiers from the Corps of Colonial Marines was not an effort unilaterally supported by all in Trinidad, and it created unlikely cross-racial alliances in opposition to this venture. For example, "a joint petition from free people of color and whites" was presented to Governor Woodford challenging the "1816 settlement of American refugees in Naparima."[158] This interracial alliance between white plantation estate owners and "the Colored and free Black Inhabitants of those

Quarters" expressed "alarm" regarding the group of newly freed "American Refugees" to their region.[159] According to Mitchell, this left the governor somewhat perplexed, for as he stated, "Many of the present Petitioners were Slaves [just] a few Years ago." However, the fact that they "possess[ed] some of the finest Estates in the Island . . . and ha[d] sent their Children for Education to England" perhaps explains these manumitted slaves shifting allegiance and making common accord with whites and coloreds.[160] Woodford thought that the former Trinidadian slaves in the region would have been a "much more real Ground of Alarm to the few white Settlers of those Quarters at that time, than is to be apprehended from the present New Comers."[161] Initially residing in the southeastern region of Naparima, black North Americans were met with added hostility. Neighboring planters who owned estates and enslaved laborers thought them an ominous symbol of freedom and independence. The black soldiers and their families were, therefore, forced to relocate further south, near Princes Town, where they were separated into six "company villages," reflective of their former military companies.

Two years later, the British established a parallel group of military company villages for its newly relocated West India Regiments. From 1795–1815 this was a militia assembled in phases: 1795–1807—"recruits bought directly from suppliers in Africa," 1808–1815—"recruits were prisoners of war and recaptives," 1812–1815—"voluntary recruits from Sierra Leone."[162] In other words, the British assembled a sundry militia from Black Carolina Corps and corps of black rangers, prisoners, and recruits from Caribbean colonies and directly from Africa, particularly Sierra Leone.[163] Following the War of 1812, of the twelve total regiments formed, the Sixth West India Regiment and the Third West India Regiment occupied land in Eastern Trinidad in 1819 and, with continued demobilization of the troops, by 1825 a number of these primarily African-born soldiers were relocated to Trinidad's Manzanilla area, a considerable distance away from the slave estates.[164] Both sets of African-descended militia settlements [North American and West India] emerge within the colonial record in 1831 with complaints to Acting Governor Sir Charles Felix Smith that as "Refugees and Disbanded Soldiers," "His Majesty's Govt. will not sanction expence for their Religious Instruction."[165] More than a decade later, the issue of religious instruction was not resolved and their "religious state" was described as "most deplorable" and also relapsing in the "errors of Mahometanism, under the guidance of three Mandingo priests," with one Protestant missionary admitting, "I have recently visited the settlements of the disbanded black soldiers at Manzanilla, at the request of the bishop, and although I am the nearest Protestant minister, . . . I find that I should be unable to pay them that close attention which their spiritual wants require, solely from the difficulties arising from the distance and the bad state of the roads."[166]

Although possessing racial overlap with others in the British colony, the North American "New Comers" in the company villages stood out in this Anglo-colony for their "pattern of language" that undoubtedly complicated the religious, cultural, linguistic, and social milieu of African-descended communities in Trinidad.[167] They introduced further diversity and complexity to the intricate *nation-al* self-understandings of Trinidad's communities of African ancestry. Before departing the United States, they held the legal status of chattel slave. After relocating to the Hispano/Franco/Anglo colony of Trinidad, they became "British subjects," and entered into a society with a recognized class of land and slaveholders of mixed racial heritage. Finally, they navigated the even more ambiguous national identity as "ex-Americans" or "Merikans."[168] These North American settlers added their own distinct layer of southern US Atlanticized African identity to this multifaceted Caribbean context, making Trinidad more richly multilingual, multicultural, multireligious, and ambiguously multinational.

Governor Woodford capitalized on the influx of hundreds of black North Americans by using them as free labor to clear the southern part of the island and to build Trinidad's municipal infrastructures. Equipped with skills such as rice planting and tree felling from their days of slavery in South Carolina, they soon began to work in various capacities throughout the colony. However, so as to make "a clear distinction between their status and that of the slaves," they were resistant to being "fully integrated into the plantation system."[169] Describing African American resettlement in Trinidad, Brereton states:

> Each refugee was allotted 16 acres of land, and the villages were put under the control of unpaid sergeants and corporals who were to have minor disciplinary powers, and a white superintendent. The "Americans," as they were called, were expected to maintain road communications between San Fernando and the southern and eastern coasts, and to open up a district that was still largely uncleared in the 1820s. . . . After 1831 the Company villages ceased to be separate settlements under the special control of the government, and gradually, as sugar cultivation spread into the southern district, they were more and more integrated into the general economic and social life of the island.[170]

Perhaps overlooked in American Atlantic history is that following the abolition of British slavery, colonial officials in Trinidad looked once more to free African Americans in the United States as a possible solution for mitigating the shortage of labor in the colony. From 1838 to 1844, a legal ordinance authorized payment of a fee for each immigrant laborer a colonial recruiting agent enticed to Trinidad.[171] This recruiting venture aggressively pursued free African Americans dispersed throughout the United States. Agents attempted to draw them to Trinidad through rhetorical strategies that invoked the restrictive American laws policing the lives of free African Americans and emphasized the reality of racial prejudice in the United States. Trinidad's governor appointed both white and African-descended recruiting agents to travel throughout New York, Maryland, Pennsylvania, Delaware, and New Jersey to galvanize support for widespread emigration.[172]

In 1840, recruiting agent William Burnley personally traveled to New York on this mission and subsequently wrote in a letter to the secretary of state in London that the colony's recruiting efforts would have to target "educated" African Americans because African Americans who were not educated or were only nominally so were creating "a feeling of disgust amongst the whites" and obstructing the larger matter at hand in the island. Assuring the secretary of state that there was an existing pool, Burnley confirmed:

> I had much communication with men of this description when last in the United States. I assured them that they would be treated and considered in Trinidad as British subjects; that the alien laws were in that colony in abeyance, and that they would be competent equally with naturalized subjects to hold property and to fill public situations.[173]

Burnley and local clergy envisaged additional African Americans would have a positive effect on the "native labourers" who were emancipated in Trinidad believing "that the introduction of the immigrants from the United States of America . . . will tend, by the better example they have shown, to improve [native labourers'] moral conduct."[174] Burnley described African Americans as "shrewd, sensible people and competent to manage their own affairs" and confessed that he was "so well satisfied with the domestic habits" that he was "convinced that they will not settle without their families."[175] His only concern was that they possessed an "extreme dearness of their food" and that the duties on imported food goods would be "so high" as to be prohibitive.[176]

Despite Burnley's concerted efforts, recruiting agents were not able to produce the significant numbers of black North American immigrants expected from this potential labor source. In 1840, two African American delegates had been sent by the free community in Maryland to investigate Trinidad. The planter class extended its hospitality to them, and they were graciously received at a dinner hosted in their honor. Although the delegates returned with mixed reviews, by 1847 close to 1,301 African Americans had left the United States bound for Trinidad, yet a number still consequentially lower than anticipated.[177]

In the end, suspicions and rumors circulating among free black populations in the United States undermined and worked to the detriment of Trinidad's plan to recruit large swaths of African Americans. Given the context of US slavery, this free population was distrustful of "the intentions of white men, however coaxing they might sound."[178] It was rumored among free US blacks that they would only receive "lizards, monkeys, and parrots" for their meals.[179] Moreover, interest in Trinidad was thoroughly subverted when those who had initially migrated to the island returned with unfavorable reports. After 1850, Trinidadian colonists made additional strategic efforts to recruit African Americans, hoping that the recently passed Fugitive Slave Act would work to their advantage. As incentives, recruiters emphasized the opportunity "to naturalize immigrants after twelve months residence" and to secure "a grant of homestead and two acres of Crown Land."[180] But given minimal African American response, an insufficient yield of Asian immigrants during their first attempt, and a sizeable class of formerly enslaved laborers refusing to work the plantation estates, white colonists again—although with great apprehension and ambivalence—turned once more to the continent of Africa as a labor resource.

"Liberated" Africans in Postemancipation Trinidad

Transitioning from the slave trade to what can best be described as the indenture trade, British Trinidad once again positioned native Africans as an essential labor source for its postslavery economy. Thousands of West and Central Africans supplied this new workforce.[181] The British navy "liberated" them from slave ships, and these "liberated" Africans would face a fate of permanent diaspora, never to return to their original homelands. Instead, many were caught in a web of multiple resettlements in British territories on the continent of Africa, and thousands of others were reexported to destinations in the Caribbean/Americas as indentured laborers in plantation colonies. An estimated 30,000–40,000 disembarked in the British Caribbean from the 1830s to 1860s.[182]

The discussion of liberated Africans is taken up more extensively in chapter 4 with the examination of the historic 1870s and 1880s legal cases against liberated Africans John Cooper (aka Hou Quervee) and Mah Nannie on charges of obeah and sorcery. For this immediate postemancipation context, it is important to situate liberated Africans within the contours of Trinidad's developing inter-society pluralism and diverse racial and *nation-al* blackness, inclusive of formerly enslaved and mixed-race populations, as well as North American and West India soldiers. And although these combined African-descended populations constituted the vast majority of Trinidad's inhabitants, Dayo Nicole Mitchell cautions that "the *varieties* of experience as a person of color belied any notion of a cohesive class."[183]

Trinidad, in particular, obtained close to 1,000 liberated Africans prior to British emancipation. In 1834, there is evidence of the governor, Sir George Hill, announcing the arrival of "207 Prize Africans" from Havana, Cuba, to be "employed as Agricultural Free Laborers" in Trinidad. Upon entry, they were "divided into 20 lots of 10 each (5 males and 5 females) keeping those together attached by relationship or friendship" and then "distributed in 20 lots upon 20 different estates."[184] The administration's preference for these "freed Africans" was that they would be "all fresh captured Africans" and not have resided in Cuba for more than two years.[185] Emphasizing their "fresh African" designation, the governor issued a receipt to each of the estate owners who received a lot of ten Africans, indicating their sex, "African and Baptismal Names," and a reminder that "the Africans are at present, from their ignorance of the languages used on this Island, unable to make known their wants or complaints." Thus, the administration requested they be placed under "special observation" by their employers.[186]

A rapid influx of reexported Africans occurred between the 1840s and 1860s, when, according to Rosanne Adderley and Johnson U. J. Asiegbu, "the island received over 7,000 immigrants from Africa" from Sierra Leone and Saint Helena and a small population from Brazil.[187] Given the continued demand for labor in the postslavery era, British officials engaged in deliberate strategies to recruit liberated Africans.[188] Depending on the point of origin and the year of arrival in Trinidad, liberated Africans could range from "English-speaking, Christian educated" to those recently rescued and depicted by the British as in a state of "extreme uncivilization."[189] European employers required multiple sources of labor that necessarily drew from a spectrum of laboring classes, and they provided financial incentives to offset passage expenses from Africa. However, unlike East Indians arriving during the same period, incentives to liberated Africans did not include a "free return passage."[190]

Liberated Africans entered the Caribbean forming *nation* cooperatives that reinforced social belonging and social cohesion. They added new texture to the region's religious, cultural, and linguistic landscape and did not readily fit into preexisting Afro-Creole communities. Given their significant numbers, liberated Africans undoubtedly contributed to the wider pollination of culture, religion, language, and custom in Trinidad. With their arrival, Trinidad's population surged: "African-born individuals" constituted some 37 percent of the island's population.[191]

Throughout official colonial documents, newspapers, travel narratives, and correspondence, writers associated liberated Africans with *nation* appellations. Colonial nomenclature included a basic "tribal" and *nation* typology of differentiation. By 1889, noted Trinidadian linguist J. J. Thomas identified the belonging groups of the indentured populations as "Mandingoes, Foulahs, Houssas, Calvers, Gallahs, Karamenties, Yorubas, Aradas, Cangas, Kroos, Timnehs, Veis, Eboes, Mokoes, Bibis, [and] Congoes."[192] Forming distinct *nation* enclaves through residential patterns, these African groups would make a significant impact on the religio-cultural milieu in Trinidad. Over the course of two decades, these liberated Africans (or what the Spanish called *emancipados*) of largely Yoruba, Kongo, and Rada descent introduced, alongside the ex-enslaved, a new infusion of Africanity into Trinidad's post-emancipation matrix.[193]

Much scholarly attention is given, for example, to the cultural imprint of the non-enslaved population of Yoruba who arrived in Trinidad in significant numbers beginning in the late 1830s. Regarding the Yoruba, historian David Trotman asserts:

> [Those] who settled in British Guiana and Trinidad between 1838–1870 came not as slaves but as immigrants. They were recruited from the large number of Africans who had been liberated by the Royal Navy from slave ships bound for Cuba, Brazil, and the United States and settled in Sierra Leone and Saint Helena. These Africans were offered the choice between apprenticeship in Sierra Leone or St. Helena, enlistment in the West India Regiment, or service in the Royal Navy. After 1838, the option of emigrating to the West Indies as plantation labor was another available alternative.[194]

This particular population is frequently credited with the emergence of Trinidad's Yoruba-Orisa and Rada traditions and also with the endurance of West African language forms/linguistic traditions, as documented in the works of Maureen Warner Lewis.[195]

Finally, as they were dually attributed with being the forerunners of new African religious traditions as well as harbingers of obeah and sorcery, liberated Africans were not exempt from being at the center of social and legal tensions. Fortified obeah laws in the late 1860s targeted liberated Africans through deliberate civic entrapment or interpersonal accusations. European colonial officials deployed obeah legislation and the judiciary to launch direct attacks on liberated Africans and their religious customs. Liberated Africans thus came to share a common history of obeah persecution with Trinidad's ex-enslaved population, who had suffered severely half a century earlier.

Officials initially hoped that liberated Africans would assimilate through language acquisition and religious conversion to Christianity—a hope for the colony as a whole, given its national, linguistic, and religious plurality.[196] Consequently, increased Anglicization of the colony, inclusive of the liberated inhabitants, emerged as a major British objective.[197] The Trinidad Association for the Propagation of the Gospel, housed under the Diocese of Barbados, employing two missionaries, several schoolmasters, and eight churches, understood immigration in the 1840s as an opportunity, believing that, if "properly conducted . . . on Christian principles and in a Christian spirit—Trinidad may be a *Missionary Country;*—an asylum . . . to multitudes from the darkness and misery of heathenism."[198] Instead, British colonists found populations of liberated Africans reticent to relinquish their traditional customs and ways. In addition to European surveillance of their religious practices, liberated Africans endured obeah accusations from black Creole populations. Monica Schuler and Rosanne Adderley both cite several instances in Jamaica and Trinidad of these intra-black allegations.[199] In Trinidad, the liberated African community, quite specifically, was seen as a locus of "particularly powerful practitioners of Obeah."[200]

Because colonial officials had no real reference or vocabulary for the range of African religious practices being performed in Trinidad, the totalizing supernatural concept of obeah would continue to surface from the slavery to postslavery era, and liberated Africans, especially those identified as Yoruba or Rada, were susceptible to obeah accusations and convictions. Various cases made reference to either a "Yaraba woman" or incantations in "Yaraba," and helped cultivate a wider societal perception that, as one Catholic missionary in Trinidad summed it up, "*African blacks* still retain certain pagan practices of their countries."[201] Moreover, in nineteenth-century Trinidad, "Yoruba-dominated villages" were formed in numerous areas of the island including Montserrat and Yarraba Village, Oropuche, Princes Town, St. Joseph, Third and Fifth Company Villages, Couva, Carenage, and Sierra Leone Village in Diego Martin.[202] According to Roslyn Howard, "The Yoruba immigrants initially segregated themselves in a separate village in the capital, Port of Spain, and the already diverse population of Trinidad became augmented by an influx of African-born peoples . . . who had never suffered the indignities of enslavement in the New World."[203] As a result, there developed increased colonial anxiety about the Yoruba and Rada groups, especially because it was "argued that allowing the immigrants to congregate in 'large numbers' would encourage them to 'form a society of themselves and . . . retain the savage habits of their nation.'"[204]

Throughout the nineteenth century, both old *nations* of enslaved Africans and new *nations* of liberated Africans would be essential in transitioning Trinidad into a deepened multicultural, multilingual, and multireligious society consisting of a decimated indigenous community, former slaves, European planters and colonial officials, free mixed-race coloreds, Asian immigrants, Black North American descendants, and liberated African inhabitants. The institution of slavery and a postslavery agricultural market in Trinidad were the common denominators that joined these disparate populations into a seamless web of coloniality. As we shall see in the chapters that follow, enslaved Africans and liberated Africans, operating in the colonial economic frontier of Trinidad, would have their religious heritages held captive in colonial imaginations of obeah while steadily laying a foundation for religious belonging and sovereignty that would reconstitute, innovate, and endure over the ensuing two centuries.

Let Them Hate
So Long as They Fear

2

OBEAH TRIALS AND SOCIAL CANNIBALISM
IN TRINIDAD'S EARLY SLAVE SOCIETY

Obeah surfaced in the eighteenth and nineteenth centuries as an imaginative coloration in the social, legal, and literary cultures of the wider imperial Anglophone Atlantic. Its resonant nomenclature in North America of "obi" and "ober" identified "men and women who employed their power to poison and to cure."[1] In Trinidad, Obeah's curative features remained invisible to British colonists. Resolute regarding the "unfreedom of slaves," they crafted social portraitures violently designed to instill fear and suppression through penal brutality.[2] Throughout the British Atlantic, the colonial imagination perceived Obeah as an illusory threat encompassing African sorcery, witchcraft, revolt, divination, poisoning, fetishism, superstition, and supernatural weaponry. The concept of obeah utilized in British colonial law had long since lost its associative and etymological connections to West African Akan, Igbo, or Ibibio, and other heritages which linked "practitioner, healer, or herbalist—or even doctor" with such terms and practices inclusive of "medicine, law, religion, magic, or judicial practice."[3] Instead, obeah was deemed injurious in profession, material instrumentality, belief, and practice throughout the Caribbean.

Obeah functioned as a supernatural, nondiscursive *metalanguage* enacted between European and African populations with "its powerful, all-encompassing effect on the construction and representation of other social and power relations."[4] The term "obeah" served in the colonial lexicon as a summating rhetorical device for categorizing "all kinds of slave religious and medical practices: herbalism, divining, spirit possession" and in most cases colonial authorities "always used it to mean 'witchcraft' rather than religion."[5] The metalanguage of obeah was thus simultaneously real and mythic, an elusive social, religious, and legal category in colonial Trinidad. It operated as "a formless, unstable, nebulous condensation" with no exact boundaries, while at the same time possessing a "unity and coherence" for European colonists who agreed on obeah's social malignancy, portentous meaning, and connection to a nefarious African persona.[6] Above all, colonizers in the Anglophone Atlantic dreaded obeah as a form of African sorcery completely divorced from the category of genuine religion, and the African body was targeted as the location for enacting colonial exorcisms of personal trepidation and social fear. Obeah existed at the center of a precarious social universe of moral complexity where colonial officials, estate owners, overseers, and African captives operated in complete ethical divergence. Charles H. Long, historian of religions, avows that "slavery and its practice defined an agonistic site—a battlefield, or better a minefield, that camouflaged and obscured within its pacific domesticity a strange and depressing dialectic of evil."[7] Within this "dialectic of evil," obeah encompassed the "*social bodies* of black persons" as they navigated and resisted societal and economic evil.[8]

This chapter scrutinizes the severe legal responses to Obeah in nineteenth-century Trinidad and elucidates them as structural expressions of Euro-colonial supremacy in the face of African displays of power. Punitive legalized torture and juridically authorized amputations of the extremities of accused Africans reflected deliberate colonial obliteration of competing social power and demonstrated colonists' performance of policing perceived religious deviation and heterodoxy. These strategies of confinement were a crucial element of a wider European *colonialcraft* of "rational management" that exercised brutal force and "relentless terror" in order to enact the complete social consumption of enslaved African bodies.[9] Along these lines, this chapter addresses the metaphysical "poetics of the flesh" in which authorities used flesh to "demonize corporeality" and where "social hierarchies become flesh" and "deadly policies."[10] Within the discourse of flesh, "*body-words*" are vocabularies of imperial power and "body-fictions" the content of colonial mythologies.[11] In British Trinidad, these "*body-words*" communicated that the enslaved black body was "judiciously and maliciously constructed," an "artifact produced for social control," and ultimately a colonial relic of authentication.[12] The black body "speaks" in colonial Trinidad, and the black body struggles against an "anatomo-politics" that renders it malignant in an imperial world and imprisoned in a perpetual web of "corporeal malediction."[13]

Conceptually, this chapter explores the colonial cult of obeah fixation under the regime of Governor Thomas Picton. Governor Picton's canon of punishments was not sanctioned by the colonial legislature. Rather, it operated in a realm of "extralegal subjection," outside of the Crown's oversight and authority, and functioned within a white popular belief system about Africans and their seemingly insurgent spiritual practices. In colonial Trinidad, "*obeah* was religious, but it was also political, economic, social, juridical, cultural and scientific."[14] As the reader will soon discover, this popular belief system was a lived religion with an extensive repertoire of colonial devotional practices.[15]

This chapter will demonstrate that Governor Picton's lived practices of African religious suppression constituted a web of technologies of torture. He is credited with "the introduction of various devices intended solely to coerce" information; "the use of the piquet and the torture rack to extort confessions from recalcitrant witnesses"; coercive psycho-torture tactics; public corporal rites of intimidation; brutal executions; extreme forms of haptic violation, involving branding, mutilation, burning, decapitation, public decomposition, amputation, and dismemberment; and sadistic afflictions such as being "placed naked on a nest of stinging ants," being beaten until skin "excoriated from . . . posteriors," or being thrown into open graves and "covered over . . . while yet alive."[16] These "disciplinary technologies" and instruments of black harm would proliferate well into the rulership of Governor Woodford (1813–1828) who would introduce the use of the penal treadmill into Trinidad for those prisoners sentenced to hard labor. White colonists readily attributed unexplained illnesses and deaths of enslaved persons, cattle, or other livestock to Africans or "Negroes," who—akin to their counterparts in neighboring colonies—purportedly invoked supernatural influence and sorcerous power in order to undermine, dismantle, and destabilize the stronghold of slavery in Trinidad. Invoking a "colonial corporeality" and singular fixation, Picton eradicated these racial-spiritual threats through "the violence of empire."[17]

Constructions of the black body in the British Caribbean reflected what anthropologist Gananath Obeyesekere identifies in *Cannibal Talk* as the "metaphysics of savagism" trapped in the European imaginary of "man-eating myth."[18] Like "the Other, the Savage, the Alien," the enslaved African was mythically tethered in this metaphysics of savagism to "lack of civility, Satanism, or the worship of demons, the absence of civilized morality that impels savages to commit acts of brutality."[19] Obeyesekere concludes that schemas of "savagism shrink discursive space," and in the case of Trinidad, obeah was "grafted onto savagism, giving the settler . . . the license to lie and the license to take hearsay as truth."[20] Thus, obeah became what I designate as the *signified imaginary* of European colonists, who signified upon their original imaginary of African religions to further create the distilled criminalized and racialized category of obeah. Charles Long argues this style of "signification constituted a subordinate relationship of power expressed through customs and legal structures."[21] Ultimately, the metaphysics of obeahism and savagism reveal the colonial imaginary of those whom Obeyesekere terms "British cannibals" and the violent "dialogical misunderstandings" that occur when the imperial anthropophagy of slavery, conquest, and colonialism devours the subjective humanity of vanquished black people.[22]

The obeah discussed in this chapter is not the Obeah through which African people drew upon an inherited repertoire of "health and healing and weaponry and warfare" traditions, as discussed in Dianne Stewart's *Three Eyes for the Journey: African Dimensions of the Jamaican Religious Experience*.[23] Instead, I interrogate obeah as it relates to the materiality of black social bodies in the colonial imagination and wider colonialscape of Trinidad. Obeah accusations flourished in a nineteenth-century Trinidadian universe where enslaved labor and maltreated bodies were consumed in colonial "imaginary terrors" and white social cannibalism.[24] This and the successive chapters of volume I focus on obeah as colonial performance of public devaluation and civic consumption narrativized through British colonial law and legally possessed black bodies.

Obeah as Social Insurgency

Obeah's inclusion in the legal lexicon of the British Caribbean appeared in 1760, shortly after the slave uprising of Tacky's Revolt in Jamaica with "An Act to Remedy the Evils Arising from Irregular Assembly of Slaves," the first anti-obeah legislation in the British colonies.[25] The law stated, "Any Negro or other Slave who shall pretend to any Supernatural Power, and be detected in making use of any Blood, Feathers, Parrots Beaks, Dogs Teeth, Alligators Teeth, Broken Bottles, Grave Dirt, Rum, Egg-shells or any other Materials relative to the Practice of Obeah or Witchcraft in order to delude and impose on the Minds of others shall upon Conviction . . . suffer death or transportation."[26]

Following suit, obeah laws proliferated throughout the British Caribbean: in Trinidad in 1800, in Barbados in 1806 and 1818, and throughout most all other British colonies, such as British Honduras, British Guiana, St. Vincent, Grenada, Antigua, and Dominica, over the next three decades.[27] British Caribbean colonial intra-discourse on Obeah legislation often centered on the public "assembly of slaves," "poisoning," "supernatural power," the use of "instruments" or materials for "witchcraft," and the "fraudulent" intentions and imposition on "the minds of others" as a means of policing African spiritual and social behavior and of maintaining civil order in slave societies overwhelmingly inhabited by Africans.[28] Trinidad's slave codes, ordinances, and prosecutions would also single out amulets, fetishes, and charms as malevolently potent devices of obeah. In all, colonial lawmakers targeted obeah as subversive and seditious activity within an ordered slave society, and this targeting functioned as a boundary-producing social apparatus of civil regulation.[29]

In order to legislate civil order in burgeoning Atlantic slavocracies, European enslavers and colonial settlers had to tackle the legal conundrum of African humanity. Chapter 17, Law 1, of the Spanish slave codes decreed that "slaves have no legal personality," yet made provisions for Africans as an "inferior kind of subject."[30] British law, however, asserted the "legal nullity of the slave's personality" and reduced all subjectivity to saleable, inheritable, and mortgageable private property.[31] Further, legal historian Alan Watson identifies a substantive difference in English and Spanish colonial slave law, namely, "the lawmaking power remained in Spain" for the latter, while for the former some instances of "basic laws were . . . made by the colonists in the colonies," leaving ample room for local autonomy.[32]

The absence of protective legal subjectivity for enslaved Africans figures significantly in colonial legal history. According to Saidiya Hartman, "criminality" became "the only form of slave agency recognized by the law."[33] An enslaved African navigated the repressive regime of slavery under "the confines of surveillance and nonautonomy" that presumed the African "a legal person only insofar as he is criminal."[34] Hartman determines that "the slave was recognized as a reasoning subject who possessed intent and rationality solely in the context of criminal liability. . . . In positing the black as criminal, the state obfuscated its instrumental role in terror by projecting all culpability and wrongdoing on to the enslaved."[35] Obeah understood as "social evil" and as offense in colonial law thus served merely to divert "the locus of culpability" away from European slaving colonies and the copiousness of "slavery's crimes."[36]

British authorities in the new colony passed obeah laws within three years after the acquisition of Trinidad from Spain in 1797. The rigors of managing Trinidad's newly ordered slave society, especially given the portentous threat of Haiti's insurrectionist fate, meant a rapid deployment of British military, civil, and legal authorities in the early formation of the colony. With the demise of Saint-Domingue, France's most profitable sugar economy, Trinidad came under military gubernatorial leadership that sought to fortify its social interior against insurgency. Reinforcing fears of insurrection, the Spanish colony's former treasurer, Don Cristobal de Robles, whom Governor Picton spoke of as "the most respectable Spaniard he had ever known," portrayed Trinidad in the following way:

> I will give you my honest and candid sentiments as to the situation of the Colony. The population is mostly composed of refugees and desperate characters who have been implicated in the rebellion and massacres of all the neighbouring Islands; their principles are incompatible with all regular Government, and their inveteracy to your nation is irreconcilable. . . . At your arrival they were actually masters of the Island. . . . To these you may add the Spanish *peons* or people of color, a set of vagabonds who casually come over from the Continent and, who are ready to join in any disorder . . . and a great population of slaves who have been sent here from the other Islands for crimes dangerous to their safety. These people are now apparently quiet, but they are more dangerous as they are only waiting for a favourable opportunity to show themselves, and in this meanwhile they are studying you and your garrison. . . . If you do not give an imposing character to your government before the climate diminishes the number of your soldiers, your situation will be embarrassing.[37]

De Robles admonished Governor Picton that "if these men do not fear you, they will despise you, and you may easily foresee the consequences. . . . There is but one line of conduct by which you can extricate yourself from all of these difficulties."[38] He sought to impress upon Picton the unboundedness of his gubernatorial power: "The circumstances of the conquest have combined in you the whole powers of the government. You are the supreme political, civil, criminal and military judge . . . you are not shackled by modes or forms of prosecution." And he concluded, "If you do substantial justice you are only answerable to God and your conscience."[39] Throughout his reign, Picton would live up to his authority as supreme ruler of Trinidad. He possessed "all civil and military power. He had his own court, and as a judge, he exercised an original jurisdiction in both civil and criminal cases." Under his rule, there existed "no right of appeal" in criminal cases.[40] It was not until well into his administration that representatives of the Crown sought to delimit Picton's sovereign rulership.

As a military leader, Governor Picton believed fortifying the colony against foreign and internal threat was his first order of business. Picton, along with every other administrator of an English colony, was on high alert following the eruption of revolts in France's Caribbean territories. Historian Elsa Goveia writes, "The rebellions of the free coloured and slaves, which followed the spread of the French Revolution in the French islands, and especially in the great colony of St. Domingue, were horrifying to the West Indians in the British islands, who feared for the survival of their own society when they saw the revolutionary assault launched against the barriers of colour elsewhere."[41] Goveia captures the mood of the West Indies during these turbulent moments: "Whites foresaw a dissolution of their society and trembled for their safety."[42] As a result of this fear, British colonial rulers such as Governor Picton targeted all offenses that threatened to undermine the empire's slave territories, designating insurrectionary and rebellious acts, seditious conversation, and poisonings as capital crimes, which carried severe penalties.

Capital crimes also included obeah offenses, which were regarded as a form of insurgency and spiritual enmity, allegedly accompanied with plant-based and charmed poisonings. Susan Scott Parrish, in "Diasporic African Sources of Enlightenment Knowledge," contends that "Africans became a crucial source for colonial knowledge of the natural world" and given their majority numbers throughout the Caribbean, "the diffuse colonial anxiety became concentrated in an exaggerated alarm about the possibility of slaves using (or misusing) plants to poison their masters."[43] Unsurprisingly, the botanical and etiological aspects of plant-based epistemologies known to enslaved African populations eluded colonial comprehension of Obeah. Africans employed Obeah as a pragmatic range of medicinal approaches and divinatory epistemologies for physical protection and spiritual security.[44] While they continued to turn to their own spiritual and pharmacopeial reserves to heal their communities, even assuming designated roles as nurses and caretakers on plantation estates, Europeans in Trinidad devoted limited resources to African healthcare.[45] The insufficient availability of European-trained doctors led Trinidad's propertied elite to readily adopt what Richard Sheridan calls "a policy of amelioration," gearing approaches to slave healthcare toward short-term treatment rather than long-term remedy.[46] Because the gaze was largely upon Africans and their alleged obeah practices, what remained uninterrogated in the colonial record was the popular folk medicine of white colonists during slavery. Among the elite slaveholding class, there existed folk prescriptions against the ailments that afflicted both them and their enslaved in Trinidad. These remedies included "types of bush tea, buds of bois cannot, young sprouts of fowl foot as cooling drinks for the kidneys, thornless cactus for the chest; and most planters had some special 'cure all' such as 'tizane' of Cedros: a mixture of sour orange, of muscovado sugar, of tafia, gin, brandy, mint, nutmeg, ginger, split peas and a large pepper cut up in slices, the whole taken hot."[47]

Trinidad was a part of the "medicalized empire" of the British Crown, which sought to protect its inhabitants from the racially and microbially diseased environments of the West Indies.[48] In the absence of organized health strategies for both free and enslaved populations, Trinidad's colonial government opted to hire a public vaccinator in 1819 under the auspices of the Vaccine Establishment. This colonial branch required vaccination of "all persons arriving in the colony, including slaves," within one week of arrival, and all those residing therein.[49] The proclamation for vaccination was issued after an outbreak of smallpox was discovered in the colony. The directive was so serious that "all Medical Practitioners" were "required and ordered, under pain of suspension of their Licenses, to take every means to extend Vaccination to the utmost of their power." Likewise, the proclamation stipulated, "a Fine of *Two Hundred Pounds Currency* is hereby declared in inoculating, or in permitting himself, his Children, his Servants, or his Slaves, to be inoculated with Small Pox, from and after the date of this order, which fine shall be recoverable before the Complaint Court of the Honorable Chief Judge."[50]

Despite these efforts, colonial-era medical practices remained substandard since trained biomedical experts were scarce. Trinidad's dearth of professionals was especially pronounced for the first three decades after its establishment as a British colony because the island had only twenty-nine licensed medical practitioners, seven licensed apothecaries, and four druggists. These figures indicate that at best Trinidad had one doctor for every 780 slaves, a ratio that grew even worse (one doctor for every 1,450 inhabitants) when extended to include the total population in the territory.[51] Moreover, doctors who did not have direct employment contracts with estate owners charged considerably higher rates to treat Africans. The Trinidad Infirmary and Marine Hospital in Port of Spain charged ten shillings for enslaved patients, while other doctors charged up to thirty-six pounds for certain services, such as midwifery for difficult deliveries.[52] Thus, given the "primitive state of botanical and medical sciences at that time, diseases of plants, animals and men due to purely natural causes could easily have been put down to poisoning by obeah men."[53]

The range of epidemics, diseases, and physical abnormalities endemic to the British West Indies forced enslaved people, as well as estate owners, to supplement their limited health system with the curative skills of Africans dubbed "negro doctors" by those controlling colonial public health.[54] According to historian Barry Higman,

> "Negro doctors" possessed as much medical knowledge as many of the white journeyman practitioners. . . . "Negro doctors" were often more successful than the whites in obtaining cures through their use of hot baths of herbs, or fermentations. . . . Slaves lacked confidence in the white physicians and so were reluctant to take their medicine, and claimed that the slave doctors never prescribed anything to be taken internally.[55]

European antidotes relied on "bleeding, blistering, and purging." Yet, African medicinal knowledge of the "virtues of some indigenous plants," the administering of "hot baths," and even African forms of "inoculation" against yaws became indispensable to the health of the colony.[56] According to Parrish,

> White colonials believed that Africans possessed zones of knowledge that they themselves did not. Colonial attitudes towards Africans' nature expertise were . . . ambivalent. Colonials credited Africans with the capacity to perform empirical work more extensively than they themselves could but also cast African knowledge as potentially subversive. . . . Whites began to view the Africans and Creole blacks around them as a toxin in the environment.[57]

This more comprehensive perspective on Obeah, inclusive of its etiological approaches to physical disease and its use as a form of protective resistance against the social disease of slavery, yields a richer and generative understanding of Obeah's functionality in Trinidad's slave society as both a means toward physiological healing and a weapon for epistemological and instrumental insurgency.[58]

Fear and apprehension abounded among European colonizers, as they saw "the Obeah man as more of a master revolutionary than a master healer."[59] On Trinidad's plantations in particular, the Obeah man, according to historian David Trotman, "represented a figure of authority . . . respected and/or feared by the slave community," who "competed with the slave owner for the allegiance of the slaves—an allegiance that must belong solely to the slave owner if the system of slavery was to succeed."[60] Herein lay both the danger of Obeah and the vulnerability of Africans in a slave society dependent on complete and total domination and submission.

For both European colonists and the accused Africans, Obeah represented a "hidden communication," concealed exchanges with the spirit world that assumed multivalent materializations across the social landscape.[61] Historian Vincent Brown specifies that "as far as colonial officials were concerned, the ban on Obeah was a ban on alternative authority and social power."[62] Thus, Africans criminalized through obeah allegations suffered greatly in Trinidad. Indictments for sorcery, poisoning, and spiritual fraud broadly collapsed as obeah and the "black arts" resulted in severe punishments that ranged from solitary confinement and permanent banishment to bodily tortures, floggings, mutilation, and physical dismemberment. Under Trinidad's autocratic and slaveholding governor, Thomas Picton, "behind all these severe punishments lurked the constant fear of slave rebellion and the dread that the slaves would become more afraid of the obeah man than of their master."[63]

Governor Thomas Picton, Obeah, and the "Violence of the Law"

Born of humble beginnings in Wales and rising to the rank of lieutenant-general, Sir Thomas Picton was Trinidad's civil and military governor from 1797 to 1804, assuming charge after the defeat of the Spanish military and, more acutely, in a period overlapping with Saint-Domingue's insurrection.[64] Similar to Saint-Domingue, Trinidad's white inhabitants, and particularly British citizens, were far outnumbered by free coloreds, who represented a significant landowning class. This, coupled with a substantial enslaved population under his rulership, led Governor Picton to conclude in his 1803 address to the Council in Trinidad that "Men of Colour" were "all irreconcilable enemies of His Majesty's Government" and warned that Trinidad was ultimately a "Camp surrounded with enemies."[65] Later he would justify "the severities" he applied to African-descended populations as "fully authorized by [his] station and circumstances."[66]

Much to his dismay, shortly after securing power, Governor Picton in March 1799 received the directive to accept "in a proper and suitable manner" a group of French planters and their 300 enslaved captives from Saint-Domingue who had temporarily taken up residence in Jamaica.[67] Governor Picton admonishingly informed the king, "For my own part I do not see how it can fail to produce equally alarming apprehensions here."[68] Although he profoundly disagreed with the decision to accommodate hundreds of enslaved people from an explosively destabilizing French colony, Governor Picton was obedient to the order from the king, and "all but 39 of the 300 Saint-Domingo Negroes . . . had been allowed to land despite the protests of the Cabildo [the municipal administrative council] and some of the inhabitants."[69]

During the first two years of his appointment, in letters written in 1799 from Port of Spain to Admiral Sir Henry Harvey, Picton exhibits much fear and angst regarding the free inhabitants of Trinidad. He specifically wrote of a "Black man named Bornedau who was discovered, by an intercepted Dispatch . . . to have carried on a treasonable correspondence . . . which had the object of Insurging the Negroes and Coloured people of the Colony."[70] As a result, he was banished from the island. Moreover, in his March 19, 1799, letter, Picton is deeply alarmed about the state of the garrison and the "weak force" at his disposal, given there is "much Danger to be apprehended from the People of Colour who are all French and amount to double the effective number of the Garrison."

As a result of Picton's trepidation and racial forebodings, the privileges free coloreds exercised under Spanish rule in Trinidad were revoked. Those who were officers in the colonial military were "stripped of rank and assigned to guard the houses of white officials," free "coloured doctors had to pay for a license to practice while whites were given theirs for free," and all free coloreds were now legally mandated to obey nightly curfews. Each evening the colonial jail bell rang at 9:30 p.m., indicating the end of their public mobility.[71] Much to their humiliation, they were also subjected to limitations on their public assembly, to elevated taxes on their social gatherings, to requirements to provide proof of their free status and their pledged oath of allegiance to the colonial regime, to mandatory segregation in public modes of transportation,[72] to prohibitions against carrying sticks on public streets, and to be obliged to carry a torch at night.[73] The last of these mandates mirrored lantern laws of the previous century in North America, where those who were enslaved were required to carry a lit lantern at night as a mode of supervision and surveillance. Simone Browne analyzes lantern laws in eighteenth-century New York as marking "black, mixed-race, and indigenous people as security risks." The lit lantern, or in the case of Trinidad the lit torch, "made it possible for the black body to be constantly illuminated from dusk to dawn, made knowable, locatable, and contained" and "part of the project of a racializing surveillance."[74] Moreover, extreme racial restrictions were enacted in Trinidad, for "whites feared that the extension of the most minimal legal rights to the coloureds would undermine the structure of race supremacy."[75] Thus, in the aftermath of the Haitian Revolution, "the local authorities and whites in general probably feared the free coloureds more than the slaves."[76] In this climate of societal distrust, Trinidad's British colonial government under Governor Picton systematically barred free coloreds from officer rank in the military, "posts in the civil service," and made them constant victims of social "contempt and discourtesy."[77]

Further, according to social and political historian Leighton James, "Trinidad had recently been seized from the Spanish, and Picton felt vulnerable, both from the threat of re-conquest and the fact that the number of slaves there greatly outnumbered his small force."[78] Governor Picton ruled a colony that had experienced great transformation during the shift from Spanish to British rule, going from a population of several hundred slaves inhabiting the colony before the Spanish cedula to a slave population that was a hundredfold greater at the height of Picton's reign. Moreover, as a military officer with recent active combat experience battling European enemies, he was now faced with leading a colony of "English, Scotch, Irish, Welsh, Spaniards, Germans, Swiss, Italians, Americans and French," which posed its own Euro-Atlantic hazard from former or future enemies.[79] Picton was not without British citizens, but Trinidad most attracted in this period what one traveler called "British runaways . . . from other West India islands," "men who would disgrace," and men with "dreams of avarice."[80]

Race was a metric of division within the colony of Trinidad, but so was economic class among its white national inhabitants. At the top of the social hierarchy were elite proprietors, while "lower in the social scale was the mass of whites, Frenchmen, Spaniards, Englishmen, Scots, Irish Catholics and an indeterminate but small number of Italians and Corsicans." They collectively arrived in the colony motivated by economics and some fleeing to Trinidad to "elude their creditors in the other islands."[81] According to one source, "washed-up attorneys, managers and overseers, self-professed lawyers and doctors, entangled merchants, heavily encumbered planters . . . these were the people who migrated to Trinidad from the British Islands in the late eighteenth century." They were to a large extent "a landless class" seeking fortune, opportunities for land acquisition, or rebuilding of lost wealth.[82] "As a soldier," Governor Picton deduced "that Trinidad was at all times susceptible to an attack by hostile forces, or to insurrection fomented by foreigners within."[83] Picton's immediate present bore witness to this susceptibility, as he saw the British military weaken over time in the face of war with France and battles in the Caribbean. By 1796 some 40,000 British soldiers had been killed and another 40,000 "rendered unfit for service."

Governor Picton had much to protect in safeguarding the future of Trinidad. Contemporaries estimated that Trinidad's economic "potential was greater than that of pre-revolutionary St. Domingue."[84] According to Picton, "this Island itself after Cuba and Hispaniola is incontestably the finest in all of the West Indies, whether the general fertility of the soil or the extent of cultivatable lands be considered. It is capable of producing more Sugar, Coffee, Cotton, and Cocoa, than all the Leeward Islands together."[85] With Picton as its governor, Trinidad experienced the flourishing of agriculture; export of sugar doubled from 7,800 hogsheads when he assumed power in 1797 to 15,461 hogsheads of sugar four years into his governorship. Trinidad also saw an increase in commerce, "annually carrying articles of British manufacture for the Main, to the value of $8,000,000."[86]

Governor Picton's intolerant and despotic political posture reflected the need to preserve this "economic boom" and growing lucrative slave colony, and thus he set a precedent for the exceedingly harsh and punitive handling of enslaved Africans and free coloreds convicted of felonies, poison/obeah-related offenses, or any other offenses that imperiled the slave order. He was also driven to rid the colony of any and all seditious behavior and to arrest inhabitants for "attending public meetings and signing petitions."[87] Those who appeared to be a threat to the social order were charged and imprisoned within despicable conditions. The infrastructure of Trinidad's jails was perhaps the "vilest" in the West Indies; Picton racially segregated white prisoners in "specially provided rooms on the top storey of the jail," while the enslaved and free coloreds endured the "stench below."[88] "To be imprisoned in such a jail . . . was itself a torture; to be detained there pending trials, as was often done with slaves, was to be horribly punished before sentence was even passed," observed William Fullarton, appointed commissioner of Trinidad. During his visit in 1804 Fullarton determined that "the Prison itself was in such a state of Pestilential nastiness, with 30 or 60 wretches some in chains others naked and many of them nearly starved to Death."[89] While investigating the colonial jail under Picton, Fullarton "found lying on the lengths of bare boards, bound and fettered, five slaves belonging to Baron de Montalembert, a French planter. They were nearly naked and had been lying there for some time. On enquiring, he was told that a few days previously they had been sent to jail by their master on suspicion of having poisoned other slaves and were soon to be tortured since that was the only way to extract the truth from them."[90]

Journalist Pierre McCallum's *Travels in Trinidad during the Months of February, March, and April, 1803* offered (in the form of letters to a member of the British Parliament) a most unfavorable representation of civil authority under Governor Picton. In his correspondence, he likened Trinidad to "a colony governed by the Inquisition" and rendered a dreadful description of its penal system:[91]

Incarcerated in a nauseous prison, without a breath of fresh air, respiring the putrid exhalation copiously emitted from your fettered fellow-prisoners, the clangour of their chains, together with their hideous yells, must assimilate your situation to that of the infernal regions. Your mind should either be racked with horror, or corroded with despair and resentment against him who thus hell-doomed you, but, all this was extremely gratifying to Governor Picton, whose sole delight was to torment indiscriminately.[92]

McCallum's letters illuminated the heinous conditions that those of African descent accused of spiritual malevolence suffered and endured. Depicting the scene as an abuse of civil power, McCallum vividly describes how "in some adjacent cells were lodged about thirty or more Africans of all ages, accused of witchcraft, necromancy, &c: all these unfortunate creatures were shackled and rivetted to the ground, much exhausted with a long and tedious confinement, and extreme heat in a dirty hole; it is remarkable they sustain existence, upon the simple diet of impure water and plantains."[93] McCallum's letters to England were an attempt to expose Governor Picton's extreme intolerance of "all possible challenges to the dominant hegemony" and his use of "the coercive aspects of the legal system" to mobilize against all perceived social threats, which Africans intensely embodied.[94] Some historians have argued that Picton "created as odious and obscene a tyranny as any country has ever known."[95] Through absolute control, harshness, and legal severity, the colony of Trinidad was governed by a pseudo-ruling philosophy likened to that of *oderint dum metuant*, a guiding principle of the third Roman emperor, Caligula (Gauis Julius Caesar Germanicus), known for his extreme cruelty, perversion, and unrestrained power during his reign from AD 37 to 41. Notorious for his "irascible temper," writers iconized Picton as Caligula as he incarnated the Roman emperor's motto—"Let them hate so long as they fear."[96]

European contemporaries characterized Governor Picton as a "rough, foul-mouth devil as ever lived" and castigated him for his "brutally authoritarian" political regime[97] (see figure 2.1). He began his administration with a message of fearless ferociousness to his adversaries, immediately dismissing the members of the Cabildo yet retaining one member, St. Hilaire Begorrat, deeming him the "greatest villain" among them and appointing him "one of the members of the next Council," as Begorrat "knows all that is going on."[98] The new governor publicly avowed in the Cabildo's presence, "If he [Begorrat] neglects to inform me of any emeute I will hang him forthwith."[99] Relatedly, Picton vowed to banish anyone who "either refused to take the oath of allegiance [to

FIGURE 2.1 Thomas Picton, governor of Trinidad (1797–1804), was notorious for authorizing excessive brutality and torture when punishing enslaved Africans and free colored persons in criminal cases. Lieut. General Sir Thomas Picton, K.B., engraved by R. Cooper from original picture by M. A. Shee, Esq. R.A. Published March 1815 by T. Cadell & W. Davies, Strand, London. Reprinted by permission of Paria Publishing.

the king of England], or became compromised, directly or indirectly, in the incessant attempts to disturb the peace of the Colony."[100] When the colony transitioned to British authority, some 900 residents of Trinidad refused to take the said oath, many opting instead to assume residency in nearby Venezuela.[101] Regardless of national origin, Governor Picton made determined efforts to weed out the sources of any potential unrest. He engaged in a complex "politics of security" in order to safeguard the British colony under his charge and this especially included the harshest of approaches to Trinidad's most sizeable population—the enslaved.[102]

Diana Paton's analysis of slave trials in eighteenth-century Jamaica applies also to the British colony of Trinidad under Picton's rule because in both contexts, "the punishments they inflicted . . . enacted rituals that . . . dramatized and sustained the power relations of this colonial slavery society."[103] Throughout the British Caribbean, severe punishments exogenously executed transformed colonial public spaces into theatres of torture and mutilation. Paton documents the observations of a British traveler who "described matter-of-factly the hanging, decapitation, and mutilation of a 'Gang of Negroes discovered who poisoned a great number of persons, their fellow slaves.'"[104]

Given the uncertainties of a slave society, Obeah was especially subjected to "colonial exaggeration or misinterpretation," and "African poisoning, in particular, seemed the inevitable expression of all slaves' mangled gnosis."[105] Under Governor Picton, Trinidad predicated its colonial laws against Obeah upon a European belief in both obeah's seditious efficacy and the civil need to contain its power. Colonists often attributed the power of Obeah to the devil and dubbed its experts "spell-doctors," "obeah-men," and "obeah women," who served as the devil's spiritual specialists and agents.[106] The view possessed in Anglophone colonies was one of Africans as "heathenish, brutish, and an uncertain kind of people" deemed "unfit to be governed by English law," and, for colonial officials such as Governor Picton, in need of "repressive rules."[107]

Reinforcing an unspoken objective of civil order and supernatural control, Article XI of the 1800 Slave Code in Trinidad stated, "Any Negro who shall assume the reputation of being a spell-doctor or Obeah-man, and shall be found with an amulet, a fetishe, or the customary attributes and ingredients of the profession, shall be carried before the Commandant of the District, who will take cognizance of the accusation; and provided the crime be not capital, inflict proper punishment."[108] With additional referential subtexts to poisonings, the ordinance further stipulated, "But should it appear probable that the culprit has been the cause of death of any person by his prescriptions (as very frequently happens), the Commandant will then transmit him to the gaol, as a criminal, to be prosecuted and dealt with according to law."[109] Beginning with Jamaica, British obeah legal ordinances thematically organized their content around references to poisoning, the capability to inflict physical harm, and the use of material ingredients for supernatural purposes. For example, Barbados's "An Act for the Better Prevention of the Practice of Obeah (1818)," stated that "any person who shall willfully, maliciously and unlawfully pretend to any magical and supernatural charm or power in order to promote the purposes of Insurrection or rebellion of the Slaves within this Island, or to injure or affect the life or health of any other person, or who willfully and maliciously shall use or carry on the wicked and unlawful practice of obeah shall upon conviction thereof, suffer death or transportation as the Court by which the said offender may be tried shall think *proper*." It subsequently banned the possession of "any poison" or "any noxious or destructive substance" with the attempt to administer with "evil intentions." It was also rendered illegal to pretend to "have the power of divination," or to engage in "Fortune telling or . . . pretend to possess the charm or power of discovering or leading to the discovery of any lost or Stolen goods, Articles, or Things."[110] Obeah thus, in Trinidad and throughout the British colonies, became shorthand for the legal nomenclature that appeared in colonial cases as, variously, sorcery, poisoning, black arts, divination, charms, or use of herbs.

Trinidad's early slave period provides an especially revealing context for what I term "lived colonial law" and its range of tacit practices and meanings under Governor Picton's penalizing philosophies. Much like "lived religion," colonial law had its official statutes, decrees, and edicts. In fact, many of its written regulations were meant to protect the enslaved from excessive punishments and abuse, to provide oversight of overseers and estate managers, to ensure means of sustenance and provisions for the enslaved, and to authorize official investigations of offenses. Yet its practice, as enacted, exercised, and performed by colonial officials in the public realm, was quite the opposite. In Governor Picton's Trinidad, the spatial zone between colonial legal authority and "the working of the law in daily life" was racialized, spiritualized, and unbridled.[111] Trinidad, along with the slave colonies of the Atlantic, "remained a place of multiple legalities and perpetual violence."[112] The disjuncture between England's authority over the law and Trinidad's application of the law within a racialized slavocracy permitted colonial malfeasance to operationalize the structural subjugation of African inhabitants.

Just a few years before Picton began his reign in Trinidad, "fear of magic and poison seemed to grip the entire white populations" in late eighteenth-century Saint-Domingue, and a white planter class was "obsessed by the black sorcery which [it] believed to be omnipresent, detected poison everywhere."[113] Picton's governorship targeted and isolated the purported incendiary African magic of obeah as an insurgent crime warranting the severest punishments, which fueled his license to disregard the boundaries of "constitutional normalcy."[114] According to Chris Evans in *Slave Wales: The Welsh and Atlantic Slavery 1660–1850*, "Picton appointed tribunals against slaves practicing Obeah, a term encompassing both African magic and all forms of African religious ritual and . . . punishments for practicing what was deemed witchcraft included burning, hanging, whipping and mutilation."[115]

Obeah practices were directly linked to insurgency and viewed as a lethal hazard to the colony of Trinidad. According to Michelle Goldwasser, "Picton feared a black rebellion [and] African magic created the energy for revolt."[116] He viewed "African magic" in the form of obeah as necessarily injurious to a fruitful colony dependent on domesticated slave labor and a plantation economy. In fact, British colonists resembled their Francophone Caribbean neighbors whose "magico-religious outlook . . . contributed greatly to their fear of the slaves, to whom they attributed dark powers."[117] In an oscillating dialectic between "French fears and African suffering," Alfred Métraux speaks of the "imaginary terrors and demented obsessions" European residents possessed as they settled amidst slave populations.[118] He argues that "the fear which reigned in the plantations had its source in deeper recesses of the soul: it was the witchcraft of remote and mysterious Africa which troubled the sleep of people in 'the big house.'"[119]

One year after outlawing the practice of Obeah in Trinidad, Governor Picton's fears only intensified when in 1801 incidents of mass slave deaths occurred on several plantation estates throughout the colony raising suspicions of the role of Obeah and its supposedly prescriptive poisonings. The governor and other white colonists attributed these poisonings to "obi," believing "the knowledge that these people possess of poison is truly awful and incredible . . . this miserable imposition has cost hundreds and thousands of lives in the West Indies."[120] In response to the alleged widespread poisonings "both of human beings and of cattle," Governor Picton established a legal substructure and appointed a special commission of seven persons, composed primarily from members of the planter class, "to investigate and adjudicate upon cases of poisoning."[121] Subsequently, Picton granted full authorization to the Commission to impose torture upon the individually accused, as appropriate: "And in Consequence of His Excellency being obliged to superintend the Business of His Majesty's Service, he gives an ample Commission, to Don Hilary Begorrat, Attorney General, to the End that he may substantiate and pass Sentence on said Cause, inflicting Tortures if necessary."[122]

In his published letters McCallum deemed the "commission illegally issued by Governor Picton."[123] In less than a year "about twenty negroes were tried by it and convicted as poisoners," and all met a final fate of execution, severe corporal punishment, or banishment.[124] McCallum harshly criticized Picton for not being more "acquainted with the manners and customs of the Africans" and realizing that "they are fond of collecting and carrying about with them any kind of bauble they may promiscuously meet with, either in the fields, rivers, or elsewhere."[125] Rather than disregard the harmless "trifles the Africans carry about them," Picton instead rendered Africans "of no value" and "put them to death" for 'imaginary crimes,'" much to McCallum's consternation.[126] McCallum was not unaware that internal threats to the colony could readily arise among its African population. To the contrary, he saw a likely threat imminently emerging from among the soldiers of the West India Regiment stationed in Trinidad rather than from among those preoccupied with spiritual practices of Obeah and divination. McCallum's fears were revealed when he stated, "There are two Negro Regiments stationed here, composed of negroes taken from the French colonies. . . . The arming and training of so many of these hirelings, after the mournful scenes and horrid barbarities of their committing we have witnessed in St. Domingo, is surely not the prudent dictate of wisdom." He believed the presence of the "Negro Regiments" in Trinidad, if left unchecked, "will yet prove a curse to the British Empire."[127] Although McCallum could not have predicted the famous 1837 Dâaga rebellion in Trinidad that would arise from the soldiers of the First West India Regiment, he nevertheless foreshadowed three decades earlier during Picton's rule a constituency of unrest in Trinidad among the black non-enslaved.[128]

In a slave colony, white slaveholders lived in unending fear of being poisoned by those who had both access to their food source and, more importantly, knowledge of plant-based toxins. Poisoning was a complex act in colonial slave society. It was a silent armament and technique of attack and retaliation, as the true "livestock" and pillars of the slave system— masters, mistresses, animals, and enslaved Africans—were vulnerable to its deadly effects. One enslaved individual accused of killing "eight slaves, and several others [that] nearly died" on a Tragarete plantation disclosed in an August 1804 confession, "I wished to poison you (my master) and your family. You know I fill your water jar with water each day and I was tempted three times to put in arsenic, but a certain fear held me back. If I had not had the misfortune to [mistakenly] kill Crepin [an eleven-month-old who died in "agony after three days with a swollen throat and terrible convulsions"], I would have killed you, your family and all your slaves."[129]

Amid the hysteria over suspected poisonings, Governor Picton sought to legislate as severely as possible colonial order and control in Trinidad's slave society. This meant the enactment of newly established punishments, including twenty-five lashes for the enslaved who did not go to bed by 9:00 at night, an increase from twenty-five to thirty-nine lashes of the whip for any given infraction, and the termination of Saturdays as off days.[130] Within the colony, Picton very much embraced his Spanish comrade Don Cristobal de

Robles's notion of "substantial justice" and positioned himself as de Robles phrased it, as "the supreme political, civil, criminal and military judge." Even when charges of excessive torture and mistreatment were levied against him, Picton reminded those who criticized his judicial practices that "the Colony of Trinidad was committed to my Military Command as a Soldier: I am no Lawyer." He impenitently stood by his approach in matters of governance and law, stating, "The first Object . . . is Self-Preservation, to which every other Consideration, of whatever Importance, must yield."[131]

Criminal offenders suffered mightily under Picton. During his early rule, the colonial office compiled a "List of Persons put to death and who suffered different kinds of Punishment" within the first year after the commission was formed. The list contained twenty-four names and the meticulously documented punishments enacted from August 13, 1801, to April 3, 1802: one person—burnt alive (Pedro); seven persons—hanged and burnt (Teotis, Bouqui, Manuel, Thisbe, La Fortune, Miguel Gordon, Robineau); three persons—heads cut off and put on poles on the public roads (Bouqui, Thisbe, Robineau); two persons—branded on both cheeks (La Rosa, Andres G.); three persons—ears cut off (Yala, Youba, Louis Caesar.); four persons—feathered and ears cuts off (Faustin, La Rosa, Andres G., Fara); one person—flogged through the streets (Ginny Larkin); two persons—led through the streets as an ass (Catherina Vangoull, Noel); seven persons—ordered to assist at executions (Leonard, Yala, Youba, Louison, Felix, Antonio, Rosa); one person—hanged at St. Joseph's (Manuel).[132] In practice, the commission functioned as "a kind of inquisition, a sanguinary tribunal," and an agent of an expansive colonial and racialized "metacosmic imagination."[133] The documented evidence of brutal mutilation as punishment for obeah-inflected offenses in the British Caribbean affirms Diana Paton's characterization of African experiences with British "legalized violence" as encounters of "terror."[134] One apologist for the governor argued that, given the internal anxieties around potential insurrection and unrest in the slave colony and the external anxieties regarding the Spanish threat of reterritorializing Trinidad, "if Picton acted with severity in order to establish a firm Government on the ruins of a weak one, it is not a matter for either surprise or blame."[135] Yet some among his contemporaries were staunch critics of Picton's lived practices of torture, arguing that instead of engaging in "honourable warfare" as his military station merited, instead, "when he waged war, it was with pretended Witches, and Sorcerers, and with Women and Children; or, if he had men to encounter, it was not with the sword that he destroyed them, but with the halter, the Torture, and the Faggot!"[136] Similarly, barrister-at-law John Sanderson openly critiqued Picton in *An Appeal to the Imperial Parliament*, castigating Picton's "tortures to extort confession of sorcery, witchcraft, and obeism, . . . public mutilations in the marketplace for such chimerical crimes, and even the burning of the living and dead together in the streets of Trinidad." Much to his dismay, Sanderson concluded these acts have "stained the character of that unfortunate colony with the blood and ashes of the devoted victims of superstitious cruelty, practiced under the authority of ignorant judges."[137]

Regardless of one's historical verdict on Governor Picton's rule, the record indicates that the unrestrained punishments Picton meted out to those accused of practicing obeah and other alleged insurgent crimes bespoke "the violence of the law," as conceptualized by Saidiya Hartman.[138] A deep apprehension and paranoia permeated the colonial mindset that feared the overwhelming number of Africans in Trinidad as possessing the power, as in Saint-Domingue, to steer their spiritual customs toward the malevolent ends of dismantling the European slave system. In combatting the peril of obeah in Trinidad, Governor Picton attacked Obeah's perceived destructiveness with the most acute forms of ruthlessness in order to annihilate the numinous menace to an island he greatly wanted to develop as another of Britain's profitable slave colonies.

Picton, himself a member of Trinidad's plantocracy, amassed considerable wealth from his simultaneous professions as governor, slaveholder, and plantation owner. In his dual roles as governor and planter, Picton fashioned a slave society in Trinidad constructed socially and legally on coerced discipline and punishment "seldom tempered by mercy."[139] His lived colonial law reserved juridical torture and mutilation primarily for the bodies of Africans. From 1797 to 1804, Picton's reign resulted in far more than the proliferation of the legal vocabulary of obeah in Trinidadian legislation. It enforced the subsequent mapping of the scourge of obeah onto African bodies through the "epidermalization of blackness"—a process that, as Harvey Young states, entails "the inscription of meaning onto skin color."[140]

Obeah and "Judicial Terror": Theorizing Body, Flesh, and "Erotic Epistemology"

Danielle Boaz insightfully engages the transatlantic legal and spiritual landscape that connected colonial Trinidad to England. Boaz chronicles the criminalization of England's witchcraft acts as early as the sixteenth century. She scrutinizes practices that were legally designated as felonies, such as "invoking or conjuring spirits, practicing witchcraft, or using enchantments or sorceries . . . hav[ing] knowledge in physiognomie [sic], palmistry, or other like crafty science, or pretending that they can tell destinies, fortunes, or such other like fantastical imagination."[141] Likewise, earlier British laws prohibiting these kinds of practices resurfaced in Britain's colonial territories and associated such offenses with "the devil and other evil spirits."[142] Boaz shows how the language prohibiting the practice of witchcraft, sorcery, enchantment, conjuration, the occult, fortune-telling, palmistry, cunning folk, or "crafty science" (particularly that found in the Witchcraft Act of 1735) was recycled in the legal nomenclature of the British Caribbean, including Trinidad's obeah statutes.[143] British colonists redeployed their old-world imaginaries of witchcraft, occultism, and supernatural powers as new-world conceptions of obeah directed at enslaved Africans.

Corporal punishments such as burning, ear cropping, beheading, and execution for witchcraft in Great Britain had dissipated by the 1700s. Yet in the British colonies in the Caribbean and the Americas, the African body figured as the new site for the dreadful revival and reemergence of these torturous practices.[144] Colonial psychology understood the enslaved African body as "morbid otherness" with a "degenerate constitution," diseased and harmful if "living in close physical proximity to whites."[145] Within this Atlantic setting, we see the tandem association of the enslaved African as a "social nonperson" and as a being made materially worthless by torture, defacement, and dismemberment.[146] Maiming aligned with the consistent issuing of corporal punishment in British colonial slave courts, as "mutilation for noncapital crimes—the chopping off of ears, noses, feet, and so on—continued long after European courts discontinued such abuses," according to Vincent Brown.[147] These punitive technologies were professionalized and brokered in Trinidad's economy of torture under Governor Picton. For example, the salaried jailer, Vallot, was compensated for discharging a maximum of thirty-nine lashes, according to law. William Payne, an executioner for hire, was paid per execution. The accompanying physician was paid an hourly fee "for assisting in the infliction of the torture" and for "report[ing] to Governor Picton in writing the state and condition of the convict so punished."[148] Payne's responsibilities included documenting for the colonial record his duties of flogging, lacerating, beheading, and burning convicts.[149] In this complex social and economic market of punishment, Payne, believing he was undercompensated for this labor, presented Colonel Fullarton during his tour of the prison with a list and admonished him to "do something about his emoluments since he had only received two joes for sixteen persons he had some time ago flogged, beheaded, or burnt"[150] (see figure 2.2).

No. VI.

List of Persons flogged, pilloried, mutilated, hanged, and burned, by
William Payne, *Executioner, delivered by him to Colonel* Fullarton,
when he visited the Jail, in company with Messrs. Black, Beggorat,
and other Members of the Cabildo, and with Mr. Adderley, *and other*
Gentlemen.

Hanged and burned at St. Josephs, and head cut off, -	1 man.
Ears clipt off at ditto, - - - -	2 ditto.
Ears clipt and stampt, - - - -	4 men.
Flogged under gallows, - - - -	1 ditto.
Punished at pillory, - - - - -	1 ditto.
Led through town and pilloried, - -	1 ditto.
Ears clipt in market, - - -	1 ditto.
Ditto in the jail-yard, - - -	1 ditto.
Mulatto man and one negro man flogged through town,	2 ditto.
Ears cut off in the jail-yard, of two black men, -	2 ditto.

Received in part two joes.

(Signed)   WILLIAM PAYNE.

A true Copy.
T. W.

FIGURE 2.2 List of the punishments inflicted by William Payne, a salaried executioner
for the colony of Trinidad, in the year 1803. In the diaspora, executioners were often of
African descent. From *A Statement, Letters, and Documents, Respecting the Affairs of Trinidad*
(London: McMillan, Bow-Street, Covent-Garden, 1804), 47. Reprinted by permission of
the National Archives of Trinidad and Tobago.

The fearful and unstable context of slavery only intensified colonial, fetishistic approaches to black bodies in response to the threat of obeah and
insurgency.[151] The socioeconomic landscape of slavery allowed the "abstrac-
tion" of obeah to be performed in the materiality of Africans, thus locating
"within the seen (body) an aspect that is largely imagined," hence blurring
"the physical Black body and the conceptual Black body."[152] In theorizing the
black body in colonial Trinidad, both the physical and the conceptual body
converge in the understanding that the black "captive body was an extension
of the imperial body" subsumed under a larger meta-narrative of colonialism,
modernity, and European "social fantasy."[153]

This social fantasy, in the estimation of Saidiya Hartman, "disavowed
white violence" through "the criminality imputed to blacks" and "acted to

dissimulate the barbarous forms of *white enjoyment* permitted within the law" throughout the wider Caribbean.[154] Hartman's perceptive invocation of "white enjoyment" and social gratification to interpret these acts of ascribed criminality and black violence conveys the complex affects associated with a perverse system of Atlantic chattel slavery predicated on the sustained proliferation of the global pleasure goods of sugar, tobacco, coffee, tea, and cocoa produced in Trinidad and elsewhere.

Further, the social fantasy of British Atlantic slave geographies (with the United States as no exception) included a pretended "construction of a nonantagonistic, organic, and complementary society" held in symmetry and stability by white paternalism and African submission.[155] Enslaved Africans' exertions of power of any kind posed direct threats to the social fantasy, necessitating a swift annihilation subsequently "transformed (by death) into discourse," according to Harvey Young.[156] White authorities thus rendered the black body as socially discursive space by making the inextricable link between "hyperembodiness" (signifying civic deviance) and the "hypervisibility" of its torturous consequences (signifying white dominance).[157]

In theorizing acts of recruiting "dead bodies and parts of bodies to demonstrate their power," Vincent Brown masterfully proffers that the mutual alliance between civil and planter authority constantly shaped new social memory regarding Africans as embodied weapons, their malevolent religious practices, and their subjugated status within the British colonies.[158] The slavescape throughout the Caribbean and the Americas established African disfigurement and malformation as civic rituals. The schedule of plantation data and returns through 1824 detail bodily abnormalities and deformities of violence as commonplace identifying "marks," which include "lost the fourth toe of the left foot," "deep scar on the left shoulder," "lost the first joint of the middle toe, left foot," "cast in the eye," and "lame in the right leg."[159] These gratuitous new-world marks became more salient than their old-world country marks as public symbols of identification.

Through the racialized criminalization of Obeah, Picton's colonial governorship gave unambiguous authorization for the legal and public consumption of African-descended bodies. One historian argued that "the brunt of [Picton's] severities fell most heavily on the slaves and the free coloureds."[160] Punishments enacted on these bodies exceeded normative boundaries of British law and generated practices of grave repression. Colonial law and its *meta-law* of violence functioned as agents of social regulation and constraint in Governor Picton's Trinidad, where the alleged obeah activities of its African inhabitants symbolized supernatural peril within the colony. Europeans were "convinced of the power (natural and supernatural) of obeah and of the use of poison."[161] Ushering in an era of "judicial terror" similar to that seen in other parts of the Caribbean, Picton sanctioned mutilating punishments for African defendants alone, exempting entirely white and nonblack bodies from these same penalties.[162]

On December 29, 1801, Pierre Francois and Bouqui (two enslaved "Negroes") along with Leonard (a "Mulatto") were "vehemently suspected" and found guilty of sorcery, divination, and poisoning by means of charms. As the recorded account indicated, Pierre and Bouqui suffered horrific physical punishments, with the former "condemned to be burnt alive" and the latter "to be hanged, and his body to be burnt" after having been "confined in a solitary dungeon for six months previous to his being tried."[163] Despite pronouncements of innocence, following the ruling Pierre and Bouqui were "conducted to the chapel," where Bouqui "was baptized by the curate of Port of Spain"; both were then "heavily ironed" and "heavily fettered," and after that "heard prayers."[164] In late afternoon, Pierre was chained to a stake with kindling beneath him and draped with a shirt of brimstone (sulfur); Bouqui was hanged and beheaded, and his "headless trunk was laid on a stake alongside of Pierre Francois"; and then "both the living and dead were consumed in flames."[165] Leonard, the mulatto, however, escaped execution and mutilation, as he was "forever banished" from Trinidad.

These and other acts of torture exemplify the antiblack violence of Picton's rule.[166] Enslaved Africans convicted of obeah or the "black arts" in Trinidad were consumed through rituals of social cannibalism in which black flesh became "the spectacle of punishment" and executions became "spectacularized murders."[167] There was a ferocity and finality of death that characterized these brutal acts. Yet, further still, there lingered a profound deathlessness and immortality of the vanquished black nefarious body—a haunt that loitered in the physical colonialscape and subsequent imaginary. Regarding the fate of Bouqui and Pierre, the archives reveal that the "frequent burnings of this sort which took place, together with the smell of the brimstone, obliged many, who lived near the gallows, to leave their houses rather than inhale emissions of black flesh."[168] Pierre McCallum renders the scene depicting Pierre Francois and Bouqui's obliteration so inexplicably shocking that "the negroes rushed off with horror from these barbaric scenes, yet it was a matter of astonishment they did not instantly massacre the white population."[169]

Scarcely a year after the public executions of Francois and Bouqui, Governor Picton's colonial court convicted an enslaved man named La Fortune, owned by a Mr. Luzette, of "having by his knowledge in the black arts, discovered the

Use of Herbs,—of having by poisons caused sickness among many Slaves on different Estates,—of having distributed and sold pretended Charms, and of having dangerous Connexions" with the Devil.[170] The trial records indicate that La Fortune feared his deeds had been discovered, and anticipated "his Master would deliver him into the hands of Justice." La Fortune then "attempted to take away his life." Unsuccessful at determining the fate of his own body, he received the harrowing sentence that he was "condemned to be hanged, his head to be cut off, and exposed on the Estate to which he belonged, and his body to be burnt." At the time of execution, La Fortune had suffered greatly after six months' imprisonment and "was so emaciated and weak, as to be carried before the tribunal by two jail negroes" and, "being unable to walk, he was dragged to the usual place of execution."[171]

Beneath the performance of display, the root of violence against the black body appeared most obvious in its reliance on torture. Less than thirty days after La Fortune's graphic execution, enslaved Thisbe and her husband, Felix, stood before Picton's tribunal on January 29, 1802, charged with poisoning and conversing with the Devil. Seventy out of one hundred and fifty enslaved Africans reportedly died within nine months on the Coblentz estate, causing great alarm in the colony. And deaths on other estates, including that owned by St. Hilaire Begorrat, only contributed to the heightened suspicions of poisoning and supernatural warfare. Also causing great suspicion was that the deaths were not among "the slaves direct from Africa who were subject to high mortality rates" but among "well seasoned slaves from Jamaica."[172] Begorrat—who had migrated to Trinidad from Martinique—and his colleagues suspected poisoning, since incidents of this nature had been previously alleged in Martinique. Investigating one death on his own estate, Reunion, Begorrat ordered Thisbe, a "nurse in the plantation hospital," and all other enslaved laborers to assemble and witness him and Dr. Le Bis "with great solemnity [open] up one of the dead slaves in front of them all and [begin] to search with precision for traces of poison."[173] An analogous ritual of disembowelment was also reported in North Naparima when between 1803 and 1805, an estate suffered the "loss of twenty negroes and negresses of the same sickness; along with 22 mules and four oxen." At Reunion estate, Begorrat and Le Bis found inside the enslaved victim's intestine "a piece of bread," which the doctor "fed to a dog and pig, both animals dying one hour after eating it." Begorrat's use of this method proved effective in singling out Thisbe, the person he most suspected. Her very attributes of attending to the sick in healing capacities and helping to keep them fed and nourished would have necessarily made her vulnerable to poisoning accusations. Placing

Thisbe at risk would have also been knowledge of "botanical and medical sciences" that could be misconstrued as poison.[174] According to De Verteuil, "Completely demoralized and without being accused, she [Thisbe] fled the scene, taking refuge with a neighboring planter and begging him to help her, and save her from her devilish master."[175] Thisbe and her husband were subsequently arrested and accused of poisoning. Her husband Felix's fate is described later. Regarding Thisbe, after being "confined in dungeon for five months" and under the "agony of *excruciating torture*," she maintained that her husband, Felix, was innocent of any crime. Thisbe, however, was ordered to be "suspended by the hands about . . . five or six inches from the ground which induced her to confess her crime immediately and declare all her accomplices."[176] Her case summary notes that "torture had been applied to Thisbe, in Consequence of which she declared herself Guilty of poisoning," and "on her own confession, extorted by Torture, and without any other Evidence, Thisbe was condemned to be hanged, and her Body afterwards burnt." Governor Picton orders her husband, Felix, to assist in Thisbe's demise.[177] Despite this, it is reported that Thisbe declared before her death, *"This is but like a drink of water to what I have already suffered"* and *"I hope my husband will be spared for he is innocent. I trust I am going to God."*[178] Thisbe was subsequently decapitated, and her head was taken to Diego Martin and exhibited on a public pole as a symbol of physical and agential decomposition.[179]

The fate of Thisbe and her husband in colonial Trinidad seemed inevitable within the context of such coercive judicial methods. Picton's regime relied on torture as the primary strategy for extracting confessions of guilt. While colonial administrators in Britain's older territories, such as Antigua, St. Kitts, and St. Vincent, attempted to legislate against torture and slave mutilation, "torture cells" factored powerfully into Governor Picton's gruesome interrogation techniques.[180] Thisbe "suffered in the month of February 1802" thus attests one nineteenth century account. And as we chart Thisbe's harrowing fate from plantation estate to torture cell to head pole, she did, indeed suffer. Yet, beyond the scope of this study, we await future works from scholars like M. Jacqui Alexander who, in the capacity of scholar/healer, seeks to provide a more "textured tapestry" of Thisbe (Congolese name: Kitsimba) and moves beyond the exogenous inflictions of violence and torture to "one who had lived" a life.[181] The work of Alexander will ultimately "transmute [Thisbe's/Kitsimba's] body and the pain of its dismemberment to a remembering of this body" beyond its criminalized colonial recollections.[182]

The colonial exertions of power over African "criminals" extended beyond the physical into the psychological. Governor Picton's court engaged in its own lived colonial law practices of instituting measures of associative guilt and inflicting psychological anguish. Without any proof or evidence, mere suspicion that someone knew of another's crime provided cause for conviction as an accomplice in Trinidad. Therefore, Thisbe's legal condemnation associatively extended to her husband, Felix, and Antoine, likely an estate-mate for allegedly "having had some knowledge" of Thisbe's purported criminal activity. Trinidad's larger arena of social instability and colonial angst coupled with notions of presumed black culpability rendered the entire network of black accused vulnerable to prosecution, conviction, and death. In addition to charges of associative criminality, those with intimate ties to the accused endured the psychological torture or "psychic brutality" of being "condemned to assist" in the executions of their friends and loved ones.[183] Thisbe's estate-mate Antoine was simultaneously convicted of the black art of *jonglerie* (explored further in the following pages) and "condemned to assist at the Execution of Thisbe." As Thisbe, Felix, Antoine, and later Yala and Youba would illustrate, the black tortured body was not a gendered body under Picton's rule. Enslaved and free women were not spared the cruelty of torture nor the fate of execution and dismemberment. Further, Thisbe's husband, Felix, was "condemned to assist at her Execution, to have his Ears cut off, and to be forever banished [from] the Island."[184]

Sentences in Trinidad resounded with older inherited European somatic approaches to criminality, punishment, and evil strongly predicated on the belief that the human body conspired as both offender and malevolent host. Centuries after Heinrich Kramer and Jacob Sprenger's famous *Malleus Maleficarum*, which wedded torture with supernatural crime and sanctioned the use of trials by red-hot iron, trials by boiling water, torturous suspensions by one's thumbs, and human burnings, we find Thisbe's complete incineration and Felix's excised ears as gruesome evidence of European resurgences of extreme mutilating punishments inflicted on the bodies of the Caribbean's black inhabitants.[185] The black body was in and of itself a fearsome weapon incarnated and enfleshed and had to symbolically undergo social disfigurement and public mutilation in order to annihilate its dangerous metastasizing resistance. Focusing on the black enslaved body as a source for meaning-making in Trinidad reveals most clearly the socio-cannibalistic behavior and consumption of this subjected body and the intricate "outworkings" and machinations of colonial dominion. Within colonial Trinidad and the wider British Caribbean, *tableaux vivants* featuring black bodies and charred and amputated black body parts functioned to mitigate and to neutralize active colonial fears as well as to fortify colonial exertions of power.

As was the case with La Fortune's decapitated head and Felix's amputated ears, British colonists established a public culture of remembrance through their social practices of what I designate "souvenir penalties" (from *se souvenir*, "to remember, to recall, to recollect"). Souvenir penalties designated "which body part would be removed at what time for each individual criminal."[186] Colonial officials often sanctioned these rituals of social remembrance and erotic display following black executions. Some of the most prominent souvenir penalties stipulated "that the severed pieces, especially ears, be nailed to significant landmarks," including public municipalities, courthouses, "the gallows, watch hut gates, or quite often to great trees," such as the revered silk cotton tree.[187] These souvenir penalties of flesh served a dual function as visual and material modes of colonial communication.

The practice mirrored North American spectacle and souvenir cultures that appeared in the mid-nineteenth century regarding the public hyperconsumption of enslaved black bodies, most notably that of slave rebellion leader Nat Turner. According to one source, the postmortem ritual of Turner had him "skinned" and "his skin . . . made into a purse," while his "flesh was turned into grease, and his head and body were permanently separated."[188] Other sources argue that Turner's body was "delivered to white physicians for dissection" and his skeletal remains became part of the private holdings of a southern doctor, functioning as a symbolic trophy of memory and remembrance.[189] In "practicing a politically potent form of necromancy," both North American and Caribbean colonial structures "used the bodies of the executed to proclaim their dominion."[190]

As a symbol of power, Governor Picton himself kept a gibbet or gallows "outside the Governor's house to the edification of all beholders," who might find a "corpse hanging by the neck" on display for some alleged act of sedition or treason; Picton also used it to threaten "suspected persons" that "the wind shall pass between the soles of your feet and the earth."[191] These collective civic rituals can best be interpreted as *exhibitus cultus*—a "visual vocabulary" of colonial preeminence obtained through the public and social vanquishing of black embodied weaponry.[192] Practices of *exhibitus cultus* persisted under Governor Picton's rulership in line with Hartman's observation that the "exercise of power was inseparable from its display."[193] Thus, the executions of Pierre, Bouqui, and La Fortune appear as more than solely spectacularized executions equipped with public exhibition. They are part of a colonial pageantry of what Spillers calls "pornotroping"—the socioerotic exhibition of black torment and suffering.[194] Most vividly, within these public rituals, burnt African men and women transmogrify into new creations of the *cultus.* Bouqui, Pierre, La Fortune, Thisbe, are no longer corporeal body and flesh, but through the alchemy of white terror, Trinidad colonists invented a novel Atlantic devotion through blackness that I classify as *charmains* (charred remains)—the aftermath of burnt racial offerings. Ritual *charmains* belong to the sweeping compendium of relics and charms housed in the archives. Bouqui and Pierre's documented experience of such sanctioned heinousness bespeaks the evils of a colonial pornocracy where pain, pleasure, and the putrid were made to commingle in an erotic ritual display. Simone Browne aptly discusses "the violent regulation of blackness" and how discipline, spectacle, punishment, and torture worked collectively as "acts of making the black body legible as property" and as a "vendable object to be bought, sold, and traded."[195] These practices gave rise to the use of the commodified African body in the Atlantic world as a symbolic artifact of libidinal spectacle terror as well as "the source of an irresistible, destructive sensuality."[196]

Thus, within this profound ritual intersection of sensuality and social cannibalism, black bodies became a consumptive symbol and fetishized site for mapping a larger sociology of colonial power. Obeah, divination, and the "black arts" collectively represented a "social and demonological stereotype" of Africans in Trinidad.[197] Hence, the supernatural cannot be divorced from the "interlocking, interdependent nature of systems of domination," that seek its eradication and substantiate antiblackness in colonial Trinidad.[198] In his essay "Bodies in Time and the Healing of Spaces: Religion, Temporalities, and Health," Charles Long contends that "the black body has always appeared in a fetishized body. . . . As a form of fetish matter, it carried all the characteristics of any fetishized body—portable, with no inherent value, fluctuating between notions of desire, exorcism, denial, and invisibility, yet possessing an overwhelming materiality."[199] This sense of overwhelming materiality of the black body and presence dominated the public colonial realm with its innumerable inhabitants, indispensable labor, corporeal vulnerability, and criminalized executions.

The fabric of Trinidad and the slaveholding Caribbean was woven more generally with the threads of colonial government, economic avidity, socioracial and class stratification, and a sanctioning judicial system all choreographed around the black body of labor, object, and desire. Under Governor Picton, the black body was at the center of the arrests, imprisonments, interrogative tortures, and public executions caught in the dramaturgical web of colonial apprehension and angst. The slave colony was a locale where black bodies were at once needed and discarded, essential and dispensable, costly and caustic, apparent and invisible. Long labeled this Atlantic phenomenon "erotic epistemology," wherein the white imagination held a keen awareness and knowingness of African presence and a constant oscillation between its desirability and disposability.[200] Long theorizes an erotic epistemology "of the sensual," whereby the social ontology of "race" makes it "possible for people to see and know each other intimately." Yet it is a seeing and knowingness that violently comingles bodies, fluids, flesh, smells, emissions, and imaginaries into a climax of intimate perversion. Slavery authenticated a profound intimate violence between the soma and the sensual. During auctions and sales in the United States, bondpersons would be inspected by "professional slave testers" who would "lick the chins of the slaves for a heavy taste of salt, [as a] sign of sickness" and bondswomen, more specifically, endured acts where "the skin of their private parts is peeled back" and "they are sniffed."[201] This epistemic sensorium was pervasive throughout the Americas and the Caribbean as African-descended populations were grotesquely transfigured into violated physicalities, culturally deficient containers, and spiritually malevolent hosts while at the same time copiously satiating a white economic and erotic appetite.

Governor Picton himself traversed the complex sensual/sexual and colonial boundaries of the above "transnational erotics," as M. Jacqui Alexander would more broadly define it, as he publicly debased and mutilated bodies of Africans and proliferated images of Trinidad's mixed-race inhabitants as violent and insurgent while having his private and personal erotic desires heterosexually consummated through a mistress from the free colored population, Rosetta Smith.[202] In history, Smith is depicted either as an independent female entrepreneur or as Picton's female counterpart, notorious and ruthless. Kit Candlin's study of "female agency in the southern Caribbean" positions Smith among a handful of free colored women in Trinidad who were "able to exploit the poorly controlled edges of empire for their own advantage."[203] As Picton's known and very public mistress, Smith was situated in proximity to the epicenter of empire. According to Candlin, "women, such as Rosetta Smith on Trinidad, owned slaves and estates, but they also used their sexuality to gain the protective attention of significant white men."[204] What is known about Smith is that she was previously married, her husband suffered bankruptcy, and she surfaces in the records between 1800 and 1815 as the single purchaser of property. In the slave registers she is listed as a purchaser and owner of at least thirty-four slaves, and her relationship with Governor Picton lasts for approximately five years until his departure from the colony.[205] Smith was proficient in at least three languages—French, Spanish, and English—and used them in commerce as she negotiated business affairs in South America and other parts of the Caribbean.[206] Candlin indicates that in addition to the governor, Smith had elite connections in the colony, traveled freely throughout the nearby region, and was part of a free colored class that, despite racial impediments, "managed to maintain the same (if not a greater) degree of transnational mobility as their poor European or Creole neighbors."[207]

Governor Picton's relationship with the free colored Rosetta Smith was both real and enduring. Smith resided in the Government House with Picton (at times she self-identified as Rosetta Picton), and they had four children together (naming the eldest Thomas Picton Jr.); their children were educated in England, and they were heirs to Smith's property and received bequests from Picton. Recent scholarship offers a more layered approach and interpretation of Rosetta Smith vis-à-vis Picton and represents her as an "astute business woman," manager of a slave-catching business with Picton, co-owner of a plantation estate, and recipient of colonial government contracts.[208] Yet the writings of her nineteenth-century contemporaries in Trinidad portray the Smith-Picton couple as engaged in illicit dealings in slave trading, unsavory and exploitive business practices, and indiscriminate abuse of prisoners and citizens.[209] According to McCallum, in 1803, Smith wielded influence in Trinidad "with the power of torturing at her command." If those arrested among the "modest and innocent" failed to pay her a bribe, "the unfortunate accused would be either hanged, burnt, put in the bastille, or otherwise punished"—all because of the influence of Rosetta Smith, whom McCallum deemed Picton's "Inquisitorial-General" because she reportedly supported the suffering of the commission's victims.[210]

When viewed through the theoretical lenses of Long's erotic epistemology and religious and performance studies, one can interpret the visually and violently erotic hanging, decapitation, cadaver display, and final incineration of each victim criminalized for practicing obeah and the "Black Arts" as a colonial "performance event."[211] As colonial theater, the enslaved black body was "staged as a 'criminal body'" with the crime and body "given a compulsory visibility"; physical dismembering became part of a ritual of public re-membering enhanced by the "ability to reactivate the expired performance event."[212] More importantly, in this public performance, the complete viewership and audience of the colony—enslaved Africans, white inhabitants, estate owners, colonial administrators, free coloreds, travelers, and visitors to the island—collectively witnessed the complete and utter annihilation of the anti-colonial, anti-imperial black weapon. Physical dismemberment and incineration functioned not only to destroy the sources of revolt, resistance, and insurrection but also to wholly obliterate the black body itself as *enfleshed weaponry*.

Informed by the foundational works of Hortense Spillers and Sylvia Wynter, Alexander G. Weheliye suggests that in an Atlantic world of race and black "fleshly surplus," interpretations of colonial contexts such as Trinidad (and North America) are inescapable from the racial "biopolitics" and "biopower" that inform and substantiate them.[213] Weheliye fittingly quotes Frantz Fanon's colonial psychoanalytics: "We know how much of sexuality there is in all cruelties, tortures, beatings."[214] Hence, colonial economy, terror, eroticism, torture, power, and profit violently converge in the dermatic sphere of anti-blackness. Predictably, iterations of this heinous social performance enacted across the British colonies climaxed with the public pageantry of the severed and weaponized black body parts—the civic "souvenir," the social "keepsake," the racial "relic," the colonized "fetish"—as the symbolic scripting of ultimate colonial power and supremacy.[215] This notion of pageantry, power, and erotic epistemology is akin to the encounter between the black imprisoned body and white civic authority in James Baldwin's essay "Going to Meet the Man," where following a police officer's torturous prodding of black testicles and the desire to "pick him up and pistol whip him until the body's head burst open like a melon," the officer, "to his bewilderment, his horror, beneath his own fingers, he felt himself violently stiffen—with no warning at all."[216] Orlando Patterson insightfully concludes that these affective violent interactions and savage encounters with black body and flesh reflect a form of relational "intimacy," and in the sensual perversion of these encounters, "intimacy was usually calculating and sadomasochistic."[217]

Obeah and *Jonglerie*

While obeah was a normative part of the colonial taxonomy that broadly designated sorcery, witchcraft, and poisonings, a lesser-known criminal subcategory of obeah, *jonglerie*, also appeared as a legal designation in the colonial record in Trinidad. Direct mention of *jonglerie* did not predominate in the criminal proceedings of supernatural crimes in Trinidad, as did obeah, though *jonglerie* was well known and widespread among a litany of supernatural arts since antiquity.

When the term is Anglicized as "jugglery," its more contemporary connotative associations with minstrels, mimes, or circus trickery far understate the layered dimensions of the historical preternatural and occult meanings attached to jugglery throughout the centuries. Its most common meaning evoked sorcery and enchantment, starting no later than Plato's associative notion of "jugglery and prophecy" in his *Laws* where he connected "clever men" with "ingenious devices," "deceit," and understandings of the "curious arts."[218] In the fifth and sixth centuries CE, the term surfaced in the writings of Christian figures such as Theodoret, Augustine, Africanus, Eusebius, Chrysostom, and Origen, who readily circumscribed their references to jugglery with a litany of verbal reinforcements, including references to Satan, demons, phantoms, oracles, magical arts, divination, astrology, and familiar spirits. Theodoret's letters speak of "the *jugglery* of . . . sorcery" in connection to "the relics of . . . false religion."[219] In his noted text *City of God*, Augustine refers to juggleries and avers that the "ten commandments are: Abandoning of prayer to idols, of lies, avarice, murder, adultery, theft, of the teaching of jugglery and magic, of duplicity of mind, which betrays doubt on religion."[220] Mention of "magic and jugglery" appears in *The Extant Fragments of the Five Books of Julius Africanus*,[221] as well as in Eusebius's refutation of "unholy forms of initiation and ill-omened mysteries" he denotes as "jugglery, by oracles."[222] Chrysostom in his *An Exhortation to Theodore after His Fall* warns against "magic and astronomy and the theatre of the whole satanic system of jugglery."[223] In his famous contestation with Celsius, the early patristic thinker Origen summarized his opponent as "express[ing] his opinion that the Jews were induced by the incantations employed in jugglery and sorcery (in consequence of which certain phantoms appear, in obedience to the spells employed by the magicians)."[224] From antiquity into modernity, "jugglery" remained a significant component of religious and social discourse.

By the early nineteenth century, English-language authorities such as *The Synonymous, Etymological, and Pronouncing English Dictionary* (1805) traced the etymologies of "juggle," "jugglingly," and "juggler" to the French word *jongler* and retained glosses that conveyed deceptive intentions. "Juggle" referred to "a trick by legerdemain" or "an imposture, a deception, a fraud," and "jugglingly" meant "in a deceptive manner, with artifice." "Juggler" expressed many pejorative characterizations, including "one who practices sleight of hand, one who deceives the eye by nimble conveyance, a hiccius-docius, a hocus-pocus, a trickish fellow, a cheat."[225]

Later in the same century, European travelers' journals along with obeah trials firmly cemented the term "jugglery" to the religious practices of African populations, as in the case of Brantz Mayer, the editor of *Captain Canot; or, Twenty Years of an African Slaver* (1855). Mayer affirmed the veracity of Canot's written correspondence with the following comment: "The frankness of

Canot's disclosures may surprise the more reserved and timid classes of society; but I am of opinion that there is an ethnographic value in the account of his visit to the Mandingoes and Fullahs, and especially in his narrative of the wars, *jugglery*, cruelty, superstition, and crime." Canot's description of "Mandingoes and Fullahs" paralleled accounts of black criminality familiar to colonial administrators in the British Caribbean.[226] Both Canot in Africa and British colonial officials in Trinidad understood encounters between European and African supernatural realms as exceptionally dangerous and even life-threatening to European social order, physical safety, and psychic welfare. In Canot's journal and written correspondence, these dangerous cultural and supernatural collisions inevitably resulted in European psychological disorders, as illustrated in the case of Canot's friend Joseph, who, "possessed by *Africo-mania*," fell under the spell of Africa's "people, habits, and superstitions," as well as the enchantment of the "full-blooded *cuffee*" woman and the "philharmonic ecstasies . . . of a bamboo *tom-tom*."[227] Failure to maintain rigid and impermeable boundaries between the two cultures would not only prove socially injurious to Europeans and their colonies, but also prove physically and psychologically deleterious to their essential well-being as Europeans. Thus, within the nineteenth-century context of a global slave economy, "*Africo-mania*" in Africa and obeah in the West Indian colonies indexed European fears of the socially and culturally prohibitive.

British authorities in Trinidad documented their spiritual warfare against Africans using the French variant *jonglerie*, acquired from the lingua franca and administrative tongue used by the colony's multinational, multilingual inhabitants and powerful French estate holders. The appearance of *jonglerie* in the Anglographic legal record represented more than a linguistic convenience, as it seemed to indicate growing knowledge of a wider world of African-based material culture. The 1802 allegations against Thisbe, Felix, and Antoine discussed earlier referenced charges of "the Crimes of '*Jonglerie, divinations, vintes de piailles et de Charmes.*'"[228] A peddler culture among the enslaved throughout the Francophone Caribbean valued items such as *piailles*, "small pouches thought to have mystical powers," and endowed the "wearing of piailles" with the attributes of protection, healing, and power.[229] In Saint-Domingue, similar qualities empowered *ouanga* and *makandal/macandal*, which white colonists customarily understood as "sorcery bundles and implied blasphemy, pacts with the Devil, and insurrection," and possession of which was "decreed a capital crime."[230] These items mirrored the spiritual fabrication of charms and amulets throughout the African-Atlantic world, including Brazil, where Africans "made *bolsas de mandingas*, pouches of cloth or leather filled with ritually significant materials such as roots, feathers, powders, and pieces of paper inscribed with Christian or occasionally Islamic prayers or other writing, attached to the body to provide protection and strength to the wearers," according to Diana Paton.[231]

For the alleged crimes of *jonglerie*, performing acts of divination, and the selling of potent pouches and charms in Trinidad, Antoine suffered a fate as dreadful as those visited on his comrades, as his sentence required him to assist in the execution of Thisbe, "to be marked on the forehead, and to be banished."[232] Louisa, presumed an accomplice of Antoine, was "convicted of being initiated in the Art of Jonglerie with Antoine" and "condemned to be banished."[233] In addition to illuminating the colonial pattern of a three-pronged approach to punishments for obeah-related offenses, the cases of Antoine and Louisa show the fixing of African religious cultures as mania, as witchcraft, or as jugglery. This rendered them typological mediums of spiritual terror in the European imagination and justified a spectrum of legally sanctioned torture, maiming, and postmortem mutilation.

Contesting Epistemologies and Punishing Bodies in British Atlantic Perspective

Colonial authorities discovered in February 1802 that Yala and Youba had allegedly engaged in the criminal "Art of Divination." Seen within the cultural world of enslaved people throughout the Atlantic colonies, their actions can be interpreted as enacting rituals and empowering objects for protection, defense, and spiritual immunity through the performance of divinatory rites that served as a fundamental mode of spiritual communication in most Africana religious cultures. Governor Picton's colonial administration, however, imposed its own distortion that Yala and Youba had made "an improper use of the credulity and weak Minds of the Negroes, in Order to impose upon them by the false Art of Divination, to persuade them that their wicked attempts would pass unpunished."[234] Their case added a novel dimension to standard obeah persecutions, as both of the accused apparently disputed the colonial framing of their spiritual work as a "false Art" predicated on an "improper" attempt at deceit. Their contestation of the indictment resulted in an added charge of "Guilty of Perjury in their Depositions," and they were "condemned by the Court to be banished."

Yala and Youba's case differed from other obeah cases and punishments in another remarkable way. In the aftermath of the legal ruling, Picton *directly intervened* in the judicial process, "not thinking the Sentence adequate to the

Offense" and overruled the initial decision concerning the two defendants. Instead of banishment alone, Picton condemned them "to assist at the Execution of the Negro Manuel," an associate charged alongside the pair, and then "to have their Ears cut off and to be banished."[235] Manuel had been imprisoned for nearly six months "with his feet fixed in iron stocks." Unable to walk, he was led to the gallows in a cart, hung for approximately ten minutes, then "taken down, decapitated, and his body burnt."[236] The governor mapped the crime of obeah onto a racial symbol that warranted the basest of physical and psychological punishment. Reflective of this, Yala and Youba's amended punishment symbolized how colonial courts, legal ordinances, magistrates, and even colonial governors colluded to obstruct, subvert, and extinguish all spiritual agency of enslaved Africans.

In March 1802, immediately following the convictions of Yala and Youba, the ignoble pattern of coupling obeah convictions with mutilation sentences reappeared in the cases of Michael Gordon, Joseph Faustin, and Aubinot. Their collective crimes included "use of a poisoned whip and [being] the cause of death and other loss on the estate of his master," "poisoning by means of charm," knowledge of the black arts, divination, and sorcery. The conviction of Gordon carried the sentence of death by hanging. Aubinot had been confined for eight months, was frequently tied to a post, was tortured every evening, and was ultimately executed, decapitated, burned, and "his head exposed on [a] pole near the burying-ground." However, because Faustin was "violently suspected of having contributed to the Death of many Persons," the court sentenced him "to assist at the Execution [of Gordon] with a Rope about his Neck—to have his Ears cut off—to be marked on the Cheek [with a red hot iron] . . . and to be transported."[237]

These recurring civic performances of punishment and execution in Trinidad reinscribed black bodies as receptacles of poison and sorcery. Within these rituals of punitive deterrence, convicted enslaved black bodies, like those of Yala, Youba, Gordon, Faustin, and Aubinot not only underwent public execution but also suffered excisions, the searing and singeing of the face, and civic immolation while still alive. Religious scholars such as James Noel and Clarice Martin theorize this complicated interplay between the European colonial imaginary and the enslaved black physical canvas. As Noel posits, in "being reduced to chattel, Africans represented a new form of materiality" whereby "their bodies as matter become imagined collectively" as disposable body parts and accessible sites for ontological disfigurement.[238] Similarly, Martin theorizes that the African body was "somatically distinct" and a strategy for "racializing evil" in the world of slavery. In colonial Trinidad, spiritual ties to obeah and witchcraft rendered Africans "ontologically polluted" against a European Christian backdrop.[239] Thus, civic acts of dismemberment were, in practice, social metaphors for marking African defiance and deviance and for making public what were seen as hidden spiritual acts of impudence and revolt against colonial imperialism and Christendom. Records from August 1801 to April 1802 evidence Picton's vicious social cannibalization of at least twenty-four people of African descent accused of "sorcery, divination, witchcraft, and poisoning by means of charms."[240] The sentences for Jean Louis, La Rose, and Noel, all three convicted of "poisoning, Divination, and other such Crimes" in April 1802, included a litany of mutilations enacted following the psychological punishment of assisting in the execution of another condemned enslaved African. Once they had completed the first task, their sentence required them to endure "29 strokes of the Whip, having their Ears cut off, and [being] marked on the right cheek with a hot Iron."[241]

In her compelling historical study of punishment in colonial Jamaica, Diana Paton underscores the "cataloguing of captured slaves through their identifying marks" and "subjection to the violence of branding and flogging" that created new enfleshed inscriptions on the bodies of the enslaved, especially runaways, in the eighteenth century.[242] In nineteenth-century Trinidad under Governor Picton's rule and the auspices of his commission, a novel catalogue of torture and a taxonomy of bodily display were created and inflicted upon its enslaved population: for example, burning persons alive, hanging and burning the corpses of the deceased, beheadings, displaying decapitated heads along public roads and plantation estates, branding persons on both cheeks, clipping and cutting off ears, featherings, public floggings, bodily draggings down streets, parading persons through the streets as though they were asses, and ordering persons to assist at executions.[243] Philosopher Calvin L. Warren postulates the concept of "ontological terror" to theorize the impact of this phenomenon of violence and the collective tapestry of torturous punishments and "corporal pain" inflicted on enslaved and free blacks. For Warren, blackness is an ontological invention with acute function and utility in the white imagination. In particular, Warren sheds new light on and posits new directional questions and analyses related to "the terror of antiblackness," racial metaphysics, Being, violence, ontology, and black nihilism while compellingly scrutinizing a wider discourse of humanity and freedom in the modern era.[244]

Across the British Caribbean, documents chronicling obeah crimes and their anguishing physical penalties proved analogous to the civil violence enacted on the criminalized black populace in Trinidad. For example, one could be "burnt alive" in British Jamaica or beheaded and displayed in British Grenada.[245] In an 1806 instance of this latter punishment, an enslaved man "tried as the law directs by two Magistrates, and three white men, as Jury" for the attempted poisoning of the manager of an estate had been "found guilty." This prosecution also included the suspicion of a larger conspiracy among the enslaved, as "it appeared on the Trial, by the Report of the Magistrates, that the Man was connected with a great many others, and practiced what is termed Obye—by which malpractice owns the excessive weakness of mind of the Negroes, and their dire superstitions."[246] Beyond the alleged influence over mentally weak and superstitious people, however, was the acknowledgment that "it is well known that this Country (all the West Indies) produces more Vegetables that have very deleterious and poisonous qualities." The Caribbean's botanical fecundity fueled a deeply engrained colonial apprehension that Africans had unlimited access to deadly pharmacopeial knowledge.[247] The impression among nineteenth-century colonists was that people "enslaved and oppressed" most readily used obeah when they quite "naturally looked for some safe mode of retaliation."[248]

In a society that reinforced European domination over Africans, European whites lived with great uneasiness and fear of African reprisal through mastery of their natural surroundings. As Dianne Stewart tells us:

> The most offensive and hazardous application of Obeah was as a weapon against White oppression and the slave regime. Throughout the Caribbean, Whites lived in constant fear of being poisoned and marked for death via Obeah practices. They learned that the Obeah practitioner was a professional herbalist. Obeah custodians knew how to combine natural vegetation to bring their enemies to horrible deaths. Evidently, on the plantations where Obeah experts were enslaved and Whites were enslavers, Whites were perpetual enemies and targets of annihilation.[249]

Indeed, officials in Grenada in the case above discovered that the convicted man had allegedly devised an elaborate poisonous "composition of pounded Glass, little filings of Copper, and the Powder of more Vegetables which could not be ascertained," which reveals the sophisticated material knowledge that enslaved Africans possessed. This discovery required the proper punishment, which in the eyes of the white authorities meant that the offender must be "sentenced to be hanged, his Head, when dead, to be cut off, then placed on a Pole."[250]

British North America utilized a comparable public language of legal violence sanctioned by judicial colonial statutes. A. Leon Higginbotham, in his groundbreaking text *In the Matter of Color: Race and the American Legal Process*, chronicles the consistency across North America with which black enslaved bodies became meaningful landscapes for charting criminality in colonial legislation. Authorities in Virginia deemed it "lawful" for county courts to administer a punishment to an "incorrigible" slave "by dismembering, or any other way, not touching his life, as they in their discretion shall think fit." Doing so allowed victims to be presented as public examples for "terrifying others from the like practices."[251] As in the British Caribbean, the mundane semantics of ordinance and law in North America masked "the human suffering imposed by statutory fiat."[252]

Colonial South Carolina, the destination for over 40 percent of the enslaved Africans imported to North America between 1700 and 1775, likewise enacted especially cruel judicial processes against its enslaved black population.[253] In the decades leading up to and following the infamous Stono Rebellion in 1739, "the most brutal displays of inhumanity to Blacks were sanctioned under the colony's rule of law" through a wide range of penalties reliant on maiming and mutilating Africans. Guilty verdicts on charges ranging from absconding to poisoning entailed punitive mandates that saw enslaved Africans "publicly and severely whipped, not exceeding forty lashes," "burned with the letter R in the forehead" or the cheek, and branded "in some part of his face with a hot iron, that the mark thereof may remain." Other punishments included "burning in the hand," the cutting of the "cord of the slave's leg," gibbeting, the excision of ears, "have his nose slit," beheading with the head "displayed on the courthouse chimney," genital castration, and "other punishment, as the said justices shall think fitting."[254] The investment of the colonial regime in these penalties appeared in follow-up provisions, such as "If a slave should die as a consequence of castration, without neglect on the part of whoever ordered it, the owner will be compensated from the public treasury."[255] Even the French colony Louisiana replicated the practices of its British neighbors, as it affirmed that "slaves could be tortured in official investigations, and judges were left free to sentence slaves to be burnt alive, to be broken on the wheel . . . , to be dismembered, to be branded, or to be crippled by hamstringing."[256] Accused of planning a slave insurrection in 1731, an African named Samba Bambara and his accomplices were "clapt in irons" and "put to the torture of burning matches." Ultimately, Samba and his eight companions "were condemned to be broke alive at the wheel, and the woman to be hanged before their eyes," according to the Superior Council of Louisiana.[257]

Within this tortuous milieu in colonized North America, black materiality and market economy merged. There was much money to be made by colonial marshals and constables in the public consumption of black mutilation.[258]

According to Higginbotham, "For whipping, branding, or cutting off the ear of a slave, the marshal received two shillings and six pence payable by the owner, attorney, or manager of the slave's plantation."[259] By 1735, compensatory incentives for these same punishments escalated to twenty shillings, and as much as five pounds when the sentence required execution.[260] Moreover, in the absence of an entire human corpse, those who could produce certain body parts of guilty runaways were also heavily compensated in what can be rendered an alternative amputating economy of black materiality. A hefty remuneration of fifty pounds "for every scalp of a grown negro slave, with the two ears" could be obtained in lieu of capture and return of live runaways. Also, those hired for "carrying out and setting up the heads and quarters of the two Negros" Champion and Valentine in "severall [sic] parts of the County" earned $2,000 in Virginia in 1733.[261] The widely advertised exhibitions of the amputated black body reflected "the desire of the colony to publicize for deterrent purposes" and, as in a 1707 Pennsylvania case, "to make the Slaves examples of Terror to others of their Complexion, by a most Severe Corporal Punishment."[262]

Criminal acts related to obeah and poisoning received especially harsh reprisals in British North America's legal reign of terror upon enslaved bodies. The Swedish professor Dr. Peter Kalm remarked of his 1748 travels that enslaved Africans in both the North and South had skills in the "dangerous art of poisoning" and "never disclose the nature of the poison, and keep it inconceivably secret."[263] The awareness of African expertise informed legislative action during this period, as in Virginia where the colony passed what became a succession of "medicine laws" against Africans, stating that any "negroe, or other slave, [who] shall prepare, exhibit, or administer any medicine whatsoever" would be subjected to death.[264] Colonists believed wholeheartedly that "many negroes, under pretence of practicing physic, have prepared and exhibited poisonous medicines, by which many persons have been murdered, and others have languished under long and tedious indispositions."[265] A 1751 amendment to South Carolina's Act for the Better Ordering and Governing Negroes and Other Slaves in this Province (1747) attempted "to prevent, as much as may be, all slaves from attaining the knowledge of any mineral or vegetable poison" by fining those who violated the prohibition of the employment of enslaved people by "any physician, apothecary or druggist." The same statute warned that "in case any slave shall teach or instruct another slave in the knowledge of any poisonous root, plant, herb, or other sort poison whatever, he or she, so offending, shall, upon conviction thereof, suffer death as a felon." Further, the law threatened "corporal punishment, not exceeding fifty stripes" for those enslaved people, "commonly called doctors," who gave "any medicine, or pretend medicine, to any other slave."[266] Other laws in these mainland colonies served to prosecute people, such as an enslaved man named Sharper charged in Virginia in 1773 for allegedly seeking out a "Negroe Doctor or Conjurer" to "procure Poison" in order "to destroy White people."[267] Another enslaved man in Virginia, Tom, was indicted for "having prepared and exhibited Medicine," which necessarily aligned him with the spiritual "art of conjuring or poisoning."[268] Found guilty, Tom was condemned to be "hanged by the Neck until he be dead."[269]

Historian Vincent Brown's categorization of these acts of punishments as "legal terror" is by no means hyperbole in the context of Britain's slave colonies, where "executions consisted of sporadic, localized dramas" primarily used to "dramatize . . . power" and "to set an example" for other enslaved Africans.[270] What we ultimately see in both North America and the Caribbean vis-à-vis the black body are displayed mutilated emblems of white rule and sovereignty before a public colonial viewership. Severed "Negro" head poles posted on plantation estates and along municipal roads, and detached black ears posted in civic and public spaces or tacked on silk cotton trees—likely to admonish the enslaved that they better listen to colonial authorities—became acceptable ciphers of black social regulation throughout the British Caribbean, including Trinidad. According to Brown, by "using dead bodies as symbols, masters marked their territory with awe-inducing emblems of their power"[271] (see figure 2.3).

The British colonial imaginary grappled paradoxically with the random disposability and expendability of African bodies on the one hand and the necessary indispensability of their black bodies for a profitable slave economy on the other. The context of chattel slavery only intensified a fetishistic approach to black bodies in that slavery both legally and economically assumed what Michael Meranze calls a "direct and violent seizure" of the wealth-producing African body.[272] Meranze theorizes connections between fetishism and legal "bodily sanction" that we see juridically and publicly spectacularized in charred, headless, earless, hot-iron-branded black body parts that constituted the amulet-like trophies of white colonial power in Trinidad.[273]

Colonial ambiguity surrounding obeah derived from the reality that "whites both believed in and doubted the efficacy of black supernatural power."[274] Obeah not only threatened the complete sovereignty of colonial political rule but also subsequently disturbed the spiritual authority of a dominant Christian order in support of slavery. Hence, "violent performances" of marking, mapping, and mutilating as "tool[s] of intimidation" came to represent not just a new colonial praxis equated with the "cosmic warfare"

FIGURE 2.3 Publicly displaying the bodies and heads of enslaved Africans on estate plantations and near municipalities was a common strategy deployed by British officials to instill intimidation and to punish obeah and alleged insurrectionist-related offenses. As one colonial official stated, its purpose was to "leave a Terrour on the Minds of all the other Negros for the future." From *Account of the Insurrection of the Negro Slaves in the Colony of Demerara on the 18th of August, 1823* (Demerara, Georgetown: A. Stevenson at the Guiana Chronicle Office, 1824), fold-out plate 12, following page 88. Courtesy of the John Carter Brown Library.

against obeah but also the methods for the conquest and subjugation of African bodies and epistemologies in the British colonial public.[275]

Obeah and Christianity: An Illusion in Spiritual Warfare

Obeah, when viewed as a noxious spiritual system, presented "a tenacious and superstitious rival to Christianity" in Trinidadian society.[276] The rivalry between Obeah and Christianity ventriloquized larger sociocultural conflicts in a distorted colonial relationship of contested morality, agency, and power. Because Europeans understood its sources of power to be rooted in negative and demonic spiritual forces, Obeah undermined the Christian God's spiritual authority, which Spanish, French, and British colonists in Trinidad upheld. Maarit Forde maintains that "the discourse on civilization and modernity that helped to rationalize religious persecution in British Caribbean colonies also served to produce a moral community."[277] "Across several centuries," the British colonial apparatus in the Caribbean proved ruthlessly intolerant of the "existence of alternative cosmologies and noninstitutionalized ritual practice," which disrupted its "ways of knowing."[278] In particular, the ruling elite in Trinidad could in no way sanction competing "ways of knowing," such as Obeah, that stood for dismantling the social and racial economy.

For a slave society predicated on complete regulation and subordination of African populations, contested ways of knowing were classified as "superstition," casting Africans beyond the purview of intelligibility and into a maligned, discursive realm. The term "superstition" framed an antipodal discourse, and as Sharla Fett reminds us, "the frequent pejorative use of the word directed at the enslaved . . . points to its importance in maintaining boundaries."[279] More importantly, "superstition" as commonly deployed against Africans served "to distinguish between enlightenment and ignorance, progress and primitivism, reason and irrationality, and medicine and quackery."[280] The discursive vocabulary of "superstition" in both Trinidad and North America served not only to "ridicule entire traditions" originating in Africa but also to establish these traditions as obvious and formidable targets of religious and legal interdiction.[281]

While Governor Picton's slave ordinances sought the annihilation and purgation of all forms of the obeah superstition, his Slave Codes of 1800 invoked Christianity and made provisions to articulate the duties and moral responsibilities of Christian masters in their governance of the enslaved. Picton's unusual position as colonial administrator accounts for his reach into private plantation affairs, as the governor functioned officially as both an operative of the Church of England and a representative of the Crown.[282] Immediately after Article XI, which outlawed the practice of obeah, Article XII of the Slave Codes of 1800 stated:

It is the duty incumbent on Christians, not only to feed and clothe those who are dependent upon them, but also to instruct them in their duty towards their Maker. Planters who have attended this precept have found the benefit of it in the improvement of their slaves' dispositions. It should be therefore the essential duty of the master to teach his slaves the first elements of the Christian religion, to prepare them for Baptism; and we expressly recommend to the parish curates the observance of this part of their office, reminding them that it is the principal object of their mission to preach the gospel to the poor.[283]

Although he required proselytization in Article XII, Picton provided little to no organizational or supportive means for Christianizing enslaved Africans in early British Trinidad. Further, Picton's successors as governor showed the same disinterest in structuring Protestant estate missions for the enslaved. The disregard for religious instruction revealed the determination from Governor Picton onward to combat African religious criminality with stern civil authority alone.[284]

Christianization, however, factored into a much larger religious debate in the colonized Atlantic. While cited as a legal obligation in Atlantic slave codes, the religious education of Africans was highly contested throughout the Caribbean. European colonists demonstrated ambivalence on the question of religious instruction and its potential impact on enslaved non-European populations despite the regular renewal of Catholic and Protestant missionizing efforts. Indeed, missionaries, the colonial government, the planter class, and the enslaved all held divergent views on the efficacy of Christian instruction. In Britain's Jamaican colony, for example, missionaries had to adopt an apologetic posture toward slavery to "assure the plantocracy that Christianity actually produces better, more dutiful, and reliable enslaved workers."[285]

In the Francophone Caribbean, French colonists expressed decided opposition to African Christianization to ensure the physical protection of estate owners. An eighteenth-century French colonist remarked that "the safety of the whites, less numerous than the slaves, surrounded by them on their estates, and almost completely at their mercy, demands that the slaves be kept in the most profound ignorance."[286] By the end of the century, however, the French Code Noir of 1789 included the heading "Education" and impressed upon colonial slave masters the following:

Every one who has slaves, of whatever class and condition he may be, is obliged to instruct them in the principles of the Roman Catholic Religion and in the necessary truths in order that they may be baptized within the year of their residence in my Dominions, taking care to explain to them the Christian Doctrine. . . . On those and other days when they are obliged to hear Mass, the Owners of the Estate shall be at the expense of maintaining a priest to say mass for them and to explain to them the Christian doctrine as likewise to administer the Holy Sacraments.[287]

The Spanish Crown, conversely, shared none of the French and British reticence and advocated for the Christianization of African slaves in Trinidad. The Crown obligated Spanish masters to go so far as to regulate the behavior of slaves on sacred holidays when they were not required to work. Further, the Crown expected masters to hold Mass on the plantation and afterward "allow slaves to divert themselves innocently in their presence," though prohibiting interaction with people of the opposite sex or slaves from other estates.[288]

African Obeah and European Christianity wrestled for spiritual supremacy throughout most of the British West Indies. Legal sanctions and, at times, Christian instruction were deemed the appropriate methods of defense for combating the unrestrained spiritual energies of Africa. Yet even in instances when Africans appeared receptive to Christian teachings in the wider British West Indies, missionaries still complained that enslaved Africans readily regarded the sacraments as forms of "Christian-Obea," speculating that in many instances "blacks generally thought of Christianity as another form of Obeah."[289] Further, British Trinidad experienced a delay of some forty years before structured Christian missionary activity to Africans occurred. Hence, the threat of Obeah loomed over Trinidad, with white colonial rule, Christian morality, and the gainful apparatus of subjugated slave order understood as Obeah's targeted adversaries.

Obeah and the Aftermath of Governor Picton

Obeah in Trinidad and throughout the British Caribbean was interwoven into the "intra-imperial social system" of colonialism and slavery.[290] Within this context, juridical laws and excessive punishments enacted against African populations demonstrated the ways "flesh and race conjure each other," creating a proliferation of social meaning around what Mayra Rivera calls "constructions of racialized flesh."[291] The archives on early British Trinidad expose "colonial discourses' indelibly marked conceptualizations of flesh" that interpreted black bodies within a new "carnal imaginary" that publicly situated African-descended people within the brutal intersection of white colonial pathologies and "white mythologies."[292] Myth, ritual, devotion, belief, performance, ontology, and practice formed the nucleus of colonial lived religion as enacted in Trinidad under Governor Picton.

Colonial law and social psyche legally assigned obeah definitions distinct from the meanings Africans attached to their practices. Diana Paton summarizes the colonial objective quite accurately in asserting, "Obeah law was intended not to suppress only those practices that could lead to collective rebellion but to criminalize the whole complex of African divination and spiritual protection."[293] Thus, in their refusal to "accept African religious practices as genuine forms of worship," Trinidad's colonial inhabitants cultivated a judicial system that administered prosecutions and corporal punishments "as harshly as the laws allowed."[294]

The documented obeah, black arts, *jonglerie*, sorcery, charms, divination, and poisoning cases tried under the colonialcraft of Governor Picton enacted a complete "deprecation of flesh" vis-à-vis black bodies. Physically and figuratively, anti-obeah executions throughout the Caribbean targeted not only the body of the African-descended accused but also an "invisible ontology" possessing a "presumed inward, invisible content" of moral degeneracy, deviance, and decadence.[295] It is within this context where a colonial cult of obeah fixation most readily exemplifies George Kelsey's point that "racial traditions and practices" are undoubtedly a "religious matter." [296] He concludes that the "faith character of racism" or "idol of race" are determinant factors for how self-designees of racial supremacy navigate "attitude, decision, and action."[297] One might aptly point to Rivera's notion of the "spiritualization of flesh," where black flesh is not simply "marked by otherness" but in its spiritualization is transmogrified as evil and ritualized as malevolent.[298]

In the end, however, Picton's severity did not go unnoticed, as he faced trial for several dozen criminal charges in England in 1806. British authorities investigated him in 1803 for customarily using torture and execution in lieu of formal trials or hearings. Colonel William Fullarton, one of the chief investigators, strongly condemned Picton's governing and legal practices, which he categorized as a "system of severity."[299] As he was charged with documenting "these Extraordinary Transactions in Trinidad" for Lord Hobart, secretary of state for the Colonial Department, Fullarton regarded his investigation of Picton and the work of the Commission as a matter of "Public duty" and "character" and found intolerable the number of "mulattoes, free negroes, and negro slaves, accused of witchcraft, sorcery, divination and poisoning," whose fates included being "tortured, condemned, mutilated, hanged, beheaded and burned alive under this Commission."[300] Historians Lauren Benton and Lisa Ford argue that Governor Picton's despotic leadership was a test case that called for greater "imperial oversight of colonial legal orders" while also laying the foundation for "a more powerful vision of global order" by the British Empire.[301] The thirty-six allegations against Picton presented to the British Privy Council included "the criminal charge of Death inflicted without any Trial" or "Execution without any form of Trial" for at least twenty-nine

British subjects.[302] The final charge proved exceptionally alarming and most startling to British authorities in portraying Picton as using suspicion of "Sorcery, Divinations, and Poisoning" to authorize "mutilation tortures, and Cruel Deaths, by burning alive and otherwise, inflicted without due forms of Law on the Mulattoes, free Negroes, and Negro Slaves."[303] An outraged Picton remarked of Fullarton and his accusers, "They are formidable in nothing but their Wickedness like their beggarly Leader," ultimately declaring, "I hold my Head high and claim Justice against an infamous Conspiracy." But Fullerton pledged that "the most satisfactory evidence will be provided that people have been Hung first and tried after and tortured before they were accused to ascertain whether there was reason for commencing . . . against them" and that "some women had been burnt alive without any evidence having been produced of their guilt [while] others had been put to torture as no witnesses whatever [testified] . . . against them and were hung on their own extorted confession."[304] Picton's critics denounced his actions, allegedly maintaining that "judicial torture . . . was unknown to English law."[305]

The British Privy Council launched a full inquiry into Governor Picton's alleged practices as "essential *for the Public Service*" and recommended that Colonel Fullarton document "every individual of whatever Country, Color, or Condition who has been *imprisoned, banished, fettered, flogged, mutilated, tortured, to extort confession, hanged, burned alive, or otherwise punished*," in addition to seeking information about "trials, sentences, periods of confinement and punishments and of all those who have died in Prison."[306] The case of Louisa Calderón, a fourteen-year-old free colored arrested for theft and who endured "the room of torture" in 1801, garnered much public outrage and eventually led to a verdict of guilty against Picton.[307] Her torture entailed the piquet or suspending her from a pulley with all of her weight lowered onto a spike[308] (see figures 2.4 and 2.5).

Surprisingly, Picton's legal counsel attempted to turn the Calderón incident into a defense tactic by seeking to "contrast the supposed mildness of Calderón's treatment with the limitless agony to which slave prisoners were subject."[309] The fixation on Calderón's torture as a point of either public sympathy or criminal liability relied on the scale of social valuation and its analytic of comparison that completely disregarded the treatment of people deemed Trinidad's most contemptible. For those crimes of social ignominy and callousness against enslaved Africans, Governor Thomas Picton would go unpunished. For the crime against Calderón, he would be found guilty in 1806—as Diana Paton insightfully points out, most likely because "she was a free light-skinned woman who was easily positioned as a sentimental

Inhuman Torture !!

FAIRBURN's EDITION

OF THE

TRIAL

OF

THOMAS PICTON,

Late Governor of Trinidad,

AND

Colonel of the 54th Regiment of Foot,

FOR TORTURING

LOUISA CALDERON,

IN THE ISLAND OF TRINIDAD,

In the Month of December, 1801,

BY SUSPENDING HER BY A ROPE TIED TO HER WRIST, AND
A SHARP SPIKE THE ONLY RESTING-PLACE FOR HER FOOT.

WHICH WAS TRIED AT

The Court of King's-Bench, Westminster,

On MONDAY, Feb. 24, 1806,

BEFORE

LORD ELLENBOROUGH & A SPECIAL JURY.

TAKEN IN SHORT-HAND.

" I ask not of your passions, but of your justice, a verdict of GUILTY
against this Defendant."   *Garrow.*

LONDON :
Published by JOHN FAIRBURN, 146, Minories,
Price Sixpence.

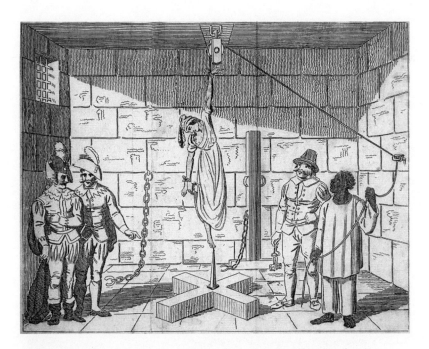

FIGURE 2.4 (LEFT) AND FIGURE 2.5 (ABOVE) Cover page and image of Governor Thomas Picton's February 24, 1806, published trial records. Picton was accused of abusing his station and among his charges was the unlawful torture of fourteen-year-old colored adolescent Louisa Calderón in December 1801. Printed in *Inhuman torture!! Fairburn's edition of the trial of Thomas Picton, late Governor of Trinidad and Colonel of the 54th Regiment of Foot, for torturing Louisa Calderon in the island of Trinidad in the month of December, 1801 . . . Which was tried at the Court of King's-Bench, Westminster on Monday, Feb. 24, 1806 before Lord Ellenborough & a special jury* (London: J. Fairburn, 1806).

victim."[310] Historian James Epstein similarly argues "the atrocities against slaves in Trinidad were condensed and displaced onto the spectacle of Calderón's martyred body."[311] However, with the support and financial backing of Trinidad's wealthy planter class, an 1808 appeal eventually cleared Picton of all charges, shielding his civic offenses and authorizing his torturous practices.[312] Picton's successor Sir Thomas Hislop, who served as governor through 1811, further exculpated Picton; as he reviewed "the copies of the commissions under which Picton had had slaves tried and executed for sorcery and poisoning, he entered into a detailed defence of the latter, commenting that severe measures of justice were inseparable from the government of a slave society."[313] Like his successor Hislop, supporters of Picton would champion him "for his inflexible preservation of good order."[314] Through the many charges and allegations, Picton maintained his innocence and believed he had done his duty to "King and Country," firmly asserting that if appointed as governor again in the Crown Colony of Trinidad, he would "pursue the same line of conduct," for in his political philosophy, "great disorders require great remedies."[315]

Obeah cases would significantly decline in the immediate decades following Picton's tenure. When enslaved Michel and Salveste appear in the 1824 Return of Criminal Causes charged with the crime of "practising necromancy, or obyism," they each escaped death, with Michel being acquitted for "default of proof" and Salveste sentenced "to suffer corporal punishment, by receiving thirty-nine stripes, in presence of the slaves of the neighboring estates, in the quarter in which he resides."[316] Akin to other British colonies, obeah restrictions resurfaced at the time of emancipation within larger legislative ordinances related to "Vagrants, Rogues, and Vagabonds, and incorrigible Rogues." In 1838, Trinidad's Governor George Fitzgerald Hill issued an ordinance under "Definition of Rogues and Vagabonds, and punishment of their offences," stating:

> Every person pretending or professing to tell fortunes or to discover by means of any subtle art, craft, or device, lost or stolen goods, or the person or persons by whom such lost or stolen goods had been taken, or professing or pretending . . . by means of any tricks, device, preparation or other such manner or thing, to exercise any undue influence over the mind of any person or persons; every person vending or practising obeah, or any such art, using any subtle craft, palmistry, means or device, to deceive or impose on any other person or persons; . . . shall be deemed a rogue or vagabond, within the true intent and meaning of this Ordinance.[317]

As a consequence, the Ordinance deemed, "And it shall be lawful for any Magistrate or Justice of the Peace to commit such offender, being thereof convicted before him by the confession of such offender or by the evidence on oath of one or more credible witness or witnesses, to prison, there to be kept, with or without hard labour, for any time not exceeding two calendar months." The punishments, then, for obeah offences in emancipated Trinidad after the 1830s proved less draconian than during Picton's governorship under slavery.

As shall be described in the next two chapters, despite a short-lived lull, the colonial world of Trinidad persisted in its socially consumptive practice of criminalizing African inhabitants while maintaining a discursive imaginary of obeah as part of a white colonial "invented fantastic."[318] Obeah as aesthetic subject found new life in the white literary imagination of nineteenth-century Europeans, and particularly set in Trinidad, after emancipation with the 1854 publication of Marcella Fanny Noy Wilkins's novel *The Slave Son*. Figurations of obeah also endured in prosecutions of liberated Africans with the resurgence of harsher corporal punishments in the obeah prohibitions legislation of 1868. In epic ways, liberated Africans, such as John Cooper and Mah Nannie, challenged colonial violations and were among those of African descent who in rare instances received both legal vindication and monetary remuneration. Obeah, despite shifting imaginaries in white colonial publics, nevertheless remained a fixed prosecutable crime in Trinidad well into the next century.

Obeah, Piety, and Poison in *The Slave Son*

REPRESENTATIONS OF AFRICAN RELIGIONS IN TRINIDADIAN COLONIAL LITERATURE

"And the time is come, thanks to Mrs. Stowe! when my subject is no longer irrelevant to the topics of the day. I present myself however not so much to take rank among the champions of civil emancipation . . . as to invite supporters for its completion in the social advancement of the coloured race."
—MARCELLA FANNY NOY WILKINS, *The Slave Son*

The Slave Son, published in 1854 by Marcella Fanny Noy Wilkins, opens with an ode of gratitude and indebtedness to North American writer and antislavery supporter Harriet Beecher Stowe. With obvious hemispheric and international impact and influence, Stowe ushered in a new genre of women's abolitionist and antislavery literary fiction with her 1852 landmark publication of *Uncle Tom's Cabin; or, Life among the Lowly*. Unlike Stowe's *Uncle Tom's Cabin*, previously published in serialized form in *The National Era* from June 1851 to April 1852, *The Slave Son* emerged from scattered stories written

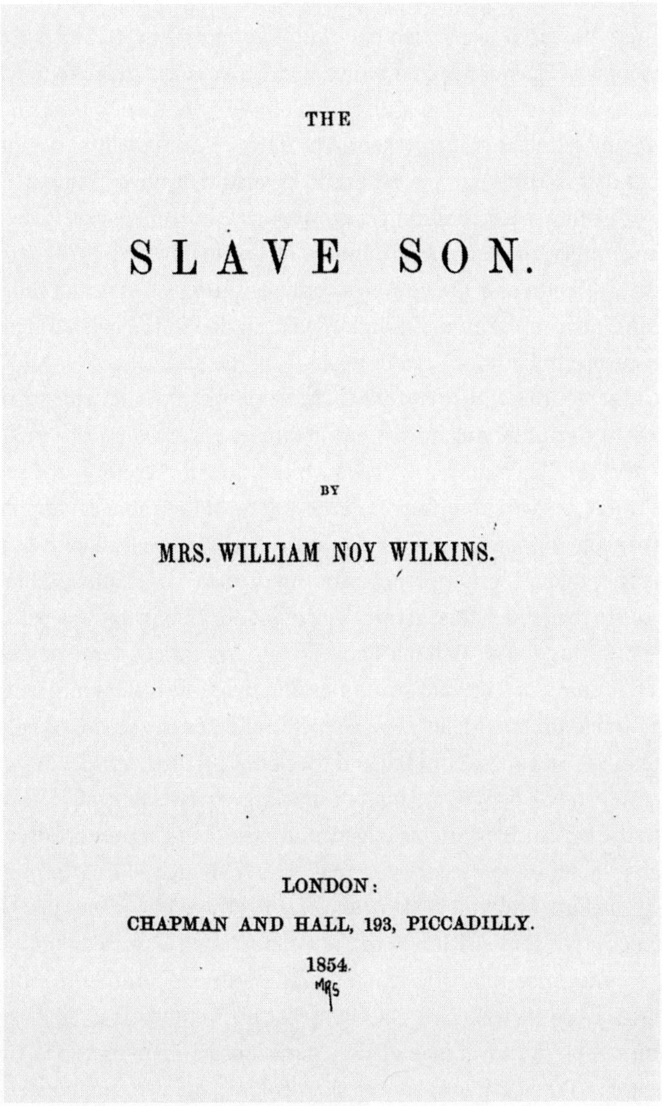

THE

SLAVE SON.

BY

MRS. WILLIAM NOY WILKINS.

LONDON:

CHAPMAN AND HALL, 193, PICCADILLY.

1854.

FIGURE 3.1 *The Slave Son* was published in London in 1854. Inspired by Harriet Beecher Stowe's *Uncle Tom's Cabin*, Marcella Fanny Noy Wilkins sought to champion "the social advancement of the coloured race" more than a decade after the British abolished slavery in its Caribbean colonies. Courtesy of the New York Public Library, digitized by Google (http://books.google.com/books?id=HgIoAAAAMAAJ&oe=UTF-8).

over several years and gathered into a novel in 1854, when the Irish-born Wilkins felt "inspired to publish the completed novel in its finished form by the success of Harriet Beecher Stowe's *Uncle Tom's Cabin*" (see figure 3.1).

Though significantly less popular than Stowe's book in its time and underutilized by scholars in the present, *The Slave Son* nonetheless provides an important text in the Anglophone literary world that unveils transatlantic notions of gender, race, economy, and national tensions, as well as intra-European conflict, in the colonial context. It further illuminates the political currency of religion and the complex representation of Africana religions (Obeah and African traditional religions) entangled in the layered tensions between European Catholics and Protestants in the Atlantic world. Additionally, the nineteenth-century novel became a powerful vehicle for women's engagement in public discourses traditionally reserved as the exclusive domain of elite white males. Privileged white women, therefore, utilized the novel as transgressive subterfuge for entering forbidden social and political domains and giving voice to matters conventionally unspeakable for women, such as rape, torture, cruelty, the suffering of slaves, race mixing, and, in this instance, the taboo supernatural secrets of obeah or what was perceived as sorcery. In this sense, Wilkins's novel counterpoints to some degree the colonial flattening of Trinidad's complex and dynamic *nations* into vendible and exploitable units. *The Slave Son* also complicates the standard colonial construction of Obeah in Trinidad and the wider Atlantic world.

Marcella Fanny Noy Wilkins figured in a larger movement of Irish immigrants to the British West Indies constituting the "largest proportion of the whites" by the mid-seventeenth century.[1] The Irish arrived in Trinidad during the eighteenth and nineteenth centuries for three major reasons.[2] First, the connection of some Irishmen to the Spanish militia carried them to the colony. Second, Irish men and women made Trinidad another destination in the postslavery era following the Great Famine in the 1840s.[3] Finally, Irish immigrants took full advantage of the Spanish cedula's invitation to Catholics to settle in Trinidad's burgeoning slave colony, an invitation bolstered by generous land incentives for plantation estate development. This created an emerging prominent Irish presence in Trinidad in the late eighteenth and early nineteenth centuries as a landed (rather than indentured) class. They were able to achieve this level of respectability amid larger British and US American nineteenth-century denouncements of Irish as "a separate race," "inferior to the Anglo-Saxon," "human swinery," and "white negroes."[4] Scholars argue that "in the West Indies, from the very inception of every colony, social conditions would inexorably force a fundamental alteration or mutation of the ancient scheme of rank and position," thus elevating the Irish well beyond their historical caste in Europe.[5] In fact, the wealthy and prominent Irish planters John Nugent, John Black, and John Nihell were three of the five members of a "Council of Advice" appointed by Governor Thomas Picton in 1801. Picton considered them among the most respectable and opulent proprietors of the Colony.[6] A few years later, Nihell, who would be appointed chief justice, and Black, in particular, would prove staunch allies and supporters of Picton when he was made to stand trial for administrative torture.[7] Lord Robert Hobart, British tory, member of Parliament in the Irish House of Commons, and secretary of state for War and the Colonies from 1801–1804, also entertained the prospect of recruiting dissenting Irish and Scottish Protestants who would be encouraged to indenture along with their Protestant clergy.[8]

What is known of Wilkins's actual biography remains scant and inconclusive, yet it serves the important purpose of showing how her novel might be situated within larger female-gendered and Atlantic discourses. To begin, Wilkins was born on March 5, 1816, as Marcella Fanny Nugent in Dublin.[9] She may have had familial connections to the wife of former Jamaican governor General George Nugent, but no definitive substantiations have yet conclusively confirmed this.[10] Within Wilkins's novel, hints of her own biography appear as she discusses her Irish slave-owning family in Trinidad and in other instances uses her characters to criticize Britain's treatment of poor whites within its boundaries, subtly referencing the Irish. She met and married an artist, William Noy Wilkins, with whom she had two children. Their marriage struggled as William suffered from severe mental illness, and he eventually relocated to Australia and went into obscurity. With Stowe's lucrative career as her inspiration and incentive, Wilkins moved to England from the Caribbean and sought to sustain herself and her children financially, apparently through the means of her literary, journalistic, and editorial writings.

Yet, her domestic situation and home life contrasted drastically with that of Stowe. Lise Winer indicates that in 1858, Wilkins applied to the Royal Literary Fund and according to the application of this mother of a nine and five year old, she sought assistance because her husband was "incapacitated by physical and mental infirmity" and "she had been advised by physicians to 'remove her husband . . . to a distance from his [professional] pursuits & domestic troubles.'"[11] The application also described her current project on labor and gender as "a work on the condition of the factory girls."[12] Twenty-six years later, she applied once again to the Royal Literary Fund for support, listing publications that pre-date The Slave Son and extend to the 1880s.[13] Conjecturing on her financial situation, it was perhaps the income she made from her publications, the inheritance income from her mother's bequest, support from her son who became an engineer in South Africa, and any support awarded by the Royal Literary Fund that constituted her total earnings. Far from the economic structures of domestic patriarchy that sustained most nineteenth-century married women, Wilkins openly confided in her 1884 Royal Literary Fund application, "Have been married, but do not know if my husband is living or not."[14]

The publication of Harriet Beecher Stowe's novel in 1852 reinforced gendered ways in which women could through the use of literary fiction find critical voice, agency, and self-determining wealth in the age of social reform (1840–1860) (see figure 3.2). Although largely invisible in the public aspects of abolitionism, women like Stowe managed to carve out spaces and important spheres of influence through the cultivation of literature and a clandestine women's readership.

Humbly representing their female works as stories, tales, and "a little gossip," Stowe's *Uncle Tom's Cabin* and Wilkins's *The Slave Son* symbolized subversive rhetorical stratagems for levying social indictments against the institution of slavery, the debasement of Africa's progeny, the disruption of home and family, and the utter corruption of human souls. They entered into this discourse on slavery from two different social and geographical trajectories: Stowe as a North American, a New Englander descending from a long line of liberal Protestant ministers and reformers, and Wilkins most likely from Irish Catholic family heritage turned Caribbean plantation and slave owners. By her own admission, Wilkins's family viewed enslaved Africans as "repulsive" and likened them to a "species of cattle" or other "domestic animals belonging to the household."[15]

Both writers, however, were moved and deeply stirred by the 1845 publication of *Narrative of the Life of Frederick Douglass*, which gained international attention through Douglass's lecture tours of England and Ireland from 1845 to 1847[16] (see figure 3.3). Douglass was sympathetic to the parallel circumstances of oppression, poverty, and political disenfranchisement that both Irish and African descendants faced. He analogized Irish conditions as "much the same degradation as the American slaves" and, on occasion, was known to have self-referenced as "something of an Irishman as well as a negro" seeking to disrupt the cycle of miseducation in the United States whereby the Irish were taught "in this Christian country to hate and despise colored people."[17]

Scholars such as Bridget Brereton, Rhonda Cobham, Mary Rimmer, Karen Sanchez-Eppler, and Lise Winer insightfully speculate that the heroic

FIGURE 3.2 Harriet Beecher Stowe (1811–1896), author and abolitionist, whose novel *Uncle Tom's Cabin* sold millions of copies internationally, outsold only by the Christian Bible. Stowe toured Britain promoting her novel in 1853, just one year before Wilkins's novel *The Slave Son* appeared in press in London. Stowe's *Uncle Tom's Cabin* was published in 1852. At its height, Stowe received $10,000 a month in royalties as 300,000 copies sold in its first year of publication and over two million copies sold globally within five years. "Harriet Beecher Stowe," by William Notman, © National Portrait Gallery, London. Reprinted by permission of the National Portrait Gallery.

FIGURE 3.3
As her contemporary, Frederick Douglass was sympathetic to Harriet Beecher Stowe and spoke publicly of her as an anti-slavery advocate and ally. This stance of support would place him in stark opposition to Martin Delany, who questioned Stowe's credibility as a true abolitionist. Courtesy National Archives, photo no. 558770.

mixed-race protagonists George Harris in *Uncle Tom's Cabin* and Belfond in *The Slave Son* were directly inspired by the personage of Frederick Douglass. They contend that "Belfond not only shares Douglass's heroic stature, mixed-race heritage and impressive eloquence, but many of the details of Wilkins's description closely echo Douglass's *Narrative* and the autobiographical accounts of slavery that characterized his lectures in Britain between 1845 and 1847."[18] More importantly, both women drew a literary circumference around the North American South and the British Caribbean, as they novelized the most charged sociopolitical and economic dilemma facing the Atlantic world. At the same time, they strategically channeled their antislavery and anti-racism causes through Victorian gendered prisms of family, the sanctity of the home, motherhood, and the inviolability of religious piety.

The Severed Black Ear

Several measures testify to the significance of Harriet Beecher's Stowe's *Uncle Tom's Cabin* as a celebrated literary work in the mid-nineteenth century. Situating the "transatlantic Stowe" within a global context of readership, the novel not only had tremendous influence within North America but also amassed a wide international audience.[19] The book sold 3,000 copies on publication day, followed by another 7,000 sales within the next few days, and 10,000 copies by the end of the first week. It then reached 300,000 sales in the United States and approximately another million and a half in England during its first year of publication; it became the first novel by an American to sell a million copies and was "the biggest best-seller of the nineteenth century after the Bible."[20] Yet the magnitude of the book's impact cannot be fully understood without including mention of an especially powerful reader response sent to Stowe in the aftermath of the book's publication. Her husband, Calvin Stowe, opened an anonymous parcel that included the severed ear of a black man accompanied by a card "deriding her defense" of the "Damn niggers."[21]

This black man's amputated ear and its corporal presence haunt any contemplation of Stowe's fictive narrative on race, religion, and slavery. As we have seen, in North America and the wider Atlantic world, white encounters with black enslaved bodies have been tracked, surveyed, plotted, and charted through a language—a colonial vernacular, so to speak—of African bodily correspondence. Both Stowe's *Uncle Tom's Cabin* and Wilkins's *The Slave Son* had readers enter into worlds that were in many ways fictive mirrors of slave societies that visited "physical suffering" and brutality upon its African captives. Walking a strategic tightrope between the violent social polarities of black dismemberment and brutality were these two pronounced woman-gendered voices of literary activism and persuasion seeking to reform their societies from their blurred public/private locations.

Stowe's husband supposedly disposed quickly of the ear, rendering it invisible to Harriet. Yet, what impact might it have had upon Stowe had she seen it before transforming her serials into a novel? What would it have meant to a woman who had only once traveled to the South (she went to Kentucky in 1834)?[22] How might she have revisited and recast her metaphorical renderings of the pious Shelbys, Augustine St. Clare, Senator Byrd and his wife, and the Quaker Hallidays? How might the black severed ear have altered her vision of Christian reform and redemption in the South had she come in contact with this excised symbol of white Southern debasement? How might questions have been raised regarding the nature of evangelical Protestantism and the way its very practice accommodated slaveholding and the theological mutilation of the black ear? How would a somatic encounter with the permanently dismembered, one-eared black man have impacted her allegorical representations of Uncle Tom? How would Stowe's pristine southern novel have been disrupted had Uncle Tom's ear been severed and Stowe's gentle protagonist forced to navigate the length of the narrative plot in incised deformity? What if the ear could speak—an amputated mouthpiece that would chronicle its journey from the excision moment, perhaps on a brutal plantation, to its careful packaging and posting to the home of Harriet Beecher Stowe? What story would it tell and, as an auricular symbol of sound, what stories has it heard about its physical and social disposability? Thus, the severed ear and its density of meaning still haunt us—haunts me—as a mutilated ancestor in our readings and rereadings of *Uncle Tom's Cabin*.

Figuratively, the black man's severed ear possessed multiple intentional meanings. First, within the context of American patriarchy and gender suppression, it said to the woman who authored the ominous book and to her husband that she had breached the normative social boundaries ascribed to women in the nineteenth century. Second, it relayed the message that despite her literary efforts at abolitionism, her insidious work would incite the opposite effect and be responsible for the continued dismemberment of countless enslaved black bodies. Third, it revealed the established geo-authority and legal sovereignty of the slaveholding South vis-à-vis the North. It sent a message that despite Northern abolitionist and literary methods, white southerners still possessed the power to own and to visit indiscriminate violence upon black bodies at will.

In US southern slave codes and the French Code Noir that governed French plantation colonies, the severed black ear symbolized a powerful punitive trope, and its amputation was authorized by law as a penalty for crimes such as striking a white person, stealing, lying, and running away. According to the Code Noir, "those who absconded for more than a month were to have one ear cut off and to be branded with the fleur de lys on one shoulder; those who ran away more than twice were to be put to death."[23] Similarly, South Carolina slave codes enacted penalties for runaways, as documented by A. Leon Higginbotham, that required "after a third offense . . . one ear . . . to be cut off" following punishments of whippings and brandings.[24] Likewise, as the previous chapters graphically depicted, in Trinidad, black bodies convicted of countless criminalized offenses were subjected to penalties of having one or both ears cut off, having the tips of the ears cut off, being feathered and having the ears cut off, or having the ears cut off and nailed on a building in a colonial municipality. Public mutilation punishments were inflicted not just upon individual black bodies but upon the collective body of black persons, who were forcibly made to consume the visual spectacle as well as symbolically "hear" through the severed ear(s) the message of unbridled white power and authority. Such colonial laws of Trinidad and the wider Atlantic sanctioned a culture of the mutilation of black bodies that endured throughout North America well into the next century, establishing "branding, mutilation, amputation, and killing of blacks" as part of a larger social grammar of racial repression and control.[25]

In the midst of US southern sanctioned violence during slavery, Stowe's *Uncle Tom's Cabin* tells a classic, and complex, tale of life among America's southern plantocracy, their families, and the range of conditions facing their enslaved captives and victims (see figure 3.4). Among those terrorized under the severe system of slavery was Uncle Tom. Stowe envisioned him as someone "whose truly African features were characterized by an expression of grave and steady good sense, united with much kindliness" and an exemplar of "benevolence." He was a "patriarch in religious matters," "his whole air [was] self-respecting and dignified," he possessed a "humble simplicity," he "sp[oke] in a voice as tender as a woman's," and he belonged to a "kindly race."[26] However, Stowe's literary sympathizers come to celebrate above all Tom's devout piety, his "self-denying suffering love," his "unquestioning sacrifice."[27] More than anything else, the important symbolic meaning of Uncle Tom, for Stowe, lies in his inner resistance to allowing the conditions of slavery to transform him into a degraded brute who relinquishes his humanity. As the very first chapter title indicates, Tom represents for the author, and hopefully for her readership, not simply social chattel or property but "a Man of Humanity."[28]

Stowe wanted her readers to understand that the allure and venom of institutional slavery were so strong and so inherently debasing that all its participants, both white and black, remained vulnerable to its corrupting effects, inevitably giving birth in its extreme form to the brutish Simon Legree.

Controversial in its depiction and extratextual legacy, Uncle Tom, as the pious, Christ-like, passive, servile, non-rebellious, and asexual symbol, met with great ambivalence over generations of black public figures, from Martin Delany and Frederick Douglass in the nineteenth century to James Baldwin in the twentieth. Delany, an ardent black nationalist, insisted that the fate of African Americans in the United States had to rely on "the *intelligent* and *experienced* among *ourselves*," and he admonished Frederick Douglass in an open letter: "With all due respect and deference to Mrs. Stowe, I beg leave to say, that she *knows nothing about us* . . . neither does any other white person—and, consequently, can

UNCLE TOM'S CABIN;

OR,

LIFE AMONG THE LOWLY.

BY

HARRIET BEECHER STOWE.

VOL. I.

TENTH THOUSAND.

BOSTON:
JOHN P. JEWETT & COMPANY.
CLEVELAND, OHIO:
JEWETT, PROCTOR & WORTHINGTON.
1852.

FIGURE 3.4 Title page of the 1852 Cleveland, Ohio, edition of *Uncle Tom's Cabin.*
Courtesy of the Internet Archive (https://archive.org/details/uncletomscabin1853
/Uncle%20Tom%27s%20Cabin%20%281852%29%20Vol.%201/page/n5/mode/2up).

contrive no successful scheme for our elevation; it must be done by ourselves."[29] Delany's skepticism of Stowe only heightened when her leanings toward colonization became evident in her "holding up the little dependent colonization settlement of Liberia in high estimation" and as she "subscribed to, and recommended their principles in her great work of Uncle Tom."[30]

Delany found Stowe's efforts on behalf of the black downtrodden to be paternalistic and chided Douglass "that no enterprise, institution, or anything else, should be commenced *for us*, or our general benefit, without *first consulting us*." He continued, "Other than this, [Stowe] is treating us as slaves, and presupposing us all to be ignorant, and incapable of knowing our own *wants*."[31] Even in the fictive arena, Delany encouraged authors of African descent to speak for themselves. He advocated for the novels and narratives of people of African descent to be the authoritative sources on the subject of slavery. Accusing Stowe of pilfering the details of her narrative from famous black authors of the day, Delany asserted, "I am of the opinion that Mrs. Stowe has draughted largely on all the best fugitive slave narratives—at least on [Frederick] Douglass's, [William Wells] Brown's[,] [Henry] Bibb's, and perhaps [Lewis] Clark[e]'s"[32] (see figure 3.5).

Delany's ultimate retort was to publish a literary response and counterexample to Stowe's Uncle Tom's Cabin entitled Blake; or The Huts of America. Delany's Blake is in many respects one of the most important hemispherically oriented novels. Among the first novels written by an African American in the United States, it depicts a cross-diasporic consciousness and awareness that many of his black North American and black Caribbean contemporaries possessed. In the eighteenth and nineteenth centuries, this awareness gained constant reinforcement through maritime travel and the ongoing diasporic migrations of black people. Carolus Henrico Blacus (Blake), Delany's African Caribbean protagonist born free in Cuba, forcibly sold into US slavery under false pretenses, eventually escapes from bondage and joins an insurrectionist movement of rebellion in Cuba intended to reverberate throughout North America. According to Floyd Miller, Delany sought to foreground in Blake the themes of "self-reliance," "blacks leading their own rebellions," and "avoiding undue dependence upon whites and white institutions," including "relying too heavily on the religion of their masters."[33]

Unlike Delany, Frederick Douglass was sympathetic to the literary and activist contributions of Stowe. Douglass refuted Delany in writing: "There is nothing in the position of Mrs. Stowe which should awaken against her a single suspicion of unfriendliness towards the free colored people of the United States, but on the contrary, there is much in it to inspire confidence in her

FIGURE 3.5 Abolitionist, soldier, and ardent nineteenth-century black nationalist Martin Robison Delany strongly critiqued Harriet Beecher Stowe and her depictions of the enslaved and free populations in *Uncle Tom's Cabin*. *Blake; or the Huts of America* was published serially in 1859 in direct response to Stowe. Unlike Douglass, Delany was born a free person and throughout his life envisioned the continent of Africa, the West Indies, or South America as possible sites for African American resettlement. Accepted into Harvard Medical School in 1850 but immediately dismissed due to student and faculty racism, Delany went on to establish his own physician's practice and is known for his medical assistance during the 1832 cholera outbreak and his strong military leadership as a ranked major during the American Civil War. Source: National Afro-American Museum and Cultural Center. Courtesy of the Ohio History Connection, NAM_SC24.

friendship. . . . We recognize friends wherever we find them. . . . We believe that lady to be but at the beginning of her labors for the colored people of this country."[34]

Novelist and essayist James Baldwin would align with Delany in revisiting Stowe's Uncle Tom's Cabin nearly a century later in his famous essay "Everybody's Protest Novel" first published in Zero in 1949, Notes of a Native Son (1955), again in his Nobody Knows My Name (1961), and also in his 1960 address to Kalamazoo College, "In Search of a Majority." Published and republished within the contexts of post–World War II and black nationalist and civil rights fervor, respectively, Baldwin launches scathing critiques labeling Uncle Tom's Cabin a "bad novel" with a "self-righteous, virtuous sentimentality." Baldwin levels two piercing critiques against Stowe's novel. The first has do with Stowe's depiction of Uncle Tom's phenotypic blackness and its relationship to his Christian identity. For Baldwin, Uncle Tom must be benign, with a self-effacing humility, and practice an "incessant mortification of the flesh" to be Christian in the ways Stowe needs him to be. Baldwin finds this inherently unnatural and concludes that "Tom, therefore, her only Black man, has been robbed of his humanity and divested of his sex. It is the price for that darkness with which he has been branded." Stowe's literary Uncle Tom thus "domesticates native black resistance and the capacity to rebel."[35] What Baldwin finds most insidious in Stowe's Uncle Tom's Cabin is the "theological terror, the terror of damnation" that permeates the novel. In Baldwin's eyes, it is a novel that brings to light a "catalogue of violence" in its representation of slavery. Baldwin ultimately contends that within this terror with its fear of damnation and its mutilating catalogue of violence, Stowe leaves "unanswered and unnoticed the only important question: what it was, after all, that moved her people to such deeds."[36]

Representing Diversity

Both The Slave Son and Uncle Tom's Cabin engaged the "dramatic reality" of slavery, though Stowe and Wilkins projected very distinctive perspectives on those enslaved. Stowe's portrayal flattened the cultural and social diversity of African-descended people, making Uncle Tom along with her mixed-raced characters equally oppressed under North American plantation slavery. Religiously, she also asserted a strong evangelical Protestant authorial voice focused on themes of repentance and conversion as necessary prerequisites to redemption and salvation. Wilkins's The Slave Son, in sharp contradistinction, portrays those identified as "Mulattoes," "children of caste," or "coloured" as occupying an important social and racial space of meaning, as most Caribbean colonies accorded mixed-race populations limited access to social privileges and, in the case of Trinidad, allowed them to own property, purchase and own slaves, and develop free enterprise. Further, *The Slave Son* does not refer to native African populations as an undifferentiated aggregated whole, but rather indicates an acute awareness of the various African *nations* that made up the African inhabitants of the island in the nineteenth century. However, similar to Stowe, Wilkins engages in problematic caricatures of native Africans and their descendent groups and does so by designating certain social stereotypes to African *nations* common in popular discourse in Trinidad.[37] The "Koromantyn nation," or Akan-Asante, she references as "proverbially brave," "profound admirers of courage," and "fearless."[38]

Within the novel, Wilkins, in furthering her literary typologies, has Quaco, an enslaved Koromantyn, declare, "You think me care for flog—me Koromantyn? Flog good for Koromantyn skin—make me feel brave for no care at all."[39] Those of the "Loango" were depicted as "the effeminate race"; the "Eboe" were considered "a desponding people" and "the laziest and most useless of those imported from Africa," who "frequently commit suicide at the first opportunity, from a belief that when dead they will immediately return to their own far country."[40] The "Mandingo nation" was labeled "a sly, cowardly, treacherous race, made ten times worse by being reduced to slavery," and the "Congo nation" was depicted as "honest, fine people, as the world knows."[41] In addition to these indigenous African *nations*, Wilkins accounts for people of African descent who arrived in Trinidad from neighboring islands, such as Martinique and Grenada, either accompanying their migrating enslavers or as free persons of color.

Equally diverse in the novel and in colonial Trinidad was the population racially designated as "white." Semi-biographically, Wilkins, herself of Irish origin, illustrated a multinational, European presence of Spanish, French, and English in her literary Trinidad, with each group deliberately maintaining strong ties to their historical, cultural, and linguistic origins. As a reflection of this, the language in Wilkins's novel weaves together a combination of English, French, Spanish, and African Creole dialects as linguistic expressions of Trinidad's multifarious population. Wilkins is careful in the novel not to present a homogenous "white" society in Trinidad free of intra-social and national tensions and prejudices. In fact (and perhaps because of her own Irish sympathies), she devotes space to a lengthy discussion between Mr. Dorset ("an English character who represents the ameliorationist view of slavery") and Mr. Cardon (Catholic) criticizing England's hypocrisy. Although having an antislavery stance, this imperial power demonstrated no advocacy for "the poor in England" (many of Irish descent) and neglected to realize that, as Mr. Cardon states, "they are slaves, like my Negroes."[42] It is postulated that Wilkins may have politically held Irish Patriot leanings and was likely in support of "the establishment of an independent Irish republic" and used the literary landscape to subtly embed her political principles.[43]

Wilkins exhibits exceptional subtlety in her representation of religion, as she drew from the multi-national and multireligious setting of Trinidad. Although the Protestant British dominated the island at the time Wilkins was writing her novel, the colony's strong Spanish roots and large French population made Catholicism a dominant religious feature in Trinidad. Wilkins praised the Spanish Catholics, "to the shame of my brother Protestants," for encouraging "the rites of marriage" and "the observance of religious service" among its enslaved population. On Spanish Catholic estates, Wilkins contends, "the Negro maid woman bore a recognized title to respect; she had influence with the master's family, and privileges on the estate which were never accorded to the unmarried."[44] More importantly, she credits Spanish Catholicism and its priesthood in Trinidad with a level of egalitarianism presumably absent from Protestant denominations with regard to Africans and indigenous communities. According to Wilkins, "far from sharing the general prejudice against a tinge of African blood, they professed it a part of their ministry to level all ranks and conditions. They had all the dead buried within the same sacred enclosure, without excluding (as was the case in other colonies) slaves or Mulattoes; and permitted in their churches no pews or any kind of private seats, so that within the precincts of their temples the scene presented was one of perfect equality, the Negro, the Mulatto, and the Indian kneeling fearlessly by the side of the white man, praying to the same God and benefiting equally by the offices of the minister."[45]

Wilkins goes far beyond Stowe's portrayal of the lived religion of African-descended people through her protracted and extensive treatment of the religious practice of obeah, its influence on African plantation culture, and its ambivalent relationship to Christianity. Stowe offers a commentary on minor "superstitions" among enslaved black and lower-class white populations, but Wilkins instead represents obeah as a supernatural system that allegedly impedes the spread of Christianity among some enslaved Africans and is symbolic of an alternative moral and ethical system antithetical to Christian principles. However, much to Wilkins's credit, she does not present this malevolent obeah as the only form of religious practice and expression among enslaved Africans, and in surprising ways she establishes herself as one of the few white authors of her time who attempts to accord respectability and credence to the indigenous religious beliefs and customs of African communities.

Obeah, the "Great Spirit"

"Think of your freedom, every time you see UNCLE TOM'S CABIN; and let it be a memorial to put you all in mind to follow in his steps, and be as honest and faithful and Christian as he was" is the final message Harriet Beecher Stowe has her character George Shelby pronounce to the recently emancipated blacks under his care (see figure 3.6). Stowe's literary work moves her readers toward a crescendo of Christian piety, with Uncle Tom from their community, not Jesus, serving as their symbolic sacrificial inspiration. God's providence abounds, and because "both North and South have been guilty before God," Stowe ends with a call for America's national repentance in order for the "Union to be saved" and to forestall the impending "wrath of Almighty God!"[46] In Stowe's estimation, America's repentance will reverse the "public evil" and "common capital of sin" the nation has made of slavery and allow God to govern a world of "Christianized humanity." Stowe hopes for a world that "has at last outlived the slave-trade" and that in its stead an "enlightened and Christianized community" of white and newly converted blacks in North America will emerge.

Wilkins's fictive narrative does not reach such a neat crescendo at the end but instead complicates the smooth morphological process toward universal black Christian conversion with complex dimensions of obeah and African indigenous religions present among its African characters. Although similar expressions of African-related religious practices undoubtedly would have been present among black North American enslaved populations, Wilkins, unlike Stowe, chooses to engage them as existing supernatural entities rather than conveniently deny their existence for the sake of Christian primacy.

In *The Slave Son*, Wilkins is careful in her literary distinction between those Africans who participated in obeah and those who enacted the traditional religion of the Koromantyns on the Palm Grove estate. Neither of these African-derived religions could ever gain parity with Christianity in Wilkins's estimation, yet she does represent Koromantyn indigenous practices as possessing a sophisticated cosmology, an intricate theology and ritual life, and a system of moral and ethical standards. And while Wilkins followed her legal and political contemporaries in furthering the normative colonial view of obeah as an evil, socially menacing, and dangerous spiritual practice, she

FIGURE 3.6 To its nineteenth-century white readership, *Uncle Tom's Cabin* depicted enslaved communities as the personification of Christian virtues and devout piety. "Prayer Meeting in Uncle Tom's Cabin," illustration on wood by George Cruikshank for Harriet Beecher Stowe, *Uncle Tom's Cabin* (London: John Casseli, Ludgate Hill, 1852). Digitized by The Institute of Museum and Library Services through an Indiana State Library LSTA Grant (https://archive.org/details/uncletomscabinooinstow/page/n59 /mode/2up?q=prayer+meeting).

differed from her European counterparts and insightfully viewed the evil of obeah as a spiritual byproduct of the European slave system.

For Wilkins, not only did the wretchedness of slavery produce a "kind of evil which pertains to physical suffering; but there lies hidden within it a deeper woe than this,—the debasement of the mind, the deadening of every virtue, the calling into action those weapons of defence which nature has given to the weak—cunning, deceit, treachery, and secret murder."[47] Obeah fits within this schematic as a set of dreadful practices void of Christian ethical and moral principles. The "Obiah" (obeah) priest in the novel is depicted as a contemptible and disfigured hermit who lives in the woods, on the margins of human community, whose immediate companions are wild dogs and snakes, who possesses culinary and herbal knowledge of poisons, and whose work is anxiously perceived within the wider society as witchcraft and sorcery directed toward inflicting harm on white planters and their families. Wilkins emphasizes to her readers a unidimensional image of obeah that bespeaks moral corruption, an impediment to African enculturation, and a source of social chaos. The obeah of Wilkins's literary imagination mercilessly poisons masters, mistresses, and babies while randomly killing livestock and enslaved Africans in order to enact revenge against slave masters. Further, obeah cements evil pacts with the dregs of white society and incites indiscriminate revolts and rebellions on plantation estates.

Within the novel, Africans and Europeans alike share a belief in obeah cosmology. Mr. Cardon states that he knows "very well what is thinning the ranks of my Negroes" but feels inept at combating its forces.[48] Mrs. Cardon is also convinced that the deaths of her four children and daughter-in-law were directly caused by the malpractices of obeah. On several occasions throughout the book, white characters inquire as to the nature of obeah, providing Wilkins with a forum for several descriptive representations. In one instance Mr. Cardon states, "This murdering work, or Obiah, as they call it, has been going on again upon my estate now for the last two years—not only cattle gone scores and scores of times over, but my best and choicest Negroes. . . . If I could only find out the sorcerer, or Obiah man, as they call him, I would hang him upon the very first tree; but the Negroes are made to take such hellish, heathenish oaths, never to reveal how, when, where, and by whom the poison is administered that it becomes hopeless to attempt to finding out the criminals."[49] Moreover, when Mrs. Dorset asks, "What is this Obiah?" she is told, "Madame . . . it is the Negro's power; they say it is witchcraft. I believe it to be poison. . . . This Negro witchcraft crawls round the white man's domicile, seizing in its deadly grasp the fairest and sweetest."[50]

Throughout the novel, Obeah is symbolized as the "poisoning work," the enactment of the "Obiah spell," the deadly practice associated with necromancy or divining by communicating with the dead. Scholars speculate that the character of St. Hilaire Cardon is a fictionalized depiction of the former Cabildo member turned Governor Picton supporter and Diego Martin estate owner, St. Hilaire Begorrat, who died just three years shy of the publication of *The Slave Son*.[51] As the previous chapter explained, the historic Begorrat who arrived in Trinidad from Martinique was completely convinced that obeah poisonings were devastating the enslaved population on his plantation estate in Diego Martin and throughout Trinidad, and he thus became an avid supporter of Governor Picton's anti-obeah commission and an advocate of its gruesome acts of civic torture. Wilkins has her fictive character, Mr. Cardon, subtly articulate Begorrat's views when Cardon expresses that "Obiah had spread its ravages to such a fearful extent, [in Martinique] that a Court was instituted."[52]

Unlike the indicted obeah practitioners (Thisbe, Felix, Antoine) who resided on and surreptitiously threatened Begorrat's plantation estate, Wilkins strategically isolates the "Obiah priest" outside of the realm of human community and places him in the uninhabitable forests and woods of Trinidad so as not to lose the sympathy of her white readers and have them mistakenly believe that *all* African-descended inhabitants among them participate in this antisocial practice. He is dubbed "the Negro sorcerer," the "wizard," and the "priest of dark science" who possesses a "fiendish visage" and displays "strange appendages—snakes hanging and coiling about him, caressing him."[53] Daddy Fanty, as he is called in the novel, is an illegal runaway who works in what Wilkins understands as the occult world of "Obiah," devising "numberless amulets, such as bags of all sizes, egg-shells, deer's horns, and parrot's beaks." Cosmologically, Daddy Fanty seals and protects his work by having his clients swear the "Wanga oath" and "drink the Wanga" or the "drink of secrecy . . . which would punish him who violated the promise given."[54] In one scene, in a covenantal consumption of the "Wanga," the client is made to repeat, "Obiah's power, Obiah's spell, Pains of earth and pangs of hell, Alight on him who dares rebel, Against the Obiah's law! . . . And Obiah's secrets you shall keep, And in its magic you shall steep, Till comes your turn in death to sleep, For such is Obiah's law!"[55]

In Wilkins's literary imagination, obeah was made to function on several levels. First, it was represented as a "science" or body of "knowledge" whose ceremonial rites were dedicated to "destruction," even "murdering babes," under control of the "Spirit of Death."[56] Second, obeah's power was anthropomorphized in the person of the "Obiah priest" who operated as its deadly ambassador. He is described in the text as the "harbinger of sickness, decline, and death."[57] Finally, obeah represented an alternative moral and ethical system of human governance and community.

In an exchange between Daddy Fanty and Belfond, the Obiah priest tries to convince Belfond (who although biracial is related to the priest through his mother) that Obiah is a form of resistance, defense, and self-protective weaponry that Africans have at their disposal in order to combat the "white man's Obiah" of slavery as well as that of his "guns and cutlasses." According to Daddy Fanty, "it is only Obiah and cunning and sly ways that will enable Negroes to put their foot upon the high ground; use the Obiah, my child; be wise, and then you will get to look the white man in the face. The white man's Obiah is weak before the Negro's Obiah, if all would only use it: the Negro's Obiah commands life and death; fire water, birds, and brutes, all obey the Negro's Obiah. Did you see such power as that with the white man?"

Wilkins then has the protagonist, Belfond, seek to persuade the Obiah priest to embrace a nobler ethical posture by urging him, "Let your power do good, not evil; your Obiah is no real friend to the Negroes; he is no friend who kills his friend."[58] Yet within this exchange, Wilkins, similar to James Baldwin's criticism of Stowe, leaves uninterrogated "the white man's Obiah" of slavery, colonization, and violence.

So as to continue the marginalization of Obeah and render it harmless to a readership who may have heightened anxieties regarding it, in the very next chapter Wilkins has the Obiah priest encounter the white sailor Higgins, and after a moment of physical conflict, the Obiah priest is left defeated. "The sorcerer knew he had no resource: his Obiah failed him here; it could do nothing against the sudden action of superior physical force upon a sickly, feckless, powerless old man as he was."[59] Readers encounter the Obiah priest twice again before the close of the novel. One time is when he is clandestinely and ironically employed to assist Laurine in getting help for Belfond. However, this good deed is short-lived, and readers encounter Daddy Fanty one final time at the end of the novel when he once again emerges in Wilkin's depiction as a malignant spiritual force who inevitably brings about moral coercion and instigates a slave insurrection on the Palm Grove estate.

Marcella Wilkins, the author, was one among several women on the island who, as residents, had first-hand knowledge of Africans on family-owned plantation estates and found ways as women to secure financial independence in Trinidad's colonial economy through plantation ownership. Most noted among Trinidad's female entrepreneurs and Wilkins's contemporaries was Maria Bridgens (born Maria Shaw), who married furniture designer, architect, and famed Trinidadian artist Richard Bridgens in 1816.[60] Following the death of her father, Colonel David Henry Shaw, Maria Bridgens inherited the St. Claire estate; she left England and eventually established herself within a class of self-sufficient propertied and landed women in Trinidad who owned and operated slave-owning estates. In 1834, when Governor Sir George Hill authorized the importation of "207 Prize Africans" from Havana, Cuba, to be contracted "free labourers," Maria Bridgens surfaced as a woman among the male estate proprietors who received possession of ten of these Africans. Her name appears in the historical record on "the Document signed by the persons who obtained these Africans containing the conditions to which they thereby bound themselves to comply."[61] Bridgens was among twenty-one estate owners and proxies for estate owners who signed to "acknowledge to have received from His Excellency the Right Honourable Sir George Fitzgerald Hill, Governor and Commander-in-Chief . . . several Male and Female African Negroes lately arrived from Havannah . . . To be employed as Agricultural Free Laborers on the Estates in the said Lists or Lots," after which they were given a receipt for ten of the Africans "together with a Memorandum of their Sexes and their African and Baptismal Names."[62] Despite Wilkins's and Bridgens's different paths to financial security and wealth-building, women rarely emerged as active participants in the colonial slave economy of Trinidad.

Although both Wilkins and Bridgens were directly tied to estate-owning families and perhaps distantly aware of the religious practices of some enslaved Africans, it was Maria's husband, Richard, who would gain recognition for describing plantation estate life in his 1836 publication *West Indian Scenery, with Illustrations of Negro Character, the Process of Making Sugar, &c. from Sketches Taken to, and Residence of Seven Years in, the Island of Trinidad*, which featured twenty-seven lithographs depicting the plantation, agricultural, social, industrial, disciplinary, and spiritual life of Africans. In her biographical study of Richard Bridgens, Judy Raymond notes that he chose to illustrate not "his [own] peers or countrymen, but the appearance, dress, speech, customs, and homes of the enslaved people who worked on the estates."[63] During his seven-year occupancy in Trinidad, beginning in 1825, Bridgens was by no means an antislavery sympathizer. Rather, he was among the planter class and presumably resided with his wife on her active sugar plantation, which likely informed the subject matter of his art. One of the most well-known of his sketches depicts a group of enslaved Africans observing a ritual that is being led by a supposed Obeah practitioner (see figure 3.7). Bridgens's caption beneath the image, "Negro Superstition, the Doo di Doo bush or which is the thief," seeks to depict a ceremonial "ordeal in use among Negroes, for extorting a confession of guilt from persons suspected of theft or other crime." He speaks of the "solemnity" of the ceremony; the "dignity of magic powers" conferred on the "Dadie" or "reputed sorcerer," and the efficacy and "numerous confessions" this ceremonial trial has obtained.[64]

Bridgens's more benign pictorial depiction of Obeah and Negro superstition lacked Wilkins's literary representation of Obeah practices as disreputable and ontologically evil. Instead, Wilkins reserved her literary affections for the indigenous African religions of those directly from the continent. Although she labeled these practices "heathen," uncultured, and uncivilized, they represented a population that was unconverted and redeemable. Wilkins ascribes to indigenous African religions a moral proximity to Christianity and attempts to bring a sense of complexity to the inner fabric and meanings of African rites and practices. Moreover, Wilkins radically distinguishes her

FIGURE 3.7 British artist, architect, and designer Richard Bridgens's lithograph, *Negro Superstition, the Doo di Doo Bush, or which is the Thief*, depicts a ceremony apparently "passed by the eye of the Author" being led by a "Dadie" or "reputed sorcerer" on a plantation estate in Trinidad. Bridgens explains the ceremony as "exorting a confession of guilt from persons suspected of theft or other crimes." Over time, the lithograph has become a popular visual depiction of obeah in the British Caribbean. Bridgens's representations of enslaved African life in the Caribbean have gained distinction over time and the purchase of a first-edition original sells for nearly £25,000. Source: Richard Bridgens, *West India scenery: with illustrations of Negro character, the process of making sugar, &c. from sketches taken during a voyage to, and residence of seven years in, the island of Trinidad* (1836), plate 21.

depiction of obeah from continental indigenous traditions, giving readers a subtle assurance that the best of "heathen" African traditions might be translated into the higher principles of Christianity. By successfully demonizing West Indian Obeah as a nefarious and iniquitous foil, Wilkins could ultimately shift the gaze toward what could now be seen as the benign and harmless practices of African religion and convince her wider readership of the eventual assimilability of Africans into white society with proper exposure and instruction.

Embodying the tenets of African sacred tradition was the character Anamoa, a Koromantyn who is enslaved in Trinidad. When he attempts to defend the honor of his daughter, Talima, he is mercilessly beaten and eventually succumbs to his injuries. Quite intriguingly, Wilkins makes Anamoa—a non-Christian—the Uncle Tom equivalent and parallel in her novel. A member of African royalty, he had suffered betrayal and treason, and ended up being sold into the slave trade. Now old and feeble and recently reunited with his long-lost daughter, Anamoa becomes a victim of the violent whip of the slave driver. Anamoa is described as a "fallen king," "generous," and "kind." On his deathbed, he says: "Children, my last word—be true to one another. Truth, honesty, goodness to the tyrant, remember, O children, is treachery to yourselves. Children, may Assarci, the spirit of mercy, spread his golden wings over you! I am going."

In one of the few instances throughout the text where she directly addresses the reader regarding Anomoa's fate, Wilkins pleads:

> But, hush Reader! give me a moment's patience before you breathe a word of doubt. It was not the triumph of Christ they spoke of, nor the glory of the coming kingdom of Heaven. *They had never received tidings of the holy Gospel, to bring comfort to their souls, to give hope to their grieving hearts,—they were heathens.* The unexplained prayers at muster-roll were as Latin to them; the word Jesus . . . was to these poor Negroes simply a hard word which they could scarcely pronounce. Yet God forsakes not even his lowliest creatures in the season of their trouble and pain. . . . Over the dark untaught soul of the dying Negro hovered the pitying angel of mercy; and wrapped in the African superstition that death bears the exile to his native place, came the dim foreshadowing of a better world—the promise of rest, of peace, of happiness, forever. There was no mourning, but encouraging words and cheerful expressions; and many a message of love to their far-distant friends did these creatures whisper to the exile returning to his home. "Children," said he, "the Great Spirit calls me to him; he whose eye is the light-giving sun has ordained that, at the first ray of tomorrow's light, my spirit shall ride away to the region of my birth."[65]

Whereas readers are given a unidimensional portrait of Obeah as evil, murderous, poisonous, and shamelessly immoral, Wilkins provides a textured illustration of African traditional religion: sophisticated cosmology, iconography, and theology; customary rites; and ethical codes that govern human community. Readers enter into a world where nature is sacralized and the silk cotton tree is transformed into the sacred "Fetish tree of the estate."[66] Humans exist in this world where the "great Accompong," the Creator, and the merciful Assarci, who governs the Earth with "mercy" and "regeneration," assists humans in diverting the afflictions of the evil spirit "Obboney."

Gods such as Assarci are honored through various rituals and beliefs: the pouring of "libations" on the ground; the burial of the dead nearby so that the living may "watch the sacred dead"; believing that in death human souls travel "back to Africa" carrying with them the messages of those who remain; and they "bear our messages to distant homes, say how we weep, and how we hope to join the loved ones again."[67]

In memorializing Anamoa's solemn deathbed moment, Wilkins writes, "The bands of life were rent asunder, and that poor Negro's soul, upon which the light had never shone, now stood trembling and heavy-laden before the great God who had created it, seeking that promised refuge of the weary and the oppressed."[68] Unlike Uncle Tom, who dies a martyred Christian, Anamoa dies a martyred "heathen" with unrelenting fidelity to his indigenous African beliefs. Wilkins's readers are moved with deep understanding for Anamoa despite his non-Christian religious convictions. She is effective at invoking a sense of sympathy and compassion for Anamoa's African humanity in ways that transcend his immediate religious, cultural, and racial differences. Seeing her novel as an attempt to lessen the social and racial cleavage between Africans and her white readership, Wilkins hoped it would ultimately aid in advancing her vision of "a thorough equalization of the races, which shall procure for all equal rights by written, law, social law, and the law which comes from Christ; to the exercise of the talents he has received from God, not to the hue of his complexion." Furthermore, Wilkins anticipated that when whites permitted "the coloured man" to take his "place among his fellow-men on earth, [he] may do credit to the generous and glorious nation which has freed him."[69]

Countering Slavery's Brute-ification

Despite their differences, *Uncle Tom's Cabin* and *The Slave Son* were united in the gravity they bestowed upon the system of slavery as a site for psycho-physical trauma, the brutalization of African bodies, and what I term the *brute-ification* of human personalities. According to Stowe, "what is peculiar to slavery, and distinguishes it from free servitude, is evil, and only evil, and that continually." She goes on to reveal that "the great object of the author in writing has been to bring this subject of slavery, as a moral and religious question, before the minds of all those who profess to be followers of Christ, in this country."[70] For Stowe's North America, "slavery, as the ultimate evil, meaning the total domination, victimization, and demonization practiced on human beings," was the crucial source of her religio-racial and literary crusade. For Wilkins's Trinidad, one had to also add the evil of social degradation based on color perpetuated even after the overthrow of the slave system.[71] Given their different historical contexts, Wilkins understood Stowe as writing in an active moment of slavery as one desirous of civil emancipation for African descendants, while Wilkins's own postslavery Caribbean context now necessitated what she understood as "social advancement." Thus, both women committed to engaging in acts of literary persuasion to convince their readers of the wickedness of slavery, the absence of social threat posed by mixed-race populations (who appeared further along in the process of religious and social advancement), and the need to support assimilation and Christianization efforts after emancipation. And finally, as we shall see at the conclusion of the chapter, they envision for their readers the future possibilities of a unified multiracial nation based ultimately on Christian sovereignty.

Stowe and Wilkins concurred that from the North American mainland to the islands of the Caribbean, slavery's presence and its afterlife symbolized unbridled violence, moral defilement, and societal contamination for all who participated in it. Both African and diaspora-born captives suffer greatly in both women's novels. They endure heinous punishments, torturous acts, and verbal assaults collectively designed to expel Africans from full humanity and make them a "thing" according to Stowe and a "brutified slave" according to Wilkins. Through the words of Wilkins's main character, St. Hilaire Cardon, this sentiment is reinforced: "The mind of the Negro is not the same as ours: it can't calculate, it can't combine the various faculties, it can't reflect; it has its will, its memory, its understanding, like the brutes. . . . Therefore next to the brute I place the Negro, and his race must bow before the intelligent whites."[72] Thus in both nineteenth-century women's novels, Africans become animalized as nigger, dog, beast, baboon, ourang-outang, black monkey, black devil, ugly raccoon, pack of trash, and so on. The black body in the novels is, among other things, "cut and thrashed," "flogged," whipped into "chopped" flesh, infested with raw wounds saturated with lemon juice and rubbed with "some salt and pepper," given a "violent kick," made to wear an "iron mask," and recipient of a "soiled plate . . . smashed . . . on the head."[73] The challenge became for the novelists to dismantle the construction of Africans as mentally and physically brutish and persuasively convince their readers that these states were a conse-quence of social *condition*, not of divine *essence* or *nature*. However, given their respective white audiences, they most strategically evade direct indictment of those who, in actuality, engineered the alleged brute-ification of Africans.

Wilkins and Stowe believed in the efficacy of appealing to an emotional and sympathetic chord in their readership. Through a literary technique of empathetic inversion, they sought to de-objectify the social meaning and category of *slave* and place Africans into juxtaposed human roles as fathers, mothers, daughters, sons, husbands, wives, adolescents, elders, and Christians in relationship to their readers. Thus, when Stowe's runaway asks the white mistress Mrs. Bird, "Have you ever lost a child? . . . Then you will feel for me. I have lost two, one after another—left 'em buried there when I came away; and I had only this one left," the maternal reader empathetically connects not with an objectified runaway slave but with a woman, wife, and mother who buried two children and is now desperately protecting her one remaining child. Stowe strategically addresses her female audience directly on this subject with an appeal: "I beseech you, pity the mother who has all your affections, and not one legal right to protect, guide, or educate, the child of her bosom! . . . I beseech you, pity those mothers that are constantly made childless by the American slave-trade! And say, mothers of America, is this a thing to be defended, sympathized with, passed over in silence?"[74]

Wilkins seeks to invoke a similar sentiment during the reunification of father (Anamoa) and child (Talima): "The old Negro looked up, a scream rent the air, and Talima, throwing herself upon his neck, sank fainting at his feet. It was his child, his long-lost African child, whom he thought his old eyes were never again to behold."[75] In this instance, the reader can interpret Anamoa's and Talima's emotions not as those of enslaved Koromantyns who presumably possess heathen ways and customs but as those of a father and daughter torn apart and reunited within a context of human tragedy. Through this literary device of ascribing humanity to Africans, Wilkins and Stowe hoped to mitigate and transcend racial and social distance, heighten the notion of African social integration, and universalize human suffering and the human condition.

Stowe and Wilkins extend this sentimental approach in their representations of mixed-race characters. The physical descriptors of their mixed-race female characters Eliza, Laurine, Emmeline, and Cassy are detailed in both novels, often with a predictable exoticism. They are described with the phrases "gentle maiden," "the prettiest," "silken hair sweeping in waving tresses almost to her feet," "long and moistened lashes," and "modest in their demeanor." These mixed-race women are said to "have a refinement of feeling," to be "the most beautiful woman in Louisiana," and to possess "the peculiar air of refinement, that softness of voice and manner . . . a particular gift to the quadroon or mulatto women," "beauty of the most dazzling kind," and "a personal appearance prepossessing and agreeable." The authors, however, seemed compelled to unmask the price of this beauty and "the temptations

which make beauty so fatal an inheritance to a slave."[76] Theirs were slave societies that sexually fetishized enslaved women, resulting in sexual violation and,
in Stowe's novel, commodification in the form of "the public and shameless
sale of beautiful mulatto and quadroon girls" in New Orleans.[77] Yet, even with
this burden, women like Stowe's Eliza and Wilkins's Laurine are model pious
believers; Laurine worships "at the holy shrine of the Virgin, the protectress
of maidens."[78] Despite Laurine's undying love for Belfond, her pleadings to
him—"Belfond, don't ask me to do what is wrong . . . I could not use stolen
money. . . . The Holy Virgin protect us! but let us be honest"—would indeed
resonate with devoted Catholic readers.[79]

In addition, mixed-raced men and women are depicted as more intelligent
and more adept than African-born persons at navigating the social terrain of
the white world. They exist in each novel as the only characters of African descent who do not speak in dialect. In both novels, George and Belfond are
championed as skillful runaways whose intelligence, ability to pass for white
gentleman, dexterity, and strong sense of love and devotion to the Christian
women in their lives enable them to be triumphant in the end. As we follow their
dangerous and dismal journeys toward freedom, the reader is aware of their
righteous dignity, their love for liberty, and their "desire to be man, and not a
brute . . . to call the wife of his bosom his wife, and to protect her from lawless
violence, . . . to protect and educate his child, . . . to have a home of his own,
a religion of his own, a character of his own, unsubject to the will of another."[80]
In short, George in North America and Belfond in the Caribbean want the same
rights and freedoms that the United States and England revered and protected
within its sovereign borders and colonies for its free white populace.

Hence, these mixed-race figures were skillfully portrayed as no different from the authors' readership, uniting both characters and readers in a
collective desire for home, family, education, virtue, freedom, and religion.
Mixed-race population posed no threat to the smooth governance of existing
society and helped white readers in the Western Hemisphere to reimagine and
acquire psychological distance from the actual mixed-race populations that
participated in Haiti's insurrection in the previous century. Such fears could
be allayed through Stowe's and Wilkins's portrayals, and Wilkins's readers in
particular were guided to see the symbol of "the lighter complexion" not as
revolt or rape but as that "which secretly but surely involves the grafting of
European intellect on the warm strong feelings of Africa."[81] Unlike the "pure
Africans" who might need to undergo more extensive processes of religious
and cultural reform, the mixed caste, by virtue of European genetics, inherited
these naturally, thus lessening the social and racial cleavage.

Gender, Masculinity, and the "Living Gospel"

Marcella Noy Wilkins and Harriet Beecher Stowe were keenly cognizant of their positionality as women within a wider public discourse on slavery and social reform. They offered gendered perspectives on reform that cultivated the power of domesticity and transformed the private sphere into a source of activism. As nineteenth-century women, they endorsed an ideology of what Kathryn Sklar calls "domesticity-based feminism" or, more commonly, "domestic feminism," whereby the home could be viewed as a dynamic source of power, authority, and influence.[82] Wilkins, in particular, sought to demarcate the boundaries of influence within which women could exert their gendered power and control. As she understood it, "the political emancipation of the coloured race is a deed for the men."[83] The public spheres of influence related to politics and legislature were not the arenas she saw women readily inhabiting. Instead, women were to work on behalf of the "social advancement" of Africans, cultivating within them whenever possible those aspects of family, home, and religion that proved foundational to society. Catharine Beecher, sister of Harriet Beecher Stowe, similarly underscored the boundaries delineating women's sovereignty. According to Beecher:

> A man may act on society by the collision of intellect, in public debate; . . . he may coerce by the combination of public sentiment; he may drive by physical force, and he does not outstep the boundaries of his sphere. But all the power, and all the conquests that are lawful to women, are those only which appeal to the kindly, generous, peaceful and benevolent principles. Woman is to win every thing by peace and love . . . But this is to all be accomplished in the domestic and social sphere.[84]

In her *Treatise on Domestic Economy for the Use of Young Ladies at Home and at School*, which she later revised with her sister Harriet and republished in 1869 as *The American Woman's Home, or Principles of Domestic Science*, Catharine Beecher argued for "the moral superiority of females" and insisted "that by dominating domestic life, women could redeem American culture."[85] Through deploying the principles of domestic science, women are empowered to utilize the "domestic circle" as the seat of their influence on wider social issues according to Stowe and Wilkens. As is the case with Stowe's characters Mrs. Bird and the Quaker Rachel Halliday and Wilkins's Mrs. Dorset, women within their domestic spheres have the capacity to enact subtle influence, provide protection and safety to their enslaved female counterparts, and defy social laws and conventions that prevented such protections. These women characters would stand as literary icons for their nineteenth-century female readership, demonstrating the force, weightiness, and subtle subversion and moral persuasion contained within their domestic spheres of governance. According to Jean Fagan Yellin, "*Uncle Tom's Cabin* shows individual women using the power of sympathy to enable them to act effectively in private against slavery when the servile institution threatens the domestic sphere. Stowe's female Christians act successfully against slavery without walking out their own front doors."[86]

The social institution of the *home* would represent in both novels an important transformative and politicized entity. Not only did it function as an incubator for social change, but it also, like its public counterpart the church, held the power to induce religious transformation and conversion. For female audiences with antislavery sympathies who resided in slaveholding households, Mrs. Dorset, whose husband owned slaves, could provide an ideal model for how to negotiate their positions of moral ambivalence. Like Mrs. Dorset, plantation mistresses could illustrate an exemplary Christian home to their slaves and exemplify for them the virtues of charity, compassion, and sympathy. Because the ultimate political and social goal was emancipation and enslaved persons would one day create homes of their own, it was the duty of white Christian women in their immediate proximity to impart replicable models.

In following the examples of Mrs. Dorset and Mrs. Halliday, women could ultimately hold the power of religious conversion within their domain. By juxtaposing it to the notion of home, Stowe made "homelessness" a sin to her readers, according to John Allen, and "the homelessness of slaves complements maternal love as a means of creating empathy in readers and a corresponding distaste for slavery."[87] Hence, countless slaves and newly freed slaves, long bereft of the power of home, could, like George Harris, ultimately experience its power and be transformed through Christian women like Mrs. Halliday: "This, indeed, was a home,—home,—a word that George had never yet known a meaning for; and a belief in God, and trust in his providence, began to encircle his heart, as, with a golden cloud of protection and confidence, dark, misanthropic, pining, atheistic doubts, and fierce despair, melted away before the light of a living Gospel."[88] For Stowe and Wilkins, women throughout North America and the Caribbean would enact the source of their true collective power when they could indeed view and govern their homes as a "Living Gospel."

Connected to the concept of the home as the locus for a Living Gospel was the powerful role of what Elizabeth Ammons calls the "Mother-Savior."

Ammons situates the "Mother-Savior" concept within a wider discourse on "matrifocal values" where what is privileged is "an ideal of community as something defined by family (rather than work), measured by relationships (rather than products), and ruled by women (rather than men)."[89] Paradoxically, although motherhood is valorized in the novels of Stowe and Wilkins, it was, in actuality, an acutely complex and ambivalent role for most nineteenth-century white women. Stowe's own mother, who died when Harriet was just five, was reflective of "other women of her generation" who "bore a child every two to two and a half years until death or menopause."[90] Ammons points out that "Stowe's own experience of motherhood was difficult," as she gave birth to seven children, (including a set of twins during her first year of marriage) and one of her seven children "died as a baby." Likewise, we learn briefly of Wilkins's personal challenges in the domestic sphere, as she states in the introduction that the "cessation of family cares and the return of health enabled me to listen to the suggestion of my friends and submit the work to the Public."

In both novels, women characters across racial lines were similar to their nineteenth-century female white readership in bearing children, suffering their devastating loss, and subsequently mourning their death. Thus, the Mother-Savior in each novel not only had the important duty of instilling Christian values in her family but also had the capacity to transcend the barriers of race and status and relate to enslaved women who had suffered the loss of a child. In North American and Caribbean societies, where high infant mortality was cross-racially shared, both novels employed strategies to invoke a common bond of maternal grief and sorrow. Through the collective work of Mother-Saviors and the influence they had in the domestic sphere, the larger nation could be transformed and its future generations molded by women to uphold and protect it.

Readers are admonished by Wilkins and Stowe that the institution of slavery, with its pervasive evil, holds the capacity to corrupt and threaten the Mother-Savior and the fatherly patriarch needed to sustain the family unit. Thus, it was possible that if they were not mindful in their important roles as mistresses, white women like Stowe's non-maternal Marie St. Clare (mother of little Eva) could emerge and prove "quite a hard mistress in domestic life."[91] Marie St. Clare possessed an "unconscious selfishness" and was described as "a woman with no heart"; "from her infancy, she had been surrounded with servants, who lived only to study her caprices; the idea that they had either feelings or rights had never dawned upon her, even in distant perspective."[92] Similarly, white mothers in the Caribbean could internalize the normalized brutality of slavery and transform into Madame Angélique Cardon, in Wilkins's novel, "who had found a soiled plate set before her instead of a clean one, smashed it on the head of the sable attendant," and then announced to her dinner guest, "I assure you their heads are very hard."[93]

Moreover, men especially were not immune to the seductive evils, pleasures, passions, and unrestrained power of slavery. If left unchecked, Christian paternity and responsible masculinity would soon give way to a slave society of unbridled power and violent abuse. In the extreme case, white men had the potential to become despicable, merciless, "foaming with rage," "ruthless," "tormentor[s]," "tyrant[s]," and "brutal" like Simon Legree. And, what in some ways was even worse, they could be like the majority of the slaveholding husbands of their female readership, who sexually accommodated themselves to the system of slavery, theologically adjusted their religious beliefs to oblige slavery's presence, and redefined the boundaries of "family" in order to reconcile the unspoken and ambiguous "master-father" role vis-à-vis their mixed-blood offspring.[94]

While the theme of family permeated both women's novels, the knotty questions of paternity as it relates to mixed-race children remained intentionally muted. Wilkins and Stowe lived in Caribbean and American worlds where mixed-race persons abounded, their fate following that of their mother and their paternity silenced. This combustible social issue disrupted the marriages of white masters and mistresses, allowed little room for parental recognition and acknowledgment, and left those like George Harris, Belfond, and even Frederick Douglass legally, socially, and domestically *fatherless*. When describing the Palm Grove estate where her biracial heroine was born, Wilkins writes, "There were many children of caste born on this estate much about the same time, and as they all bore a great resemblance to one another, scandal assigned them to one and the same father, even to the master himself; but as this has little to do with the tale in question, we shall pass it over, and proceed."[95] Both Wilkins and Stowe made literary choices to "pass it over, and proceed," leaving the thorny questions of adultery, sexual violation, concubinage, paternity of biracial children, and cross-racial sibling ties to remain in the unspoken crevices of the text. In strategically gendered ways, the master-father is intimated, yet diversions allow readers to avoid perhaps their most haunting fears about slaveholding households so as not to deepen the real wounds white mistress readers undoubtedly experienced regarding this delicate social issue.

The censorship and erasure of the master-father figure do not preclude it, however, from becoming a trope for accepted white masculinity within the text. Here, Wilkins and Stowe portray to their readers the paradoxical symbol of masculinity and how their respective societies permit one to be an elite, propertied *gentleman* like Augustine St. Clare, St. Hilaire Cardon, and Mr. Dorset while owning and participating in chattelizing Africans, fathering enslaved children, and condoning punitive and disciplinary violence.

However black masculinity would come to be defined in these novels, Wilkins and Stowe show great care in not dismantling the constructed norm. They remained loyal to mainstream fabrications of black masculinity, in many respects undermining the integrity of their own objectives. Black men had to be carefully constructed as brute-ified, domesticated, infantilized, or feminized in order to be acceptably redeemable. Those who did not fit within this typology, such as the African figure Anamoa, had to be rendered old and feeble and ultimately nonthreatening to the current social order. Both novels present mixed-race men similarly. Undoubtedly, Stowe and Wilkins developed characters such as George Harris (Stowe) and Belfond (Wilkins) as literary devices to convey their convictions that mixed-race men possessed the "masculine solution."[96] Like their hero Frederick Douglass, these mixed-race facsimiles embodied "heroism," "boldness," and "determination."[97] Yet, though they had visages similar to those of their white counterparts, neither George nor Belfond was allowed the agency or freedom to give "full vent" to his rage, to define liberty outside of British and North American moral values, or to move too far beyond the fold and the influence of Christian virtues.

In positing a "maternalization of Christian theology," Stowe, however, to a greater degree than Wilkins, proffers Uncle Tom as a feminized masculine character imbued with prayer, piety, and pacifism.[98] Cynthia Griffin Wolf offers an insightful reading of the masculine character of Uncle Tom that shifts the gaze from one in which it is "a manifestation of weakness" or a "blind and passive submission" to one in which Uncle Tom's nonviolent passive resistance and prudence mirrored the approaches of black abolitionists conditioned by hostility encountered in the North. Wolf notes further that Stowe ensured that "Tom's strategies are always ultimately effective in saving his loved ones," thus comforting the reader with the assurance that nonviolence provided better protection than "acts of aggression" and their retaliatory consequences.[99] Moreover, for a society not yet reconciled to "its fear of the dark," the familial and relational title "Uncle" appended to Tom allows readers to minimize their fears of the "large, broad-chested, powerfully-made man, of a full glossy black, and a face" with "truly African features."[100] According to James Baldwin, "Uncle Tom is, for example, if he is called uncle, a kind of saint. He is there, he endures, he will forgive us, and this is a key to that image. But if he is not uncle, if he is merely Tom, he is a danger to everybody. He will wreak havoc. . . . When he is Uncle Tom he has no sex—when he is Tom, he does—and this obviously says much more about the people who invented this myth than it does about the people who are the object of it."[101] In my estimation, Stowe's "careful political leverage in the creation" of "Uncle" Tom allows this black uncle to remain a part of the larger American family and national home both she and Wilkins seek to create.[102] His fate—though threaded with tragedy in protecting Emmeline and Cassy—also represents, for Stowe, triumph over a slave system that tried to foster an inner brutalization among its captives, one that many of Wilkins's black female characters were unable to escape.

In *The Slave Son* the daunting responsibility of the Mother-Savior seemed virtually impossible for black women and made the system of slavery even more morally insidious, for it allegedly robbed this population of enslaved women of their natural instincts to fulfill this function. It is important to note that in both novels only those female characters of the mixed-race caste can rise above their enslaved condition and not let it preclude their embodiment of the Mother-Savior role. There is a glaring juxtaposition between these characters and the African and dark-skinned women in the novel, who appear bereft of most of their natural maternal instincts. Prolonged acts of repeated sexual violence, the sale and separation of children from their mothers, and the inability of slave mothers to protect their children from physical harm were major factors *The Slave Son* attributed to this de-maternalized state. According to Wilkins, "Now the Negro women are either passionately fond of their children, or they are hopelessly indifferent to them, and it was to the latter class that Laurine's mother belonged. . . . The slave had fallen to the condition of a brute; her maternal instinct, if indeed such had ever existed with her, had vanished with the calls of the infant, and she had come to look upon her [mixed-race] offspring as an alien with whom she had nothing to do. . . . Slavery had annihilated all power of thought, care, will, even self-preservation; she was by no means a rare instance, there were many like her even on the estate to which she belonged."[103] Even in Stowe's book, Uncle Tom's wife, the dark-skinned Aunt Chloe, lacks the instinct of what Dianne Stewart explores as "motherness" in volume II.[104] Aunt Chloe refers to her children, Mose and Pete, as "niggers" and "aggravating young uns," threatening to take them down "a button-hole lower"; the only physical touch she extends to her children comes in the form of "a slap."[105]

Aunt Chloe's mishandling of her black children necessarily foregrounds a critical discussion on the representation and treatment of black children throughout *Uncle Tom's Cabin* and *The Slave Son*. Black children in both novels are belittled, become targets of brutal violence, garner meager sympathy, and are left virtually unprotected. In *Uncle Tom's Cabin*, they are referred to as "little dirty things," "little dirty babies," a "creature," a "monkey," possessing "wild diablerie," "depraved," "goblin-like," "ugly," "heathenish," "sooty little urchins," "that thing," and "wicked." Although readers of *Uncle Tom's Cabin* are first introduced to young Topsy as "a neglected, abused child," with "great welts and calloused spots" on her back and shoulders, readers are not invited to feel sympathy for the child. Instead, even abused, she is made to function as comic relief in the novel, with St. Clare taking a "kind of amusement in the child," calling to her, "'Here, Topsy' . . . giving a whistle, as a man would to call the attention of a dog, 'give us a song, now, and show us some of your dancing.'"[106] Similarly, black babies and children in *The Slave Son* experience vicious abuse, often without sympathetic consideration from the adults around them. Within the Caribbean context, they are corralled away from their mothers, who are compelled to work in the fields, and kept in "rearing houses." Vicarious punishments could even be inflicted upon a baby for infractions its mother committed. In Coraly's case, "her infant was taken from her as a punishment, and locked up; the squalling brat took convulsions and died."[107] Finally, when Talima, the child of Anamoa the Koromantyn, tried to intervene on behalf of her father by "interposing her body between him and the whip," Mr. Dorset attempted to plead on her behalf, saying, "But the girl—she has done nothing." But Mr. Cardon ignored him, ordering, "Strike away at her, driver, and let her have it well; when she has fainted, we'll go on with her daddy."[108]

In contradistinction, the white children in the novels, Eva and Léonce, are depicted as angelic and delicate and as treasures protected by both white and black characters at all costs. Tom risks his life diving into the river to save Eva from drowning; during a slave insurrection, Laurine, instead of joining in the collective resistance, risks her life to ensure Léonce's safety on another plantation. Black children, on the other hand, are consistently the victims of slave owners' violence, infanticide, verbal abuse, and abandonment, with very little invocation of reader sympathy and in the virtual absence of any white or black adult characters placing themselves at risk or sacrificing on their behalf. It is only through the character of the frail, dying, and socially powerless child Eva that white acknowledgment of this abuse of black children is named: "I love you, [Topsy] because you haven't had any father, or mother, or friends;—because you've been a poor, abused child!"[109] By this display of Christian compassion, Topsy experiences an inner metamorphosis, and Stowe is able to demonstrate the piercing power of Christian love and its transformative ability in relationship to enslaved blacks. Ultimately, this exchange between the white child of the master and the black child of the slaveholder symbolizes for Stowe the hope in a future generation whereby the vision of a cooperative, cross-racial model of Christian co-existence could one day be possible in North America.

"I Merely Did His Dictation"

Utilizing a seemingly benign genre, Stowe and Wilkins believed in the "evocative potential" of fictional literature as a medium of "intercultural communication" whereby the lofty ideals of social reform could be palatably consumed by their readership. These white female romantic racialists understood themselves as engaging in translation work between their white readership and the characters they reify. Harriet Beecher Stowe's Uncle Tom's Cabin and Marcella Fanny Noy Wilkins's The Slave Son represent important literary experiments in nineteenth-century women's narrative commentaries on the societal effects of the transatlantic slave system and its aftermath in North America and Trinidad. Transfiguring the literary novel into a "vehicle of social criticism," Stowe and Wilkins were able to carve out an acceptable, yet potentially subversive, social space for women's voices.[110] They laid at the threshold of women's homes, within the purview of women's power, the ability to influence a future world in line with God's greater laws and principles of universal liberty. Both women established their literary writings as authoritative representations of African-descended communities, their Christian religious lives, and, in the case of Wilkins, African traditional religions and other traditions deemed supernaturally dangerous and antisocial, such as Obeah. According to Alfred Kazin's introduction to the novel, Harriet Beecher Stowe, in particular, "was consumed by a personal, achingly assured emotional religion that might be called a nineteenth-century invention; it was so particularly and immediately addressed to the healing, redeeming power that she felt, as a Christian woman, directly in touch with God."[111] Referring to Uncle Tom's Cabin, Stowe once remarked, "I did not write it. God wrote it. I merely did His dictation."[112]

In the end, through distinct gendered and racialized perspectives of the Atlantic world, both Stowe and Wilkins provided important nineteenth-century literary examples of how the power of God's imagined script might readily redeem the enslaved and formerly enslaved throughout North America and Trinidad. Yet even within their sympathetic literary depictions of African peoples, neither author escaped the white colonial imagination of religious and cultural violence and romantic racial ascription reflective of US and Trinidadian society during slavery.

Beyond the pages of fiction that expanded colonial and romantic impressions of African peoples and their religious cultures, in the next chapter pages of colonial legal records return us to the terror of state violence in cases of mislabeled and maligned religious identity. These cases serve to document liberated Africans' unfortunate entanglements with colonial obeah and their determination to confront colonial criminalization of their African religious traditions in the same legal arena that callously produced an enduring obeah genealogy in Trinidad and other regions of the African diaspora.

Marked in the
Genuine African Way

LIBERATED AFRICANS AND OBEAH
DOCTORING IN POSTSLAVERY TRINIDAD

O n April 3, 1872, the *Trinidad Chronicle* published the minutes of a session of the Supreme Civil Court of Appeal. Contained within was one of the most extensively documented cases of obeah in Trinidadian legal history levied against a liberated African.[1] The case began with the arrest of John Cooper (Hou Quervee) on the evening of November 25, 1871, and the accusation and charge of "*Practicing Obeah*" or "*en sorcier.*" Cooper was eventually found guilty by the Port of Spain Police Court and given the harsh punishment of twenty lashes with a cat-o'-nine-tails and six months imprisonment at hard labor. An extensive appeal was recorded the following year as Cooper and his attorney filed a countersuit for monetary damages for the premature and unlawful infliction of corporal punishment (flogging). After much testimony and deliberation, the British colonial court, in a historic ruling, exonerated the liberated African, and Cooper was awarded a financial indemnity of fifty pounds sterling out of the total five hundred of the initial suit. As the appeals process in this monumental case unfolded, it surfaced the internal social conflicts regarding "popular and professional medicine" in Trinidad. It likewise exposed how liberated Africans were able to disrupt medical control and religious authority in postslavery colonial society.[2]

The significance of John Cooper's case is determined not merely by its extensive documentation in late nineteenth-century colonial records and newspaper accounts but also by its importance as a successful appellate litigation that left an enduring mark on Trinidadian legal history. Unlike the mutilating and disfiguring punishments associated with pre-Emancipation obeah trials, described in chapter 2, John Cooper's prosecution was symbolic of a shift in the social perception of obeah. Under slavery, obeah's odious threat largely encompassed human and cattle poisonings, perceived spiritual warfare against the estate ruling class, and potential slave insurrection. In postslavery Trinidad, obeah legislation was largely redefined as monetary deception, baseless superstition, "a medium for extortion," and medical quackery. Yet the ambiguity around its practice was that Obeah's esoteric and botanical technologies were needed and necessary in a society that had not made provisions for adequate medical care for its free African populations. Health, healing, and wellness services were among the top reasons spiritual priests and practitioners such as John Cooper were consulted. As in many Atlantic contexts, spiritual intercession mitigated the misfortunes related to physical and psychic health, addressed interpersonal tensions and relationships, prevented personal and legal calamity, and, as was the occasion with John Cooper, intervened on employment challenges.

In nearly 100 pages of case summary, testimony, and proceedings chronicled in Britain's Colonial Office records for Trinidad, John Cooper's lone signature of an "X" is the only mark that exists of his distinguishable presence in the historical archive[3] (see figure 4.1). Yet, historians are fortunate that this extensive record was preserved. Most obeah cases were tried without a jury in magistrate's court or "police court" and were "presided over by magistrates most of whom had no legal training and were part of the local elite."[4] According to Diana Paton, recorded archives of these cases were kept only in the event of a formal appeal of the original decision, which John Cooper officially filed in 1872, rendering his case visible in the annals of Caribbean colonial history.[5] The mark left by this liberated African is symbolic of a larger marking and mapping of African curative and resistance traditions in the Caribbean and their subsequent illegality in postemancipation Trinidad. Analogous to his "X signature" circumscribed by white colonial script, populations of African descent in the diaspora enacted religious markings for securing protective refuge while also encircled by colonial scripts of legal subjugation and repression. This chapter not only examines the shifting depictions of obeah in the legal and public imagination of postslavery Trinidad but also explores what Diana Paton calls the context of "legal practice and cultural discourse"

FIGURE 4.1 John Cooper's signature mark as printed in the original court documents of his case summary and appeal. Reprinted by permission of the National Archives of the United Kingdom, ref. CO 295/261.

as it relates to the "subterranean traditions" of African diasporic communities.[6] Finally, this chapter understands "marking" much as Claudia Mitchell-Kernan does, in that "marking is essentially a mode of characterization," and as such, John Cooper's case is an important marking in the historical record of rival medico-spiritual traditions in colonial society.[7]

Liberated Africans and the Arrival of New Nations in Trinidad

Rosanne Marion Adderley's "*New Negros from Africa*," Monica Schuler's "*Alas, Alas, Kongo*," the works of Maureen Warner-Lewis, and Richard Anderson and Henry Lovejoy's edited volume. are among the most comprehensive scholarship on the liberated *nations* of Africans in the Caribbean.[8] Resettled in the region as indentured labor from colonial territories in Africa, these African-born populations were often referred to in the historical and scholarly literature as "liberated" or "recaptive." From 1808 to 1863, some 164,333 Africans were rescued from illegal slave ships, with close to 61 percent of them initially disembarking in Sierra Leone.[9] These British acts of "liberation" were managed largely by the Liberated African Department and proved not wholly philanthropic and benevolent in motive. According to Monica Schuler, "Britain and France cleverly exploited their own anti-slave trade efforts by 'liberating' Africans from the slave trade and requiring them to migrate to the plantation colonies of these two countries as indentured servants."[10] Scholars such as Richard Anderson interpret the dual complexity surrounding liberated Africans as "simultaneously an act of emancipation *and* colonization" whereby liberated Africans "were assigned new tasks designed to fulfill the labor and defense needs of Britain's Atlantic empire."[11] Although rescued from lives of perpetual enslavement, they were, nonetheless, compelled to "a future of forced migration and liminal freedom, but also lives of mobility around the Atlantic."[12] In particular, the more than thirty thousand Africans who were dispersed throughout the British Caribbean greatly alleviated the labor challenges that colonies such as Trinidad were consistently experiencing.[13]

From 1841 to 1867, Trinidad received a sizeable number of liberated Africans into its borders. Statistically, some 3,383 arrived from Sierra Leone, another 3,510 from the Kru coast near Liberia, and an additional 3,396 from St. Helena, with perhaps more than half having "Yoruba" ethnic backgrounds.[14] This Yoruba dominance may be seen in statistical data gathered from the holding stations in Sierra Leone for heterogenous liberated Africans. Though enslaved Yoruba people did not figure prominently in the transatlantic trade through the eighteenth century, the Oyo Empire's fall and the wars that followed generated many more Yoruba captives.[15] A decade of British patrols policing the recently outlawed Atlantic trade resulted in a majority of Yoruba-origin liberated Africans in Sierra Leone by the 1820s. This proportion held steady for another two decades, as records for 13,237 Africans in 1848 indicated origins in Yorubaland. A similar share of Yoruba among liberated Africans likely reached Trinidad and British Guiana. Liberated persons came from many different nations, though it appears that Yorubas arrived in especially high numbers relative to other African groups.[16]

African *nation* association must be seen as fluid when designating and distinguishing liberated African populations in the nineteenth century. The liberated African population represented a montage of African *nations* that commingled and cohabited in places like Freetown, Sierra Leone, over years. Thus, Trinidad received Africans of many *nations* from the 1840s through the 1860s, and what became operative were constellations of identities and practices that distilled themselves through dominant meta-*nations* such as "Igbo," "Calabar," "Congo/Angola," "Nago/Yoruba," "Ashanti," "Mandingo," "Moco," "Foula," and "Rada." Even *nation* names themselves gained currency through experiences of dispersal, as the label and concept for a unitary "Yoruba" identity emerged early among liberated communities from Sierra Leone, who refashioned the Hausa term for Oyo's people for this new purpose.[17] These larger meta-*nations* were important markers of meaning for African populations fostering collective identities, cultural structures, linguistic exchanges, and durable communities in the midst of mobility and diaspora. We could go so far as to say, as does Peter Cohen, that "the Yoruba" people in the diaspora developed "as a product of displacement and dispersion" having no fixed nomenclature to be unreflectively extended into the world of captivity.[18] Indeed, the varied *nations* "Nago" (used in Brazil, Haiti, and Jamaica, etc.), "Lucumi" (Cuba), "Aku" (Sierra Leone), and "Yoruba/ Yaraba" (Trinidad) compel us to read the *nation-al* designations associated with liberated Africans in the colonial record not as bounded categories by any means but as expanded and protracted identity locaters of communal meaning. In ever-changing diaspora contexts, their plasticity was their power.[19]

By the 1840s, Trinidad had become a multicultural, multilingual, and multireligious society consisting of declining indigenous populations, ex-enslaved persons, European colonists, free blacks, mixed-race coloreds, black North Americans, Asian immigrants, and liberated Africans. In postslavery Trinidad, African traditions remained maligned and non-enslaved liberated African communities and their religious heritages soon became legally "spectered" as obeah. Native-born Africans, according to Rosanne Adderley, were perceived as "particularly powerful practitioners of Obeah."[20] She notes that documents from the late 1850s directly identified "'Negroes from Africa' as the predominant guilty parties" in obeah practice.[21] Due to the perceived merit of their African birth, newly arrived liberated Africans were understood by white colonist as having stronger and "greater . . . 'powers'" in the spiritual realm of obeah vis-à-vis Creole practitioners "because the newly arrived immigrants had a more recent connection to the African sources of their craft."[22]

Between the 1860s and the 1880s, the new African populations disproportionately found themselves defendants in colonial obeah cases. This is not surprising, for in 1866 when Daniel Hart published his *Trinidad and Other West India Islands and Colonies*, the general sentiment regarding the majority of Trinidad's newly arrived populations of Africans and East Indians was that they were "heathen" and "semi-barbaric." Hart quite sharply admonished:

> It must be kept in mind that the Immigrants are almost universally heathens, and if not savages, yet semi-barbarians at the best, being of the lowest classes in their own heathen country, characterized by many heathen vices, and in particular disregard of truth and justice, and even of life itself. Shall this uncivilized heathen be allowed to grow and spread, unchecked and uncorrected, and one of the finest of our West Indian Colonies become the abode of barbarism? Humanity and sound policy at once reply: "It is not to be."[23]

Nineteenth century historians of Trinidad associated both "Africans" and "Hindoos" with witchcraft, sorcery, and the "cruel superstitions of Buddhism, Brahminism, or Fetichism."[24] Louis Antoine De Verteuil understood "Obeahism" as a predatory force exerted upon the "poor," and the "ignorant classes" of Trinidad. According to his 1884 publication, De Verteuil expressly understood its nefarious use "to seduce the affections of a female, to effect a separation between a man and wife, to possess with a devil, to afflict with sickness, to procure the ruin or the death of an enemy—such are of the objects of Obeahism in Trinidad."[25] Similar to its historians who penned observations about Obeah, even established Catholic clergy in Trinidad believed that "*African blacks* still retain certain pagan practices of their countries."[26] The arrival of liberated Africans into communities that already had significant numbers of African-born people still engaged with ancestral traditions proved quite disturbing to Trinidad's European settler populations.[27]

Liberated Africans "followed a pattern" well established by their predecessors in that they toiled grudgingly on the plantation estates for their required time, felt "stranded in a European-dominated world," and "refused to submit to its values and concerns."[28] When given the opportunity, according to Monica Schuler, liberated Africans "organized their communities with as little reference to the European world as possible."[29] The "cultural-communal longevity" of *nation* traditions among liberated Africans relied on the clustering of large numbers of people from shared African backgrounds, particularly for Central Africans and the Yoruba in the British Caribbean colony of Jamaica.[30] This phenomenon was similarly reproduced in Grenada, Martinique, and Trinidad, where sizeable numbers of liberated Africans were imported, resulting in "recognizable Yoruba or Central African cultures."[31]

Specifically referencing Trinidad, Schuler argues that the Yoruba-ization of local culture was heightened by the island's geographical, economic, and political isolation coupled with the intercultural capacities of Catholicism. The analytical possibilities for understanding African religious cultures across the diversity of African-descended populations appear endless. However, presently there are too few studies that seek to parcel out the "exceptional human qualities of endurance, resourcefulness, and creativity" displayed by Africans in diaspora contexts across the centuries.[32] The ways scholars interpret diaspora cultural encounter and the production of its historiography are ripe for radical transformation if studies of religious and cultural production in the Caribbean take into consideration not only the early communities of the enslaved but also their dialogical and dynamic encounters with late-arriving free, liberated African communities and their accompanying "immigrant religion[s]."[33] From studies like Schuler's and also David Trotman's, "Yoruba and Orisha Worship," we might be able to unearth the evolving eighteenth- and nineteenth-century understandings of what it meant to be of African descent and engaged in continuous meaning-making endeavors in a socially ambiguous and often unstable and precarious diaspora. Theoretically, it is important to emphasize that within a context of multivalent influences and intra-population diversity, "these African traditions formed a *heterogeneous mosaic*," as Trotman indicates, "rather than a *homogeneous system*."[34] And Dianne Stewart addresses in greater depth this subject of African diaspora cultural encounter and religious formation in volume II.

Late nineteenth-century European travel literature offers insightful glimpses into the portrayal of liberated African populations who were subjected to the constricting obeah laws in 1860s to 1880s Trinidad. Through the eyes of European travelers, Trinidad was a place where first-generation liberated Africans squatted on land throughout the island. Viewing the colony from the perspective of the traveler, one author beheld in the 1870s a settlement of "Africans of various tribes—Mandingos, Foulahs, Homas, Yarribas, Ashantees, and Congos."[35] Europeans when confronted with these sundry populations created elaborate ethno-portraitures that served to delineate and validate their limited knowledge of African *nations*. In Trinidad, Congos supposedly occupied the "lowest position in the social scale," leading "for the most part, a semi-barbarous life, dwelling in miserable huts." The "Yarribas" (Yorubas), in stark contrast, were seen as possessing "superior intellect while still uncivilized." Yet, what was said of both in a March 1868 article in the *Trinidad Chronicle* was that "the district known as Caratal and other districts are inhabited by negro-kind from the Yaraba down to the Congo, who though nominally Christian, live under the influence of Obeah superstition and who are, more or less, barbarous in their manners, and impatient of control."[36] Even with these efforts to distinguish among African groups, African traits and personality are, nevertheless, filtered through a European imaginary possessing a synthesis and cohesion of value and use only to Europeans.

European travel narratives about Trinidad proved most revealing on the subject of religion. In postemancipation settings, where exposure to Christianity likely came through sparse clerical and missionary encounters, there remained a general societal sentiment that Obeah was a foreboding presence. Therefore, it was believed that although many postslavery Africans might "belong nominally to some denomination of Christianity; . . . their lives are more influenced by their belief in Obeah."[37] Throughout European reflections, Obeah would consistently be characterized as the "mischievous imposture" of true religion.[38] Most noted among the European travelers to Trinidad was Anglican clergyman, Cambridge professor, and novelist Charles Kingsley, author of *At Last: A Christmas in the West Indies* (1871). In a seven-week visit to Governor Arthur Gordon of Trinidad, to whom the book is dedicated, Kingsley in seventeen chapters chronicles his explorations by steamship and road as he journeyed throughout Trinidad. Formulaically indicative of nineteenth-century travel literature, Kingsley sought to map a comprehensive narrative landscape that included details on the physical terrain; the fauna and flora; the diverse inhabitants and their customs, interactions, and religions; comparisons of West Indian and European lifestyles; important historical events such as the West India Regiment and the famous 1837 revolt of Daaga; over forty illustrated images of the natural, social, and religious world of Trinidad; and the reflective "homeward bound" journey back to England.

Colonial officials lauded his account as reputable and respected ethnography, but Kingsley, in his portrayal of Africans, is unable to resist their association with obeah. He speaks of obeah's originary source, saying that "the Portuguese first met with it on the African coast four hundred years ago." He then goes on to declare to his readers:

> But surely it is an idolatry, and not a nature-worship. . . . Any worship, or quasi-worship, which may linger among the Negroes now, are likely to be the mere dregs and fragments of those older superstitions. . . . We shall not be surprised to find that a very important, indeed the most practically important element of Obeah, is poisoning. This habit of poisoning has not (as one might well suppose) sprung up among the slaves desirous of revenge against their white masters. It has been imported, like the rest of the system, from Africa.[39]

This "imported" system with its pernicious "dregs," "fragments," and "habit of poisoning" is what colonial law sought forthrightly to restrain and regulate throughout nineteenth-century Trinidad.

Obeah and Colonial Legislation in Postslavery Trinidad

Legal ordinances in postemancipation Trinidad deepened the prohibitions against the formerly enslaved and newer *nations* of Africans concerning their movement and mobility, their assemblage for ritual ceremonies, and their collective participation in Carnival masquerades and other public gatherings. Through this narrowly restricted gaze of colonial sightedness, African religious and social practices were dangerously and reductively refracted, with the criminalization of Obeah and other African-related practices most pronounced.

Legislation in the British Caribbean immediately following emancipation, and particularly ordinances on vagrancy, associate obeah with fraud, pretense, and deception.[40] Still, in these legislative records a wide aperture of meaning regarding vagrancy was at play in the context of Trinidad. The term was inclusive of a social dimension restricting idleness, prostitution, begging, and disorderliness. Yet, the definitional net of vagrancy also encompassed a supernatural dimension, outlawing all activities associated with "pretending or professing to tell fortunes, or using or pretending to use any subtle craft or device, by palmistry, obeah, or any such like superstitious means, to deceive and impose on any of Her Majesty's subjects."[41]

By 1868, shortly after the last consignment of liberated Africans arrived in the Caribbean and only three years prior to the arrest and conviction of John Cooper, British officials in Trinidad passed a detailed ordinance reinforcing previous legal repressions of African religious practices in Trinidad.[42] Similar to early ordinances, "any 'African' worship was automatically classified as Obeah," and Obeah's practice and the commodification of its services were all considered prosecutable.[43] Under the heading "Superstitious Devices," the 1868 Obeah Prohibition Ordinance stated:

> Any person who, by the practice of Obeah or by an occult means or by an assumption of supernatural power or knowledge, intimidates or attempts to intimidate any person, or obtains or endeavours to obtain any chattel, money or valuable security from any other person, or pretends to discover any treasure or any lost or stolen goods, or the person who stole the same, or to inflict any disease, loss, damage or personal injury to or upon any other person, or to *restore any other person to health*, and any person who procures, counsels, induces, or persuades or endeavours to persuade any other person to commit any such offence, is liable to imprisonment for six months, and, subject to the Corporal Punishment Act.[44]

The ordinance in Trinidad also legalized a search and seizure component that directly targeted the "Articles used in Obeah and Witchcraft." If discovered, spiritual artifacts were confiscated and presented as tangible evidence against the defendant in judicial proceedings. According to the material aspect of the law:

> Where it is shown, upon the oath of a credible witness that there is reasonable cause to suspect that any person is in possession of any article or thing

used by him in the practice of Obeah or witchcraft, any Justice may, by warrant under his hand, cause any place whatsoever belonging to or under the control of such person to be searched . . . and, if any such article is found in any place so searched, cause it to be seized . . . for the purpose of being produced in evidence in any case in which it may be required.[45]

With the rigid strictures of slavery and repressed mobility removed through emancipation, white colonists determined new ways of inhibiting the collective social and ceremonial actions of Africans in the colony. These new legal ordinances targeted African participation in what colonists interpreted as social rituals of aggression and dissent. During John Cooper's era of the 1870s and extending into the 1880s, in addition to obeah, ceremonial practices of Bongo, Canboulay, and Carnival masking were specifically isolated and labeled degenerate in the legal ordinances.

Bongo ritualized communication with the spirits of the dead. It assumed the form of a dance that typically accompanied a wake as a "ritual farewell for the dead" intended to be "bright and entertaining in order to cheer up the spirit on its journey from this world."[46] Since the days of slavery, Trinidad's colonizers found African funerary practices especially barbarous and distasteful. One newspaper account reported that "one of the lingering relics of a slavish and barbarous age . . . is the abominable and heathenish practices which attend the watchings over the dead."[47] Colonial periodicals offered harrowing descriptions to the Trinidadian public of Bongo rituals. Historian Bridget Brereton summarizes:

> The body was exposed in a small room. Around seven in the evening hymns were sung and the choruses shouted out; cake and grog were served. Only friends and relatives were inside the house, but outside a crowd of up to a hundred people assembled. They beat drums, sang "lewd" songs and danced the bongo. "When the spirit has taken possession of the circle, then you begin to know what a Bongo is." . . . Wakes were said to be especially bad around Cambridge Street in the city, where a "colony of Africans" was settled, for the "rites of their native country" were extremely noisy. Wakes were "orgies over the dead," which started with psalms and ended with obscene songs and dances. They were a blot on civilisation, and, in short, ought to be suppressed.[48]

In an attempt at Bongo's total obliteration, an 1883 law stated, "Every owner or occupier of any house, building yard, or other place who shall permit any persons to assemble and dance herein the dance known as 'bungo' or any similar dance, shall be liable to a fine of forty-eight dollars."[49] Seizure of ritual artifacts was also permissible, and it became "lawful for any constable . . . to enter any house, building, yard, or place where any persons may be so assembled, and stop such dance or seize and carry away all such drums, gongs, tambours, bangees, chac-chacs or other instruments of music, and the same shall be forfeited."[50] This ordinance included the Calenda and Belaire drum dances as well, which were collectively deemed "immoral."[51]

In 1881 and 1884, the Canboulay had become a major source of public contention between African masqueraders and civil authorities in areas such as Port of Spain, San Fernando, and Princes Town. A ritual heavily associated with slavery, the Canboulay "commemorate[d] the occasions during slavery when cane fires would break out on the estates and slaves from surrounding estates were sent to help put out those fires," creating a social space where "slaves from different estates could meet and mix freely."[52] After emancipation, the Canboulay evolved into a "dance of protest"[53] enacted in a processional of lighted torches "accompanied by chants and throbbing drums."[54] The colonial governor, William Robinson, eventually enacted an official legal ordinance in order to impede these public encounters.[55] The ordinance directly stated that "the procession generally known as the Cannes-brulees or Canboulay will not be allowed to take place, and further Regulations for giving effect to this prohibition are promulgated in a Proclamation bearing even date herewith."[56] The proclamation went on to conclude that "any person who does any act or takes part in any dance, procession, assemblage or collection contrary to any such Proclamation shall be guilty of an offence punishable on summary conviction and may be fined in any sum not exceeding Twenty Pounds or imprisoned with or without hard labour for any term not exceeding Six Months."[57]

Finally, Carnival, too, became a target for colonial legal censorship. The performance of Carnival in colonial Trinidad represented the relaxing of public etiquette, the inversion of social hierarchies, the defiance of civil restrictions, and the transgressing of physical boundaries. In addition to providing a forum for revelry, merriment, and unrestrained public space, Carnival also provided disenfranchised Africans with a resistant context for engaging in intentional acts of white physical aggression. As with the Canboulay, Afro-Trinidadians utilized the public space of Carnival to mitigate hidden social conflicts and tensions. Therefore, Carnival became an important vehicle of social outlet for Trinidad's African populations.

"Masking" had a twofold meaning within the context of Trinidad's Carnival. Masking, as performance, enabled the embodiment of alternative personalities. Through Carnival, masqueraders could reinvent and refashion themselves beyond the boundaries of their normal status and personae. During Carnival there were many instances of humans assuming the form of animals as well as of transvestism, where men engaged in gender switching and assumed the outward form of women.[58] Another major reason for its being outlawed was that the mask was also a public weapon providing temporary social agency and power for Trinidad's marginalized black populations. Under the protection of the mask, Afro-Trinidadians meted out random acts of physical violence to whites and to black rivals. Obeah Prohibition Ordinance No. 6 of 1868 spoke directly to this subversive use of masking: "Any person who being masked or otherwise disguised, shall unlawfully assault, or beat any other person shall, upon conviction before a Stipendiary Justice, be imprisoned with hard labour for any term not exceeding six months."[59] Over time, the punishment for this crime was doubled to "imprisonment for twelve months."[60]

In September, 1881, a confidential document was submitted to the Colonial Office entitled, "Mr. Hamilton's Report on the Causes and Circumstances of the Disturbances in Connexion with the Carnival in Trinidad."[61] The report to London, inclusive of recommendations for future amelioration, addressed recent events in Trinidad's Carnival involving a Captain Baker who ordered that the torches of the masqueraders be extinguished, which was interpreted as "a step towards the suppression of the Carnival" and a "wilful and wanton interference with their . . . honored customs and amusements" regarding "Camboulay," and resulted in acts of public disturbance. The report identified long-standing tensions with the police that became exacerbated during Carnival. Such tensions were expected given (1) the previous history of the Alguazils when "the free coloured people were forced to do the work of the police . . . which included hanging, flogging, and burning"; (2) that "the force is largely comprised of Barbadians who are not liked by the Trinidadians"; and (3) the existing "antipathy to the office of policeman," resulting in a force not "drawn from the people." The immediate social conflict was settled when the governor clarified that the police's efforts were not one of suppression of ritual but one of protection against "the danger of fire in the dry season." The broader issues surrounding Carnival and its "senseless and irrational amusement" and "unbridled licentiousness" were still in need of resolution, with possible solutions ranging from "Carnival if left alone will die out" to "Carnival should be stopped altogether." The Right Honorable Hamilton eventually recommended that "the Carnival should be allowed to be held, but its proceedings should be carefully regulated"; that it should "be restricted to daylight, . . . from 6 a.m. to 6 p.m. on the Monday through Ash Wednesday"; that "torchlight processions and dances should be allowed, but that they should be restricted . . . where they can be held without danger or annoyance to the inhabitants"; that "in the interest of the maintenance of law and order, that [the police] should be fully supported in the execution of their duties"; and, finally, that similar attention be given to the East Indian "Coolie Festival, or Hosea" and its careful regulation "so as to prevent them from developing into another description of Carnival."

Carnival was no longer the festive celebration Trinidad's white gentility enjoyed during slavery but had become an active and shared social space with emancipated and liberated Africans, much to the disdain of the elite. As a consequence, European colonists responded with sheer revulsion at African appropriations of Carnival. A late nineteenth-century article on Carnival printed in the Port of Spain Gazette remarked "that never before was Trinidad so over-run with open violence and immorality, and with Obeahism and other secret abominations."[62] Bans on masking had begun as early as 1846 and were amended continually in the late nineteenth century. In part, these collective legal limitations on public activity were subsequently a ban on the supposed inherent vices of the African personality. J. H. Collins in his 1888 book A Guide to Trinidad argued that Afro-Trinidadians possessed "invincible laziness, outward devotion and piety combined with a superstitious belief in spirits and Obeah, a love of ceremonies and display, sexual immorality, dishonesty, lack of thrift and ambition, and a tendency to steal."[63] By the late nineteenth century, this wide-scale anti-African sentiment was concretized in the religious, social, and legal climate of Trinidad.

Carnival with its power of social inversion facilitated an arena for African populations of the lower classes to readily assume the role of gentility, dressing up in elaborate costumes and imitating the mannerisms of the colonial elite. Perhaps more surprising, however, were the moments of social transference embodied by the white elite, who donned the "costume of the field labourers" and began to imitate the very African practices they deliberately criminalized and despised.[64] One account stated that the white plantocracy would pretend to "unite in bandes representing the gangs of different Estates, and with torches and drums to represent what did actually take place in the cane districts" in addition to enacting "black drum dances, such as the 'bamboula,' 'belair,' 'calinda' and 'ghouba.'"[65] With apparent cross-fertilization from the concurrent minstrelsy tradition in North America, this Trinidadian form of minstrelsy extended beyond Carnival to the theatrical stage with local performances such as Poor Old Joe, dramatized in "white-in-blackface" caricature.[66] These performances at the same time strategically alleviated and assuaged through parody their very real colonial fears. By embodying the African in theatrical form, European colonists perhaps thought they could symbolically diffuse the potency of this social threat and the perceived erratic spiritual traditions of Obeah. It is within this Euro-colonial social imprint of Africans that John Cooper and Mah Nannie's cases, discussed later in the chapter, must be situated. Believing it their duty to maintain order and balance in a society governed by British authority and Christian moral law, the colony's formidable religious threat—Obeah and comparable practices under African authority—had to be subdued.

Liberated Africans and Nation-Building in Sierra Leone

Obeah legislation in Trinidad was a disputed landscape for contesting health epistemologies and authorities of medicine. Liberated Africans arriving in Trinidad between the 1840s and the 1860s did not disembark tabula rasa. Quite the contrary, they arrived in Trinidad from geographies in West Africa with sophisticated approaches to nationhood and group identity, complex religious and theological cosmologies, and acute distrust of European medicine and healthcare. Prior to their transport into Britain's Caribbean territories or entry into the African Colonial Corps or West India Regiment militia, British colonial literature recounted the ways liberated Africans readily resumed the cultural rites of their various nations in its colonies of Sierra Leone and St. Helena.[67] Rosanne Adderley suggests some liberated Africans may have arrived with "Christian baptism" having been performed, yet "had long lived without the supervision and guidance of a regular Christian minister."[68]

In Sierra Leone's Kissy Village in the 1840s, half of the town was described by Robert Clarke in the colonial record as "Eboe" as well as "Akoo" (used interchangeably with Aku, "Yarribah," or Yoruba). Other groups documented as the "nations of liberated Africans" in the 1848 Sierra Leone census include the Paupahs, Hausas, Mokos, Congos, Calabahs, Kromantees, Kakanjas, Binnees, Bassas, and Mozambiques, who displayed "national marks" demarcating the cultural bodies of liberated Africans in Sierra Leone.[69] In terms of habitation, liberated Africans expressed a strong "desire to live separately" in their own enclaves and settlements.[70] With regard to religious diversity, some liberated Africans were described as "zealous followers of Christianity," others as having "assumed the garb and religion of Mahomet," and still others who followed "Pagan" forms of worship. Regarding the "Akoo" or "Yarribah" ritual ceremonies in Sierra Leone, it was stated that "their several modes of worship are indicated by the devotee wearing necklaces of beads, and the colour and size of the bead distinguishing the worshippers."[71] In creating sacred ritual space for "Yarribah,"

> buildings of a square form are appropriated to the worship of the gods, at which the people assemble with the priests. . . . The [stone] idols are placed at the corner of the hut, and are called Olisha, or Orisha. Before these they prostrate themselves, petitioning for riches and children, barrenness bearing stigma with these people. The clay idols are looked upon as gris-gris; . . . the idols are generally adorned with Cowrie shells. . . . Water is worshipped in small earthen pots. . . . When at worship they kneel close to the pots.[72]

Most profound within these European colonial accounts in Sierra Leone were complex renderings of African creation stories, names of deities, and spiritual technologies. According to the chronicler Clarke in his 1840s account, "The Akoos entertain the following belief of the first creation of man:—Odua (God) made one man and woman, and put them on a high hill. . . . The man and woman Odua made, had six children, and these were set out by their parents to build a town for themselves, and become subject to the king of the Akoos."[73] The narrative then takes a presentist turn, saying, "The following is their account of the separation of the whites from the blacks":

> Odua asked Oeibo (white man), and Ouba-oyo, (the King of the Akoos,) what they would take. Oeibo said he would take water; Ouba-oyo, that he would sit down and fight for Odua. Thereupon Odua makes a bowl, and puts a cover to it, which he gives to Oeibo, telling him to carry it to the sea and there open it; after which he was to put it on the water, and get into it and paddle it with a golden stick, when he would find it to move wherever he pleased. . . . It [Jffeh or Ife] was the first place that God made, and where he put the first man and woman; it is also the place of departed spirits, for whose accommodation a market place has been erected, called Ouga Attehah, or the market of the dead,—where the dead buy and sell. In this place, the surviving relatives of a person lately deceased, may obtain an interview with the departed friend; but they would die if they should speak.[74]

Within the pantheon of deities, "the worshippers of thunder and lightning, wear a necklace of white and black beads, alternating with a red one" and "those who adore large rivers or lakes, are known by wearing white necklaces." According to the observer, "while worshipping the thunder and lightning, some of the Akoos roll around the idol's wooden balls intended to represent the thunder bolts, which they believe to fall during the storm. Indeed they often previously place a hatchet in the house which may be burnt up by the lightning, which the Jugglers show as having fallen from the clouds."[75] Detailing divinatory technologies, Clarke states that "the Akoo were known for having a 'swarm of Jugglers or Fortune Tellers' . . . of which the palm nuts are consulted," and "they count out sixteen palm nuts, having each four seed holes, which are kept very carefully free from dust."[76] Other ritual paraphernalia identified within the descriptive detailing of sacred divinatory items included a bone, a seed, a shell, and "yam flour . . . placed on the floor of the hut" for drawing with the "fore and middle fingers symbolical lines." Described as "Conjurors" in the literature—seemingly priests of the ancient system of Ifa divination—"the individuals who pay divine homage to the palm nut, permit their Priests to wear beads . . . their colour being white and green . . . the palm nuts intended to represent the Deity, are not indiscriminately selected, but those only are chosen, which have placental or four seed holes."[77]

The same *nations* of liberated Africans in Sierra Leone would come to populate Trinidad in the mid-nineteenth century. Their religious practices would serve as the cultural basin for refortifying their *nation* identities upon arrival in Trinidad. Clarke's 1843 descriptions above bear witness to the cultural endurance and religious tenacity of the liberated Africans' traditions and customs that would come to resurface in Trinidad. As David Northrup commends the innovation of liberated Africans in their expanded notions of *nationhood*, "the nations created in Sierra Leone are striking evidence of how malleable (and how strong) national consciousness among groups can be."[78]

Obeah Regulations and Competing Notions of Health in Postslavery Trinidad

Unlike the health and social challenges faced by Africans in colonial Trinidad, newly liberated Africans in Sierra Leone were consistently negotiating dire health challenges related to their extended time on foul European slave vessels experiencing an "immense number of deaths during the first six weeks after their arrival to Sierra Leone."[79] After journeying in the wretched hulls of slave ships, African bodies upon rescue and arrival to Sierra Leone or St. Helena exhibited extreme health atrocities and diseases associated with the torrential voyage. When colonial officials inquired: "what was their state of health during the middle passage?," African passengers were described as suffering from "inflammatory fever," "sores and ulcers," and "pulmonary affection."[80] One senior assistant surgeon to the colony of Sierra Leone assessed their condition upon disembarkment as "so deplorably emaciated, that the skin appears to be tensely stretched over, and tied down to the skeleton," the "belly is as it were tacked to the back, whilst the hip bones protrude, and give rise to foul slough- ing and phagedenic ulcers"; their bodies contained "extensive gangrenous ulcerations, situated on the extremities, often detaching the soft parts from the bones, which becoming carious, are exfoliated."[81]

The "principal diseases" plaguing them because of the unhygienic and con- taminating conditions of the slave ship were "dropsical, dysenterie, pulmonic, and rheumatic complaints of long standing, and of the most intractable nature" and "the contagious disease, small pox." Colonial medical profession- als who worked in Sierra Leone recalled the pronounced images of "the squa- lor, and extreme wretchedness of the [African] figure . . . heightened in many cases, by the party-coloured evacuations with which the body is besmeared." Collectively speaking, *vesseled Africans* were reduced to an "emaciated, totter- ing, and debilitated body."[82] In addition to their physical conditions, liberated Africans showed through their mental countenance that they had endured "suffering, moral and physical, of the most profound and agonizing nature," which "merged in melancholic and raving madness."[83] One medical profes- sional gloomily remarked, "This truly pitiable state of the newly arrived Liberated Africans, must have been observed by every member of the profession, who has had any opportunity of seeing them."[84]

Even in physical and mental states of unfathomable anguish, liberated Africans were understandably suspicious of all European attempts at medical assistance. They deeply distrusted British medical physicians and were highly reluctant to use European health facilities in Sierra Leone. Doctors residing in the colony stated quite emphatically that Africans were "averse to having recourse to European methods of treatment." It was recorded that liberated Africans would not submit to treatment "until they have tried all the native remedies with which they are acquainted."[85]

The distressing health conditions persisted after liberated Africans arrived in the Caribbean. One incident concerning those disembarking in Trinidad from a vessel called the *Growler* was of particular concern. In a correspondence from Trinidad addressed to the Colonial Land and Immigration Office on April 19, 1848, the *Growler* had apparently delivered a shipload of Africans who had experienced "disastrous mortality" that "has continued after their disem- barkation." It was estimated that of "the 441 Emigrants embarked at Sierra Leone, 135 are now dead,—and 28 are ill and expected to die,—168 are ill but expected to recover, and only 109 are in good health." Ironically, the governor of the colony of Sierra Leone, George Macdonald, described the liberated

Africans upon departure as being "as fine a body of Emigrants as ever left this Country."[86] The surgeon, Dr. Robert McCrae, who accompanied the voyage sent confirmation to the Emigration Commissioners that the 441 had been "selected from about a thousand of both sexes and all ages, at that time in the Liberation Africans Yard, with . . . scrupulous attention to their state of health, and likelihood of being serviceable as laborers after their arrival in the colony." Surgeon McCrae admitted that some Africans were "rather thin" and "emaciated" but attributed it more to "their recent privations during the period of captivity, than to the existence of active disease." Having been "very recently liberated out of a slave vessel," details such as "foul state of holds," "deteriorated atmosphere on board," "a skin disease called Craw-Craw (onchocerciasis)," and "fatal disease" exposed the physical conditions tolerated by African captives during their multi-Atlantic passages. McCrae proffered his professional theory that the deplorable conditions and preexisting disease on board slave vessels before transport to Sierra Leone, coupled with the twenty-three-day voyage to Trinidad, resulted in the high mortality and disease-ridden state upon disembarkation.[87]

Although disease, illness, and mortality were constant afflictions in these transatlantic voyages, unlike the intermediary locations where liberated Africans initially disembarked, such as Sierra Leone, St. Helena, and even the United States colony of Liberia, Trinidad acutely restricted liberated Africans' practice of their traditional religions, ritual assemblages, and theurgical wellness systems. Surgeon McCrae described that quite the opposite was the practice in Sierra Leone where Africans were co-practitioners in the healthcare process and those "found to be sick and requiring Hospital Treatment" were given the necessary attention and then "placed under the immediate observation of native attendants familiar with their language and habits."[88] The doctors of Sierra Leone and St. Helena relied on Africans as medical partners in the healing and caring of the infirmed. "Native attendants" were trusted as skilled authorities and experts possessing specialized technologies for observation, cure, and recovery. This dubious partnership worked in an environment where Africans were suspicious of European medicine and motives.

Conversely, the aspersive allegations of obeah along with its suspected articles of harm and/or fraud cast Africans as adversaries of healthcare and a growing medical economy in Trinidad that sought to regulate and control the contours of health and healing. Africans' pharmacopoeic knowledge was rendered poisonous, their medicinal skills for diagnosis and healing were labeled fraudulent, and their material technologies and curative systems were reduced to superstition or obeah. To white colonists, Obeah defied

Trinidad's Western healthcare system by purporting to employ supernatural forces, to spiritualize diagnoses, and to make use of animal, herbal, and other perceived nonscientific instruments to bring about healing.

Healthcare was inadequate in most colonial Caribbean societies. As discussed more thoroughly in the following pages, local newspaper articles from the *New Era* and the *Trinidad Chronicle* indicate this was certainly true of healthcare in Trinidad. The *Trinidad Chronicle* admits that "a West India population, within 40 years of slavery," has experienced a "slowness" to "sanitary science" and the doctrines of "sanitary reform," resulting in outbreaks of smallpox, typhoid, and leprosy.[89] Within colonial conditions of widespread pestilence and deadly disease of pandemic proportions, such as Trinidad's 1871 smallpox contagion, the search for health and wellness created spaces for the collision of the seemingly dichotomized sacred African and medical European epistemologies.

Unfortunately, in a world where African modalities of healing were relegated to marred superstition and criminal offense, seeking African forms of health remedies would be a direct social threat to European respectability. Thus, an article in 1872 in the *Trinidad Chronicle* admonishes those who might have consulted Afro-healing specialists and turned to African heritage rituals for alternative healthcare. The author warns of an incident of "superstitious rites enacted within our hearing, in the suburbs of this town, last week, by people, most of them Africans, . . . but some of them creoles, of Scottish parentage on their father's side, that would open the eyes of some on the need of education."[90] From this brief account, it is clear that the "superstitious rites" of Africa were strongly juxtaposed with educated and enlightened approaches to healing and disease prevention. It was thought that these "quasi-religious exercises" combined with "pagan fatalism" prevented African communities in Tacarigua from taking the necessary health precautions. In reference to an outbreak of smallpox, the author concluded that belief in these practices left these communities "ready prey to an easily avoided pestilence."[91]

A commonplace colonial belief was that the superstitious customs of Africans were a subterfuge for healthcare. Those understood as practicing obeah would allegedly "pretend to cure diseases; they invariably declare that such diseases are produced by wicked practices, and . . . can be cured only by the administration of medicines aided by incantations."[92] Trinidadian historian Louis Antoine De Verteuil ultimately declared to his nineteenth-century readership, "Some of the quack doctors and Obeah practisers have a wide reputation, and practice extensively; they are generally negroes from Africa."[93]

For more than a half-century, the British worked to heavily control the qualifications for doctors and healthcare providers on the island. While still a slave colony, Trinidad's Governor Woodford diligently sought to standardize what it meant to be a medical professional with the 1814 formation of the Trinidad Medical Board, which had resonances in Spanish rule and held licensing power over general practice, surgery, and drug and medicine sales.[94] Woodford's proclamation required "every Person or Persons who now practice Medicine or Surgery or who act as Apothecaries or sell any Medicines or Drugs in the said Island" to appear before the board and "produce any permission, licence or authority" certifying their practice.[95] Licensure required a medical degree from a European or American university, certification from a recognized authority, or an examination by the Medical Board.[96] Comparable efforts to protect the sacrosanct boundaries of medical practitioners would continue well into the twentieth century with the passing of the 1903 legal ordinance indicating, "any person who shall willfully and falsely pretend to be, or take or use the name or title of physician, surgeon, doctor of medicine, licentiate in medicine and surgery . . . or practitioner in medicine, or takes any step, title, addition, designation, or description implying that he is qualified to practice medicine, surgery or midwifery," shall be subjected to fines, hard labor, or imprisonment.[97] Despite consistent efforts to draw rigid boundaries around medical accreditation, there still persisted among some white residents a lack of confidence in and distrust of licensed doctors' medical knowledge. Famed author E. L. Joseph expressed this sentiment in the 1840s when he stated, "Duellists kill with powder and ball, doctors kill with powder and pill."[98]

African-descended populations, both slave and free, confronted discrimination and interdictions regarding access to medical licenses in Trinidad. Even wealthy mixed-race European-trained applicants were no exception.[99] Strict prohibitions were placed on the sale or issue of drugs "to any slave" without written permission, with the penalty being two hundred dollars for a first offense and double that amount plus loss of their medical license for a second offense. Excluding non-whites from the registry of medical authority was common not only in Trinidad but also in antebellum North America. Sharla Fett, in exploring similar occurrences in the antebellum South, speaks of the competing juxtapositions of white "standard orthodox medicines" and black "doctoring knowledge."[100] In other words, while African-descended persons laid claim to doctoring traditions through inherited knowledge, "white doctors made a . . . claim to medical authority vested in learned knowledge, class standing, professional training, and male entitlement."[101] Within larger

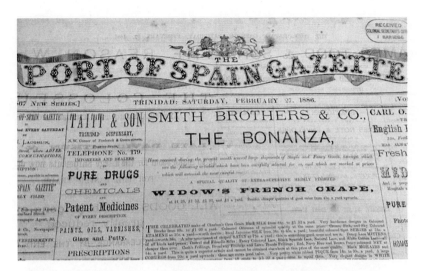

FIGURE 4.2 Advertisements for pharmaceutical drugs and medicines that were marketed to European colonists in nineteenth-century Trinidad. In contrast, colonists did not view African medicinal and healthcare practices as lawful and legitimate and subjected them to prosecution as obeah and witchcraft under the 1868 Obeah prohibition ordinance. *Port of Spain Gazette*, February 27, 1886. Reprinted by permission of the National Archives of Trinidad and Tobago.

"hierarchies of scientific and medicinal knowledge," African curing epistemologies clandestinely practiced both in North America and in the Caribbean were placed well below the scale of legitimate medicine.[102]

Newspapers such as the *Port of Spain Gazette* were replete with public advertisements representing a new era in the postslavery curative economy (see figure 4.2). Health, healing, and restorative medicine in colonial Trinidad were highly competitive. The Caribbean colonies relied on a prescriptive drug and medicine economy that was largely based on importation. This import-reliant structure generated a flourishing medical advertisement culture.[103] Targeting a literate, colonial citizenry, advertisements for medicines assumed various forms, some inclusive of photos and testimonials, but collectively these advertisements generally boasted of government stamps of approval, of their many years of operation, of positive guarantees, and of a widespread European consumer market (see figure 4.3).

These advertisements also became a window into the history of the nineteenth-century health and disease culture confronting colonial residents. In colonial Trinidad, diseases for which medical cures were advertised included both acute and chronic maladies such as bronchitis, "leprosy, or

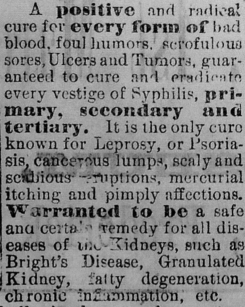

Reuter's Life Syrup No. 2!

A **positive** and radical cure for **every form of** bad blood, foul humors, scrofulous sores, Ulcers and Tumors, guaranteed to cure and eradicate every vestige of Syphilis, **primary, secondary and tertiary.** It is the only cure known for Leprosy, or Psoriasis, cancerous lumps, scaly and scabious eruptions, mercurial itching and pimply affections. **Warranted to be** a safe and certain remedy for all diseases of the Kidneys, such as Bright's Disease, Granulated Kidney, fatty degeneration, chronic inflammation, etc.

The best of all stimulators and correctors of the Liver, promptly removing torpidity, hardening, and enlargement, liquifying the bile, causing it to flow freely into the bowels, thereby preventing and removing constipation, dyspepsia and indigestion, thus removing the cause of headaches, dizziness, nausea, palpitations, hysteria and fainting. A fair trial of the **Life Syrup No. 2,** is all that is asked. We positively Guarantee

A COMPLETE CURE!

FIGURE 4.3 Advertisement for a standard elixir, Reuter's Life Syrup No. 2, prescribed as a cure for various ailments, including leprosy, cancerous lumps, psoriasis, and chronic inflammation. *Port of Spain Gazette*, February 27, 1886. Reprinted by permission of the National Archives of Trinidad and Tobago.

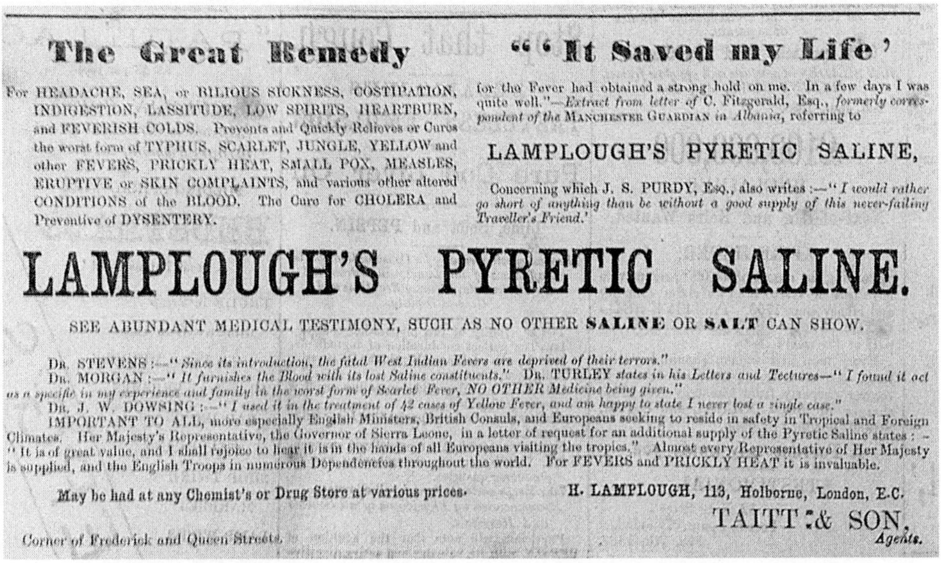

The Great Remedy

For HEADACHE, SEA, or BILIOUS SICKNESS, CONSTIPATION, INDIGESTION, LASSITUDE, LOW SPIRITS, HEARTBURN, and FEVERISH COLDS. Prevents and Quickly Relieves or Cures the worst form of TYPHUS, SCARLET, JUNGLE, YELLOW and other FEVERS, PRICKLY HEAT, SMALL POX, MEASLES, ERUPTIVE or SKIN COMPLAINTS, and various other altered CONDITIONS of the BLOOD. The Cure for CHOLERA and Preventive of DYSENTERY.

"'It Saved my Life'"

for the Fever had obtained a strong hold on me. In a few days I was quite well."—*Extract from letter of* C. Fitzgerald, Esq., *formerly correspondent of the* MANCHESTER GUARDIAN *in Albania*, referring to

LAMPLOUGH'S PYRETIC SALINE,

Concerning which J. S. PURDY, Esq., also writes :—'*I would rather go short of anything than be without a good supply of this never-failing Traveller's Friend.'*

LAMPLOUGH'S PYRETIC SALINE.

SEE ABUNDANT MEDICAL TESTIMONY, SUCH AS NO OTHER **SALINE** OR **SALT** CAN SHOW.

DR. STEVENS :—"*Since its introduction, the fatal West Indian Fevers are deprived of their terrors.*"
DR. MORGAN :—"*It furnishes the Blood with its lost Saline constituents.*" DR. TURLEY *states in his Letters and Tectures*—"*I found it act as a specific in my experience and family in the worst form of Scarlet Fever, NO OTHER Medicine being given.*"
DR. J. W. DOWSING :—"*I used it in the treatment of 42 cases of Yellow Fever, and am happy to state I never lost a single case.*"
IMPORTANT TO ALL, more especially English Ministers, British Consuls, and Europeans seeking to reside in safety in Tropical and Foreign Climates. Her Majesty's Representative, the Governor of Sierra Leone, in a letter of request for an additional supply of the Pyretic Saline states : — "It is of great value, and I shall rejoice to hear it is in the hands of all Europeans visiting the tropics." Almost every Representative of Her Majesty is supplied, and the English Troops in numerous Dependencies throughout the world. For FEVERS and PRICKLY HEAT it is invaluable.

May be had at any Chemist's or Drug Store at various prices.   H. LAMPLOUGH, 113, Holborne, London, E.C.

TAITT & SON, *Agents.*

Corner of Frederick and Queen Streets.

FIGURE 4.4 Prescription advertisements often included authenticating testimonies from medical doctors and attorneys to enhance the credibility and legitimacy of their marketing claims. *Port of Spain Gazette*, February 27, 1886. Reprinted by permission of the National Archives of Trinidad and Tobago.

Psoriasis, cancerous lumps, scaly and scabious eruptions, mercurial itching, and pimply affections," "constipation, dyspepsia and indigestion," as well as "hysteria and fainting." Likewise, "pulmonary affections" and "scrofulous diseases" were treatable with Scott's Emulsion of Pure Cod Liver Oil, with Hypophosphites.[104] There were also more benign disorders such as headache, nausea, fainting attacks, worms, "bad blood, foul humors, scrofulous sores, Ulcers and Tumors" and "skin diseases of every kind and at every stage." For example, Lamplough's Pyretic Saline boasted itself as "the Great Remedy" with "abundant medical testimony" as it "prevents and quickly relieves or cures the worst forms of TYPHUS, SCARLET, JUNGLE, YELLOW AND OTHER FEVERS, PRICKLY HEAT, SMALL POX, MEASLES, ERUPTIVE OR SKIN COMPLAINTS, and various other altered conditions of the BLOOD. The cure for CHOLERA and Preventive of DYSENTERY" (see figure 4.4). The advertisement is surrounded by expert testimonials from two attorneys as well as three medical doctors, one of whom states, "Since its introduction, the fatal West Indian Fevers are deprived of their terrors." European companies held the power of cure through boastings of "fresh drugs," "pure chemicals," "homeopathic medicines" containing "no opium nor any deleterious drug," and "the latest improvements in the dispensing arts."[105]

Advertisements by local apothecaries and pharmacists commonly vaunted about importation from London, but not surprisingly, Africa was never privileged as an important source of origin for medical knowledge and remedies. As we will see later in this chapter, John Cooper and Mah Nannie were read as threatening in a colonial economy of competitive medicinal healthcare. African healing practices codified as obeah existed side by side with Western medicine, and the "copresence of these two orientations" toward health, wellness, and prevention resulted in much social and legal tension.[106]

Quite paradoxically, the healing technologies of Africans were both readily criminalized and profoundly essential in late nineteenth-century Trinidad. "Colonial healthcare" in 1870 took the form of the establishment of the public Government Medical Service, which proved wholly insufficient for the medical needs of all of Trinidad and especially its African communities. In the absence of adequate healthcare facilities, African doctoring practices helped to sustain the health of African-descended populations, and "the continued inaccessibility of services sent many people to Obeah practitioners."[107] According to Laurie Jacklin, "innumerable . . . people used indigenous healers, Obeah, and private physicians, but these encounters in the private sector are not documented in the records of colonialism."[108] These African *doctors* "conducted a brisk business in herbal therapeutics, to help Afro-Trinidadians cope with their conditions of life."[109] While publicly prosecuting Africans through the end of the nineteenth century and well into the twentieth, colonial officials secretly depended on Trinidad's African *nations* to be self-reliant in their approaches to healthcare. In an 1891 private correspondence, one official most revealingly remarked that the "African portion of the population can take care of themselves when left alone in the woods."[110]

To Restore Any Other Person to Health:
The "Case of John Cooper, Convicted of Obeah"

In the "socio-medical landscape" of Trinidad, the "social role of punishment" for obeah took on new meaning, and some fifty-three Black Trinidadians were convicted for practicing obeah between 1868 and 1899.[111] John Cooper (Hou Quervee) and his brother, known as Mah Nannie/Robert Antoine or Papa Nanee (alternatively written as Nannee or Nanny), were two of the liberated Africans among the "4,240 African born" persons residing in Trinidad in the 1870s, and subjected under the 1868 Obeah Prohibition Ordinance, they were unfortunately brought before the colonial magistrate for allegedly engaging in illicit social and supernatural practices.[112] As discussed earlier in the chapter, living in a colonial society with inadequate sustained healthcare placed African populations in precarious and unsteady conditions. Even when medical resources were available, they were scanty and in rural areas of Trinidad largely nonexistent, leaving Africans to draw upon the medical resources and knowledge within their own communities. Laurie Jacklin explains that in the "scarcity of the GMS [Government Medical Service] resources in the rural areas," African communities consulted their local "Obeah practitioners and herbalist medicine" specialists. Citing David Trotman, she writes, "There were no doctors within ten to fifteen miles of rural areas like Moruga, LaBrea, and Toco. There were no government health services in these areas, since the health centers outside of Port-of-Spain tended to be located only in those areas where there was a heavy concentration of indentured East Indian labor," leaving Africans largely unattended.[113] Within this chasm, liberated Africans like John Cooper became valuable resources for negotiating the comprehensive challenges of physical and social health.

In the "Case of John Cooper, Convicted of Obeah," case number 5518, dated May 9, 1872, the handwritten minutes begin with the testimony of the inspector general of police, who testified that "John Cooper, a black, was entering Port of Spain about 5 a.m. on the 25th Novr., [1871] with a bundle" (see figure 4.5). According to the testimony, Cooper's "demeanor attracted the attention of a constable," and under Section 55 of the Law of 1868, Cooper was stopped "for the purpose of examining the bundle." Cooper was "taken to the station and charged with being in possession of fowls suspected to be stolen." What ensued in the record was a complex set of verbal negotiations in which Cooper sought to defend himself against an initial crime of theft. However, in doing so, his explication inadvertently entrapped him in an alleged confession to the crime of obeah. The court summary was as follows:

> Cooper proceeded to account for his possession of the fowls by stating that he had received £10 from one "Edward" and another £10 from one "John" to *work* for them in order that they might not lose their situations. "To *work* for a person" meaning, amongst the class of persons to which Cooper belongs, to practice Obeah for him. Cooper said the fowls had been used for this purpose, and gave a circumstantial account of the process. The practice of Obeah is under sec. 30 of Law 6 of 1868, an offence punishable by imprisonment and flogging. Cooper was accordingly *charged on his own statement* with the practice of Obeah.[114] (See figure 4.6.)

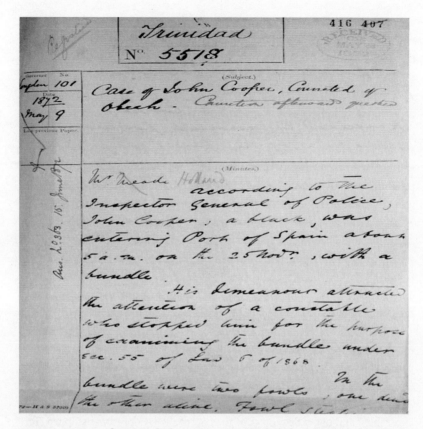

FIGURE 4.5 No. 5518, "Case of John Cooper, Convicted of Obeah," May 9, 1872. These handwritten minutes from John Cooper's case file chronicle the series of events that led to his arrest in 1871. Reprinted by permission of the National Archives of the United Kingdom, ref. CO 295/261.

When John Cooper introduced the notion of "work" in his legal statement, he was drawing upon a long lineage of African and African diasporic "health work" traditions that endured in the Americas and the Caribbean. Spiritual *work* is an indigenous designation that contributes to Africana Religious Studies an essential conceptual category. Work conceptualizes the labor of religion, a process through which ritual preparation and ritual enactment

Superstitious Devices.

Assumption of supernatural power or knowledge.

30. Every person who, by the practice of obeah or by any occult means or by any assumption of supernatural power or knowledge, shall intimidate or attempt to intimidate any person, or shall obtain or endeavour to obtain any chattel, money, or valuable security from any other person, or shall pretend to discover any lost or stolen goods, or the person who stole the same, or to inflict any disease, loss, damage, or personal injury to or upon any other person, or to restore any other person to health, and every person who shall procure, counsel, induce or persuade, or endeavour to persuade any other person to commit any such offence shall, on conviction before any Stipendiary Justice, be imprisoned with or without hard labour, for any term not exceeding six months, and if a male, may be once privately whipped during the continuance of such imprisonment, and if a female, may during such imprisonment be kept in solitary confinement not exceeding three days at any one time, and not exceeding one month in the whole, as such Justice shall direct.

Articles used in obeah and witchcraft may be seized.

31. If it shall be shewn, upon the oath of a credible witness, that there is reasonable cause to suspect that any person is in possession of any article or thing used by him, in the practice of obeah or witchcraft, it shall be lawful for any Justice of the Peace, by warrant under his hand, to cause any place whatsoever belonging to or under the control of such person, to be searched, either in the day or in the night, and if any such article shall be found in any place so searched to cause the same to be seized and brought before him or some other Justice of the Peace, who shall cause the same to be secured for the purpose of being produced in evidence in any case in which it may be required.

FIGURE 4.6 Excerpt from the 1868 Obeah prohibition ordinance detailing obeah and witchcraft offenses and the sentences associated with criminal conviction. Reprinted by permission of the Law Library, Judiciary of the Republic of Trinidad and Tobago.

operationalize a sacred economy of medicine, healing, devotion, sacrifice, and intervention. Contravening white colonial physical economies of slavery and indentureship, the "work" of African curative economies constitutes alternative labors, employments, currencies, contractual transactions, and deliverables. Thus, when John and Edward employed John Cooper "to work for them in order that they might not lose their situations," in the Africana religious universe, they were employing a person they believed to be an expert spiritual laborer to intercede on their behalf during a time of social uncertainty. Coupled with the intercessory sacrifice of the fowl in Cooper's possession, the healing intention was "to cut [the fowl's] throat and sprinkle [blood] on the ground to do good to the person who had employed [Cooper] to *work*." Cooper's African theurgical system of remedy and restoration was, nonetheless, misapprehended and relegated to the disreputable realm of colonial obeah where it was prosecutable and punishable. Despite the punitive legacy of eradicating the spiritual work of African devotees, Brent Crosson in writing about Obeah in contemporary Trinidad, still acknowledges the religious category of "work" as a necessary imperative "to balance opposing forces, decipher hidden powers, and redress problems caused by those powers."[115]

The case "was tried by William Lovesy, the new Police Magistrate," who ordered: "John Cooper of Port of Spain aforesaid Laborer is convicted before me for that he did on the 24th day of November 1871 at Cimaronero Ward and within the limits of the said Western District of the County of St. George *by the practice of Obeah*." Cooper might have been unaware that disclosing the financial transactions associated with obeah's spiritual economy would redound to his disadvantage, for "in Trinidad in the late nineteenth and in the twentieth century, money paid for the services of a ritual specialist served as the primary incrimination evidence."[116] During the trial, "questions were put to [Cooper] to which he answered, '*C'est Vrai.*' He spoke broken English and French. A Yaraba and had great difficulty in explaining himself. He is an uneducated man an African." However, the circuitous exchange where the record indicated "He said 'yes' to everything" was seemingly sufficient, as "the result left no doubt upon the magistrate's mind that the fowls had been used for the purpose of Obeah." He was judged guilty and subsequently sentenced to imprisonment "in the Royal Gaol at Port of Spain for the term of Six Calendar months with hard labor and being above sixteen years of age to receive twenty lashes with a cat-of-nine-tails."[117] However, in an unprecedented act of legal intervention, Cooper, unlike Trinidad's formerly enslaved, sought judicial and financial recourse and challenged the magistrate's ruling on appeal in 1872. In a monumental decision, the conviction was overturned, and Cooper was awarded monetary damages; furthermore, a new legal regulation regarding punishment was enacted by the governor.

Using the extensive documentation of this case, scholars can access and weave together John Cooper's presence in colonial legal history. His case was chronicled, as mentioned previously, in over eight dozen documents totaling more than hundred pages amassed from Port of Spain Police Court records: the original complaint against John Cooper (prepared by S. P. Pierre), the records of Cooper's sentencing in the Western District of the County of St. George (the Minutes of Meeting of the Court of Appeal), the correspondence between Governor James Robert Longden and the principal secretary of state for the colonies, a summary prepared by Charles Hobson on behalf of the colonial court, the Notes of Evidence of the Supreme Civil Court in Trinidad, and an appeals statement and correspondence prepared on behalf of John Cooper by R. M. Griffith, Esq. The cast of performers in this intricate legal production, which began in 1871 and lasted many months, included the plaintiff and appellant, John Cooper; the counsel for the appellant, Charles William Warner (also rendered "Warren"); Conway Lovesy, stipendiary justice of the peace of the town of Port of Spain; Chief Justice Joseph Needham; First Puisne Judge Horace Fitzgerald; Second Puisne Judge Henry Court; Michael Fitzpatrick, sergeant major of police and the respondent; Philip Pierre, clerk of the peace for Port of Spain; Charles Henry, court translator; and witnesses Edward Tanner and John Waterloo.

In April 1868, the Summary Administration of Justice Ordinance was passed, which gave the governor the power to appoint stipendiary justices of the peace who were assigned to districts and could adjudicate and determine cases.[118] In Trinidadian jurisprudence, "every Stipendiary Justice had the jurisdiction to hear and determine in a summary manner all offences that by any Ordinance that was in force then or in the future may be heard and determined before one or more Justices of the Peace."[119] This, then, was the venue in which Cooper's original trial was conducted. Upon appeal, the case was turned over to the Supreme Civil Court, whose oversight was in the hands of the chief justice and two puisne judges (judges of lesser rank).[120]

A careful read of the John Cooper case unveils at least two salient elements concerning the colonial imagination and what it determined to be accurate information on the nations of Africa, their modes of communication, and the intricacies of their religious traditions. First, European colonists throughout the British Caribbean possessed a very collapsible knowledge of African ethnicity and nationhood. Not only did they operate out of their own constructed ethno-typologies of African peoples, but they simultaneously created an array of unverifiable and stereotypical ethno-lores that were associated with categorizations such as John Cooper's supposed "Yaraba" heritage, for example.

Second, Cooper's case unmasked a complex exercise in colonial translation, exchange, and unsuccessful attempts to communicate with John Cooper through imperial languages, due to the colonial recognition of "the mixture of nationalities and languages existing in this Island." Within these official multilingual and intercultural encounters, Cooper was forced to navigate the power dynamics of Trinidad's legal system through sovereign colonial languages. However, we find only a micro-glimpse of Cooper's own linguistic proficiency and aptitude. When Cooper attempted to speak on behalf of his own defense, he most likely struggled to translate his African language of origin into colonial speech. Yet his desired statement/testimony is absent from the legal record because it was recorded as something "nobody understood." Tragically, this lack of understanding, resulting in Cooper's largely muted historical voice, proved detrimental in a rush to facile judgment concerning his guilt or innocence.

Archival silence leads to even greater speculation and ambivalence concerning the recorded veracity of Cooper's confession of obeah. In his monograph *Troubling Confessions: Speaking Guilt in Law and Literature*, Peter Brooks problematizes the act of confession in Western legal history.[121] Confession as a complex "speech act" can be "unstable and unreliable," according to Brooks, and cannot be disconnected from its complicated sources of "self-incrimination," coercive interrogative motives and torturous practices, or performative narration in a discursive space where confessions "cohabit with both truth and lie."[122] Upon closer scrutiny, we discover that Cooper's alleged voluntary plea of "guilty" was admittedly not rendered "using that word but by repeating in French and in English—'c'est vrai, c'est vrai—it is true, it is true.'" What then ensued was an act of hermeneutical maneuvering in that "the interpreter in his evidence before The Court of Appeal says *he* interpreted these words as meaning '*guilty*.'" More specifically, in the translator's own words, "I translated to the Magistrate 'C'est Vrai.' It is true. I translated 'It is true' as meaning Guilty. *He did not say Guilty; that was not what he said*. He said he had received ten dollars to work *Sorcier* for the Overseer."[123]

Cooper's trial lasted "about half an hour," and "there was no other evidence given. No other Witnesses called"; nor did the translator recollect "any Caution being given by the Magistrate of Police." Analyzing the symbiotic relationship between confession and interrogation, Brooks argues that in most cases the "interrogator maintains control of the storytelling, so that the suspect is put in a position of denying or affirming" (i.e., Cooper's "C'est vrai"), "often affirming through denials that lead to entrapment—the unfolding narrative that . . . is largely the interrogator's own making, his 'monologue.'"[124] Therefore, as was possibly the case for John Cooper and his colonial interrogators, "controlling an interrogation in this sense means *imposing* a controlling narrative."[125]

Brooks's hypothesis of competing and controlling narratives complicates the lenses through which to interpret John Cooper's case. For example, during the appeal, the clerk of the police of Port of Spain, upon cross-examination, revealed that "the Appellant did not seem to understand the charge and he was asked to plead Guilty or Not. He did not appear to understand these words and I explained these to him and he said it is true." The initial case, tragically, ended with great uncertainty as to Cooper's proven guilt or comprehended confession. He was kept imprisoned and, in what appeared to be a rush to administer corporal punishment, was flogged with a cat-o'-nine-tails (designed to inflict multiple wounds simultaneously, leaving deep lacerations) for the full twenty lashes "before the time allowed for appealing expired." With the help of friends from Laventille (located in nearby East Port of Spain), an attorney was retained and Cooper was eventually released pending an appeals hearing. Floggings like Cooper's remained a corporal penalty in Trinidad in the postslavery period, as in other British colonies. Obeah was included among the criminal offenses punishable by physical lashes.[126] Thomas Sealy, the superintendent of prisons in the 1870s, reported to the Colonial Office similar punishments of individuals "Practising Obeah" and recorded fourteen other instances of one to six months imprisonment and twelve to thirty-six lashes. Comparably, in British Jamaica, flogging in the 1850s and 1860s had grown increasingly associated with sexual offenses. With reference to race and flogging, Diana Paton cites editorials of the day which favored flogging penalties specifically for African-descended communities, in the belief that "it was necessary because the prevalence of sexual and violent crimes demonstrated that 'Afric's sons and daughters,' are in a fair way of relapsing into their 'original state of barbarism;'" this reinforced prior arguments from slavery that Africans "ought to be dealt with as brutes are, and flogged into tameness and submission."[127]

Filed December 4, 1871, in the Supreme Civil Court of Trinidad by solicitor William Griffith, "the Humble Petition of John Cooper of the Ward of Laventille in the Island of Trinidad" sought to carefully redress two procedural lapses and omissions committed by the magistrate court in the original trial. First, John Cooper had been "aggrieved by a certain Conviction under the hand of Conway Whitbourne Lovesy Esquire Stipendiary Justice of the Police . . . alleged . . . by the practice of Obeah obtained from one Edward the sum of Ten Dollars in money contrary to the laws, and the conviction was made without any information in writing." Second, it was argued that "such conviction was made without any evidence having been given of the Committal by the said John Cooper of the offence mentioned in such conviction." The formal appeal concluded, "I do intend to prosecute the said Appeal at the sittings of the said Court to be holden at the Court House in the Town of Port of Spain on Tuesday the second day of January next" and "that the said John Cooper is not guilty of the offence mentioned in the said conviction." The appeal was signed "John Cooper by Wm. M. Griffith his Solicitor."

On procedural grounds, it appeared from the minutes that in Cooper's original trial, there was much vagueness as to whether or not Cooper fully comprehended the criminal charge levied against him and the consequences of the subsequent plea he was asked to render. In addition, there was sufficient evidence to conclude that a legal caution was not extended to Cooper that would have warned him of the consequences of speaking and advised him that he could remain silent. There was also no "information signed by the party charging" that would have lawfully served as the equivalent of the required legal indictment. The sergeant major dismissed this oversight with the casual remark, "But Obeah cases are so rare that we do not usually take informations." Moreover, several items of Cooper's personal property were prematurely confiscated while "he was not sworn" and were subsequently being used to substantiate the charge.

During the appeal, the burden fell on the stipendiary justice of the peace and the sergeant major of police to prove and sustain a charge of obeah against John Cooper and to justify executing his additional sentence of six months' imprisonment. Aware of the rules of evidence regarding criminal trials for obeah, Governor Longden admitted "the difficulty of obtaining evidence against Obeah men."[128] In Cooper's case, the two men who purportedly paid him to do spiritual work on their behalf provided testimonies that muddied both their culpability and Cooper's credibility. One witness, Edwards, a baker from St. Joseph, flatly "denied having 'paid Cooper any money to keep him in his place'" of employment, but said he gave him "Twenty-two dollars" as "payment for work done in cutting Wood and cleaning Cocoa. . . . I paid him on the same Friday he came to town." Edwards stated on the day he "paid him the money he was talking nonsense and acting foolishly," so he "sent for James [John] Waterloo a friend of Cooper." According to Edwards, "I do not understand his [Cooper's] language" and "used to converse with him by signs" he noted, "it was through Waterloo's interpretation I knew . . . Cooper said that his child was dying." When Edwards was asked direct questions regarding Cooper's practice of obeah, he stated unequivocally, "I never gave any information to the Police of Cooper having practiced Obeah. . . . I made no charge against Cooper. I never knew Cooper to practice Obeah." Under sworn testimony Waterloo, a Barbadian, stated that Cooper was "first in my care in the year 1860," "he was under my charge," and speaks "broken English, French a very little." Waterloo corroborated the story that "that day Cooper's head was not right" and that he "appeared to have been drinking," yet testified, "I know him intimately. He is a hard working man," Contradicting the allegations of Cooper as an inebriate was the testimony of Philip Pierre, clerk of the peace for Port of Spain, "who was present when the charge was heard" and said that "at the time of the trial he did not appear to be on liquor."

Within this arena of regulated self-disclosure and performed protection, veracity and facticity become elusive. As in similar cases of obeah throughout the British West Indies, those who were often named as clients and called to testify against an alleged obeah practitioner very rarely offered corroborating evidence to substantiate the colonial criminal charge. Confessing his own frustration with the challenges of witnesses, the governor said:

> It is not the least pernicious part of the superstition that the very persons who need protection against the Obeahman are themselves afraid to give true evidence, and every acquittal of an Obeahman is attributed to the power of his Obeah. It would be vain to hope for the absolute suppression of Obeah by legislation,—religion has hitherto failed to overcome it,—and a long time must necessarily elapse before it banishes with the spread of education.

In this particular case, both testimonies proved ineffective in providing evidentiary leverage against Cooper as an obeahman.

Noteworthy in these proceedings was the sergeant major of police's attempt to connect Cooper historically to the liberated Africans who had arrived in Trinidad only decades earlier and to link Cooper spiritually to a wider genealogy of obeah originating in Africa. According to the sergeant major's testimony, "It appears that he was brought to the Colony with his father from Africa in 1860; that his father practiced Obeah, and that he himself is looked upon by his countrymen as an Obeahman." Furthermore, in the "Minute Paper," the magistrate of police's narratology stated: Cooper "is looked upon by his countrymen as an Obeah man and that his father before him exercised the same trade." These brief entries in the historical record are the closest we get to biographical information on Cooper.

Africa in this context symbolized religious lineage and supernatural primordialism. Cooper's affiliations with Trinidad's Rada community of liberated Africans, identified as "his countrymen," reinforced the sergeant major's ideation regarding the foreignness and importability of obeah and Cooper's guilt. According to his testimony, it was "difficult to suppose that

Cooper was entirely innocent of the offence laid to his charge." However, without corroborating evidence and definitive witnesses, unsubstantiated anecdotal speculation was not enough to sustain the charge of obeah against Cooper. Therefore, the Supreme Civil Court "adjudged . . . that the conviction and order be and the same is hereby reversed and quashed and that the said Appellant John Cooper to have his costs of such appeal as against the said Respondent Michael Fitzpatrick." This landmark ruling was a legal milestone for former slave colonies of Britain. For Africans in Trinidad whose social lineage was connected to recaptivity and indentureship, the public victory of John Cooper, a nonliterate liberated African, over Michael Fitzpatrick, the sergeant major of police, marked a momentary rupture in colonial configurations of power (see figure 4.7).

When the *Trinidad Chronicle* of April 9, 1872, printed the proceedings of the Meeting of the Court of Appeal of March 21, 1872, Cooper's attorney, Charles Warren, strategically labeled the appeal a "novel case," of which he was "somewhat embarrassed as to the mode of procedures," and he would be "sorry if the case should go abroad [England] to be taken as a type of the administration of justice in Trinidad. Here is a man of the humbler walks of life—a fact that ought not to weigh against his receiving equal justice with Her Majesty's subjects of greater consideration."

Viewing this case as an exception and its legal proceedings as "most irregular," Warren implored the court, "For the honor of the Queen and the laws of the colony, I hope this will be the last case of the kind to come before the Court." He persuasively argued that Cooper had been "irregularly judged" and "certain answers which the Appellant made to questions most improperly put" were erroneously "considered as a confession." He argued that Cooper had been found guilty under an ordinance "of 186[8], founded on the old obsolete statutes of King James against witchcraft practices which are now almost unknown." Moreover, the initial charge of "practicing Obeah" was substantiated even "without any overt act to constitute the offence being shewn." Most pointedly concerning recompense, Warren insisted he would "take every opportunity, and use my utmost efforts to bring this matter to the notice of the proper authorities, so as to procure adequate compensation for the unfortunate man."

Thus, within the context of the Atlantic world, where African materiality was historically the object of currency and wealth, Cooper's case proved momentous in the sense that it documented the rare moment that a person of African descent had a conviction overturned by the Supreme Civil Court and was subsequently awarded (modest) monetary damages. Successful appeals

ADJOURNED MEETING OF THE COURT OF APPEAL
On 21st March, 1872.

Before

His Honor J. Needham, Chief Justice.

   „   „   H. Fitzgerald, 1st Puisne Judge.

   „   „   H. Court,   2nd „   „

Cooper, *Appellant.*

Fitzpatrick, *Respondent.*

The Chief Justice enquired how far the proceedings had reached, as it seemed the matter
had been before the Court already.

Mr. Warner stated, that he appeared for the
Appellant, that some argument had taken place
in the absence of the Chief Justice, but no decision had been given; he wished to produce some
witnesses whose examination was necessary on
the part of the Appellant.

Attorney-General.—The Appellant in the Court
below had pleaded guilty; and the depositions
put in will prove the case for the Respondent;
the conviction followed as a matter of course on
the confession of guilt.

Mr. Warner.—What is recorded as a plea of
"guilty" was not so. Certain answers which the
Appellant made to questions most improperly
put, were considered as a confession, but he was
in a position to disprove all that is alleged in
the depositions.

C. Justice.—Then you desire to withdraw the
plea and to have the case reheard on the merits.

Attorney General.—This is the first intimation I have received in this matter as to the proceedings to be taken.

C. Justice.—We will hear the case on its
merits. The onus is shifted.

Mr. Warner.—I propose to examine Mr. Scott.

H. P. Scott, sworn.—I act as Interpreter in
the Police Court in Port-of-Spain; I acted so in
a case against Cooper, the Appellant, on a charge
of obeah; the charge was read over to him. He
made a statement in answer to a question. The
Respondent, Serjeant-Major Fitzpatrick, questioned him.

FIGURE 4.7 Court document identifying John Cooper as the petitioner in his case before the Supreme Civil Court of Appeal. Cooper sued for damages and filed an appeal to overturn his 1871 conviction under the 1868 obeah prohibition ordinance. He was exonerated, his conviction was quashed, and he was awarded a financial settlement in 1872. Reprinted by permission of the National Archives of the United Kingdom, ref. CO 295/261.

of obeah cases such as Cooper's had a detrimental effect upon the social cred- ibility of civil authorities. According to Paton, "Magistrates . . . emphasized the significance of obeah convictions as a sign that state power was stronger than the power of obeah. They enjoyed pointing out that a successful pros- ecution for obeah revealed that the defendant was not, despite what he or she claimed, able to determine [through the use of obeah] the outcome of court cases."[129]

Connected with the overturned conviction was the ensuing ruling on remuneration. Because Cooper had endured twenty lashes with the cat-o'- nine-tails, and because the timing of the punishment was illegal, monetary restitution was being sought in the "sum of Five Hundred Dollars." Awarding only a fraction of this, the final ruling reported:

> His Excellency the Governor declined to grant to your Petitioner more
> than a sum of fifty pounds sterling. Your Petitioner refuses to accept this
> sum as being a most inadequate compensation whether measured by your
> Petitioners sufferings or by the dignity of the Crown. Your petitioner be-
> lieves that a Jury, . . . would award to Your Petitioner a far larger sum by
> way of damages than the amount which he is willing to accept.

Governor Longden "felt it incumbent on him to offer Cooper [£]50 compen- sation for the flogging . . . and the Gov. does not feel justified in offering him more than [£]50." For the governor, fifty pounds sterling (the equivalent of approximately $243US at the time) seemed "ample compensation for the flogging," and even though it was substantially lower than what Cooper had requested, it symbolically marked an exceptional moment in Obeah legal history of authorized colonial reparation. Equally monumental was the im- pact of John Cooper's appeal on Trinidadian legislation. In the May 9, 1872 dispatch which declared John Cooper's "conviction afterwards quashed," Governor Longden also amended the statute on corporal punishment and declared, "In order to prevent any possibility of any man being flogged in future under a sentence which may afterwards be reversed, I have issued orders to the Superintendent of Prisons that the punishment of flogging, when ordered by a stipendiary justice or other magistrate. . . . is not to be inflicted until after the time limited for appealing against the sentence has expired nor of course if an appeal be lodged."[130]

In establishing a legal atmosphere around the case, Chief Justice Joseph Needham early on recognized, "this is an exceptional case. Let us hear every- thing that can be said." He remarked of Trinidad that "formalities are much more fully and strictly carried out here than anywhere within [his] experience," the actual proceedings of the John Cooper case rendered this assessment less convincing. For example, in the appeals process, the police magistrate (Lovesy) stated he had a "distinct recollection" of the charge "being explained to Cooper" and had "not a shadow of a doubt that he perfectly understood the nature of the proceedings" and the consequences of Cooper's presumed plea of guilty. According to the record, Cooper, the "Defendant who pleads Guilty to the charge" had "expressed a wish to make a statement." Yet the content of Cooper's statement remains undocumented and undeciphered. What was recorded was that "Cooper first made a statement which nobody understood," that the "Magistrate did not understand what the prisoner meant," that Cooper "spoke very indistinctly," and that an interpreter was needed. With his statement inaccessible and in an effort to achieve clarity, a series of questions was posed to Cooper by Sergeant Major Fitzpatrick and translated by Charles Henry; it was revealed that "he made a statement in answer to questions" and "did not make a continuous statement." What the transcript plausibly intimates is that among the liberated African nations in Trinidad, African languages persisted alongside the colonial lingua franca.

Firsthand accounts offer evidence of African linguistic endurance over a decade later. Printed in the *San Fernando Gazette* was a lecture delivered by A. R. Gray in Edinburgh on March 11, 1882. Gray had been educated at the Edinburgh Institute and his name is found on Colonial Office lists as having held several posts in Trinidad from the 1850s to the 1880s.[131] The lecture, entitled "Ways and Customs of Trinidad," detailed Alexis de Tocqueville–like impressions of his experiences in the colony living among populations of the "Chinaman," "negro or African," "Aborigines" or "Red Indian," and "coolies" from "Hindostan." He maintains that the presence of these people groups in combination with European diversity meant that the "natives of the soil of to-day possess a very conglomerate language known as Creole-French. It has a framework of pure French, and the spaces in this are filled in by words borrowed from English, Spanish, Indian, and African dialects." After detailing his impressions of the "Chinaman," Gray informs his audience that "Trinidad can show you many genera of negroes." According to Gray, there is the "true African" and the "emancipated slaves," and among the former, Trinidad has "Africans from all parts of that wonderful continent, differing as much from one another in appearance and language as an Englishman differs from a Frenchman."[132]

According to Gray, in 1880s Trinidad "there is the tall Houssa, of which the West India regiments are largely composed; there is the Yarouba, tall and tattooed; there is the Ibo; the Rada, or natives from Dahomey; the short Congo from the mouth of the river of that name; the Canga, and others, all speaking their own language and preserving intact some of the customs of their mother country." Gray goes on to proclaim to his audience that it is in Trinidad where "we can study some of the tribes, their languages and customs; and we have no difficulty in finding Houssas, Yaroubas, and Congoes; but others like the Ibos are rare." To further demonstrate his point about the proliferation of diverse African populations in Trinidad and their preponderance of diverse customs of languages, Gray ultimately holds up the Rada community in Belmont, of which Cooper is a member, as an example of Trinidad's enduring African linguistic and cultural presence. Gray states, "The Radas, seem after the emancipation to have congregated together, for there is a large village composed of this people in a part of the island." More specifically, he concludes that Belmont is "where they celebrate their heathen rites, and practice their witchcraft, or Obeah, and where, . . . they once a year have a mysterious dance round a huge sheet dipped in the blood of the sacrifices, and which no outsider is allowed to see."

It is distinctly clear within the deliberations of the Trinidad Supreme Civil Court of Appeal that while the practice of obeah was considered a felonious crime necessitating severe penalties of corporal punishment and imprisonment, the deeper meaning of Obeah's theurgical, divinatory, sacrificial, and healing practices remained largely incomprehensible to the judicial order. For example, upon hearing a series of statements and cross-examinations, Chief Justice Joseph Needham, a recent arrival from England, interjected, "I confess that I am very anxious to know what Obeah is, it is not anywhere explained in the Statute." In response, the attorney general informed him that it was explained in Ordinance No. 6 of 1868. Warner, Cooper's attorney, then strategically exploited Needham's unfamiliarity and ignorance to lighten and reframe the moment through humor: "The unfortunate prisoner's offence seems to have been the bottle of rum and because he had a bottle of rum, the Police concluded he must have been a conjuror. Tried and condemned, like poor Stephano in the 'Tempest' only on the evidence of a bottle of rum!" This remark was reported in the record as having been followed with laughter. In many respects, John Cooper's case was a source of social and spiritual relief in rendering African Obeah nonthreatening to the colonial order as well as nonpolluting to Trinidad's more recent inhabitants of Asian immigrants. Within the colonial record detailing John Cooper's case, Governor Longden concluded his summary report of John Cooper's appeal indicating he was pleased with the "fortunate circumstance that the Obeah superstition does not appear to have any effect upon either Coolies or Chinese," and he was confident in the future that "as the population of Asiatic origin increases yearly in number, while the number of Africans, being no longer recruited from Africa, constantly diminishes, it may be hoped that the superstition will gradually die away." Perhaps this aspect of the deliberations foreshadowed the levity that, along with exchanges of gravitas, characterized controversial parliamentary debates on a bill designed to repeal anti-obeah laws in Trinidad and Tobago in early 2000. More than 130 years would pass before Yoruba-Orisa (and Spiritual Baptist) activists would win the battle to nullify the laws that trapped and terrorized John Cooper in 1871.[133]

"To Protect Himself": John Cooper and the Material World of Obeah

Given the juxtaposition of the court's laughter and the new chief justice's anxiety, it was apparent in John Cooper's case that the colonial legal system largely interpreted Obeah as self-imposed ignorance. The elaborate set of spiritual technologies, body of material culture, and extensive botanic epistemologies that constituted African religious practices (Obeah) was perpetually illegible to the chief justice and other custodians of the cult of obeah fixation. It is evident in John Cooper's case that the colonial juridical understanding of Obeah was as superstitious lore with felonious linkages to fraud, not as sacred mystical technologies that protected, healed, and provided a service of efficacious "work," as John Cooper sought to explain. In the minutes of John Cooper's case, it was straightforwardly admitted that both the attorney general and the chief justice "treated the idea of the practice of Obeah with contempt." It was concluded that "Obeah is of course nonsense," while the minutes openly acknowledged that "the belief in it, the fear of it, and the extortion to which these give rise, are only too real amongst the Negroes." According to historian Vincent Brown, "Whites generally mischaracterized Obeah as simple witchcraft, thus failing to see its larger role in social and spiritual healing and protection."[134]

The repertoire of items confiscated from John Cooper included a hen, a cock, a package of powder, a parcel of powder, a bottle of rum, a bottle of sweet oil, shells, a bone, and ten dollars. These seized material artifacts are spiritual and material texts that spoke to an intricate tapestry of religious meaning and African medical technology. These medicinal items collectively constituted for Cooper an assortment of tools and ingredients for spiritual work. As indicated in the court proceedings, "the articles and money found on [Cooper] were" entered into evidence. "They were produced by Fitzpatrick before the conviction—he stated he found them on the prisoner, but he was not sworn." Upon interrogation about these sundry artifacts, he offered the following responses regarding the efficacy and cosmology of African practices of healing and protection:

> He was asked what the package of powder found on him was for; he said, to protect himself. He had a cock; he said he would cut its throat, and sprinkle the blood on the ground to do good for the person who employed him [to perform spiritual work]. The overseer wanted to keep his situation.[135]

The historical record does not indicate that John Cooper was further interrogated as to what it meant to "protect himself." However, Cooper's response to the question about the powder is revealing: "he said it was to keep his head from swelling. There was another Powder which he said was to prevent harm to him when he walked." Cooper also had "the bone of a Deer which he said was to protect himself." We are only made aware from Cooper's recorded statement that the "package of powder" would be used as a prophylactic, and so we are left to speculate as to whether this protection would be physical or spiritual and whether it would be applied topically, ingested, or used as a ritual element.

Also worth noting is that Cooper's arrest and appeal directly correspond with what one historian calls "the great pandemic of 1871–2" of Trinidad in which "terrible ravages of smallpox" were experienced throughout the island.[136] As Cooper worked to protect himself, he would have done so in the midst of a pandemic where medical practitioners were scarce, knowledge of the disease's symptomology was limited, and the "haemorrhagic forms of smallpox" were prevalent.[137] We can only speculate that both physical and spiritual fortification would have been necessary on an island that experienced more than 12,000 smallpox infections and well over 2,000 deaths, affecting every community, including those of Africans. Unwilling to misidentify himself that he was an obeah man, Cooper nonetheless professed the skills and instrumentality to "protect himself" against the backdrop of a health pandemic. The brief intimation about a child who was dying is never revisited and again, we only have to speculate what spiritual role Cooper was to play in healing affliction and prolonging life.

As a liberated African, John Cooper found himself among those overly represented as defendants in late nineteenth-century obeah cases. It was widely believed among colonial officials, including Governor Longden, that the spiritual malignancy of obeah was directly linked to native-born Africans (see figure 4.8). Even Cooper's identification as a "Yaraba," strongly reinforced existing colonial

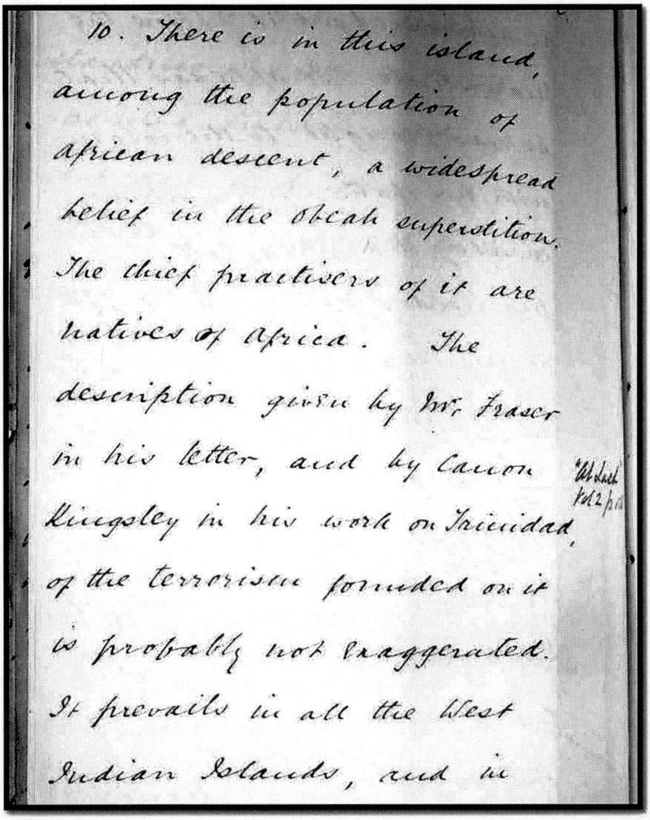
10. There is in this island,
among the population of
african descent, a widespread
belief in the Obeah superstition.
The chief practisers of it are
natives of Africa. The
description given by Mr Fraser
in his letter, and by Canon
Kingsley in his work on Trinidad,
of the terrorism founded on it
is probably not exaggerated.
It prevails in all the West
Indian Islands, and in

FIGURE 4.8 Correspondence from Sir James Robert Longden, governor of Trinidad from 1870–1874, on May 9, 1872. Colonial Office and Predecessors: Trinidad Original Correspondence, Correspondence, Original, Secretary of State. Despatches. Reprinted by permission of The National Archives (of the United Kingdom) Kew—Colonial Office, Commonwealth and Foreign and Commonwealth Offices 01 April 1872–31 May 1872, ref. CO 295/261.

typecasting. Colonial officials had no real reference or vocabulary to catalogue the range of African religious practices being performed; therefore, the totalizing supernatural concept of obeah continued to predominate in the legal sphere, with native Africans as the prime suspects. Within Trinidad's legal history, the colonial documents on John Cooper's case and those of his brother, Mah Nannie, a decade later must be scrutinized not as "an Obeah as practiced by Caribbeans" but as "Obeah as fantasized by white observers."[138]

"500 Obeah Men on This Island": Obeah and the Case of Mah Nannie

In the late 1880s, the *New York Times* reported the presence of "500 'Obeah men' on this island [Trinidad], to whom the other colored people go for assistance and advice."[139] Among those sought out for "assistance and advice" were John Cooper and his brother Mah Nannie. The latter half of the 1870s and the early 1880s saw four governors pass through the colony: Herbert Taylor Ussher (1872–1875), Robert William Harley (1875–1877), Augustus Frederick Gore (1877–1880), and Edward Laborde (1880–1882). Under each of them, there were documented police raids "among the Belmont Radas," who were believed to be "of the fetish persuasion."[140]

Stories of raids and seizures in the late 1870s and 1880s appeared alongside local newspaper accounts of violent crimes and abductions allegedly associated with the ritual practice of obeah. For example, on Prince Street, obeah was blamed for the stealing of a young boy "for the murderous purpose of the obeah-men"; a "murdered female child" was found near Piccadilly Quarry "with the heart cut out"; and a "coolie girl" was found by the San Juan railway station "with the heart cut out" and "the addition of the fingers being chopped off." All of these crimes were suspected to be obeah-related. After reporting the arrest of an unnamed suspect accused of one of these crimes, the article stated that "a great deal too much credence, deference and fear is yet shewn by the ignorant towards the miserable practisers of Obeahism. . . . The law against obeah is clear and strong, and it is most desirable the police should make every effort to bring to justice the perpetrators of those atrocities and source of so much terror and misery." Obeah's crimes, the article concluded, lingered "chiefly among the Africans and their descendants who have not been brought under the influence of the clergy and teacher, but it is not confined to them. We have known a fellow, generally quiet and seemingly harmless, a black man from one of the French Islands who had some knowledge of herbs and simples, and made up *remedes* for the poor about him, for a consideration,—who on the strength of a sojourn in France when young was presumed to be possessed of more intelligence than his fellows, but who proved to be a thief and a vagabond and was found to be practising obeah."[141] With exception, Obeah was understood as a spiritual predator unleashing bewitchment and sorcery among the untutored and less educated, making them easy victims to obeah's deception, trickery, and deceit, and posing challenges to Christianizing and civilizing efforts. Civil authorities viewed John Cooper and Mah Nannie's compound as a major epicenter of obeah activity in Trinidad.

In A. R. Gray's aforementioned published lecture, he locates the "large village" of African-born Radas in Belmont and associates it with witchcraft, obeah, mysterious dances, and secret rituals of blood sacrifices. Cooper was a member of this community, and his African-born brother Mah Nannie was similarly charged with obeah in the 1880s. (Their brother, Mah Dosou, also had obeah-related encounters with the colonial authorities.) In his 1953 study, "A Rada Community in Trinidad," anthropologist Andrew Carr records that in the 1870s, Belmont was not an exclusive community of West African Radas. As a Fulbright scholar in 1953, Carr had the opportunity to travel to Northwestern University and work with leading anthropologist Melville Herskovits.[142] According to Carr's study, the Radas were co-settlers among Mandingo, Congo, Ibo, and Yoruba populations.[143] The founding of one of the two publicly known Belmont Rada compounds was attributed to Mah Nannie or Papa Nanee, who was born Abojevi Zahwenu around 1800 in the Kingdom of Whydah in Dahomey. He was captured and subsequently indentured in the mid-1850s on an estate in Trinidad near St. Joseph; in July 1868 he purchased and took up residence on three-fifths of an acre in Belmont, in the district of Laventille.[144] According to Carr, "The compound began with one house built on the land to accommodate a small family; a chapel or voudunkwe (house of the gods), and a tent or covered shed adjoining the house on its southern side, and facing the road."[145] Mah Nannie was said to be "a member of the priestly caste" and a skilled diviner, herbalist, and medicine man who led Rada rituals and co-led large ceremonies of "combined followers" with "the Yorubas whose settlement lay about a mile away."[146]

The Belmont Rada community was the target of consistent harassment from the local police. In the criminal case of Mah Nannie, the police exercised surveillance, used informants, and deployed entrapment strategies over a period of nine years in order to apprehend him.[147] "The Police, it appeared had watched him closely but had been unable to detect him." Sergeant Mc-Collin testified that "he had known the prisoner for nine years, and that he had always heard his name mentioned as one who practised obeah. He tried his utmost to detect him, but had always been unsuccessful."[148] Repeated failure, however, did not preclude the sergeant and civil authorities from making continued attempts and eventually instigating a calculated plan to indict Mah Nannie.

Entrapment was a consistently used, yet contested, approach to seizing alleged obeah offenders. It was a risky maneuver because it could potentially backfire upon appeal as an illegal tactic, as was the circumstance with Mah Nannie. Well into the twentieth century, Trinidad's civil authorities believed "it almost always necessary to employ 'Police Spies' in order to detect & prosecute to conviction persons charged with the practices of Obeah," as Diana Paton's archival investigations reveal.[149] Colonial police relied heavily upon collusion with locals willing to be used or compensated for their role in entrapment schemes and in the confiscation of items that would be exhibited as material evidence of obeah during public hearings of accused defendants.

As noted previously, by the late nineteenth century obeah had evolved in the law from offenses of sorcery and poisoning during the period of slavery into deceitful schemes of fraud, deception, and pretext of possessing supernatural power that targeted the feebleminded and uneducated. But the "medico-legal" repression of liberated Africans persisted. Obeah's curative practices were on display in the courts as police and prosecutors attempted to engage in colonial translations of African religions and pharmacopeias. Against this backdrop, in September 1886, Mah Nannie from the Belmont community was charged with the crime of obeah. Mah Nannie's case paralleled John Cooper's in his initial conviction and its eventual overturn on appeal, much to the dismay and vexation of the police magistrate, the colony's clergy, and Trinidad's ruling elite. Details of Mah Nannie's original conviction and subsequent appeal were publicized in the Port of Spain Gazette in at least four different articles in 1886: "Prosecution of an African for Obeah," "The Appeal of Mah-Nannie, the Belmont Obeah-Man, and Quashing of the Magistrate's Conviction," "Mah-Nannie, the Obeah-Man," and "Scotched but Not Killed"[150] (see figure 4.9).

Unlike the circumstances that had led to the initial conviction of John Cooper, the charges against Mah Nannie were preceded by an elaborate plan of entrapment devised by the Trinidadian police in collusion with the Catholic clergy and fellow Africans identified in the colonial record as "police assistant" or "informant." One of these was an African "informant" named Anson, who was known to the police and had previously been used in prosecutions, such as the case of a Chinese man charged with the practice of Whe, the Chinese numbers game played with marks and bets, linked to esoteric dreams, and deemed illegal in Trinidad. The scheme began with Anson the informant bringing another man to Mah Nannie one evening under the pretense that he had "cut a man in Chaguanas, and he wishes you to prevent that man charging him in the Chaguanas Police Court." Mah Nannie agreed to help. The Obeah Prohibition Ordinance of 1868 criminalized anyone who "intimidates or attempts to intimidate any person, or obtains or endeavours to obtain any chattel, money or valuable security from any other person," or "who procures, counsels, induces, or persuades or endeavours to persuade any other person to commit any such offence" while claiming use of "an occult means or . . . assumption of supernatural power or knowledge."[151] According to the record, Mah Nannie allegedly set a fee of twelve dollars and when informed that "the parties had only brought eleven shillings, told them to go away." Instead of the informant returning with the twelve dollars, Sergeant Black arrived around 9 or 10 p.m. with a warrant, Constable Henry, and a Catholic priest, Père François, in order to search the premises of the Belmont

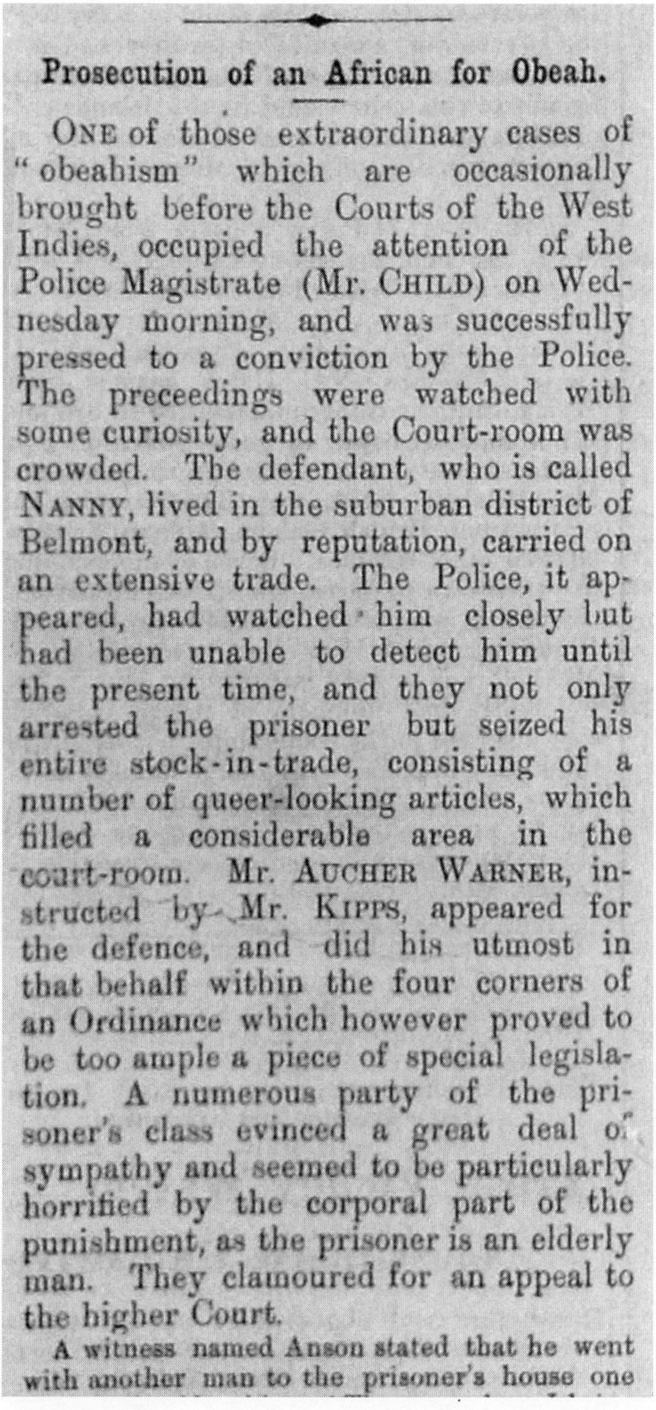

Prosecution of an African for Obeah.

ONE of those extraordinary cases of "obeahism" which are occasionally brought before the Courts of the West Indies, occupied the attention of the Police Magistrate (Mr. CHILD) on Wednesday morning, and was successfully pressed to a conviction by the Police. The preceedings were watched with some curiosity, and the Court-room was crowded. The defendant, who is called NANNY, lived in the suburban district of Belmont, and by reputation, carried on an extensive trade. The Police, it appeared, had watched him closely but had been unable to detect him until the present time, and they not only arrested the prisoner but seized his entire stock-in-trade, consisting of a number of queer-looking articles, which filled a considerable area in the court-room. Mr. AUCHER WARNER, instructed by Mr. KIPPS, appeared for the defence, and did his utmost in that behalf within the four corners of an Ordinance which however proved to be too ample a piece of special legislation. A numerous party of the prisoner's class evinced a great deal of sympathy and seemed to be particularly horrified by the corporal part of the punishment, as the prisoner is an elderly man. They clamoured for an appeal to the higher Court.

A witness named Anson stated that he went with another man to the prisoner's house one

FIGURE 4.9 A *Port of Spain Gazette* article announcing the arrest, seizure of spiritual items, and conviction of Mah Nannie on the criminal charge of obeah. Printed in the *Port of Spain Gazette*, September 11, 1886. Reprinted by permission of the National Archives of Trinidad and Tobago.

compound. Mah Nannie responded "no" in English to the constable's question as to whether he had "anything at all concerning obeah." The *Port of Spain Gazette* also recorded Nannie's firm declaration of his innocence in French patois: "'*Portez l'argent, mon pas connaitre rien comme ca,*' &c." indicating that he did not know anything about carrying (taking/receiving) any money.

What would eventually become material evidence against Mah Nannie were items confiscated from a locked room in his compound that the police forcibly entered. Mah Nannie's immediate response was to avoid confiscation by attempting to explain to the officers the religious significance of the material items. But his attempts were futile. It did not matter to the police when Mah Nannie said it "was the food for the gods . . . to eat" and admonished them, "Don't touch them, this is food for the gods" and "the gods were the two images produced." The "Trinidadiana" section of the *Trinidad Guardian* reported on the "seizure of the gods"—clay pots that later would be used as physical evidence against Mah Nannie. In seizing the various items of Africana spiritual-material culture, the police and priest believed that "this good work will break down the faith in the African Baal." Commandeered items included "small smooth stones" called "brimstone" that were "sprinkled with Sulphur." Other items confiscated included the "skin of a snake," "some stuff resembling dirt," "Guinea pepper," a "ram-goat's head," "some earth made up like pudding with wooden pins stuck in it, and glass articles resembling a druggist's scales, the globes at both ends of which contained coloured liquid." The print media characterized the Rada priests in Belmont as the "obeah gentry" and described them during the raid as "rather crestfallen at Père François's seizure of their gods, but clay is plenty, and they have a few posts left, with rudely-carved heads, fitted with glass eyes, real wool, teeth, &c.—in a close hut, locked against gentile intrusion, ready for the next great rite."[152]

Within this elaborate scheme of entrapment, witnesses such as Anson, Clarke, Louis Monroe, and Peter David (all identified as "African" in the court records) were called to testify that Mah Nannie was indeed a practitioner of obeah who claimed supernatural and divinatory powers and who charged monetary fees for perpetrating such fraud. Although they were witnesses for the prosecution, under intensive questioning each informant became hesitant and uncertain. When asked about the paraphernalia found in the locked room, Clarke responded, "I don't know if those articles are used in the practice of obeah."

Likewise, Louis Monroe became vague and pretended not to understand when queried, "Have you ever consulted this man when you were in difficulty?" Offering a confounding response, he testified before the court,

"I never gave him any advice," and further noted that Mah Nannie made "his living" through proceeds from "his garden." When Monroe was asked whether or not he frequented Mah Nannie's chapel he responded yes, but added, "We don't go there in the night." And because the charges of fraud were based largely upon evidence of extorting money, Monroe was asked, "Do you ever pay any money to the chapel?" Monroe responded in the affirmative but added that Nannie simply put the money along with his "paper" in the chapel and that Nannie "takes care" of the money "deposited with him." The defense then shifted the questioning away from fraud and into African customary practices. When asked, "Is that the custom with the Africans, that they deposit their money with an old friend of theirs," Monroe confirmed this custom, stating, "That is my country fashion; when I have money I don't give every body, I give him the money to keep in the chapel," and concluding that "a great many Africans there do that."

The testimonies of liberated Africans in Mah Nannie's case offer a glimpse into the interior world of Trinidad's Rada community. Unintelligible to the white colonists was how centrally Mah Nannie and the chapel functioned as an important nexus of Rada religious life, practice, and social organization. Mah Nannie and his followers provided compelling insight into the religious dimensions of African healing as well as the endurance of indigenous African banking systems, something invisible to those wielding colonial power.[153] Mah Nannie was a priest who healed and prayed for the sick in the community in the chapel while at the same time was a banker who utilized the chapel as a spiritual vault to secure the community's finances. Questions asked in court to elicit evidence to further incriminate Mah Nannie inadvertently revealed the phenomenon of spiritual centers simultaneously functioning as mutual aid societies and support systems, something found throughout the African diaspora.

When the interrogation turned to exploring the physical evidence against Mah Nannie, quite revealing among the material culture items was a "box with papers" that included "summons[es]" for others who might have been Nannie's clients as well as over two dozen names of magistrates, judges, and chief justices who may have authorized the summonses: Chief Justice Needham, Judge Fitzgerald, Judge Court, Mr. Garcia, Mr. Denis O'Connor, Mr. Joseph, Mr. Brown, Mr. Kelly King, Mr. Robert Gray, and so forth. What this most likely reveals is that clients may have petitioned Mah Nannie to work spiritually on their behalf in sundry legal matters. Using the exact names of colonial legal officials potentially added needed precision to intervening rituals performed by Nannie. Notes containing signed pledges from clients included for example, "I promise to pay Mr. Nanny on order, in the time that

I am well cured of my sickness, as doctor, as he is to me, the amount of $100, which I agreed with him." There were also written requests for Mah Nannie to "see" or consult with family members or to assist in procuring a "head overseer's" position that was "vacant."

In his testimony Sergeant McCollin tried to draw on his expertise of Obeah and its artifacts from his past experience "as a soldier in Africa." He testified that a shell that was confiscated from Nannie's chapel (its name was recorded phonetically as "jegga") was the same shell "used in obeah at Freetown, Sierra Leone," that "the shell was filled with dirt that seemed to be taken from a grave in the Cemetery," that "he had seen cases of this nature in Africa, and the shell was always used for practising obeah," and that "Guinea pepper [also confiscated from Nannie] was used along with it."

Mah Nannie's lawyer argued that the case had not been proven because "a few papers containing names" and "a few things which he might in his ignorance have worshipped or treated as gods" did not necessarily constitute the legal threshold for obeah. Nor had the "prisoner professed to put those things to a supernatural use," especially having received no compensation at the time of encounter. According to Mr. Warner's argument:

> The prisoner had received no money, on the contrary, he refused to receive it. The words of the Ordinance were "Every person who by the practice of obeah, or by an occult means, or by an assumption of supernatural power or knowledge." There was no proof that the prisoner practised obeah. A lot of images were not proof of occult means. This was a criminal case, and His Worship would not stretch the words of the Ordinance any further than they were already stretched. Was there any evidence to show the assumption of supernatural power or knowledge? . . . There was no evidence that the prisoner was doing a wrong thing, or anything which was apt to cause any one harm. The words of the Ordinance were: "Or shall obtain, or endeavour to obtain any chattel or valuable security from any other person or any stolen goods, or to inflict any disease, loss, damage," &c. The large penalty which was inflicted by the Ordinance would cover an extreme case in which a man was a vicious man and was trying to do harm to other people, but this man only seemed to have untaken to do good or to settle a case and not allow it to go any further so as to prevent another man from going to gaol.

In the end, the magistrate counterargued that although "the offence did not necessarily consist of committing or trying to persuade a person to commit an offence," there was "evidence of an assumption of supernatural power or knowledge," which was still considered a violation under the ordinance. The magistrate, a local, was convinced of Mah Nannie's guilt. The complex inner workings of Obeah were obscure to most white colonists and officials; yet, there existed enough mythical lore in the colony surrounding obeah to fuel indictments.

Native-born African witnesses clearly had greater credibility when testifying about Obeah and African religions. Thus, when Peter David offered his sworn testimony, his first words were: "I am an African. I know Mr. Nanny." Providing perhaps the most comprehensive testimony in defense of the legitimacy of Mah Nannie's chapel, specifically, and African religion more broadly, David testified, "I have been in Belmont a long time. That chapel has always been there. Mr. Nanny keeps the chapel. I give him lights and sweet oil, not money." When asked about the confiscated images, David affirmed, "We serve them for gods," testifying that many people frequented the chapel, particularly in times of illness. According to David, "There are some goblets, and there are certain days to go for the water for sickness. If you come with any sickness you go to the chapel and put your candle and your sweet oil and he [Mah Nannie] prays for you, and if there is any sickness he gives you water out of the goblet to drink, or you wash your hands, or however he gives it to you." He was then interrogated as to Mah Nannie's power to find lost money or to divine the nature of ailments, to which Peter David answered, "I don't know anything about that." We "serve for sickness" and "only sickness," he emphasized. What was not clearly understood in the context of the case was that, as Brereton concluded, "the Radas saved money to use as a mutual sickness, confinement, and burial fund, built up by very small payments."[154] Still, Peter David's testimony further emphasized that institutions of mutual aid existed among the Rada in Trinidad as sources of community support, common protection, and communal stability.

Having sought to establish Mah Nannie as a legitimate religious consultant for healing and remedy, the defense rested its case, closing that these practices were not in fact obeah according to the legal statutes but "that this was a form of worship among these Africans, who were as ignorant of our religion as we were of theirs."[155] To further emphasize the court's ignorance of African religions, Mr. Warner for the defense cited a book by scholarly authority Rev. J. G. Wood entitled The Uncivilized Nations of the World, which, he argued, "speaking of the peculiar religions in the central parts of Africa . . . their fetishes are innumerable and it is hardly possible to walk anywhere without seeing a fetish or two." The text stated, "The religious idea of the Fanti are, as usual in Africa, vague and indistinct. Each person has his Saman—literally a skeleton or goblin—or private fetish, an idol, rag, fowl feathers, bunch of grass, a bit of glass, and so forth; to this he pays the greatest reverence." Warner argued that this same African "ignorance" was being maintained in Trinidad, and that the residents of Belmont "believed that going to a chapel and using oil or candles it pleased the god, whoever he might be, and that they got relief. The prisoner was a kind of high priest among them . . . that was really what he was among these people, and the evidence showed no assumption of supernatural power or knowledge." In many ways Warner was attempting to explain to the court what Sharla Fett calls "a relational view of health" and to point out that for liberated Africans this relationality would include "the god," "the fetish," and "the high priest," encompassing a vast materiality and the "greatest reverence," from which liberated Africans eventually "got relief."[156]

In the end, the magistrate vehemently disagreed with Warner, and took into consideration a prior conviction in which Mah Nannie was "sentenced to be flogged for stealing fowls." He upheld the present conviction, ultimately contending "that this was not only a form of religion that he [Mah Nannie] had been practising at Belmont, but that he had been exercising his small power on his ignorant fellow countrymen in order to obtain money from them—to swindle them, in fact, by means of a pretended form of religion. . . . The prisoner had been carrying on this offence for at least nine years and obtaining money all this time from those people." After extensive testimony, debate, and display of sacred items, Mah Nannie was sentenced to "six months imprisonment and to receive thirty-six lashes with the cat-o'-nine-tails," as recorded in the *Port of Spain Gazette* on Saturday, September 11, 1886. An outcry by local residents filled the crowded courtroom in response to his conviction and the sentence: "A numerous party from the prisoner's class evinced a great deal of sympathy and seemed to be particularly horrified by the corporeal part of the punishment, as the prisoner is an elderly man. They clamored for an appeal to the higher Court." On October 19, 1886, Mah Nannie's conviction for Obeah was appealed before the higher court.

"We Serve for Sickness": The Appeal of
Mah Nannie against the Charge of Obeah

Of great significance would be the outcome of Mah Nannie's appeal to the Supreme Civil Court in the aftermath of his brother John Cooper's historic appeal and victory a decade or so previously. Mah Nannie was represented by Vincent Brown, "the coloured lawyer" and by Aucher Warner, with the appeals proceedings attracting a huge public audience curious about the fate of the African defendant accused of obeah.[157]

Various constituencies had a stake in the final disposition of Mah Nannie's case. First, local European residents and police were particularly interested in how to curtail aberrant acts of social or religious power not subject to colonial authority. Second, nonresident British authorities found little credence in the supposed power of obeah and sought to dispel the credibility of that notion among the colony's inhabitants. Third, health authorities fostering increased education and medicalization of cures found obeah beliefs and "superstitions" to be antithetical to the logic and science of Western medicine. Mah Nannie's case on obeah was reported in newspapers alongside prominent medical advertisements on "how to secure health" via the "great remedy," "a complete cure," "homeopathic medicines," "prescriptions," "fresh drugs and medicines," or "pure drugs and chemicals," substances that were often legitimized by "government stamp," "patent," "medical testimony," or "Her Majesty's Representative."[158] Finally, liberated Africans and African-descended communities in Trinidad were invested in the outcome of the contestation between African spiritual power and European legal power.

The attorney general was of the view that the case against Mah Nannie "was a very simple case" fully substantiating his guilt. However, the case was far from simple. Nannie was charged "with endeavouring to obtain money by pretending to have supernatural power." Due to the method of entrapment used to extract evidence, the chief justice, who arrived from England, had to carefully discern the distinction between "a genuine case" and "a trumped up case." More specifically, one interpretation in support of Mah Nannie was that "the police went there for the purpose of inducing the man to break the law for the purpose of catching him." On the other hand, from the perspective of the local magistrate, "it was difficult to detect offenders in cases of this kind without using that kind of strategy" and "it was impossible to detect these offences without some plan being laid."

The chief justice's approach in many ways muddied the issue of Mah Nannie's guilt, which was the primary focus of the police and the magistrate. Instead, the chief justice questioned whether it was the *informants* who had actually committed a crime, given the content of the ordinance on obeah. He read an excerpt from the 1868 Obeah Prohibition Ordinance in support of his query: "Every person who shall procure, counsel, induce, or persuade or endeavor to persuade any other person to commit such an offence, shall on conviction appear before a Stipendiary Magistrate." Thus, he concluded the court is "not quite sure if we have got the right man here," intimating that the true case was against Anson and Clarke, who had broken the law by inducing Mah Nannie "to commit such an offense." Seizing on this line of questioning,

Mah Nannie's attorney, Mr. Brown, reasoned, "It was the duty of the police to bring up the man who had committed the offence; but they had let go the men who had committed the offence and taken hold of a man who had not committed the offence, and brought as witnesses the men who had committed the offence." The chief justice concluded that although it was argued that "people who believed in obeah practices would be too frightened to come forward," the tactic of enlisting local informants "to do the dirty work" did not stand on sound legal ground, as the chief justice believed that "nobody would do that without money." It was further maintained that Mah Nannie had no "sign board before his door that might have been constructed as an offer of services," and instead the witness falsely solicited services with the goal of getting Mah Nannie to incriminate himself. The witness Clarke's testimony was revisited, and it was noted that it was "in evidence that Clarke believed the appellant was a doctor." Persuasively shifting the gaze of culpability from his client to the remaining witness, Mr. Brown concluded, "If this man had supernatural power he would not easily have been caught by Anson. Perhaps Anson has got the supernatural power of trapping people."

The Supreme Civil Court proceedings next turned to the material culture and spiritual paraphernalia confiscated from Mah Nannie's Belmont compound as physical evidence of prohibited "superstitious devices" and "articles used in the practice of obeah and witchcraft."[159] Of particular focus were "two hideous black images" described as "the two gods, which are part of the evidence," and other instruments the police sergeant "says is used in obeah." Conversely, the defense argued that the "assumption of supernatural power" should not be attributed to these items. Although Bilby and Handler posit that identifying "instruments of obeah" or "supernatural devices" was an imprecise science; nevertheless, "it was presumed that a person found to have such 'instruments' on his person or in his home was an obeah practitioner."[160] In fact, the exact opposite was argued in defense of Mah Nannie: it was maintained that "some of the images found in the place were such as we were in the habit of seeing in our houses—images of the Virgin and all that sort of thing." Moreover, the court determined that the collection of objects spoke to nothing more than "how supremely ignorant those people might be, and how they would bring things, so very much apart, together for the purpose of carrying on worship which they might think was correct, but the idea of which other people could not entertain for a moment."

Finally, the remainder of the appeals process focused largely on the debate regarding the fraudulent practice of obeah (which was illegal) versus the legal legitimacy of "the religious worship of the Africans." According to the Chief

Justice Sir John Gorrie, it behooved the court and the police to "find out if those people worshipped their gods in that way, or whether those images were being kept, as 'Mumbo Jumbos' to frighten people out of their money." Apparently, the attorney general was of the opinion that the evidence the police had gathered made the case for obeah. However, the chief justice determined "there was no evidence at all," "that those implements belong to the religious worship of the Africans," and that the prosecution's solid evidence proved that "those things were used to induce men to believe that the appellant was able by mysterious arts to help them in their sickness." Hence, "that was the practice of obeah."

Mr. Brown argued in the end that, contrary to what an obeah man did, Mah Nannie "prayed for people in their illness." The chief justice supported this interpretation, stating that "the practice of obeah is not to help people in their sickness." Most succinctly, the "defence counsel argued that this was a form of worship; Nannee was a kind of high priest, and the evidence showed no assumption of supernatural powers, which was the legal definition of obeah."[161] The attorney general sought to strategically counter the validity of Mah Nannie's priesthood, asserting that there was no proof that the Belmont Rada compound was "a genuine temple of worship"; had it been such, the police would have violated the ordinance in the "Miscellaneous" section of the 1868 summary of offences prohibiting "disturbing places of worship" as well as "molesting religious ministers in performance of their functions."[162] The attorney general appealed to scholarly authority in his assertion that "these things are not shown by any book to belong to any religious worship" and that it was "less likely that those things were there for religious worship" as "they are mixed up with other images." To this Mr. Brown intervened, "We have the testimony of the man himself of the use for which they make those things." With great authority, Brown proclaimed that Mah Nannie and the Belmont community "were not descendants of Africans but they came here themselves direct from Africa" and that Mah Nannie "calls himself their priest." The chief justice inquired if any other persons could support this claim, whereupon the "wife of the appellant was brought before the Court, and Mr. Brown called the Court's attention to the fact that her face was marked in the genuine African way" as many at that time may have been similarly marked.[163] The facial or "country" marks were highlighted as evidence to support indigenous African birth and authentic nationhood. Not completely convinced, the attorney general demanded to know "when was the last importation of Africans to Trinidad." The appellant's attorney responded with the suggestion that the attorney general could call on Mah Nannie and the others to answer his question, for they were credible witnesses as to their native African origin.

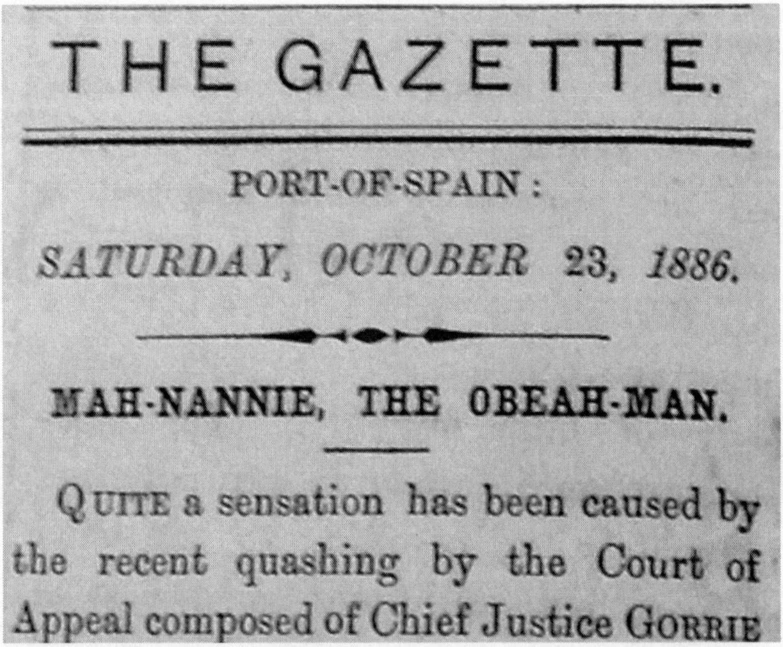

THE GAZETTE.

PORT-OF-SPAIN :

SATURDAY, OCTOBER 23, 1886.

MAH-NANNIE, THE OBEAH-MAN.

QUITE a sensation has been caused by the recent quashing by the Court of Appeal composed of Chief Justice GORRIE

FIGURE 4.10 Newspaper article detailing the successful appeal of Mah Nannie overturning his conviction on the criminal charge of obeah in 1886. Printed in the *Port of Spain Gazette*, October 23, 1886. Reprinted by permission of the National Archives of Trinidad and Tobago.

Sir John Gorrie, the chief justice from England, ultimately ruled in favor of Mah Nannie, overturning and quashing his original conviction. The police informant's use of an entrapment strategy was discredited "owing to the circumstances under which he gave that evidence," and the material items that were confiscated by the police and Père François could not be proven definitively to be obeah objects and not items used in a genuine African (albeit "supremely ignorant") form of worship. Thus, the proceedings of the appeal revealed a monumental and important legal distinction between legitimate African religious practices and fraudulent obeah practices (see figure 4.10).

Blame for this perceived legal travesty was laid at the feet of Chief Justice John Gorrie, revealing deep dissension and division within the European residential and nonresidential populations regarding Obeah. Those who were long-term residents in Trinidad had an ideation of Obeah as something deeply and darkly malevolent. Conversely, British-appointed colonial officials the whipping only. As the matter now stands, Obeahism has received a new lease of vigorous life, as its votaries will without doubt attribute MAH-NANNIE'S escape to his supernatural power—what the extent of the mischief this will work will be, we are not prophet enough to be able to predict.

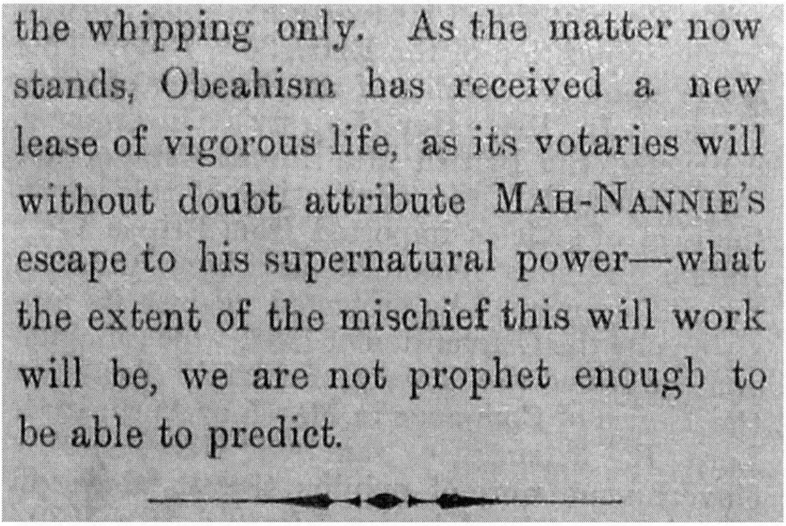

FIGURE 4.11 Mah Nannie's appeal is mocked by white colonists as a victory for "Obeahism" and its success attributed to "his supernatural power." Printed in the *Port of Spain Gazette*, October 23, 1886. Reprinted by permission of the National Archives of Trinidad and Tobago.

whose stays on the island were transitory failed to share the ominous imaginings of Trinidad's white elite and instead viewed obeah to be among the harmless and ignorant superstitious practices of African communities. Chief Justice John Gorrie was positioned among the latter. This discrepancy most illumined that British Trinidad was not of a single mind in its imaginations of obeah. Long-standing inhabitants were unwaveringly convinced that in "a case of this gravity," obeah was a real and pernicious force pervading the island. Others, like the chief justice, saw Obeah as a practice of ignorance, perhaps related to African primitive rites, yet all the while incapable of inflicting any real harm or posing any threats to health and safety.

Most interestingly, Chief Justice John Gorrie had first served in the Caribbean in the 1860s on the colonial Royal Commission and then served in Mauritius, Fiji, and Jamaica before becoming chief justice of the Leeward Islands in the 1880s, arriving in Trinidad in February 1882. As a relative newcomer, the longstanding local elite castigated Gorrie for being "little acquainted with the wide extent to which Obeahism prevails here [Trinidad], the deadliness of its operations, its secrecy and the consequent difficulty of bringing its High-Priests to punishment" (see figure 4.11).

European creole occupants were frustrated by Gorrie's inability to see the "iniquitous system" of obeah and to indict Mah Nannie, the "disciple of Obeah," as one who "works out his purpose, not unfrequently a deadly one, with more than the cunning of a venomous serpent that only comes out at night to hunt for his prey." The chief justice was dismissed as an outsider who was unaware of the "deep secrecy of the[obeah] system." He did not possess the "requisite knowledge" of the power of the obeah-man needed to guard against his "insidious" and "unscrupulous" practices and the danger of his impenetrable secrets. From the perspective of local whites, the chief justice failed to understand that obeah practitioners operated in "silence" and took every "precaution to render detection impossible."

Chief Justice Gorrie's 1886 ruling would be one among many that would place him in contention with Trinidad's elite and estate proprietors. Over the course of his career as a chief justice in Trinidad, Gorrie's initiatives would focus on "reforming the transfer of land," opposing the "contract system" that benefited estate owners, chairing the commission on trade and taxes, and working to create a "people's bank" in Trinidad. His "tendency to take the part of native races," his "predilection for the working classes," and his "leaning towards easing the burden for the negro" and "administering justice" in the colonial courts, one source indicates, made him "an idol of the negroes, while the rest of Trinidad society could hardly speak sufficiently evil of him."[164]

Immediately following Mah Nannie's successful appeal, the article "Mah-Nannie, The Obeahman" appeared in the Port of Spain Gazette on October 23, 1886. Despite the fact that he had been fully exonerated on appeal, the article nonetheless labeled Nannie an "Obeah-Man" and a "notorious disciple of Obeah." Mah Nannie's case evoked "intense interest and deep emotion" among the black "lower classes," and—much to the consternation of the writer—Nannie was being elevated to the honorific status of "hero-worship" and "martyr." Among Trinidad's European inhabitants, news of the decision to overturn the obeah ruling was "received with astonishment and apprehension," for it was understood that this population was "acquainted with the iniquities of the Obeah-system from the fearful revelations that have been made . . . in our Police Courts and in death-bed confessions, of this deeply-rooted, wide-spread, debasing and dangerous practice."

More importantly, white colonists interpreted Mah Nannie's exoneration as a direct attack on the stipendiary magistrate, the police, and the strategy of "detecting and bringing to punishment the vile and dangerous ministers of Obeahism" through the testimonies of informants. Written on behalf of the

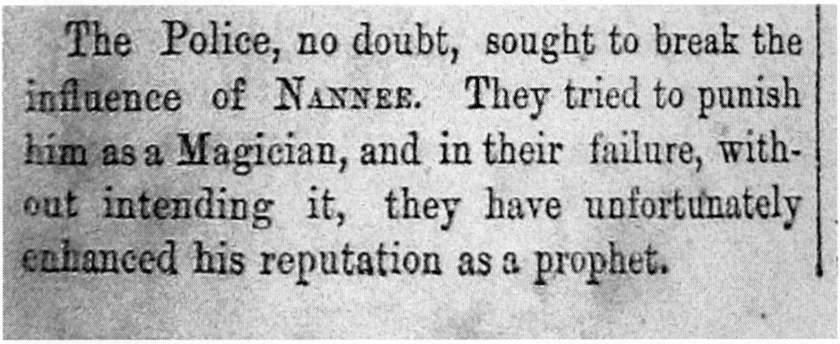

> The Police, no doubt, sought to break the influence of NANNEE. They tried to punish him as a Magician, and in their failure, without intending it, they have unfortunately enhanced his reputation as a prophet.

FIGURE 4.12 In a newspaper article entitled "Scotched but Not Killed," Mah Nannie is derided as having moved from magician to prophet following the affirmative court ruling in his favor. Printed in *The New Era*, October 25, 1886. Reprinted by permission of the National Archives of Trinidad and Tobago.

European residential constituency, the article expressed deep consternation: "we can come to no other conclusion than that the conviction was just and should not have been quashed." Furthermore, the article insisted that Mah Nannie was a man who "had for more than nine years been notorious to the Police as an Obeahman they had been unable to lay hands on." For many white residents, evidence of "all of the loathsome symbols of his diabolical arts" was apparent, the informant was credible, and the fee Mah Nannie charged was meant to do harm. As a matter of "fully discharging [their] public duty in connection with this case," they reprimanded the chief justice for his attitude and inappropriate wit regarding the stipendiary magistrate, Mr. Child, who had provoked laughter from the "ignorant" and "thoughtless." Gorrie's remarks were viewed as "out of place and uncalled for" as well as "simply offensive to good sense and taste," defying their expectation that "Justice . . . be administered with due dignity." The "gravity" of the case and the clemency granted Nannie meant that "Obeahism has received a new lease of vigorous life, as its votaries will without doubt attribute Mah-Nannie's escape to his supernatural power." Thus, the true victory was against white local colonial power, control, and authority. The groundbreaking ruling transmitted a vital message to local white colonists that Mah Nannie's "particular idolatry" was in a very public way "considered to have been stronger than the law." Ultimately, Trinidad's white Christian residents (as voiced in the local press) found most disturbing that, "in an effort 'to break' Mah Nannie's spiritual power and influence, the police tried to punish him as a Magician, and in its failure, without intending it, they have unfortunately enhanced his reputation as a prophet"[165] (see figure 4.12).

The overturning of his conviction vindicated Mah Nannie and custodians of all other African religions for which we have no name but Obeah. Mah Nannie's victorious appeal (and for that matter John Cooper's) would have been inconceivable during the tyrannical reign of Governor Picton. However, in the post-emancipation late nineteenth-century context, Mah Nannie's supporters witnessed the triumphant resolve of Africa. The *Port of Spain Gazette* reported that the "din and confusion in Court, after the Chief Justice gave judgment, were so great that the words of Judge Court could scarcely be heard, . . . and the wild rejoicing of the retreating crowds who thronged the Court sounded ominously in the ears of all who know the pernicious, deadly influence of Obeahism over their ignorant minds." As the news reached Mah Nannie's home community of Belmont, the "excitement was intense to an extreme," and as an expression of their victory, "the Police were jeered and turned into ridicule in the most insulting and contemptuous manner" by the local residents.

During the late nineteenth century and well into the next century, Obeah continued to enthrall and captivate the European colonial imagination. Obeah's historic presence indicated that neither Christianity nor imperialism would neatly prevail in Trinidad. The Obeah of African-descended populations consistently undermined these authorities of religion and politics while steadily creating fractures in the social, economic, medical, and legal structures of colonial power.

Dénouement: "Reverend Hou Quervee," Spiritual Custodian of a True African Apothecary

As Cooper's and Nannie's cases show, late nineteenth-century obeah trials attempted to overtly stabilize social, religious, and medical authority in Trinidad. However, Paton's research indicates that this pattern persisted into the twentieth century, and she documents some 121 arrests and prosecutions for obeah in Trinidad between 1890 and 1939. Particularly interesting in the wider British colonial legal landscape are analogous obeah cases in Jamaica that specifically charged obeah offenders for "practising medicine without a licence," which may have included "offering ritual and spiritual healing services."[166] Thus, Colonial legal professionals and magistrates throughout the Caribbean arbitrated the meaning of social healthcare while seeking to adjudicate the demarcations of health and religion during this period.[167]

The British machination of colonialism and its legal prohibitions against Obeah functioned as a social regulator of "discipline and civilization" to safeguard the colony against "what would otherwise relapse . . . into anar-

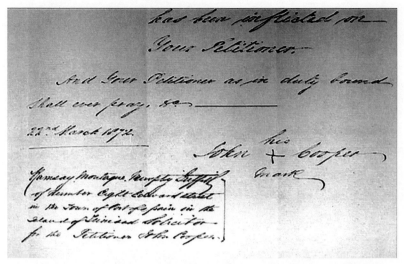

FIGURE 4.13 Excerpt from the transcript of John Cooper's case before the Supreme Civil Court of Appeal, Port of Spain, Trinidad, March 21, 1872. Printed in the *Trinidad Chronicle*, April 9, 1872. Reprinted by permission of the National Archives of Trinidad and Tobago.

chy and barbarism."[168] This exercise of control was the colonial legal mark of obeah. John Cooper and Mah Nannie, however, left an ostensibly different mark upon the legal, health and medical, and spiritual landscapes of Trinidad (see figure 4.13).

Beyond its legal significance, John Cooper's recorded case, and the subsequent case of Mah Nannie, offer rare access into Obeah's theurgical properties as practiced by its African priesthoods, and they also present an opportunity for conceptually *unslaving* religion through the study of liberated Africans in nineteenth-century Trinidad. The two cases simultaneously offer a glimpse of African people as steadfast appellants who exacted reform within the British colonial legal system. In the absence of boundary distinctions between African superstition and legitimate African theurgical practices, obeah became the comprehensive term used to depict "any religious or magical practices, including healing and conjuring of all types, which were believed to be African-derived," according to Bridget Brereton.[169] Within colonial Trinidad, a positive lexicon for interpreting the complexities of African religiosity was nonexistent. Hence, in the absence of such a lexicon, broader African religious practices were easily demonized and criminalized alongside what was targeted as obeah.[170]

> DIED—this morning, Tuesday (19th) be-
> fore daylight, after not many hours illness
> having been in health yesterday morning,—
> at his residence on the Laventille hills, the
> Rev. HOU QUERVEE, a native of Africa,
> of the Rada tribe bordering on Dahomé, re-
> garded by some of the tribe as assistant
> Curate of Belmont, *in partibus infidelium*,
> (to the Rt. Rev. Bp. or head Obeahman
> of that ilk—a worthy of the name of Keebo,
> too familiarly styled 'Mister George'), D.S.
> —Doctor in Sorcery, one of a family (the
> relationship is denied by some persons) of
> three brothers—brothers at least in ini-
> quity, say the revilers of the fetish (viz:
> Dosou Quervee—at present on Her Ma-
> jesty's bounty as an inmate of the Asy-
> lum for dangerous lunatics, Nanee, and
> himself)—who practise or practised in
> Belmont the black arts and mysteries of
> exorcism, fascination, compulsion, wasting,
> herbal-cure, terrorism and other bedevilment,

FIGURE 4.14 Excerpt from published obituary of Rada priest, John Cooper, (referred to as Rev. Hou Quervee), where he is identified, along with his siblings Dosou and Nanee, as an Obeahman and pejoratively represented as a practitioner of the "black arts and mysteries of exorcism, fascination, compulsion, wasting, herbal-cure, terrorism and other bedevilment." Printed in the *Trinidad Chronicle*, June 22, 1877. Reprinted by permission of the National Archives of Trinidad and Tobago.

John Cooper is silenced in the colonial archives immediately after his trial and appeal in 1871–1872. He resurfaces one final time in the public record through an obituary published in the *Trinidad Chronicle* on Tuesday, June 19, 1877. There he is remembered not by his Anglo name, John Cooper. Instead, the writer of the obituary addresses him as "the Rev. Hou Quervee, a native of Africa, of the Rada tribe bordering on Dahomé," and he is ascribed the appellation of D.S. (Doctor in Sorcery) and "assistant Curate of Belmont" to the "head Obeahman" Keebo or "Mister George"[171] (see figure 4.14).

Quervee was reportedly one of "three brothers"—Hou, Dosou, and Nanee—whom the writer deems "revilers of the fetish" and "brothers . . . in iniquity." Dosou was said to be "at present on Her Majesty's bounty as an inmate of the Asylum for dangerous lunatics." The Rada brothers were described facetiously as having "practiced in Belmont the black arts and mysteries of exorcism, fascination, compulsion, wasting, herbal-cure, terrorism and other bedevilment, and one or other of whom has been credited with having caused the death, by fear . . . of certain poor credulous creatures over whom they pretended to have throw[n] a spell and curse." The writer also alluded to Cooper/Quervee's prior conviction in 1871, noting that "His Reverence, having been betrayed, had the misfortune to be convicted by the Magistrate, of dealing in the Black Art," for which he "received—according to law—certain lashes . . . in Gaol; but having summoned friends from Laventille to swear he had done no obeahism, he was freed from further durance, and received a *solatium* of ten dollars for each stripe," after which time he "led a more retired life."[172] In a British colonial world where obeah practitioners and practices were demonized and criminalized, it is astounding that Cooper/Quervee's obituary withstands history and is archived in a local newspaper.

At the end of his life, having survived what Dianne Stewart characterizes as the "extended Middle Passage" and endured colonial prosecution for

retired life. He leaves to his two daughters a cow and calf, a wooden cottage nearly finished, and a bag of money saved from the earnings of his profession. We have not been instructed as to who is the happy heir of the old man's peculiar treasure—popularly credited as comprising the following, among other professional furniture and materia: jaw of cayman, fang of snake, matapel claw and tiger-cat tooth, must of quenck and spume of toad, powdered wasp and blood of rat(and kid ?), centipede head and scorpion's tail, with jars and calabashes of wild roots, barks, and junks of liane, the properties of which are known only to men of his calling, with feathers red, yellow and blue, and sundry indescribable rags and bundles—the whole, with odd bottles and vials,constituting, no doubt, a valuable stock-in-trade to gentlemen of the cloth and persuasion of the deceased.

FIGURE 4.15 Excerpt from the published obituary and informal bequest of John Cooper detailing his earthly possessions and spiritual ingredients bequeathed to his two daughters. Printed in the Trinidad Chronicle, June 22, 1877. Reprinted by permission of the National Archives of Trinidad and Tobago.

obeah, it appeared that John Cooper/Hou Quervee's numinous profession proved quite lucrative in Trinidad's colonial medical economy—he was able to bequeath to his two daughters "a cow and calf, a wooden cottage nearly finished, and a bag of money saved from the earnings of his profession."[173] Although criminalized, Cooper/Quervee's "work" functioned in an alternative spiritual economy amidst a colonial society controlled by ordinance, violent force, and authority. This Africana spiritual system operated in a clandestine culture of healing, protection, and agency in defiance of both law and standard medical profession.

Cooper/Quervee also left behind a legacy of "professional furniture and materia" that the writer deemed the "old man's peculiar treasure" (see figure 4.15). Its contents included

> jaw of cayman, fang of snake, matapel claw and tiger-cat tooth, musk of quenck and spume of toad, powdered wasp and blood of rat (and kid . . .), centipede head and scorpion's tail, with jars and calabashes of wild roots, barks and junks of liane, the properties of which are known only to men of his calling, with feathers red, yellow and blue, and sundry indescribable rags and bundles—the whole, with odd bottles and vials, constituting, no doubt, a valuable stock-in-trade to gentlemen of the cloth and persuasion of the deceased.[174]

The writer of the obituary provided no deeper insight into the inner meanings of John Cooper's material pharmacopeia at the time of his death. Yet, within the mystical world of African spiritual healthcare, these artifacts attest to the healing instrumentalities of African specialists, shine a light on the esoteric epistemologies of the natural world, and offer rare insight into the spiritual inventory of a true African apothecary.

Afterword

"This was a form of worship among these Africans, who were as ignorant of our religion as we were of theirs," *remarked Mr. Aucher Warner, defense attorney during the 1886 appeal to the Trinidad Supreme Civil Court on behalf of Mah Nannie.[1] The prosecutions, punishments, and appeals described throughout volume I reflect the choreography of the colonial imaginary enacted for nearly a century in public and legal performances of prohibition against obeah and African religions. British colonial officials' collective ignorance and criminalization of African worship and sacred medicine is a long thread that weaves across this first volume, connecting it to volume II.*

Testifying in what was described as broken English and French, John Cooper speaks the words "C'est vrai" or "It is true" through the pages of the colonial script, owning the truth and integrity of his African Rada tradition and practices. Beyond colonial imaginations and their accompanying legal repression, Cooper informs us in his 1872 declaration that "it is true"—Africans willfully practiced and "worked" the religions of their nations as protection, weapon, and spiritual healthcare for surviving and thriving in the diaspora.

As liberated Africans accused of obeah in the late nineteenth century, John Cooper (Hou Quervee) and Mah Nannie were captives of the "extended Middle Passage" in their protracted journeys from West Africa to Trinidad.[2] Rada, Yoruba, and Mandingo "High Priests," as they were referenced in colonial records, were transported post-British slavery from homes and homelands aboard slave vessels seized by the British navy, directed to colonial territories on the African continent, and subsequently transported to their final destinations in imperial diasporas throughout the Caribbean and the Americas. African religions are what sustained these populations in their new regions. Obeah and criminalization are what made those transported to the Anglophone Caribbean visible and (on rare occasions) have voice within colonial records and archives. While Christian missionaries, such as Rev. W. H. Gamble, labored to bring Africans "under the sound of truth," countless Africans who inhabited colonial Trinidad such as John Cooper and Mah Nannie worshiped under an alternative sound of truth.[3]

In Dianne Stewart's subsequent volume, she engages "Africana religious nationalism as a healing modality of becoming and belonging inspired by heritage love." Still, navigating between and beyond the colonial gaze, we find in volume II postemancipation Africans recouping, reorganizing, and repurposing their nation identities as primary indicators of religious community in Trinidad. Rada, Hausa, Mandingo, Yoruba, and Ibo were not mere colonial identifiers for the purposes of colonial registries, tax statements, plantation estate files, or criminal records. For African persons these designations represented the customs, traditions, and practices that demarcated prediaspora and transatlantic identities and histories, regardless of how those identities and histories inspired new and improvised allegiances in diaspora contexts of racial slavery. And although obeah accusations continued into the twentieth century, communities of Africans defending their religious practices against criminalization and arguing for full exoneration in colonial courts also endured.

Privileging the twentieth and twenty-first centuries, volume II examines African religions beyond the socially reductive category of colonial obeah that predominates in volume I. The second volume explores African religions as tradition-building phenomena. The themes of nation, sovereignty, kinship/family, social belonging, and motherness interlace an intricate analytical tapestry that provides access to Yoruba-Orisa religion as a source of meaning, citizenship, ethics, and African descendants' "uncooperative endurance" (to use Stewart's phrase) of antiblackness in the afterlife of slavery and colonialism. Unlike the study of early colonial literatures, travelogues, and European legal records that eclipse the structure, theology, and ethics of African religions and obscure them through distorted colonial prisms, volume II engages in the study of African religious interiority, specifically among custodians of the Yoruba-Orisa religion in Trinidad. Spanning volumes I and II is the historical consistency with which African devotees act as ambassadors of their heritage traditions, defenders of them in the face of colonial proscriptions (even under penalty of death), and embodied reservoirs of nation, knowledge, and healing.

As this study transitions into volume II, what cannot be left unsaid in my closing reflections on volume I is that these Africana resources of healing and resistance have not lost their efficacy and necessity in contemporary times. I contemplate this as both Dianne Stewart and I finalize both volumes in the midst of: (1) a global health pandemic, (2) a national race pandemic in America, (3) a centennial anniversary of the Tulsa Black massacre during which state forces dropped the first air bomb on American citizens of African descent, (4) the two hundredth anniversary of the Denmark Vesey slave insurrection plot of 1822 in South Carolina, and (5) a layer of controversy as the University of Pennsylvania and Princeton University disclose their possession of the remains of an African American child in the MOVE organization who was incinerated in Philadelphia in 1985, a victim of the second air bombing of African American citizens on US soil. Arielle Julia Brown worked as the former public programs developer and cultural planning consultant for the Penn & Slavery Project at the University of Pennsylvania. When asked for reflections on Penn's possession of these remains, Brown remarked, "Black people [are still] dispossessed of their own material future after death, after wrongful death, after violent death at the hands of white supremacy."[4]

The atemporal performance of transatlantic black carnage rituals from the colonial cult of obeah fixation and beyond end in a shared finale of exhibitus cultus and worldwide public expositions assuming the forms of Africana body parts at the altar of colonial municipalities; poled black heads at entrances of plantations; jarred, pickled, and sexualized body parts of Sarah Baartmans in museums; rancid remains on lynching trees and woodpiles; microscoped cancer cells of Henrietta Lacks; freshly killed Michael Browns on the street canvas of Ferguson, Missouri; and police-sanctioned C-4 explosions and obliteration of Micah Johnsons splattered across social media. Most recently, the world visually consumed the over-extinguishment of Jayland Walker's body in a violent symphony of ninety-plus bullets and of George Floyd's black body as a police officer's knee replicated the ancient method of torture peine forte et dure, or the technique of European weight "pressing" upon the human body until final death due to, as Floyd's autopsy revealed, "asphyxiation from sustained pressure."[5] These instances are manifestations of white libidinal power that serve as object lessons in the study of white lived religion.

To explore further one of these object lessons, the charred skeletal remains of MOVE resident, fourteen-year-old Katricia Africa, fit neatly into this ritual lineage of black carnage. Before their repatriation to her family, Katricia's remains in the University of Pennsylvania's Morton Cranial Collection were part of "the unethical possession of human remains" within the museum.[6] In addition, the bones of this African American child and daughter were prominently featured in a Princeton University Coursera class, Real Bones: Adventures in Forensic Anthropology. The course syllabus offered the following description for its first week: "This week introduces the field of forensic anthropology with a case study of the bombing of the MOVE community. Many human remains were burned and thus 'personhood' was lost."[7] I anguish at the fact that in the age of NAGPRA (the Native American Graves Protection and Repatriation Act of 1990), which brought needed sacrality to the remains of indigenous communities in university museums, the bones of an African American child could be academically dishonored. What if the bones of Katricia, her charmains, appeared in the classroom recorporealized? If they could feel, think, and speak, what would their response be to the professor's claim that "personhood was lost?" What would

Katricia's once incarnated bones think of being showcased in week one of a course where her traumatized remains are featured as "Adventures?" What if they told/taught the inner story—the story of the body bombed and incinerated at 6221 Osage Avenue; the account of a child, diasporaed in America, a victim of civil warfare, a recaptive of 3260 South Street? What would Katricia Africa's charmains recount about their status—imprisoned in a museum collection until 2021, unburied for decades, deprived of Onile's (Mother Earth's) protection, too young to be ancestored, too black to be sacralized, relegated to labs and archival storage like Thisbe, Yala, and Youba.

In her Elegy (for MOVE and Philadelphia), famed poet Sonia Sanchez graphically depicts the horrors of the May 13, 1985, Osage Avenue MOVE bombing that killed six adults and five children and destroyed sixty-one homes. Sanchez summons the reader "to hurry on down to osage st." Plaintively, she continues to describe the catastrophic destruction in the following excerpts:

> they're roasting in the fire
> smell the dreadlocks and blk/skins
> roasting in the fire
> . . . they are combing the morning for shadows
> and screams tongue-tied without faces
> look, over there, one eye
> escaping from its skins
> . . . give us this day our rest from seduction
> peeling us down to our veins
> who anointeth the city with napalm? (I say)
> who giveth this city in holy infanticide?
> . . . this country. this city.
> this people.
> collecting skeletons from waiting rooms
> lying in wait for honor and peace.
> one day.[8]

The lesson we must learn from these verses, this volume, and black charmains everywhere, is palpable: the forensic anthropological analysis of charred bones once enveloped by black flesh must never be decoupled from a forensic psychological analysis of the religious and racial crimes that have sanctioned the annihilation of black persons in the Americas and the Caribbean.

In writing this volume it was at times difficult for me to separate the social cannibalism and consumption of black flesh in Governor Picton's Trinidad from similar white imaginaries of enfleshed terror I was witnessing under modern-day civil authority in North America. The social acts of what a Philadelphia Inquirer opinion piece identifies as sanctioned "state murder" mirror the social negation of the black body in nineteenth-century Trinidad's Port of Spain.[9] Similar to La Fortune, Pierre, Thisbe, and her husband, Felix, who could not simply be arrested, sentenced, and punished, those deemed black and criminal in the United States must, too, unnecessarily suffer authorized racial, physical, and civil amputations, hyper-killings, and non-burials which equate to acts of public seduction and racial eye candy.

Writing in this historical moment, I could not help but conclude that the ritual cross-roads linking Bouqui to Breonna Taylor, La Fortune to George Floyd, Eric Garner, and Micah Johnson, Jayland Walker, and Yala and Youba to Sandra Bland and Katricia Africa is the repeated gratuitous violence of the white imaginary upon the enfleshed and de-fleshed black body across the centuries.[10] Throughout diaspora geographies and tempo-ralities from Trinidad to the United States, we see a shared white imaginary and psychic orientation regarding race, religion, the "body-words" of blackness, and its inescapability from social malignancy, criminality, and hyper-annihilation.[11] Nevertheless, the next volume illumines how African spirituality, in the structures of Trinidad's Yoruba-Orisa tradition, has prevailed beyond colonial violence. And likewise (in a study to be written by a future author), it will have to be acknowledged that the Yoruba-Orisa religion also prevails among increasing numbers of African Americans in the United States, including the cofounders of the Black Lives Matter movement and countless black activists who love African spirits and support the substance and most noble aims of the movement.[12]

Reader, as you conclude volume I, remember John Cooper's "C'est vrai." It is indeed true that colonial imaginations and romantic racialisms endure and that the hauntings of social cannibalism still persist. It is true that black bodies are still surveilled, policed, spectacularized, consumed, and discarded. Yet it is also true that Black Death Matters in all of its sacrosanctity and inviolability to African-descended persons, even as I write now, over two centuries after the time period described in this study. It is true that under the threat of old and new racialized allegations of witchcraft, sorcery, and black occult-ism, Trinidadians and African Americans continue to invoke the African Gods in affirma-tion and defense of black persons in this hemisphere. And perhaps most true is that African(a) religions in general, and Yoruba-Orisa more specifically, represent an infinite resource of spiritual power and weaponry, of shielding and sustaining protection, and of righteous resistance to the religious violence and enduring beliefs of white racecraft.[13]

Notes

Preface

1 Layli Maparyan discusses "harmonizing and coordinating" as an important component of womanist methodology in *The Womanist Idea* (New York: Routledge, 2012), 56–57.
2 Jan Vansina, *Paths in the Rainforests: Toward a History of Political Tradition in Equatorial Africa* (Madison: University of Wisconsin Press, 1990), 258.
3 Charles H. Long, *Significations: Signs, Symbols, and Images in the Interpretation of Religion* (Aurora, CO: Davies, 1995) (1986).
4 See chapter 1, n. 12.
5 "Within the discipline of religion, David D. Hall and Robert Orsi have for close to two decades been at the forefront in pioneering 'a history of practice' in American religious history through the heuristic rubric of 'lived religion.' Inspired from the French concept *la religion vécue*, Hall and Orsi sought to encourage new innovations in 'cultural and ethnographical approaches to the study of religion and American religious history' by 'enlisting perspectives' that privilege human practice as an important lens for determining how humans 'live with and work through multiple realms of meaning.' Through examining 'modalities of practice' over and against normative theologies, doctrines, or elite orthodoxies, lived religion sought to recast the disciplinary representation of religion into a more flexible, 'complex and multifaceted phenomenon.' Lived religion expanded the interpretive gaze of American religious history to include not only practice as a crucial site for engaging religious meaning but also the inclusion of non-elite popular communities as significant actors in religious production." Quoted in Tracey E. Hucks, "Perspectives in Lived History: Religion, Ethnography, and the Study of African Diasporic Religion," *Practical Matters: A Transdisciplinary Multimedia Journal of Religious Practices and Practical Theology* 3 (Spring 2010): 3.

6 Long, *Significations*, 6.

7 Karen E. Fields and Barbara J. Fields, *Racecraft: The Soul of Inequality in American Life* (New York: Verso, 2012), 5.

8 Olúpọ̀nà, *City of 201 Gods*, esp. 1–5.

9 Abdul R. JanMohamed, *The Death-Bound-Subject* (Durham, NC: Duke University Press, 2005).

10 Scholars such as Tweed, *Crossing and Dwelling*; Tandberg, *Relational Religion*; Mwale, *Relationality in Theological Anthropology*; Harris, et al., "Womanist Theology;" and Krech, "Relational Religion," have proposed the need for developing relational theories of religion and theology. Our approach to relationality is distinct from these perspectives in that it takes its point of departure from a Longian conception of orientation.

11 James, *Varieties*, 31–32. Emphasis added. On "soul-life," see chapter 3, n. 66 of this volume.

11 See James, *Varieties*.

Introduction

1 Consultations with Yoruba scholars have confirmed neither that *mojunta* is a Yoruba word nor the meaning attributed to it in this context.

2 Sam Phills, interview by author and Dianne M. Stewart, tape recording, Port of Spain, May 8, 2001.

3 *Nation*, *nationhood*, *nation-al*, *inter-nation-al*, and other related word compounds are italicized in this study to signify Africana constructions of sociocultural networks and institutions that often included governing offices and micropolitical activities but were not political state structures. Africana assertions of *nation* identities and productions of *nation* mechanisms constituted a widespread phenomenon among enslaved and indentured laborers in every corner of the European slaveholding and colonial world. For more information on these institutions and their religious frameworks, see Olabiyi Yai, "African Diasporan Concepts and Practice of the Nation and Their Implications in the Modern World," in *African Roots/American Cultures: Africa in the Creation of the Americas*, ed. Sheila S. Walker (Lanham, MD: Rowman & Littlefield, 2001), 244–55; Edison Carneiro, *Candomblés da Bahia* (Bahia: Secretaria de Edicação e Saúde, 1948); Edison Carneiro, "The Structure of African Cults in Bahia," *Journal of American Folklore* 53, no. 210 (October–December 1940): 271–78; Beatriz Góis Dantas, *Vovó Nagô e Papai Branco, Usos e abusos da África no Brasil* (Rio de Janeiro: Edições Graal, 1988); Beatriz Góis Dantas, *Nagô Grandma and White Papa: Candomblé and the Creation of Afro-Brazilian Identity*, trans. Stephen Berg (Chapel Hill: University of North Carolina Press, 2009); John Thornton, *Africa and Africans in the Making of the Atlantic World: 1400–1800* (Cambridge, UK: Cambridge University Press, 1998); J. Lorand Matory, *Black Atlantic Religion*

(Princeton: Princeton University Press, 2005); Yvonne Daniel, *Dancing Wisdom: Embodied Knowledge in Haitian Vodou, Cuban Yoruba, and Bahian Candomblé* (Champaign: University of Illinois Press, 2005); Patrick Taylor, *Nation Dance: Religion, Identity, and Cultural Difference in the Caribbean* (Bloomington: Indiana University Press, 2001); and Rachel Harding, *A Refuge in Thunder: Candomblé and Alternative Spaces of Blackness* (Bloomington: Indiana University Press, 2000).

4 In both volumes, Dianne Stewart and I adopt a semantic strategy of employing a capital "O" when referencing Africana conceptions of "Obeah" and a lowercase "o" when referencing the colonial invention of "obeah"—colonial imaginings, beliefs, discursive ideologies, and so forth.

5 CO 137/209. Records of the Colonial Office (CO), National Archives, Kew Gardens, United Kingdom.

6 "Obeah Histories: Researching Obeah Prosecution for Religious Practice in the Caribbean," WordPress, accessed May 19, 2016, https://obeahhistories .org/polydore/.

7 See Dianne M. Stewart Diakité and Tracey E. Hucks, "Africana Religious Studies," 28–77. The Caribbean experience and its relationship to neighboring regions invite conceptual treatments of African religious heritage and contemporary practice within Caribbean studies, Latin American studies, diaspora studies, Atlantic world studies, and American studies frameworks. While the material uncovered for this book requires engagement with some of these rubrics, we found compelling reasons to offer an Africana framework as this study's guiding conceptual rubric. We emphasize that our Africana framework is not insular and myopic but necessarily dialogical and resonant with other frameworks.

8 Comaroff and Comaroff, "Africa Observed," 31.

9 Comaroff and Comaroff, "Africa Observed," 32–33.

10 Young, Embodying Black Experience, 1.

11 Fields and Fields, *Racecraft*, 5.

12 Saidiya Hartman, "Venus in Two Acts," 11.

13 The epigraph is from Hall, "Negotiating Caribbean Identity," 6.

14 Hall, "Negotiating Caribbean Identity," 6.

15 Hall, "Negotiating Caribbean Identity," 6–7. Emphasis added.

16 Hall, "Negotiating Caribbean Identity," 7.

17 Patterson and Kelley, "Unfinished Migrations," 20.

18 Butler, "Defining Diaspora," 193.

19 Wood, *Trinidad in Transition*, 32.

20 Williams, *History of the People*, 66; Wood, *Trinidad in Transition*, 32.

21 A. Meredith John, *The Plantation Slaves of Trinidad 1783–1816: A Mathematical and Demographic Enquiry* (New York: Cambridge University Press, 1988), 165.

22 Brereton, *Race Relations in Colonial Trinidad*, 64, 70.

23 Brereton, *Race Relations in Colonial Trinidad*, 214; Schuler, "Alas, Alas, Kongo": A Social History, 9.

24 I invoke my concept of "diasporaed" used in my first book in order to punctuate the fact that when discussing the African captives of the transatlantic slave trade and slavery in the Western Hemisphere and their African diasporas, central to my analysis is the understanding that "diaspora" is used not as a noun but as a verb demarcating an occurrence and a series of processes that happened to those African captives who found themselves involuntarily exiled from their African homelands and enslaved in the Caribbean and the Americas. See Hucks, *Yoruba Traditions*, xxi.

One. The Formation of a Slave Colony

1 Carmichael, *History of the West Indian Islands*, 76.
2 Carmichael, *History of the West Indian Islands*, 76.
3 Besson and Brereton, *Book of Trinidad*, 11–18.
4 Besson and Brereton, *Book of Trinidad*, 118.
5 Besson and Brereton, *Book of Trinidad*, 118; Carmichael, *History of the West Indian Islands*, 77.
6 Summary of dispatch from Governor Hislop to the secretary of state on the slave rising, December 19, 1805, Public Record Office, State Papers, Colonial C.O. 295/11, Trinidad and Tobago.
7 Carmichael, *History of the West Indian Islands*, 77; Besson and Brereton, *Book of Trinidad*, 118–19.
8 Carmichael, *History of the West Indian Islands*, 77.
9 De Barros, Diptee, Trotman, eds., *Beyond Fragmentation*, xii.
10 Fraser, *History of Trinidad*, 272.
11 The term "inter-society pluralism" comes from Simpson, *Caribbean Papers*, 1/21.
12 Throughout the volume, I use "Obeah" to designate the spiritual practices of African-descended communities. In contradistinction, I use "obeah" to encompass the broad meanings of the European imaginary.
13 Gerbner, "'They Call Me Obea,'" 160–78; Stewart, *Three Eyes*, esp. 15–68, 139–88; Bilby and Handler, "Obeah: Healing and Protection," 153–83; Handler and Bilby, "On the Early Use," 87–100.
14 For more on the death-bound-subject, see Abdul R. JanMohamed, *The Death-Bound-Subject*. (Durham, NC: Duke University Press, 2005).
15 Newson, *Aboriginal and Spanish Colonial Trinidad*, 72.
16 *Cedula to all persons giving permission to wage war upon and enslave the Caribs of Trinidad and other places*, December 23, 1511, Trinidad Historical Society, Publication No. 75, 2–3.
17 *Cedula to all persons*, 2.
18 *Cedula to all persons*, 2.
19 Newson, *Aboriginal and Spanish Colonial Trinidad*, 72.

20 Benjamin, *Atlantic World*, 172.

21 Newson, *Aboriginal and Spanish Colonial Trinidad*, 78.

22 Brereton, *Introduction to the History of Trinidad and Tobago*, 5.

23 Newson, *Aboriginal and Spanish Colonial Trinidad*, 76–77, 186.

24 Newson, *Aboriginal and Spanish Colonial Trinidad*, 101.

25 Newson, *Aboriginal and Spanish Colonial Trinidad*, 101.

26 Newson, *Aboriginal and Spanish Colonial Trinidad*, 101.

27 Newson, *Aboriginal and Spanish Colonial Trinidad*, 102.

28 Brereton, *Introduction to the History of Trinidad and Tobago*, 6.

29 Williams, *History of the People of Trinidad and Tobago*, 25.

30 Williams, *History of the People of Trinidad and Tobago*, 27.

31 Newson, *Aboriginal and Spanish Colonial Trinidad*, 132.

32 Newson, *Aboriginal and Spanish Colonial Trinidad*, 132. Comparatively, enslaved aboriginals cost substantially less, between 40 and 50 pesos each.

33 John, *Plantation Slaves of Trinidad*, 12.

34 Wood, *Trinidad in Transition*, 32.

35 Newson, *Aboriginal and Spanish Colonial Trinidad*, 184, 180. "Immigration increased, and amongst the new colonists were fugitive slaves from nearby islands who obtained concessions as freemen on arrival in Trinidad. There was some anxiety as to the presumed criminal nature of some of the former slaves. In order to prevent the island from becoming a refuge for 'robbers, fraudulent bankrupts, criminals or men lost in vice,' it was resolved that all slaves who had fled from other islands should pay their price plus 6% for every year they had absented themselves, whilst those unable to pay were to be returned. In this way the Governor aimed at retaining the enterprising refugee slaves and at the same time dispens[ing] with criminal elements."

36 Although Carmichael's book includes the entire translated text of the cedula in the appendix, it is dated in error 1873 instead of 1783.

37 John, *Plantation Slaves of Trinidad*, 363.

38 The entire cedula is reproduced in full in Carmichael, *History of the West Indian Islands*, 363–69. http://caribbeanhistoryarchives.blogspot.com/2007/12/royal -cedula-of-1783.html. Accessed March 6, 2022.

39 Williams, *History of the People of Trinidad and Tobago*, 42; Brereton, *Introduction to the History of Trinidad and Tobago*, 12.

40 Brereton, *Introduction to the History of Trinidad and Tobago*, 27.

41 John, *Plantation Slaves of Trinidad*, 14.

42 James Millette, *Society and Politics*, 7.

43 Stinchcombe, *Sugar Island Slavery*, 99.

44 Brereton, "Trinidad, 1498–1962," http://www.caribbean-atlas.com/en/themes /waves-of-colonization-and-control-in-the-caribbean/waves-of-colonization /trinidad-1498-1962.html. Accessed March 30, 2022. See also Wood, *Trinidad in Transition*, 33 and John, *Plantation Slaves of Trinidad*, 54.

45 Epstein, "Politics of Colonial Sensation," 715.

46 Wood, Trinidad in Transition, 32. According to Wood, "In February 1803, a census showed that there had been a twenty-fold increase in twenty-five years and that the French-speakers, both white and coloured, were now the predominant group."

47 Millette, Society and Politics, 17.

48 John, Plantation Slaves of Trinidad, 54.

49 John, Plantation Slaves of Trinidad, 52. See her chap. 4, "The Population of Trinidad," for detailed statistics on slave population, sex ratios, Caribbean importation, age distribution, color distribution by plantation, and job classification.

50 Elsa V. Goveia. "The West Indian Slave Laws of the Eighteenth Century" in Shepherd and Beckles, Caribbean Slavery in the Atlantic World, 580–596.

51 Williams, History of the People of Trinidad and Tobago, 66.

52 Between 1802 and 1808, African captives disembarked in Trinidad from vessels originating in the Bight of Biafra (twenty-five, from which 6,536 captives disembarked); other unspecified regions of Africa (twenty-five, from which 5,579 captives disembarked); West-Central Africa (seven, from which 1,390 captives disembarked); Sierra Leone (four, from which 888 captives disembarked); Senegambia (three, from which 615 captives disembarked); the Gold Coast (three, from which 1,111 captives disembarked); and the Windward Coast (one, from which 279 captives disembarked). See Voyages: The Transatlantic Slave Trade Database, https://www.slavevoyages.org/.

53 Williams, History of the People of Trinidad and Tobago, 75.

54 Wood, Trinidad in Transition, 32.

55 John, Plantation Slaves of Trinidad, 22–23.

56 Burnley, Observations on the Present Condition, 51.

57 Williams, History of the People of Trinidad and Tobago, 76–167.

58 John, Plantation Slaves of Trinidad, 103.

59 John, Plantation Slaves of Trinidad, 104.

60 John, Plantation Slaves of Trinidad, 110, 114.

61 John, Plantation Slaves of Trinidad, 117.

62 John, Plantation Slaves of Trinidad, 106.

63 John, Plantation Slaves of Trinidad, 214.

64 Williams, Historical Society of Trinidad and Tobago, 40.

65 Williams, Historical Society of Trinidad and Tobago, 140

66 Williams, Historical Society of Trinidad and Tobago, 152.

67 Williams, Historical Society of Trinidad and Tobago, 139.

68 Williams, Historical Society of Trinidad and Tobago, 122.

69 Williams, Historical Society of Trinidad and Tobago, 122.

70 Williams, Historical Society of Trinidad and Tobago, 148.

71 Williams, Historical Society of Trinidad and Tobago, 150.

72 For a broader context, see Jennifer Morgan, *Laboring Women: Reproduction and Gender in New World Slavery* (Philadelphia: University of Pennsylvania Press, 2004).

73 John, *Plantation Slaves of Trinidad*, 207.

74 De Verteuil, *Seven Slaves and Slavery*, 28.

75 John, *Plantation Slaves of Trinidad*, 208.

76 John, *Plantation Slaves of Trinidad*, 208.

77 John, *Plantation Slaves of Trinidad*, 101.

78 John, *Plantation Slaves of Trinidad*, 212.

79 John, *Plantation Slaves of Trinidad*, 214.

80 John, *Plantation Slaves of Trinidad*, 217.

81 John, *Plantation Slaves of Trinidad*, 45.

82 John, *Plantation Slaves of Trinidad*, 165.

83 John, *Plantation Slaves of Trinidad*, 221.

84 John, *Plantation Slaves of Trinidad*, 240.

85 John, *Plantation Slaves of Trinidad*, 240.

86 Wood, *Trinidad in Transition*, 39.

87 Wood, *Trinidad in Transition*, 45.

88 Brereton, *Introduction to the History of Trinidad and Tobago*, xv.

89 Elder, "Evolution of the Traditional Calypso of Trinidad and Tobago," 72.

90 Brereton, *Introduction to the History of Trinidad and Tobago*, 14.

91 Botero, "Racial Question During Struggles of Independence," 1582.

92 Robinson, "Trinidad and Tobago," 1881.

93 Mitchell, "Ambiguous Distinctions of Descent," 42–43.

94 Brereton, *Introduction to the History of Trinidad and Tobago*, 16.

95 Brereton, *Introduction to the History of Trinidad and Tobago*, 17.

96 John, *Plantation Slaves of Trinidad*, 14.

97 John, *Plantation Slaves of Trinidad*, 14.

98 Williams, *History of the People of Trinidad and Tobago*, 47.

99 Williams, *Documents on British West Indian History*, 208.

100 Williams, *Documents on British West Indian History*, 64, 70.

101 Wood, *Trinidad in Transition*, 41.

102 Brereton, *Introduction to the History of Trinidad and Tobago*, 44.

103 MacDonald, *Trinidad and Tobago*, 24.

104 MacDonald, *Trinidad and Tobago*, 26.

105 Williams, *History of the People of Trinidad and Tobago*, 69.

106 Newson, *Aboriginal and Spanish Colonial Trinidad*, 184.

107 Williams, *History of the People of Trinidad and Tobago*, 49.

108 Williams, *History of the People of Trinidad and Tobago*, 48.

109 Farmer, *AIDS and Accusation*, 155.

110 Brereton, *Introduction to the History of Trinidad and Tobago*, 25.

111 Brereton, *Introduction to the History of Trinidad and Tobago*, 25.

112 Newson, *Aboriginal and Spanish Colonial Trinidad*, 193.

113 Newson, *Aboriginal and Spanish Colonial Trinidad*, 193.

114 Brereton, *Introduction to the History of Trinidad and Tobago*, 51.

115 De Verteuil, *Seven Slaves and Slavery*, 46.

116 De Verteuil, *Seven Slaves and Slavery*, 46; Brereton, *Introduction to the History of Trinidad and Tobago*, 37.

117 Millette, *Society and Politics*, 33.

118 Millette, *Society and Politics*, xv.

119 Millette, *Society and Politics*, xv.

120 The Commissioners to the Secretary of State, March 28, 1803, Historical Society of Trinidad and Tobago, 1–2.

121 Colonel Fullarton to the Secretary of State, March 29, 1803, Historical Society of Trinidad and Tobago, 2.

122 Fraser, *History of Trinidad*, appendix, xviii–xix.

123 Fraser, *History of Trinidad*, 310.

124 Millette, *Society and Politics*, 264.

125 Winer, *Adolphus*, xvii.

126 CO 714157 Records of the Colonial Office (CO), Index Précis of Incoming Correspondence. The National Archives, Kew Gardens, UK

127 Williams, *Documents on British West Indian History*, 216.

128 Williams; *Documents on British West Indian History*, 216. Mitchell, "Ambiguous Distinctions,"

129 Brereton, *An Introduction to the History*, 25; Campbell, "The Opposition to Crown Colony Government," 58.

130 Williams, *Documents on British West Indian History*, 212. Mitchell, "Ambiguous Distinctions," 212.

131 Winer, *Adolphus*, xvii; Robinson, "Trinidad and Tobago," 1882.

132 Mitchell, "Ambiguous Distinctions," 188.

133 Mitchell, "Ambiguous Distinctions," 6.

134 Mitchell, "Ambiguous Distinctions," 6.

135 Clement, "Shango," 17–18. Free coloreds should not be completely homogenized as many maintained different types of alliances and allegiances.

136 Clement, "Shango," 18.

137 Howell, *I Was a Slave*, 43.

138 Howell, *I Was a Slave*, 43.

139 Williams, *Documents on British West Indian History*, 209.

140 Williams, *History of the People of Trinidad and Tobago*, 70.

141 MacDonald, *Trinidad and Tobago*, 33.

142 MacDonald, *Trinidad and Tobago*, 33.

143 Simpson, *Caribbean Papers*, 1/21.

144 Brereton, *Introduction to the History of Trinidad and Tobago*, 43.

145 Memorandum by the Colonial Department, April 7, 1803, Historical Society of Trinidad and Tobago, 1.

146 Memorandum, 46.
147 "Business in the Blood: Chinese Bring Culture of Commerce to T&T," Trinidad Express, October 2, 2011; Millette, Society and Politics, 134.
148 Lai, The Chinese in the West Indies, 31.
149 Millette, Society and Politics, xv.
150 Louis B. Homer, "The Rise of the Chinese in T&T," Trinidad Express, October 7, 2012.
151 Fiona Rajkumar, "Chinese in the Caribbean," 3.
152 Bolland, Struggles for Freedom, 182.
153 Sherry-Ann Singh, "Experience of Indian Indenture in Trinidad."
154 See also Ikuko Asaka, Tropical Freedom (Durham, NC: Duke University Press, 2017).
155 Glazier, "Mourning in the Afro-Baptist Traditions," 142.
156 Rudolph Eastman, The Fight for Dignity, 39.
157 Laitinen, Marching to Zion, 46.
158 Mitchell, "Ambiguous Distinctions," 312.
159 Mitchell, "Ambiguous Distinctions," 313.
160 Mitchell, "Ambiguous Distinctions," 313.
161 Mitchell, "Ambiguous Distinctions," 312.
162 https://www.natt.gov.tt/sites/default/files/pdfs/Our_African_Legacy_Roots_and_Routes.pdf. Accessed March 5, 2022.
163 Laurence, "Tobago and British Imperial Authority," 44.
164 https://www.natt.gov.tt/sites/default/files/pdfs/Our_African_Legacy_Roots_and_Routes.pdf. Accessed March 5, 2022. Brereton, Introduction to the History of Trinidad and Tobago, 24. Laurence, "The Settlement of Free Negroes in Trinidad, 26.
165 CO 295/85 Records of the Colonial Office (CO), The National Archives, Kew Gardens, UK.
166 Burnley, Observations on the Present Condition, 61–63.
167 Hackshaw, Baptist Denomination, 3.
168 Huggins, Saga of the Companies, 3.
169 Huggins, Saga of the Companies, 23.
170 Brereton, Introduction to the History of Trinidad and Tobago, 68.
171 Wood, Trinidad in Transition, 68.
172 Wood, Trinidad in Transition, 67.
173 Carmichael, History of the West Indian Islands, 420.
174 Burnley, Observations of the Present Condition, 61.
175 Carmichael, History of the West Indian Islands, 419.
176 Carmichael, History of the West Indian Islands, 419–20.
177 Wood, Trinidad in Transition, 67; Bolland, Struggles for Freedom, 181.
178 Wood, Trinidad in Transition, 69.
179 Wood, Trinidad in Transition 69.

180 Wood, Trinidad in Transition 68.
181 Wood, Trinidad in Transition; Schuler, "Alas, Alas, Kongo," 2.
182 Schuler, "Alas, Alas, Kongo," 2; Adderley, "New Negroes from Africa," 2.
183 Mitchell, "Ambiguous Distinctions," 339.
184 Sir George Hill, Governor of Trinidad, to Right Honourable E. G. Stanley, March 9, 1834, Historical Society of Trinidad and Tobago, Publication No. 253, 1.
185 Hill to Stanley, 2.
186 Hill to Stanley, 5.
187 Adderley, "New Negroes from Africa," 9, 75, 86.
188 Adderley, "New Negroes from Africa," 79–80.
189 Adderley, "New Negroes from Africa," 78.
190 http://caribbeanhistoryarchives.blogspot.com/. Accessed March 1, 2022.
191 Trotman, "Yoruba and Orisha Worship," 19.
192 Goldwasser, "Rainbow Madonna of Trinidad," 111; Brereton, Race Relations in Colonial Trinidad, 134.
193 Adderley, "New Negroes from Africa," 61, 113. By the end of the nineteenth century, exceptions were observed among some liberated Africans, especially the Yoruba, who could be found living among Creole blacks. See Brereton, Race Relations in Colonial Trinidad, 135.
194 Schuler, "Alas, Alas, Kongo," 2.
195 Maureen Warner-Lewis, Yoruba Songs of Trinidad (London: Karnak House, 1994).
196 Adderley, "New Negroes from Africa," 90.
197 Millette, Society and Politics, vi.
198 Appeal of the Trinidad Association for the Propagation of the Gospel, more particularly to The Inhabitants of the Island and to all interested in the welfare, or their benevolent co-operation in farther extending the means of Religious Instruction and Emprobement, especially to The Immigrants from Heathen Lands, have arrived and are still arriving on its shores, lix.
199 Millette, Society and Politics, vi; Adderley, "New Negroes from Africa," 183.
200 Adderley, "New Negroes from Africa," 183.
201 Adderley, "New Negroes from Africa," 184. Emphasis added.
202 Warner-Lewis, Yoruba Songs of Trinidad, 7; Trotman, "Yoruba and Orisha Worship," 8.
203 Howard, "Yoruba in the British Caribbean," 161–162.
204 Adderley, "New Negroes from Africa," 63.

Two. Let Them Hate So Long as They Fear

1 Fett, Working Cures, 41.
2 Stinchcombe, Sugar Island, 128.
3 Handler and Bilby, Enacting Power, 5; Paton, No Bond but the Law, 183.

4   Higginbotham, "African American Women's History," 252.
5   Williams, *Hamel, the Obeah Man*, 35; Forde and Paton, 14.
6   Higginbotham, "African American Women's History," 252.
7   Long, "Bodies in Time and the Healing of Spaces," 43.
8   Long, "Bodies in Time and the Healing of Spaces," 48. Emphasis added.
9   *Egalite for All: Toussaint Louverture and the Haitian Revolution*, directed by Nolan Walker, Public Broadcasting Service, 2009, DVD.
10 Rivera, *Poetics of the Flesh*, 1–2.
11 Rivera, *Poetics of the Flesh*, 4; Debra Walker King, ed., *Body Politics and the Fictional Double* (Bloomington: Indiana University Press, 2000), vii–viii, 69–70.
12 Rivera, *Poetics of the Flesh*, 113, 7.
13 Hartman, *Scenes of Subjection*, 22, 59.
14 Murray, "Three Worships, and an Old Warlock and Many Lawless Forces: The Court Trial of an African Doctor who Practiced 'Obeah to cure' in early Nineteenth Century Jamaica," *Journal of Southern African Studies* 33, no. 4 (November 2007): 811–28.
15 Alexander G. Weheliye, *Habeas Viscus: Racializing Assemblages, Biopolitics, and Black Feminist Theories of the Human* (Durham, NC: Duke University Press, 2014), 132.
16 Millette, *Society and Politics*, 60, 57; Pierre McCallum, *Travels in Trinidad during the months of February, March and April, 1803, in a Series of Letters addressed to a Member of the Imperial Parliament of Great Britain* (Liverpool, 1805), 134, 344; Andrew J. Rotter, *Empire of the Senses: Bodily Encounters in Imperial India and the Philippines* (New York: Oxford University Press, 2019), 73.
17 James Epstein, "Politics of Colonial Sensation: The Trial of Thomas Picton and the Cause of Louisa Calderon," *The American Historical Review* 112, no. 3 (June 2007): 714; Pierce and Rao, *Discipline and the Other Body*, 4.
18 Obeyesekere, *Cannibal Talk*, 152.
19 Obeyesekere, *Cannibal Talk*, 1, 230, 152.
20 Obeyesekere, *Cannibal Talk*, 153–54.
21 Long, *Significations*, 2.
22 Obeyesekere, *Cannibal Talk*, 24.
23 Stewart, *Three Eyes for the Journey*.
24 Farmer, AIDS and Accusation, 157.
25 For more on Tacky's Revolt see Vincent Brown, *Tacky's Revolt: The Story of an Atlantic Slave* (Cambridge: Harvard University Press, 2000).
26 CO 139/21, Records of the Colonial Office (CO), National Archives, Kew Gardens, UK.
27 Handler and Bilby, *Enacting Power*, 16.
28 Handler and Bilby, *Enacting Power*, 19–21.
29 Shepherd and Beckles, *Caribbean Slavery*, 584.
30 Watson, *Slave Laws*, 61; Shepherd and Beckles, *Caribbean Slavery*, 584.

31 Shepherd and Beckles, *Caribbean Slavery*, 584, 587.

32 Watson, *Slave Laws*, 64.

33 Hartman, *Scenes of Subjection*, 41.

34 Hartman, *Scenes of Subjection*, 30, 55.

35 Hartman, *Scenes of Subjection*, 82.

36 Handler and Bilby, *Enacting Power*, 17; Hartman, *Scenes of Subjection*, 82, 108.

37 Fraser, *History of Trinidad*, 117–18.

38 Fraser, *History of Trinidad*, 118.

39 Fraser, *History of Trinidad*, 118.

40 Ivol Blackman, *Post Capitulation Trinidad (1797–1947): Aspects of the Laws, The Judicial System, and the Government* (Indiana: Xlibris, 2019), 11–12.

41 Goveia, *Slave Society*, 251–52.

42 Goveia, *Slave Society*, 252.

43 Parrish, "Diasporic African Sources," 283.

44 Long, "Bodies in Time and the Healing of Spaces," 43.

45 Higman, *Slave Populations*, 261.

46 Higman, *Slave Populations*, 261.

47 Anthony De Verteuil, *A History of Diego Martin* (Port of Spain: Paria, 1987), n.p. The section labeled "Obeah" is located at the back of the text and does not have pagination.

48 Rotter, *Empires of the Senses*, 202–3.

49 Higman, *Slave Populations*, 279.

50 Ralph James Woodford, "Proclamation Regarding Small Pox in the Island," Trinidad, March 26, 1819, Historical Society of Trinidad and Tobago, Publication No. 300, 3.

51 Woodford, "Proclamation," 3; Higman, *Slave Populations*, 261–62.

52 Higman, *Slave Populations*, 294.

53 De Verteuil, *History of Diego Martin*, 52.

54 Higman, *Slave Populations*, 266.

55 Higman, *Slave Populations*, 266.

56 Higman, *Slave Populations*, 273, 266, 271.

57 Parrish, "Diasporic African Sources," 283.

58 Paton, "Witchcraft, Poison, Law," 261; Watson, "Obeah and Empire," 5; Watson, *Caribbean Culture*.

59 Savage, "Slave Poison/Slave Medicine, 166.

60 Trotman, *Crime in Trinidad*, 228.

61 Paton and Forde, *Obeah and Other Powers*, 3.

62 Brown, *Reaper's Garden*, 150.

63 De Verteuil, *History of Diego Martin*, 53.

64 In 1804, Govenor Picton ruled as part of a three-person Commission with William Fullarton and Samuel Hood.

65 Millette, *Genesis of Crown Colony Government*, 100.

66 Millette, *Genesis of Crown Colony Government*, 109.

67 Millette, *Genesis of Crown Colony Government*, 109.

68 Governor Sir Thomas Picton, Governor of Trinidad, to the Secretary of State, May 1, 1800, Trinidad Historical Society, Publication No. 525, 2.

69 Millette, *Genesis of Crown Colony Government*, 101.

70 Governor Sir Thomas Picton, Letter 3 to His Excellency Right Admiral Harvey, 1799. This correspondence is from the unpublished and uncataloged collection of Sir Thomas Picton papers and made available at the National Archives of Trinidad and Tobago.

71 Hollis Urban Liverpool, "Origins of Ritual and Customs in the Trinidad Carnival," TDR 42, no. 3 (Autumn, 1998): 29.

72 Williams, *Historical Society of Trinidad and Tobago*, 212. On December 11, 1818, a Trinidad newspaper reported the following: "A Steam Board will be put into activity, as a passage vessel, on Monday 21—the boat is furnished with two separate cabins, for the white and coloured classes of the community . . . and a third division, at half price, is appropriated for the use of slaves or of such others as may not have the means of paying for the superior accommodation."

73 Brereton, *Introduction to the History of Trinidad and Tobago*, 49; Williams, *History of the People of Trinidad and Tobago*, 72.

74 Simone Browne, *Dark Matters: On the Surveillance of Blackness* (Durham, NC: Duke University Press, 2015), 78–79.

75 Brereton, *Introduction to the History of Trinidad and Tobago*, 50.

76 Winer, *Adolphus*, xvi.

77 Winer, *Adolphus*, xvi–xvii; Mitchell, "Ambiguous Distinctions of Descent," 38.

78 Prior, "Battle of Waterloo."

79 Fraser, *History of Trinidad*, 289.

80 Gérard Besson and Bridget Brereton, *The Book of Trinidad* (Port of Spain: Paria, 2010), 105; Millette, *Society and Politics*, 32, 115.

81 Millette, *Society and Politics*, 32.

82 Millette, *Society and Politics*, 115, 120–21.

83 Millette, *Society and Politics*, 109.

84 Millette, *Society and Politics*, 18.

85 Sir Thomas Picton, Colonial Correspondence, July 30, 1799. This correspondence is from the unpublished and uncataloged collection of Sir Thomas Picton papers and made available at the National Archives of Trinidad and Tobago.

86 De Verteuil, *History of Diego Martin*, 50–52; Louis Antoine Aimé Gaston De Verteuil, *Trinidad: Its Geography, Natural Resources, Administration, Present Condition, and Prospects* (London: Ward and Lock, 1858), 276.

87 Lauren Benton and Lisa Ford, "Island Despotism: Trinidad, the British Imperial Constitution and Global Legal Order," *Journal of Imperial and Commonwealth History* 46, no. 1 (2018): 29. Evans, *Slave Wales*, 101.

88 Millette, *Society and Politics*, 141–42.

89 Millette, *Society and Politics*, 142.
90 Millette, *Society and Politics*, 143.
91 McCallum, *Travels in Trinidad*, 126.
92 Besson and Brereton, *Book of Trinidad*, 109.
93 McCallum, *Travels in Trinidad*, 131.
94 Trotman, *Crime in Trinidad*, 228.
95 Millette, *Society and Politics*, 54.
96 Carradice, *Snapshots of Welsh History*, 29. Prior, "Battle of Waterloo," n.p.
97 Evans, *Slave Wales*, 96.
98 De Verteuil, *History of Diego Martin*, 43.
99 De Verteuil, *History of Diego Martin*, 43.
100 Fraser, *History of Trinidad*, 155.
101 De Verteuil, *History of Diego Martin*, 42.
102 Millette, *Society and Politics*, 35.
103 Paton, "Punishment, Crime," 923.
104 Paton, *Cultural Politics*, 81.
105 Parrish, "Diasporic African Sources," 297.
106 Obeyesekere, *Cannibal Talk*, 53; Watson, "Obeah and Empire," 10.
107 Benjamin, *Atlantic World*, 393.
108 John, *Plantation Slaves of Trinidad*, 215; Carmichael, *History of the West Indian Islands*, 382. The entire 1800 Slave Code is reproduced in both texts.
109 John, *Plantation Slaves of Trinidad*, 215.
110 CO 30/20 Records of the Colonial Office (CO), The National Archives, Kew Gardens, UK.
111 Paton, "Punishment, Crime," 923.
112 Eliga H. Gould, *Zones of Law, Zones of Violence*, 507.
113 John, *Plantation Slaves of Trinidad*, 215.
114 Evans, *Slave Wales*, 96.
115 Evans, *Slave Wales*, 96.
116 Goldwasser, "Rainbow Madonna," 105.
117 Farmer, AIDS *and Accusation*, 156.
118 Farmer, AIDS *and Accusation*, 156–57.
119 Farmer, AIDS *and Accusation*, 157.
120 De Verteuil, *Seven Slaves and Slavery*, 98.
121 Fraser, *History of Trinidad*, 224; De Verteuil, *History of Diego Martin*, 52.
122 CO 295/5 Records of the Colonial Office (CO), The National Archives, Kew Gardens, UK.
123 McCallum, *Travels in Trinidad*, 131.
124 Fraser, *History of Trinidad*, 224.
125 McCallum, *Travels in Trinidad*, 131.
126 McCallum, *Travels in Trinidad*, 131, 183.
127 McCallum, *Travels in Trinidad*, 26.

128 "Dâaga," Peoples of the Historical Slave Trade, accessed February 24, 2022, https://enslaved.org/fullStory/16-23-92876/. The famous Dâaga Rebellion occurred on June 17, 1837. West African-born Dâaga was a liberated African, and he and his soldiers took over the military barracks in the St. Joseph area of Trinidad. They fled with the intention of securing passage to South America and returning to the continent of Africa. However, Dâaga was captured, court-martialed, and executed before a firing squad with his last words pronouncing a curse upon his white adversaries: "The curse of Holloloo on white men. Do they think that Dâaga fears to fix his eyeballs on death?"

129 De Verteuil, History of Diego Martin, n.p., (square brackets in the original).

130 "Brutality of Picton Past Examined: A Military Hero Has Been Branded a Cruel Colonial Governor, Remembered as a 'Beast' on the Slave Island He Ruled," BBC News, March 20, 2007.

131 CO 295/5 Records of the Colonial Office (CO), The National Archives, Kew Gardens, UK; Millette, Society and Politics, 52.

132 Millette, Society and Politics, 141.

133 Susan Campbell, "Carnival, Calypso, and Class Struggle in Nineteenth Century Trinidad," History Workshop Journal 26, no. 1 (1988): 7; Jared Hickman, "Globalization and the Gods, or the Political Theology of 'Race,'" Early American Literature 45, no. 1 (2010): 156, 170.

134 Paton, "Punishment, Crime, and the Bodies of Slaves," 927, 924.

135 Fraser, History of Trinidad, 120.

136 Letters of Decius, In Answer to the Criticism Upon the Political Account of Trinidad and Upon the Defence of the Crimes of Governor Picton, in the Anti-Jacobin Review, under the Title of the "Pictonian Prosecution," (London: John Morton, 1808), 69.

137 Millette, Society and Politics, 54–55, quoting from John Sanderson, An Appeal to the Imperial Parliament upon the Claims of the Ceded Colony of Trinidad, to Be Governed by a Legislature and Judicature, Founded on Principles Sanctioned by Colonial Precedents and Long Usage (London, 1812).

138 Hartman, Scenes of Subjection, 82.

139 Evans, Slave Wales, 97.

140 Young, Embodying Black Experience, 1.

141 Boaz, Banning Black Gods, 142–43.

142 Boaz, Banning Black Gods, 143.

143 Boaz, Banning Black Gods, 144.

144 Paton, "Punishment, Crime, and the Bodies of Slaves," 939, 941.

145 Savage, "Slave Poison/Slave Medicine," 161.

146 Patterson, Slavery and Social Death, 92. Shepherd and Beckles, Caribbean Slavery, 34.

147 Brown, Reaper's Garden, 140.

148 Fraser, History of Trinidad, 225; Millette, Society and Politics, 144–45; Laws of Trinidad and Tobago, Summary Offences, Chap. 11:02, #79, 99.

149   Millette, *Society and Politics*, 143; Fullarton, *Statement, Letters, and Documents*, 47.

150   Millette, *Society and Politics*, 143.

151   Meranze, *Laboratories of Virtue*, 317.

152   Young, *Embodying Black Experience*, 7.

153   Hartman, *Scenes of Subjection*, 46, 89.

154   Hartman, *Scenes of Subjection*, 82, 87. Emphasis added.

155   Hartman, *Scenes of Subjection*, 88.

156   Young, *Embodying Black Experience*, 17.

157   Hartman, *Scenes of Subjection*, 19. Young departs from this analysis in contending that "the black body does not need to die to become discursive. It is always discursive, even while fleshed. . . . It exists within the public imaginary, appears within public policy, dwells (or is confined) in public institutions" (Young, *Embodying Black Experience*, 18).

158   Brown, *Reaper's Garden*, 147.

159   Trinidad: Report of His Majesty's Commissioners of Legal Inquiry on the Colony of Trinidad. Great Britain. Commissioners of Legal Inquiry on the Colony of Trinidad. [London]: [publisher not identified], [1827], 175–76.

160   Millette, *Society and Politics*, 109.

161   De Verteuil, *History of Diego Martin*, 52.

162   Savage, "Slave Poison/Slave Medicine," 152.

163   McCallum, *Travels in Trinidad*, 193.

164   McCallum, *Travels in Trinidad*, 192.

165   McCallum, *Travels in Trinidad*, 192, 194.

166   CO 295/6, Records of the Colonial Office (CO), National Archives, Kew Gardens, UK.

167   Hartman, *Scenes of Subjection*, 20; Young, *Embodying Black Experience*, 194.

168   McCallum, *Travels in Trinidad*, 192–93.

169   McCallum, *Travels in Trinidad*, 192–93.

170   CO 295/6, Records of the Colonial Office (CO), National Archives, Kew Gardens, UK.

171   McCallum, *Travels in Trinidad*, 194.

172   De Verteuil, *History of Diego Martin*, 64.

173   De Verteuil, *History of Diego Martin*, 52.

174   De Verteuil, *History of Diego Martin*, 52.

175   De Verteuil, *History of Diego Martin*, 51.

176   De Verteuil, *History of Diego Martin*, 51.

177   CO 295/6, Records of the Colonial Office (CO), National Archives, Kew Gardens, UK.

178   McCallum, *Travels in Trinidad*, 195.

179   Millette, *Society and Politics*, 143.

180   Shepherd and Beckles, *Caribbean Slavery*, 586–87, 29.

181   Alexander, *Pedagogies of Crossing*, 315.

182 Alexander, *Pedagogies of Crossing*, 329.

183 Weheliye, *Habeas Viscus*, 118.

184 CO 295/6, Records of the Colonial Office (CO), National Archives, Kew Gardens, UK.

185 Kramer and Springer, *Malleus Maleficarum*, part 3, question 17.

186 Brown, *Reaper's Garden*, 142.

187 Brown, *Reaper's Garden*, 142; Paton. "Punishment, Crime, and the Bodies of Slaves," 932; Higginbotham, *In the Matter of Color*, 177, 181.

188 Greenberg, *Nat Turner*, 19.

189 Fett, *Working Cures*, 158; Daina Berry, "Nat Turner's Skull and My Student's Purse of Skin," *New York Times*, October 18, 2016.

190 Brown, *Reaper's Garden*, 130–31.

191 De Verteuil, *History of Diego Martin*, 44.

192 Epstein, "Politics of Colonial Sensation," 731.

193 Hartman, *Scenes of Subjection*, 7.

194 Hortense Spillers, "Mama's Baby, Papa's Maybe: An American Grammar Book," *Diacritics* 17, no. 2 (2006): 67.

195 Browne, *Dark Matters*, 42.

196 Spillers, "Mama's Baby," 67.

197 Jonathan Durrant and Michael D. Bailey, *Historical Dictionary of Witchcraft*, Historical Dictionaries of Religions, Philosophies, and Movements (Lanham, MD: Scarecrow Press, 2012), 23.

198 bell hooks, *Outlaw Culture: Resisting Representations* (New York: Routledge, 2008), 290.

199 Long, "Bodies in Time and the Healing of Spaces," 49.

200 Keynote Address, Dr. Charles H. Long. "Signification Forward: Towards a New Publication," *Ellipsis*. Colloquium convened by the African Atlantic Research Team of Michigan State University, *September* 30–October 1, 2013.

201 Stewart, *Black Women, Black Love*, 256; Alexander, *The Rattling of the Chains*, 238.

202 Alexander, *Pedagogies of Crossing*, 19.

203 Kit Candlin, "The Empire of Women: Transient Entrepreneurs in the Southern Caribbean, 1790–1820," *Journal of Imperial and Commonwealth History* 38, no. 3 (September 2010): 351.

204 Candlin, "Empire of Women," 352.

205 Candlin, "Empire of Women," 354–55.

206 Candlin, "Empire of Women," 358–59.

207 Candlin, "Empire of Women," 357–59, 367.

208 Kit Candlin and Cassandra Pybus, *Enterprising Women: Gender, Race, and Power in the Revolutionary Atlantic* (Athens: University of Georgia Press, 2015), 46.

209 Candlin and Pybus, *Enterprising Women*, 110.

210 McCallum, *Travels in Trinidad*, 148–49, 133.

211 Young, *Embodying Black Experience*, 188.

212 Young, *Embodying Black Experience*, 12, 188.

213 Weheliye, *Habeas Viscus*, 2, 57–59.

214 Frantz Fanon, *Black Skins, White Masks* (New York: Grove Press, 1994), 159, quoted in Weheliye, *Habeas Viscus*, 97.

215 Weheliye, *Habeas Viscus*, 168–69, 179.

216 James Baldwin, *Going to Meet the Man* (New York: Vintage International, 1995), 233, 235.

217 Patterson, *Slavery and Social Death*, 12.

218 Plato, *Laws: The Dialogues of Plato* (Aeterna Press, 2015), 55.

219 *A Select Library of Nicene and Post-Nicene Fathers of the Christian Church*, 2nd ser., vol. 3, ed. and trans. Philip Schaff and Henry Wace (Oxford: Christian Literature Company, 1892). Emphasis added.

220 *A Select Library of Nicene and Post-Nicene Fathers of the Christian Church*, vol. 4, ed. Philip Schaff (New York: Charles Scribner's Sons, 1909), chap. 3.

221 *The Ante-Nicene Fathers: Translations of the Writings of the Fathers Down to A.D. 325*, vol. 6, ed. Alexander Roberts and James Donaldson (New York: Charles Scribner's Son, 1899), chap. 3.

222 *A Select Library of Nicene and Post-Nicene Fathers of the Christian Church*, 2nd ser., vol. 1, ed. and trans. Philip Schaff and Henry Wace (Oxford: Christian Literature Company, 1890), chap. 3.

223 "Two Letters to Theodore after His Fall," in *A Select Library of Nicene and Post-Nicene Fathers of the Christian Church*, vol. 9, ed. Philip Schaff (New York: Charles Scribner's Sons, 1903), 87–116.

224 *The Ante-Nicene Fathers*, chap. 3.

225 Perry and Johnson, *Synonymous, Etymological, and Pronouncing English Dictionary*.

226 Mayer and Canot, *Captain Canot*, 111 Emphasis added.

227 Mayer and Canot, *Captain Canot*, 111. Emphasis added.

228 CO 295/6, Records of the Colonial Office (CO), National Archives, Kew Gardens, UK.

229 Savage, "Slave Poison/Slave Medicine," 154.

230 Farmer, *AIDS and Accusation*, 158.

231 Diana Paton, "Witchcraft, Poison, Law," 249. See also Lara Putnam, "Rites of Power and Rumors of Race: The Circulation of Supernatural Knowledge in the Greater Caribbean," in *Obeah and Other Powers: The Politics of Caribbean Religion and Healing*, ed. Diana Paton and Maarit Forde (Durham, NC: Duke University Press, 2012), 249.

232 CO 295/6, Records of the Colonial Office (CO), National Archives, Kew Gardens, UK.

233 CO 295/6, Records of the Colonial Office (CO), National Archives, Kew Gardens, UK.

234 CO 295/6, Records of the Colonial Office (CO), National Archives, Kew Gardens, UK.

235 CO 295/6, Records of the Colonial Office (CO), National Archives, Kew Gardens, UK.

236 McCallum, *Travels in Trinidad*, 194.

237 CO 295/6, Records of the Colonial Office (CO), National Archives, Kew Gardens, UK.

238 Noel, *Black Religion and the Imagination of Matter*, 117, 3.

239 Clarice Martin, "Hagar's Mirror: Black, Gendered, and Feared Bodies in Early Christian Apocrypha, Patristic, and Medieval Literature, 200–1300 CE," Colgate University Division of Arts and Humanities Colloquium, November 5, 2019.

240 Fullarton, *Statement, Letters, and Documents*, 187.

241 CO 295/6, Records of the Colonial Office (CO), National Archives, Kew Gardens, UK.

242 Paton, *No Bond but the Law*, 11.

243 Millette, *Society and Politics*, 140–41.

244 Calvin L. Warren, *Ontological Terror: Blackness, Nihilism, and Emancipation* (Durham, NC: Duke University Press, 2018).

245 Brown, *Reaper's Garden*, 149.

246 CO 101/44, Records of the Colonial Office (CO), National Archives, Kew Gardens, UK.

247 CO 101/44, Records of the Colonial Office (CO), National Archives, Kew Gardens, UK.

248 William Drysdale, "West Indian Witchcraft: Some Remarkable Superstitions of the Negroes," *New York Times*, April 11, 1886.

249 Dianne Stewart, "Weapons of the Spirit: Distilling the 'Science' of *Obeah* and Other Powers of Engagement," unpublished manuscript, June 20, 2021.

250 CO 101/44, Records of the Colonial Office (CO), National Archives, Kew Gardens, UK.

251 Higginbotham, *In the Matter of Color*, 56.

252 Higginbotham, *In the Matter of Color*, 57.

253 Wood, *Black Majority*, xiv.

254 Higginbotham, *In the Matter of Color*, 177, 181; Parrish, "Diasporic African Sources," 294.

255 Watson, *Slave Laws*, 70.

256 Shepherd and Beckles, *Caribbean Slavery*, 592.

257 Rose, *Documentary History*, 105.

258 Higginbotham, *In the Matter of Color*, 186.

259 Higginbotham, *In the Matter of Color*, 186.

260 Higginbotham, *In the Matter of Color*, 186.

261 Rose, *Documentary History*, 239–40.

262 Higginbotham, *In the Matter of Color*, 255, 257, 291.

263 Benson, *Peter Kalm's Travels*, 1: 204–11, quoted in Rose, *Documentary History*, 50.

264 Fett, *Working Cures*, 165.

265 "An Act Directing the Trial of Slaves Committing Capital Crimes," 1748, chap. 38, in Hening, *Statutes at Large*, 104–5, quoted in Fett, *Working Cures*, 165.

266 McCord, *Statutes at Large of South Carolina*, 7:423. See also Higginbotham, *In the Matter of Color*, 198; Fett, *Working Cures*, 166.

267 Fett, *Working Cures*, 162.

268 Fett, *Working Cures*, 142.

269 Fett, *Working Cures*, 143.

270 Brown, *Reaper's Garden*, 140.

271 Brown, *Reaper's Garden*, 131, 133, 134, 137, 139 140, 142, 147, 149.

272 Meranze, *Laboratories of Virtue*, 297.

273 Meranze, *Laboratories of Virtue*, 309.

274 Brown, *Reaper's Garden*, 149.

275 Fett, *Working Cures*, 157; Mark Juergensmeyer, *Terror in the Mind of God: The Global Rise of Religious Violence*, 3rd ed. (Berkeley: University of California Press, 2003), 186.

276 Wood, *Trinidad in Transition*, 242.

277 Paton, "Witchcraft, Poison, Law," 205.

278 Forde, "Moral Economy of Spiritual Work," 205.

279 Fett, *Working Cures*, 45.

280 Fett, *Working Cures*, 45.

281 Fett, *Working Cures*, 47.

282 Caldecott, *Church in the West Indies*, 122.

283 Hart, *Trinidad and Other West India Islands*, 108; Carmichael, *History of the West Indian Islands*, 382.

284 Brown, *Reaper's Garden*, 150–51.

285 Winston Arthur Lawson, *Religion and Race: African and European Roots in Conflict—A Jamaican Testament* (New York: Peter Lang, 1998), 45.

286 Goveia, *West Indian Slave Laws*, 47. This quote was originally published in L. Peytraud, *L'Esclavage aux Antilles Françaises avant 1789* (Paris, 1897).

287 John, *Plantation Slaves of Trinidad*, 206.

288 John, *Plantation Slaves of Trinidad*, 207.

289 Brown, *Reaper's Garden*, 210.

290 Bolland, *Struggles for Freedom*, 7.

291 Rivera, *Poetics of the Flesh*, 117.

292 Rivera, *Poetics of the Flesh*, 117–18.

293 Paton, "Witchcraft, Poison, Law," 261.

294 Brown, *Reaper's Garden*, 156.

295 Fields and Fields, *Racecraft*, 201–5.

296 Kelsey, *Racism and the Christian Understanding of Man*, 28.

297 Kelsey, *Racism and the Christian Understanding of Man*, 34.

298 Rivera, *Poetics of the Flesh*, 157.

299 CO 295/10 Records of the Colonial Office (CO), The National Archives, Kew Gardens, UK.

300 CO 295/10 Records of the Colonial Office (CO), The National Archives, Kew Gardens, UK.

301 Benton and Ford, "Island Despotism," 21–46.

302 In 1803, correspondence from Lord W. Hulladen to Colonel Fullarton (in England), CO 295/6 Trinidad 1803 Commissioners Vol. 3 Dec, 21, 1803; Benton and Ford, "Island Despotism," 30.

303 Fullarton, *Statement, Letters, and Documents*, March 31, 1803.

304 Fullarton, *Statement, Letters, and Documents*, March 31, 1803.

305 Epstein, "Politics of Colonial Sensation," 720; Fields and Fields, *Racecraft*, 205.

306 Fullarton, *Statement, Letters, and Documents*. Emphasis in original. Fraser, *History of Trinidad*, 165.

307 Epstein, "Politics of Colonial Sensation," 719.

308 Evans, *Slave Wales*, 103. "Picton had introduced the piquet to Trinidad—first to the barracks yard to discipline soldiers, and two years later to the prison chamber to torture slaves—and he had ordered Calderon's torture." Epstein, "Politics of Colonial Sensation," 722.

309 Evans, *Slave Wales*, 104.

310 Diana Paton, "Review of James Epstein, Scandal of Colonial Rule: Power and Subversion in the British Atlantic During the Age of Revolution," *Social History* 38, no. 4 (November 2013): 521.

311 Epstein, "Politics of Colonial Sensation," 725.

312 Evans, *Slave Wales*, 109.

313 Millette, *Society and Politics*, 199.

314 Benton and Ford, "Island Despotism," 33.

315 An Address by General Picton to the Council, April 14, 1803, Historical Society of Trinidad and Tobago, 4.

316 Legal Inquiry on the Colony of Trinidad, 551.

317 Accounts and Papers of the House of Commons, vol. 45 (Great Britain: Parliament, House of Commons, 1848) 132–33.

318 Obeyesekere, *Cannibal Talk*, 4.

Three. Obeah, Piety, and Poison in *The Slave Son*

1 Bridenbaugh and Bridenbaugh, *No Peace Beyond the Line*, 102.

2 De Verteuil, *Sylvester Devenish and the Irish*; Rodgers, "Irish in the Caribbean," 145–55; Hilary Beckles, "A 'Riotous and Unruly Lot,'" 503–22.

3 De Verteuil, *Sylvester Devenish and the Irish*, 4, 13.

4 Rhoda E. Howard-Hassmann, *State Food Crimes* (Cambridge: Cambridge University Press, 2016), 46; Unsigned review of *Uncle Tom's Cabin, or Life Among the Lowly*, by Harriet Beecher Stowe, *North American Review* (October 1853): 477, 480.

5 Bridenbaugh and Bridenbaugh, *No Peace Beyond the Line*, 102–3.

6 Anthony De Verteuil, *A History of Diego Martin* (Port of Spain: Paria, 1987), 57.

7 Millette, *Society and Politics*, 199.

8 Millette, *Society and Politics*, 134.

9 Winer, *Adolphus*, xlii. Diana Paton identifies the author as Mary Fanny Wilkins and an American, not Irish-born, resident of Trinidad; see Paton, *Cultural Politics*, 83. In the only other references I have found, which are few, she is identified as Marcella Fanny Wilkins.

10 Winer, *Adolphus*, xlii–xliii.

11 Winer, *Adolphus*, xliii–xliv.

12 Winer, *Adolphus*, xliv.

13 Winer, *Adolphus*, xliv.

14 The direct quote comes from her answer to a question about marital status on an application to the Royal Literary Fund. See Winer, *Adolphus*, xliv.

15 Wilkins, *Slave Son*, 14. There is some speculation, however, that Wilkins could have been Protestant, but this is inconclusive. See Winer, *Adolphus*, xiv.

16 An outstanding contemporary novel fictionizing Frederick Douglass's nineteenth-century tour in Ireland can be found in Colum McCann's *Trans Atlantic* (New York: Random House, 2013).

17 Winer, *Adolphus*, xiviii.

18 Winer, *Adolphus*, xxxviii.

19 Denise Kohn, Sarah Meer, and Emily Todd, eds., *Transatlantic Stowe: Harriet Beecher Stowe and European Culture* (Iowa City: University of Iowa Press, 2006).

20 Stowe, *Uncle Tom's Cabin*, ix, xiii.

21 Gossett, *Uncle Tom's Cabin and American Culture*, 211.

22 Gossett, *Uncle Tom's Cabin and American Culture*, 196.

23 Blackburn, *Making of New World Slavery*, 290.

24 Higginbotham, *In the Matter of Color*, 177.

25 Higginbotham, *In the Matter of Color*, 177.

26 Stowe, *Uncle Tom's Cabin*, 167, 117, 32.

27 Stowe, *Uncle Tom's Cabin*, 464, 432.

28 Stowe, *Uncle Tom's Cabin*, 9.

29 Levine, *Martin R. Delany*, 224.

30 Stowe, *Uncle Tom's Cabin*, 232.

31 Levine, *Martin R. Delany*, 235.

32 Levine, *Martin R. Delany*, 235.

33 Delany, *Blake; or The Huts of America*, xxiv–xxv.

34 Levine, *Martin R. Delany*, 237.

35 Baldwin, *Price of the Ticket*; Gates, *Annotated Uncle Tom's Cabin*, xxii.

36 Baldwin, *Price of the Ticket*, 28.

37 For the broad comparative context, see Michael A. Gomez, *Exchanging Our Country Marks: The Transformation of African Identities in the Colonial and Antebellum South* (Chapel Hill: University of North Carolina Press, 1998), 17–27; Gomez, *Reversing Sail*, 63–122.

38 Wilkins, *Slave Son*, 77, 80, 86.

39 Wilkins, *Slave Son*, 80.

40 Wilkins, *Slave Son*, 116.

41 Wilkins, *Slave Son*, 218.

42 Wilkins, *Slave Son*, 121; Paton, *Cultural Politics*, 83.

43 Winer, *Adolphus*, xivi.

44 Wilkins, *Slave Son*, 30.

45 Wilkins, *Slave Son*, 26–27.

46 Stowe, *Uncle Tom's Cabin*, 494.

47 Wilkins, *Slave Son*, 10.

48 Wilkins, *Slave Son*, 116.

49 Wilkins, *Slave Son*, 129–30.

50 Wilkins, *Slave Son*, 283–84.

51 Paton, *Cultural Politics*; Wilkins, *Slave Son*, 83.

52 Paton, *Cultural Politics*; Wilkins, *Slave Son*, 83.

53 Wilkins, *Slave Son*, 158–59.

54 Wilkins, *Slave Son*, 164.

55 Wilkins, *Slave Son*, 164.

56 Wilkins, *Slave Son*, 162–67.

57 Wilkins, *Slave Son*, 244.

58 Wilkins, *Slave Son*, 166.

59 Wilkins, *Slave Son*, 176.

60 https://collections.library.yale.edu/catalog/2026552.

61 Sir George Hill, Governor of Trinidad to Right Honourable E. G. Stanley, "Prize Africans," March 9, 1834, Historical Society of Trinidad and Tobago, Publication No. 253, 1.

62 Hill, "Prize Africans," 3–5.

63 Judy Raymond, *The Colour of Shadows: Images of Caribbean Slavery* (Pompano Beach, FL: Caribbean Studies Press, 2016), 2.

64 Handler and Bilby, *Enacting Power*, 35–36.

65 Wilkins, *Slave Son*, 240–41. Emphasis added.

66 Wilkins, *Slave Son*, 203.

67 Wilkins, *Slave Son*, 243.

68 Wilkins, *Slave Son*, 242.

69 Wilkins, *Slave Son*, 19.

70 Stowe, *Uncle Tom's Cabin*, xiv.

71 Stowe, *Uncle Tom's Cabin*, xiv.
72 Wilkins, *Slave Son*, 119.
73 Wilkins, *Slave Son*, 141.
74 Stowe, *Uncle Tom's Cabin*, 489.
75 Wilkins, *Slave Son*, 149.
76 Stowe, *Uncle Tom's Cabin*, 20.
77 Stowe, *Uncle Tom's Cabin*, 486.
78 Wilkins, *Slave Son*, 55.
79 Wilkins, *Slave Son*, 263.
80 Stowe, *Uncle Tom's Cabin*, 424.
81 Wilkins, *Slave Son*, 62.
82 Sklar, *Catharine Beecher*, 277, 325; Sklar, "Reconsidering Domesticity," 1252.
83 Wilkins, *Slave Son*, 18.
84 Yellin, "Doing It Herself," 87.
85 Yellin, "Doing It Herself," 103, 86, 96.
86 Yellin, "Doing It Herself," 101.
87 Allen, *Homelessness in American Literature*, 24.
88 Stowe, *Uncle Tom's Cabin*, 161.
89 Ammons, "Stowe's Dream of the Mother-Savior," 157.
90 Ammons, "Stowe's Dream of the Mother-Savior," 157–58.
91 Stowe, *Uncle Tom's Cabin*, 176.
92 Stowe, *Uncle Tom's Cabin*, 177.
93 Wilkins, *Slave Son*, 141.
94 Winer, *Adolphus*, 34.
95 Wilkins, *Slave Son*, 59.
96 Bush, *American Declarations*, 71.
97 Winer, *Adolphus*, xxxviii.
98 Ammons, "Stowe's Dream of the Mother-Savior," 172.
99 Wolf, "Masculinity," 12–13.
100 Baldwin, *Price of the Ticket*, 230; Stowe, *Uncle Tom's Cabin*, 32.
101 Baldwin, *Price of the Ticket*, 233.
102 Wolf, "Masculinity," 13.
103 Wilkins, *Slave Son*, 63.
104 See Stewart, *Obeah, Orisa, and Religious Identity*, chap. 4.
105 Stowe, *Uncle Tom's Cabin*, 37.
106 Stowe, *Uncle Tom's Cabin*, 267.
107 Wilkins, *Slave Son*, 132.
108 Wilkins, *Slave Son*, 155.
109 Stowe, *Uncle Tom's Cabin*, 314.
110 Gossett, *Uncle Tom's Cabin and American Culture*, 195.
111 Stowe, *Uncle Tom's Cabin*, x.
112 Stowe, *Uncle Tom's Cabin*, ix.

Four. Marked in the Genuine African Way

1 Colonial trial and appeal records of John Cooper's brother, Mah Nannie, describe Nannie's wife as "marked in the genuine African way," indicating that her facial markings represented her *nation* identity.

2 Fett, *Working Cures*, 3.

3 All citations throughout chapter 4 detailing the conviction and appeal of John Cooper's case are referenced from CO 295/61, Records of the Colonial Office (CO), National Archives, Kew Gardens, UK.

4 Paton, *Cultural Politics*, 162.

5 Paton, *Cultural Politics*, 162.

6 Stewart, *Three Eyes*, 198; Paton, "Witchcraft, Poison, Law, and Atlantic Slavery," 237.

7 Gundaker, *Signs of Diaspora/Diaspora of Signs*, 131; Mitchell-Kernan, "Signifying and Marking, 161–79.

8 Adderley, "*New Negroes from Africa*"; Schuler, "*Alas, Alas, Kongo*"; Warner-Lewis, *Trinidad Yoruba*; Warner-Lewis, *Guinea's Other Suns*; Anderson and Lovejoy, *Liberated Africans and the Abolition of the Slave Trade, 1807–1896*.

9 Anderson, "Diaspora," 101.

10 Schuler, "*Alas, Alas, Kongo*," 2. See also Wood, *Trinidad in Transition*.

11 Anderson, "Diaspora," 101. Emphasis added.

12 Anderson, "Diaspora," 101.

13 Schuler, "*Alas, Alas, Kongo*," 2.

14 De Verteuil, *Seven Slaves and Slavery*, 369; Trotman, "Yoruba and Orisha Worship," 1–17.

15 Trotman, "Yoruba and Orisha Worship," 6.

16 Trotman, "Yoruba and Orisha Worship," 10.

17 Cohen, "Orisha Journeys," 18.

18 Cohen, "Orisha Journeys," 18.

19 Northrup, "Becoming African," 17.

20 Adderley, "*New Negroes from Africa*," 183.

21 Adderley, "*New Negroes from Africa*," 184. Emphasis added.

22 Adderley, "*New Negroes from Africa*," 197.

23 Hart, *Trinidad and Other West India Islands*, 90–91.

24 De Verteuil, *Trinidad*, 34.

25 De Verteuil, *Trinidad*, 161–63.

26 Adderley, "*New Negroes from Africa*," 184.

27 Trotman, "Yoruba and Orisha Worship," 19.

28 Schuler, "*Alas, Alas, Kongo*," 9.

29 Schuler, "*Alas, Alas, Kongo*," 9.

30 Schuler, "*Alas, Alas, Kongo*," 9.

31 Schuler, "*Alas, Alas, Kongo*," 9.

32 Schuler, "Alas, Alas, Kongo," 9.

33 Schuler, "Alas, Alas, Kongo," 9.

34 Trotman, "Yoruba and Orisha Worship," 10. Emphasis added.

35 Charles Kingsley, At Last, 204; Adderley, "Orisha Worship and 'Jesus Time,'" 192.

36 Kingsley, At Last, 204.

37 Kingsley, At Last, 204.

38 Kingsley, At Last, 249.

39 Kingsley, At Last, 237–38.

40 Forde, "Moral Economy of Spiritual Work," 201; Handler and Bilby, Enacting Power, 19.

41 Handler and Bilby, Enacting Power, 123.

42 Schuler, "Alas, Alas, Kongo," 8.

43 Brereton, Race Relations in Colonial Trinidad, 155.

44 Laws of Trinidad and Tobago, Summary Offences Act, Chapter 11:02, #43, 24. Emphasis added.

45 Laws of Trinidad and Tobago, Summary Offences Act, Chapter 11:02, #44, 25.

46 Anthony, Historical Dictionary of Trinidad and Tobago, 65.

47 Originally quoted in the San Fernando Gazette and reprinted in Brereton, Race Relations in Colonial Trinidad, 156.

48 Brereton, Race Relations in Colonial Trinidad, 156–57.

49 Sankeralli, Crossroads, 95–96.

50 Sankeralli, Crossroads, 95–96.

51 Njoroge, Chocolate Surrealism, 143.

52 Anthony, Historical Dictionary of Trinidad and Tobago, 96.

53 Anthony, Historical Dictionary of Trinidad and Tobago, 97.

54 Anthony, Historical Dictionary of Trinidad and Tobago, 96.

55 See Cowley, Carnival, 84–103.

56 Trinidad and Tobago, Proclamation no. 8 of 1889.

57 Trinidad and Tobago, Proclamation no. 9 of 1889.

58 Cowley, Carnival, 132; Brereton, Race Relations in Colonial Trinidad, 170.

59 Trinidad and Tobago, Proclamation No. 9, 1889.

60 Laws of Trinidad and Tobago, Summary Offences, Chap. 11:02, #6, 13.

61 R. G. Hamilton, "Mr. Hamilton's Report on the Causes and Circumstances of the Disturbances in Connection with the Carnival in Trinidad, 13 June 1881," (Confidential Print, September 1881): CO 884/4/40, 3–18.

62 Originally published in the Port of Spain Gazette on February 6, 1889; reprinted in Cowley, Carnival, 116.

63 Brereton, Race Relations in Colonial Trinidad, 198; Collens, Guide to Trinidad, 38–40, 50, 52.

64 Cowley, Carnival, 21.

65 Cowley, Carnival, 21.

66 Cowley, *Carnival*, 128.

67 Schuler, "*Alas, Alas, Kongo*," 26, 89.

68 Adderley, "Orisha Worship and 'Jesus Time,'" 195.

69 Northrup, "Becoming African," 10; Clarke, *Description of the Manners*, 37.

70 Clarke, *Description of the Manners*, 20.

71 Clarke, *Description of the Manners*, 149.

72 Clarke, *Description of the Manners*, 150–52.

73 Clarke, *Description of the Manners*, 153.

74 Clarke, *Description of the Manners*, 153–54.

75 Clarke, *Description of the Manners*, 150.

76 Clarke, *Description of the Manners*, 151.

77 Clarke, *Description of the Manners*, 151–52.

78 Northrup, "Becoming African," 17. The phenomenon of diasporaed African nation formation will be discussed more extensively in volume II of the study.

79 Burnley, *Observations on the Present Condition*, 69.

80 Burnley, *Observations on the Present Condition*, 70.

81 Clarke, *Description of the Manners*, 99.

82 Clarke, *Description of the Manners*, 84–85. The physical neglect Africans endured and their resultant bodily deterioration during the extended middle passage deserves a distinct conceptualization. Thus, the term *vesseled Africans* seems most appropriate. Here I take creative license to coin the verb, *vesseled* from the noun "vessel."

83 Clarke, *Description of the Manners*, 83–84.

84 Clarke, *Description of the Manners*, 85.

85 Clarke, *Description of the Manners*, 84.

86 Colonial Correspondence, Thomas Murdoch to the Colonial Land and Immigration Office, April 19, 1848.

87 Colonial Correspondence, Dr. Robert McCrae to Colonial Land and Immigration Office, April 13, 1848.

88 Colonial Correspondence, Dr. Robert McCrae.

89 *Trinidad Chronicle*, January 16, 1872.

90 *Trinidad Chronicle*, January 16, 1872.

91 *Trinidad Chronicle*, January 16, 1872

92 De Verteuil, *Trinidad*, 163.

93 De Verteuil, *Trinidad*, 163.

94 Higman, *Slave Populations*, 265.

95 Sir Ralph James Woodford, "Proclamation Regarding New Medical Board, December 20, 1814, Historical Society of Trinidad and Tobago," Publication No. 554, 2.

96 Woodford, "Proclamation," 265.

97 *Laws of Trinidad and Tobago*, Vol. III (Port-of-Spain: Government Printing Office, 1903), 29.

98 De Verteuil, *Seven Slaves and Slavery*, 187.

99 Woodford, "Proclamation," 265.

100 Fett, *Working Cures*, 114–15.

101 Fett, *Working Cures*, 134.

102 Fett, *Working Cures*, 46.

103 Higman, *Slave Populations*, 269.

104 These advertisements were featured in the *Port of Spain Gazette*, February 27, 1886.

105 *Port of Spain Gazette*, February 27, 1886.

106 Gundaker, *Signs of Diaspora/Diaspora of Signs*, 135.

107 Jacklin, "British Colonial Healthcare," 115, 123.

108 Jacklin, "British Colonial Healthcare," 114.

109 Jacklin, "British Colonial Healthcare," 131.

110 Jacklin, "British Colonial Healthcare," 115.

111 Trotman, *Crime in Trinidad*, 132; Diana Paton, *No Bond but the Law: Punishment, Race, and Gender in Jamaican State Formation, 1780–1870* (Durham, NC: Duke University Press, 2004), 51.

112 Cohen, "Orisha Journeys," 27.

113 Jacklin, "British Colonial Healthcare," 132.

114 Emphasis mine. In the original it is written $10, not to be confused with US currency however.

115 Crosson, *Experiments with Power*, 22.

116 Forde, "Moral Economy of Spiritual Work," 202.

117 Port of Spain Police Court, November 25, 1871, CO 295/261, Records of the Colonial Office (CO), National Archives, Kew Gardens, UK.

118 Ivol Blackman, *Post Capitulation Trinidad (1797–1947): Aspects of the Laws, the Judicial System, and the Government* (Bloomington, IN: Xlibris, 2019), 211.

119 Blackman, *Post Capitulation Trinidad*, 211.

120 Blackman, *Post Capitulation Trinidad*, 209.

121 Brooks, *Troubling Confessions*, 9, 14, 17.

122 Brooks, *Troubling Confessions*, 23, 30, 49, 17.

123 Emphases added to the original document.

124 Brooks, *Troubling Confessions*, 40.

125 Brooks, *Troubling Confessions*, 43. Emphasis added.

126 Paton, *No Bond but the Law*, 140.

127 Paton, *No Bond but the Law*, 141–42.

128 Finkelman, *Slavery and the Law*, 209.

129 Paton, *Cultural Politics*, 205.

130 Correspondence from Governor James Robert Longden to The Right Honourable, The Earl of Kimberley, May 9, 1872, CO 295/261, Records of the Colonial Office (CO), National Archives, Kew Gardens, UK.

131 Anderson, *Colonial Office List*, 418–19.

132 *San Fernando Gazette*, March 11, 1882.
133 The Spiritual Baptists are another African heritage religious body in Trinidad with a long history of religious repression and struggle for religious freedom. Although many Spiritual Baptists also participate in or are devotees of the Orisa, it is still a distinct faith tradition. This discussion is taken up in more detail in volume II of this study.
134 Brown, *Reaper's Garden*, 146.
135 Emphasis added. It is interesting that in the 1868 ordinance, immediately following the prohibition of "articles used in the practice of obeah," there was a prohibition against "*Cruelty to Animals*," which prescribed "punishment for torturing, &c, any animal," including "negligen[t]" or "ill-usage" of animals or persons "be[ing] the means whereby any mischief, damage, or injury shall be done to any such animal" (Laws of Trinidad and Tobago, Summary Offences, Chap. 11:02, #43, 68, 85). Yet the courts never appended this crime to obeah with respect to John Cooper regarding the "cock and hen" in his possession.
136 R. Seheult, "On an Epidemic of Small-Pox of Irregular Type in Trinidad during 1902–4," *Epidemiological Section*, April 1908, 230.
137 Seheult, "On an Epidemic," 230; J. D. Rolleston, "The Smallpox Pandemic of 1870–1874," *Proceedings of the Royal Society of Medicine*, November 24, 1933, 190.
138 Putnam, "Rites of Power and Rumors of Race," in Paton and Forde, eds, *Obeah and Other Powers: The Politics of Caribbean Religion and Healing*, 245.
139 Drysdale, "West Indian Witchcraft: Some Remarkable Superstitions of the Negroes," *New York Times*, April 11, 1886.
140 Brereton, *Race Relations in Colonial Trinidad*, 155.
141 *The Trinidad Chronicle*, Wednesday, April 17, 1878.
142 M. Herskovits, personal communication, September 26, 1952.
143 Andrew Carr, "A Rada Community in Belmont," *Caribbean Quarterly* 3, no. 1 (1953): 36.
144 Carr, "Rada Community," 38.
145 Carr, "Rada Community," 39; Brereton, *Race Relations in Colonial Trinidad*, 153.
146 Carr, "Rada Community," 38, 48.
147 All citations recording the details of the conviction and appeal of Mah Nannie in chapter 4 are referenced from "Court of Appeal—October 19 before Chief Justice Sir John Gorrie and Mr. Justice Court: The Appeal of Mah-Nannie, the Belmont Obeah-Man, and Quashing of the Magistrate's Conviction," *Port of Spain Gazette*, Wednesday, October 20, 1886.
148 *Port of Spain Gazette*, October 23, 1886.
149 Paton, *Cultural Politics*, 190.
150 The following four newspaper reports are the primary sources referenced throughout the chapter of the unofficial responses of local Trinidadians to the affirmative Mah Nannie appeal: "Prosecution of an African for Obeah," *Port of Spain Gazette*, September 11, 1886; "The Appeal of Mah-Nannie, the

Belmont Obeah-Man, and Quashing of the Magistrate's Conviction," *Port of Spain Gazette*, October 20, 1886; "Mah-Nannie, the Obeah-Man," *Port of Spain Gazette*, October 23, 1886; and "Scotched but Not Killed," *The New Era*, October 25, 1886.

151 Laws of Trinidad and Tobago, Summary Offences Act, Chapter 11:02, #43, 24.

152 *Port of Spain Gazette*, Wednesday, October 20, 1886.

153 Fett, *Working Cures*, 76; Dianne M. Stewart, "Collecting on Their Investments, One Woman at a Time: Economic Partnerships among Caribbean Immigrant Women in the United States," *International Journal of African Renaissance Studies* 2, no. 1 (2007): 35–57; Aubrey Bonnett, *Institutional Adaptation of West Indian Immigrants to America: An Analysis of Rotating Credit Associations* (Washington, DC: University Press of America, 1981).

154 Brereton, *Race Relations in Colonial Trinidad*, 154.

155 Emphasis added.

156 Fett, *Working Cures*, 199.

157 Brereton, *Race Relations in Colonial Trinidad*, 155; MacDonald, *Trinidad and Tobago*, 36.

158 *Port of Spain Gazette*, February 27, 1886.

159 Laws of Trinidad and Tobago, Summary Offences, Chap.11:02, #31, 68.

160 Handler and Bilby, *Enacting Power*, 21.

161 Brereton, *Race Relations in Colonial Trinidad*, 155.

162 Laws of Trinidad and Tobago, Summary Offences, Chap.11:02, #74, 70, 98.

163 Emphasis added.

164 *Dictionary of National Biography*, Supplement, vol. 2, ed. Sidney Lee (New York: Macmillan, 1901), 332–33.

165 *The New Era*, October 25, 1886.

166 Paton, *Cultural Politics*, 163.

167 Paton, *Cultural Politics*, 162.

168 Kingsley, *At Last*, 252.

169 Brereton, *History of Modern Trinidad*, 134.

170 Trotman, *Crime in Trinidad*, 223.

171 *Trinidad Chronicle*, June 22, 1877.

172 As noted earlier, the actual amount awarded in Cooper's 1872 appeal was "fifty pounds sterling."

173 In "Indigenous Wisdom at Work in Jamaica: The Power of Kumina," in *Indigenous Peoples' Wisdom and Power: Affirming Our Knowledge Through Narratives*, ed. Julian Kunnie and Nomalungelo I. Godukka (London: Ashgate, 2006), 127–42. Dianne Stewart understands the period during which Africans were liberated from slave vessels and transported to temporary and/or permanent settlements along the West African coast and in the Americas/Caribbean for registration, processing, conscription and indentured labor assignments as the "extended Middle Passage."

174 *Trinidad Chronicle*, June 22, 1877.

Afterword

1   "The Appeal of Mah-Nannie, the Belmont Obeah-Man, and Quashing of the Magistrate's Conviction," *Port of Spain Gazette*, October 20, 1886. Emphasis added.

2   In "Indigenous Wisdom at Work in Jamaica: The Power of Kumina," in *Indigenous Peoples' Wisdom and Power: Affirming Our Knowledge Through Narratives*, ed. Julian Kunnie and Nomalungelo I. Godukka (London: Ashgate Publishers, 2006), 127–42. Dianne Stewart understands the period during which recaptive Africans were liberated from slave vessels and transported to temporary and/or permanent settlements along the West African coast and in the Americas/Caribbean for registration, processing, conscription, and indentured labor assignments as the "extended Middle Passage."

3   See Stewart's Afterword in *Obeah, Orisa, and Religious Identity*, 250–51.

4   Abdul-Aliy Muhammad, "Penn Museum Owes Reparations for Previously Holding Remains of a MOVE Bombing Victim," *Philadelphia Inquirer*, April 21, 2021.

5   Lorenzo Reyes, Trevor Hughes, and Mark Emmert, "Medical Examiner and Family-Commissioned Autopsy Agree: George Floyd's Death Was a Homicide," *USA Today*, June 1, 2020, https://www.usatoday.com/story/news/nation/2020/06/01/george-floyd-independent-autopsy-findings-released-monday/5307185002/.

6   https://www.penn.museum/sites/morton/. Accessed April 9, 2022.

7   https://www.classcentral.com/course/real-bones-forensic-anthropology-21165. Accessed August 2021. The full description of the first week reads: "This week introduces the field of forensic anthropology with a case study of the bombing of the MOVE community. Many human remains were burned and thus "personhood" was lost. This is more than just a forensic anthropology case study. There were very serious issues of social and political consequences of the events that led up to the assault on the Philadelphia neighborhood and their outcome in a confrontation with law enforcement agencies." Princeton University suspended the teaching of the course in Spring 2021.

8   Sonia Sanchez, *Collected Poems* (New York: Beacon Press, 2021), 163. Emphasis added.

9   Muhammad, "Penn Museum."

10 Fields and Fields, *Racecraft*, 147.

11 Rivera, *Poetics of the Flesh*, 4.

12 Liza Vandenboom, "The Faith of the Black Lives Matter Movement," Religion Unplugged, July 10, 2020, https://religionunplugged.com/news/2020/7/10/the-faith-of-the-black-lives-matter-movement.

13 Fields and Fields, *Racecraft*.

Bibliography

Adderley, Rosanne Marion. "New Negroes from Africa: Culture and Community among Liberated Africans in the Bahamas and Trinidad 1810–1900." Ph.D. diss., University of Pennsylvania, 1996.

Adderley, Rosanne Marion. *"New Negroes from Africa": Slave Trade Abolition and Free African Settlement in the Nineteenth-Century Caribbean*. Bloomington: Indiana University Press, 2006.

Adderley, Rosanne Marion. "Orisha Worship and 'Jesus Time': Rethinking African Religious Conversion in the Nineteenth-Century Caribbean." *Pennsylvania History*, Vol. 64, (Summer 1997): 183–206.

Alexander, Errol D. *The Rattling of the Chains*. Bloomington, IN: Xlibris, 2015.

Alexander, M. Jacqui. *Pedagogies of Crossing: Meditations on Feminism, Sexual Politics, Memory, and the Sacred*. Durham, NC: Duke University Press, 2005.

Allen, John. *Homelessness in American Literature: Romanticism, Realism and Testimony*. New York: Routledge, 2003.

Ammons, Elizabeth. "Stowe's Dream of the Mother-Savior: *Uncle Tom's Cabin* and American Women Writers before the 1920s." In *New Essays on Uncle Tom's Cabin*, edited by Eric J. Sundquist, 155–95. New York: Cambridge University Press, 1986.

Anderson, John. *The Colonial Office List for 1896: Comprising Historical and Statistical Information Respecting the Colonial Dependences of Great Britain*. London: Harrison and Sons, 1896.

Anderson, Richard. "The Diaspora of Sierra Leone's Liberated Africans: Enlistment, Forced Migration, and 'Liberation' at Freetown, 1808–1863." *African Economic History* 41 (2013): 101–38.

Anderson, Richard, and Henry B. Lovejoy, *Liberated Africans and the Abolition of the Slave Trade*. New York: University of Rochester Press, 2020.

Anthony, Michael. *Historical Dictionary of Trinidad and Tobago*. Lanham, MD: Scarecrow Press, 1997.

Asaka, Ikuko. *Tropical Freedom: Climate, Settler Colonialism and Black Excursion in the Age of Emancipation.* Durham, NC: Duke University Press, 2017.

Baldwin, James. *Going to Meet the Man.* New York: Vintage International, 1995.

Baldwin, James. *The Price of the Ticket: Collected Nonfiction, 1948–1985.* New York: St. Martin's Press, 1985.

Beckles, Hilary. "A 'Riotous and Unruly Lot': Irish Indentured Servants and Freemen in the English West Indies, 1644–1713." *William and Mary Quarterly* (3rd Series) 47, no. 4 (October 1990): 503–22.

Benjamin, Thomas. *The Atlantic World: Europeans, Africans, Indians and Their Shared History, 1400–1900.* New York: Cambridge University Press, 2009.

Benson, Adolf B., ed. *Peter Kalm's Travels in North America, Volume I.* New York: Wilson-Erickson, 1937.

Benton, Laura, and Lisa Ford. "Island Despotism: Trinidad, the British Imperial Constitution and Global Legal Order," *Journal of Imperial and Commonwealth History* 46, no. 1 (2018): 21–46.

Berry, Daina. "Nat Turner's Skull and My Student's Purse of Skin." *New York Times,* October 18, 2016.

Besson, Gerard, and Bridget Brereton. *The Book of Trinidad.* Port of Spain: Paria Publishing Company, 2010.

Bilby, Kenneth, and Jerome Handler. "Obeah: Healing and Protection in West Indian Slave Life." *Journal of Caribbean History* 38, no. 2 (2004): 153–83.

Blackburn, Robin. *The Making of New World Slavery: From the Baroque to the Modern 1492–1800.* London: Verso, 1997.

Blackman, Ivol. *Post Capitulation Trinidad (1797–1947): Aspects of the Laws, the Judicial System, and the Government.* Bloomington, IN: Xlibris, 2019.

Boaz, Danielle. *Banning Black Gods: African Diaspora Religions and the Law in the 21st Century.* University Park: Penn State University Press, 2021.

Bolland, O. Nigel. *Struggles for Freedom: Essays on Slavery, Colonialism, and Culture in the Caribbean and Central America.* Belize City: Angelus, 1997.

Botero, Juan. "Racial Question During Struggles of Independence in Latin America." In *Africana: The Encyclopedia of the African and African American Experience,* edited by Kwame Anthony Appiah and Henry Louis Gates Jr., 1582–84. New York: Basic Books, 1999.

Brereton, Bridget. *A History of Modern Trinidad 1783–1962.* Exeter, NH: Heinemann, 1981.

Brereton, Bridget. *An Introduction to the History of Trinidad and Tobago.* Oxford: Heinemann, 1996.

Brereton, Bridget. *Race Relations in Colonial Trinidad: 1870–1900.* Cambridge: Cambridge University Press, 1979.

Brereton, Bridget. "Trinidad, 1498–1962." In *Caribbean Atlas,* online project co-headed by Romain Cruse and Kevon Rhiney, 2013. http://www.caribbean-atlas.com/en/themes/waves-of-colonization-and-control-in-the-caribbean/waves-of-colonization/trinidad-1498-1962.html.

Bridenbaugh, Carl and Roberta Bridenbaugh. *No Peace Beyond the Line: The English in the Caribbean, 1624–1690*. New York: Oxford University Press, 1972.

Brooks, Peter. *Troubling Confessions: Speaking Guilt in Law and Literature*. Chicago: University of Chicago Press, 2000.

Brown, Vincent. *The Reaper's Garden: Death and Power in the Atlantic World of Slavery*. Cambridge, MA: Harvard University Press, 2008.

Brown, Vincent. *Tacky's Revolt: The Story of an Atlantic Slave*. Cambridge: Harvard University Press, 2020.

Browne, Simone. *Dark Matters: On the Surveillance of Blackness*. Durham, NC: Duke University Press, 2015.

"Brutality of Picton Past Examined: A Military Hero Has Been Branded a Cruel Colonial Governor, Remembered as a 'Beast' on the Slave Island He Ruled." *BBC News*, March 20, 2007.

Burnley, William Hardin. *Observations on the Present Condition of the Island of Trinidad and the Actual State of the Experiment of Negro Emancipation*. London: Longman, Brown, Green, and Longmans, 1842.

Bush, Harold K., Jr. *American Declarations: Rebellion and Repentance in American Cultural History*. Urbana: University of Illinois Press, 1999.

Butler, Kim. "Defining Diaspora, Refining a Discourse." *Diaspora: A Journal of Transnational Studies*, 2001, 193.

Caldecott, Alfred. *The Church in the West Indies*. London: Frank Cass, 1970.

Campbell, C. "The Opposition to Crown Colony Government in Trinidad before and after Emancipation, 1813–46." In *Trade, Government, and Society in Caribbean History, 1700–1920: Essays Presented to Douglas Hall*, edited by Barry W. Higman, 57–68. Kingston, Jamaica: Heinemann Educational Books Caribbean, 1983.

Campbell, Susan. "Carnival, Calypso, and Class Struggle in Nineteenth Century Trinidad," *History Workshop Journal* 26, no. 1 (1988): 1–27.

Candlin, Kit. "The Empire of Women: Transient Entrepreneurs in the Southern Caribbean, 1790–1820," *Journal of Imperial and Commonwealth History*, 38, no. 3 (September 2010): 351–72.

Candlin, Kit, and Cassandra Pybus. *Enterprising Women: Gender, Race, and Power in the Revolutionary Atlantic*. Athens: University of Georgia Press, 2015.

Carmichael, Gertrude. *The History of the West Indian Islands of Trinidad and Tobago: 1498–1900*. London: Alvin Redman, 1961.

Carr, Andrew. "A Rada Community in Belmont," *Caribbean Quarterly* 3, no. 1 (1953): 36–54.

Carradice, Phil. *Snapshots of Welsh History*. UK: Accent Press Ltd, 2011.

Clarke, Robert. *A Description of the Manners and Customs of the Liberated Africans; with Observations upon the Natural History of the Colony, and a Notice of the Native Tribes*. London: James Ridgway, 1843.

Clement, Dorothy Caye. "Shango: A Modernizing Cult in Trinidadian Society," Master's thesis, University of North Carolina, Chapel Hill, 1969.

Cohen, Peter. "Orisha Journeys: The Role of Travel in the Birth of Yoruba-Atlantic Religions." *Archives de Sciences Sociales des Religions* 117 (January–March 2002): 17–36.

Collens, J. H. *A Guide to Trinidad.* London: E. Stock, 1888.

Comaroff, Jean, and John Comaroff. "Africa Observed: Discourses of the Imperial Imagination." In *Perspectives on Africa: A Reader on Culture, History and Representation,* 2nd ed., edited by Roy Richard Grinker, Stephen C. Lubkemann, and Christopher Steiner, 31–43. Hoboken, NJ: Wiley-Blackwell, 2010.

Cowley, John. *Carnival, Canboulay and Calypso Traditions in the Making.* Cambridge: Cambridge University Press, 1996.

Crosson, J. Brent. *Experiments with Power: Obeah and the Remaking of Religion in Trinidad.* Chicago: The University of Chicago Press, 2020.

De Barros, Juanita, Audra Diptee, and David V. Trotman, eds., *Beyond Fragmentation: Perspectives on Caribbean History.* Princeton, NJ: Markus Wiener, 2006.

De Verteuil, Anthony. *A History of Diego Martin, 1784–1884.* Port of Spain: Paria Publishing Company, 1987.

De Verteuil, Anthony. *Seven Slaves and Slavery: Trinidad 1777–1838.* Port of Spain: Scrip-J, 1992.

De Verteuil, Anthony. *Sylvester Devenish and the Irish in Nineteenth Century Trinidad.* Port of Spain: Paria Publishing Company, 1986.

De Verteuil, Louis Antoine Aimé Gaston. *Trinidad: Its Geography, Natural Resources, Administration, Present Condition and Prospects.* London: Ward and Lock, 1858.

Delany, Martin R. *Blake, or The Huts of America.* Edited by Floyd J. Miller. Boston: Beacon Press, 1970.

Drysdale, William. "West Indian Witchcraft: Some Remarkable Superstitions of the Negroes." *New York Times,* April 11, 1886.

Durrant, Jonathan and Michael D. Bailey, *Historical Dictionary of Witchcraft,* Historical Dictionaries of Religions, Philosophies, and Movements. Lanham, MD: Scarecrow Press, 2012.

Eastman, Rudolph. *The Fight for Dignity and Cultural Space: African Survivals and Adaptations in Trinidad.* Bloomington: Xlibris, 2008.

Egalite for All: Toussaint Louverture and the Haitian Revolution, directed by Nolan Walker. Public Broadcasting Service, 2009. DVD.

Elder, Jacob Delwo. "Evolution of the Traditional Calypso of Trinidad and Tobago: A Socio-Historical Analysis of Song-Change." PhD diss., University of Pennsylvania, 1966.

Epstein, James. "Politics of Colonial Sensation: The Trial of Thomas Picton and the Cause of Louisa Calderon." *The American Historical Review* 112, no. 3 (June 2007): 712–41.

Evans, Chris. *Slave Wales: The Welch and Atlantic Slavery, 1660–1850.* Cardiff: University of Wales Press, 2010.

Farmer, Paul. *AIDS and Accusation: Haiti and the Geography of Blame.* Berkeley: University of California Press, 2006.

Fett, Sharla. *Working Cures: Healing, Health, and Power on Southern Slave Plantations.* Chapel Hill: University of North Carolina Press, 2002.

Fields, Karen E., and Barbara J. Fields. *Racecraft: The Soul of Inequality in American Life.* New York: Verso Books, 2012.

Finkelman, Paul. *Slavery and the Law.* Lanham, MD: Rowman & Littlefield, 1998.

Forde, Maarit. "The Moral Economy of Spiritual Work: Money and Rituals in Trinidad and Tobago." In *Obeah and Other Powers: The Politics of Caribbean Religion and Healing,* edited by Diana Paton and Maarit Forde, 198–219. Durham, NC: Duke University Press, 2012.

Fraser, Lionel Mordaunt. *History of Trinidad Vol. 1: 1781–1813.* London: Frank Cass, 1971.

Fullarton, Colonel William. *Statement, Letters, and Documents, Respecting the Affairs of Trinidad: Including a Reply to Colonel Picton's Address to the Council of That Island.* London: B. McMillan, 1804.

Gates, Henry Louis, Jr., ed. *The Annotated Uncle Tom's Cabin.* New York: W. W. Norton, 2005.

Gerbner, Katharine. "'They Call Me Obea': German Moravian Missionaries and Afro-Caribbean Religion in Jamaica, 1754–1760." *Atlantic Studies* 12, no. 2 (2015): 160–78.

Glazier, Stephen D. "Mourning in the Afro-Baptist Traditions." *Southern Quarterly* 23, no. 3 (1985): 142.

Goldwasser, Michelle Annette. "The Rainbow Madonna of Trinidad: A Study in the Dynamics of Belief in Trinidadian Religious Life." PhD diss., University of California, Los Angeles, 1996.

Gomez, Michael A. *Reversing Sail: A History of the African Diaspora.* 2nd ed. New York: Cambridge University Press, 2020.

Gossett, Thomas F. *Uncle Tom's Cabin and American Culture.* University Park, TX: Southern Methodist University Press, 1985.

Gould, Eliga H. "Zones of Law, Zones of Violence: The Legal Geography of the British Atlantic, circa 1772," *The William and Mary Quarterly* 60, no. 3 (July 2003): 471–510.

Goveia, E. V. *Slave Society in the British Leeward Islands at the End of the Eighteenth Century.* New Haven: Yale University Press, 1965.

Goveia, E. V. *The West Indian Slave Laws of the 18th Century.* London: Ginn, 1970.

Greenberg, Kenneth S. *Nat Turner: A Slave Rebellion in History and Memory.* New York: Oxford University Press, 2003.

Gundaker, Grey. *Signs of Diaspora/Diaspora of Signs: Literacies, Creolization, and Vernacular Practice in African America.* New York: Oxford University Press, 1998.

Hackshaw, John Milton. *The Baptist Denomination: A Concise History Commemorating One Hundred and Seventy-Five Years (1816–1991) of the Establishment of the "Company*

Villages" and the Baptist Faith in Trinidad and Tobago. Port of Spain: Amphy and Bashana Jackson Memorial Society, 1992.

Hall, David, and Robert Orsi, eds. *Lived Religion in America: Towards a History of Practice*. Princeton, NJ: Princeton University Press, 1997.

Hall, Stuart. "Negotiating Caribbean Identity." *New Left Review* 209, no. 1 (1995): 3–14.

Hamilton, R.G. "Mr. Hamilton's Report on the Causes and Circumstances of the Disturbances in Connection with the Carnival in Trinidad, 13 June 1881." (Confidential Print, September 1881): 3–18.

Handler, Jerome, and Kenneth Bilby. *Enacting Power: The Criminalization of Obeah in the Anglophone Caribbean*. Kingston: University of the West Indies Press, 2013.

Handler, Jerome, and Kenneth Bilby. "On the Early Use and Origin of the Term 'Obeah' in Barbados and the Anglophone Caribbean." *Slavery and Abolition* 22 (2001): 87–100.

Harris, Janée, Natoya Haskins, Janise Paker, and Aiesha Lee. "Womanist Theology and Relational Cultural Theory: Counseling Religious Black Women." *Journal of Creativity in Mental Health* (2021): 1–19.

Hart, Daniel. *Trinidad and Other West India Islands and Colonies*. Port of Spain: Chronicle, 1866.

Hartman, Saidiya V. *Scenes of Subjection: Terror, Slavery, and Self-Making in Nineteenth-Century America*. New York: Oxford University Press, 1997.

Hartman, Saidiya V. "Venus in Two Acts." *Small Axe* 26 (June 2008): 1–14.

Hickman, Jared. "Globalization and the Gods, or the Political Theology of 'Race'" *Early American Literature* 45, no. 1 (2010): 145–82.

Higginbotham, A. Leon, Jr. *In the Matter of Color: Race and the American Legal Process: The Colonial Period*. New York: Oxford University Press, 1978.

Higginbotham, Evelyn Brooks. "African-American Women's History and the Metalanguage of Race." *Signs* 7, no. 2 (Winter 1992): 251–74.

Higman, B. W. *Slave Populations in the British Caribbean, 1807–1834*. Baltimore: Johns Hopkins University Press, 1984.

hooks, bell. *Outlaw Culture: Resisting Representations*. New York: Routledge, 2008.

Howard, Roslyn. "Yoruba in the British Caribbean: A Comparative Perspective on Trinidad and the Bahamas." In *The Yoruba Diaspora in the Atlantic World*, edited by Toyin Falola and Matt D. Childs, 157–76. Bloomington: Indiana University Press, 2005.

Howard-Hassmann, Rhoda E. *State Food Crimes*. Cambridge: Cambridge University Press, 2016.

Howell, Donna Wyant, ed. *I Was a Slave: True Life Stories Told by Former American Slaves in the 1930s*. Washington, DC: American Legacy Books, 1995.

Hucks, Tracey E. "Perspectives in Lived History: Religion, Ethnography, and the Study of African Diasporic Religion," *Practical Matters: A Transdisciplinary Multimedia Journal of Religious Practices and Practical Theology* 3 (Spring 2010): 1–17.

Hucks, Tracey E. *Yoruba Traditions and African American Religious Nationalism*. Albuquerque: University of New Mexico Press, 2012.

Huggins, A. B. *The Saga of the Companies*. Port of Spain: Twinluck, 1978.

Jacklin, Laurie. "British Colonial Healthcare in a Post-Emancipation Plantation Society: Creolising Public Health and Medicine in Trinidad, to 1916." PhD diss., McMaster University, July 2009.

James, William. *The Varieties of Religious Experience*. 2nd ed. New York: Longmans, Green and Co., 1902.

JanMohamed, Abdul R. *The Death-Bound-Subject: Richard Wright's Archaeology of Death*. Durham, NC: Duke University Press, 2005.

John, A. Meredith. *The Plantation Slaves of Trinidad 1783–1816: A Mathematical and Demographic Enquiry*. New York: Cambridge University Press, 1988.

Juergensmeyer, Mark. *Terror in the Mind of God: The Global Rise of Religious Violence*, 3rd ed. Berkeley: University of California Press, 2003.

Kelsey, George D. *Racism and the Christian Understanding of Man*. New York: Scribner, 1965.

King, Debra Walker, ed., *Body Politics and the Fictional Double*. Bloomington: Indiana University Press, 2000.

Kingsley, Charles. *At Last: A Christmas in the West Indies*. New York: Harper Books, 1871.

Kohn, Denise, Sarah Meer, and Emily Todd, eds. *Transatlantic Stowe: Harriet Beecher Stowe and European Culture*. Iowa City: University of Iowa Press, 2006.

Kramer, Heinrich, and James Springer. *Malleus Maleficarum*. New York: Cosimo Classics, 2007.

Krech, Volkhard. "Relational Religion: Manifesto for a synthesis in the Study of Religion." *Religion* 50, no. 1 (2020): 97–105.

Kunnie, Julian, and Godukka, Nomalungelo I., eds. *Indigenous Peoples' Wisdom and Power: Affirming Our Knowledge Through Narratives*. London: Ashgate, 2006.

Lai, Walton Look. *The Chinese in the West Indies, 1806–1995: A Documentary History*. Kingston: University Press of the West Indies, 1998.

Laitinen, Maarit. *Marching to Zion: Creolisation in Spiritual Baptist Rituals and Cosmology*. Helsinki: Helsinki University Printing Press, 2002.

Laurence, K. O. "The Settlement of Free Negroes in Trinidad." *Caribbean Quarterly* 9, no. 1–2 (March/June 1963): 26–52.

Levine, Robert S., ed. *Martin R. Delany: A Documentary Reader*. Chapel Hill: University of North Carolina Press, 2003.

Liverpool, Hollis Urban. "Origins of Ritual and Customs in the Trinidad Carnival," *TDR* 42, no. 3 (Autumn 1998): 24–37.

Long, Charles H. "Bodies in Time and the Healing of Spaces: Religion, Temporalities, and Health." In *Faith, Health, and Healing in African American Life*, edited by Stephanie Y. Mitchem and Emilie M. Townes, 35–54. Westport, CT: Praeger, 2008.

Long, Charles H. *Significations: Signs, Symbols, and Images in the Interpretation of Religion*. Aurora, CO: Davies, 1995 (1986).

MacDonald, Scott. *Trinidad and Tobago: Democracy and Development in the Caribbean*. New York: Praeger, 1986.

Maparyan, Layli. *The Womanist Idea*. New York: Routledge, 2012.

Mayer, Brantz, and Theodore Canot. *Captain Canot, or Twenty Years of an African Slaver*. New York: D. Appleton, 1855.

McCallum, Pierre Franc. *Travels in Trinidad, During the Months of February, March, and April 1803, in a Series of Letters addressed to a Member of the Imperial Parliament of Great Britain* (1805). Montana: Kessinger Publishing, 2010.

McCord, David J., ed. *The Statutes at Large of South Carolina, Containing the Acts Relating to Charleston, Courts, Slaves, and Rivers*. Columbia, SC: A. S. Johnston, 1840.

Meranze, Michael. *Laboratories of Virtue: Punishment, Revolution, and Authority in Philadelphia, 1760–1835*. Chapel Hill: University of North Carolina Press, 2012.

Millette, James. *The Genesis of Crown Colony Government: Trinidad, 1783–1810*. Port of Spain: Moko Enterprises, 1970.

Millette, James. *Society and Politics in Colonial Trinidad*. London: Zed Books, 1985.

Mitchell, Dayo Nicole. "The Ambiguous Distinctions of Descent: Free People of Color and the Construction of Citizenship in Trinidad and Dominica, 1800–1838." PhD diss., University of Virginia, 2005.

Mitchell-Kernan, Claudia. "Signifying and Marking: Two Afro-American Speech Acts." In *Directions in Sociolinguistics: The Ethnography of Communication*, edited by John J. Gumperz and Dell H. Hymes, 161–79. New York: Holt, Rinehart and Winston, 1972.

Morgan, Jennifer. *Laboring Women: Reproduction and Gender in New World Slavery*. Philadelphia: University of Pennsylvania Press, 2004.

Muhammad, Abdul-Aliy. "Penn Museum Owes Reparations for Previously Holding Remains of a MOVE Bombing Victim." *Philadelphia Inquirer*, April 21, 2021.

Murray, Deryk. "Three Worships, and an Old Warlock and Many Lawless Forces: The Court Trial of an African Doctor who Practiced 'Obeah to cure' in early Nineteenth Century Jamaica." *Journal of Southern African Studies* 33, no. 4 (November 2007): 811–28.

Mwale, Jones. *Relationality in Theological Anthropology: An African Perspective*. Sunnyvale. CA: Lambert Academic Publishing, 2013.

Newson, Linda A. *Aboriginal and Spanish Colonial Trinidad: A Study in Culture Contact*. London: Academic Press, 1976.

Njoroge, Njoroge M. *Chocolate Surrealism: Music, Movement, Memory, and History in the Circum-Caribbean*. Oxford: University of Mississippi Press, 2016.

Noel, James A. *Black Religion and the Imagination of Matter in the Atlantic World*. New York: Palgrave Macmillan, 2009.

Northrup, David. "Becoming African: Identity Formation among Liberated Slaves in Nineteenth-Century Sierra Leone." *Slavery and Abolition* 27, no. 1 (2006): 1–21.

"Obeah Histories: Researching Obeah Prosecution for Religious Practice in the Caribbean." Accessed May 19, 2016. https://obeahhistories.org/polydore/.

Obeyesekere, Gananath. *Cannibal Talk: The Man-Eating Myth and Human Sacrifice in the South.* Berkeley: University of California Press, 2005.

Olúpònà, Jacob. *City of 201 Gods: Ilé-Ifẹ̀ in Time, Space, and the Imagination.* Berkeley: University of California Press, 2011.

Parrish, Susan Scott. "Diasporic African Sources of Enlightenment Knowledge." In *Science and Empire in the Atlantic World,* edited by James Delbourgo and Nicholas Dew, 281–310. New York: Routledge, 2008.

Paton, Diana. *The Cultural Politics of Obeah: Religion, Colonialism and Modernity in the Caribbean World.* Cambridge: Cambridge University Press, 2015.

Paton, Diana. *No Bond but the Law: Punishment, Race, and Gender in Jamaican State Formation, 1780–1870.* Durham, NC: Duke University Press, 2004.

Paton, Diana. "Punishment, Crime, and the Bodies of Slaves in Eighteenth-Century Jamaica." *Journal of Social History* 34, no. 4 (Summer 2001): 923–54.

Paton, Diana. "Witchcraft, Poison, Law, and Atlantic Slavery." *William and Mary Quarterly* 69, no. 2 (April 2012): 235–64.

Paton, Diana, and Maarit Forde, eds. *Obeah and Powers: The Politics of Caribbean Religion and Healing.* Durham, NC: Duke University Press, 2012.

Patterson, Orlando. *Slavery and Social Death.* Cambridge, MA: Harvard University Press, 1985.

Patterson, Tiffany, and Robin D. G. Kelley. "Unfinished Migrations: Reflections on the African Diaspora and the Making of the Modern World." *African Studies Review* 43, no. 1 (2000): 11–45.

Perry, William, and Samuel Johnson. *The Synonymous, Etymological, and Pronouncing English Dictionary: In which the Words are Deduced from Their Originals, Their Part of Speech Pointed Out, and Their Synonyms Collected, which are Occasionally Illustrated in Their Different Significations, by Examples from the Best Writers.* London: T. Gillet, 1805.

Pierce, Steven, and Anupama Rao. *Discipline and the Other Body: Correction, Corporeality, Colonialism.* Durham, NC: Duke University Press, 2006.

Plato. *Laws.* Translated by Benjamin Jowett. New York: Cosimo Classics, 2008.

Prior, Neil. "Battle of Waterloo: Thomas Picton, the Hero and Villain." *BBC News,* June 18, 2015.

Putnam, Lara. "Rites of Power and Rumors of Race: The Circulation of Supernatural Knowledge in the Greater Caribbean, 1890–1940." In *Obeah and Other Powers: The Politics of Caribbean Religion and Healing,* edited by Diana Paton and Maarit Forde, 243–267. Durham, NC: Duke University Press, 2012.

Rajkumar, Fiona. "The Chinese in the Caribbean during the Colonial Era." In *Caribbean Atlas,* online project co-headed by Romain Cruse and Kevon Rhiney, 2013. http://www.caribbean-atlas.com/en/themes/waves-of-colonization

-and-control-in-the-caribbean/daily-lives-of-caribbean-people-under
-colonialism/the-chinese-in-the-caribbean-during-the-colonial-era.html.

Raymond, Judy. *The Colour of Shadows: Images of Caribbean Slavery.* Pompano Beach, FL: Caribbean Studies Press, 2016.

Reyes, Lorenzo, Trevor Hughes, and Mark Emmert. "Medical Examiner and Family-Commissioned Autopsy Agree: George Floyd's Death Was a Homicide." *USA Today*, June 1, 2020.

Rivera, Mayra. *Poetics of the Flesh.* Durham, NC: Duke University Press, 2015.

Roberts, Alexander, and James Donaldson, eds. *The Ante-Nicene Fathers: Translations of the Writings of the Fathers Down to A.D. 325*, Vol. 4. Buffalo, NY: Christian Literature Publishing Company, 1885–96.

Robinson, Lisa Clayton. "Trinidad and Tobago." In *Africana: The Encyclopedia of the African and African American Experience*, edited by Kwame Anthony Appiah and Henry Louis Gates Jr., 1881–85. New York: Basic Books, 1999.

Rodgers, Nini. "The Irish in the Caribbean, 1641–1837: An Overview." *Irish Migration Studies in Latin America* 5, no. 3 (November 2007): 145–55.

Rolleston, J.D. "The Smallpox Pandemic of 1870–1874." *Proceedings of the Royal Society of Medicine* (November 24, 1933): 177–92.

Rose, Willie Lee, ed. *A Documentary History of Slavery in North America.* New York: Oxford University Press, 1976.

Rotter, Andrew J., *Empires of the Senses: Bodily Encounters in Imperial India and the Philippines.* Oxford: Oxford University Press, 2019.

Sanchez, Sonia. *Collected Poems.* New York: Beacon Press, 2021.

Sankeralli, Burton, ed. *At the Crossroads: African Caribbean Religion and Christianity.* Port of Spain: Caribbean Conference of Churches, 1995.

Savage, John. "Slave Poison/Slave Medicine: The Persistence of Obeah in Early Nineteenth-Century Martinique." In *Obeah and Other Powers: The Politics of Caribbean Religion and Healing*, edited by Diana Paton and Maarit Forde, 149–71. Durham, NC: Duke University Press, 2012.

Schaff, Philip, ed. "Two Letters to Theodore after His Fall." In *A Select Library of Nicene and Post-Nicene Fathers of the Christian Church*, New York: Charles Scribner's Sons, 1903.

Schaff, Philip, and Henry Wace, eds. *A Select Library of Nicene and Post-Nicene Fathers of the Christian Church*, 2nd ser., Vol. 1, Vol. 3, Vol. 4. Translated by Philip Schaff. Oxford: Christian Literature Company, 1890.

Schuler, Monica. *"Alas, Alas, Kongo": A Social History of Indentured African Immigration into Jamaica, 1841–1865.* Baltimore: Johns Hopkins University Press, 1980.

Seheult, Roger. "On an Epidemic of Small-pox of Irregular Type in Trinidad during 1902–04," *Proceedings of the Royal Society of Medicine* 1 (1908): 229–302.

Shepherd, Verene, and Hilary Beckles. *Caribbean Slavery in the Atlantic World: A Student Reader.* Kingston: Ian Randle, 1999.

Simpson, George Eaton. *Caribbean Papers*. Cuernavaca: Centro Intercultural de Documentacion, 1970.

Singh, Sherry-Ann. "The Experience of Indian Indenture in Trinidad: Arrival and Settlement." In *Caribbean Atlas*, online project co-headed by Romain Cruse and Kevon Rhiney, 2013. http://www.caribbean-atlas.com/en/themes/waves -of-colonization-and-control-in-the-caribbean/waves-of-colonization/the -experience-of-indian-indenture-in-trinidad-arrival-and-settlement.html.

Sklar, Kathryn Kish. *Catharine Beecher: A Study in American Domesticity*. New Haven, CT: Yale University Press, 1973.

Sklar, Kathryn Kish. "Reconsidering Domesticity through the Lens of Empire and Settler Society in North America." *American Historical Review* 124, no. 4 (2019): 1249–66.

Spillers, Hortense. "Mama's Baby, Papa's Maybe: An American Grammar Book," *Diacritics* 17, no. 2 (2006): 64–81.

Stewart, Dianne M. *Black Women, Black Love: America's War on African American Marriage*. New York: Seal Press, 2020.

Stewart, Dianne M. "Indigenous Wisdom at Work in Jamaica: The Power of Kumina." In *Indigenous Peoples' Wisdom and Power: Affirming Our Knowledge Through Narratives*, edited by Julian Kunnie and Nomalungelo I. Godukka, 127–42. London: Ashgate, 2006.

Stewart, Dianne M. *Obeah, Orisa, and Religious Identity in Trinidad: Africana Nations and the Power of Black Sacred Imagination—Orisa*. Vol. 2. Durham, NC: Duke University Press, 2022.

Stewart, Dianne M. *Three Eyes for the Journey: African Dimensions of the Jamaican Religious Experience*. New York: Oxford University Press, 2005.

Stewart, Dianne M. "Weapons of the Spirit: Distilling the 'Science' of Obeah and Other Powers of Engagement," Unpublished manuscript, June 20, 2021.

Stewart Diakite, Dianne M., and Tracey E. Hucks. "Africana Religious Studies: Toward a Transdisciplinary Agenda in an Emerging Field." *Journal of Africana Religions* 1, no. 1 (2013): 28–77.

Stinchcombe, Arthur L. *Sugar Island Slavery in the Age of Enlightenment: The Political Economy of the Caribbean World*. Princeton, NJ: Princeton University Press, 1995.

Stowe, Harriet Beecher. *Uncle Tom's Cabin*. New York: Everyman's Library, 1994.

Tandberg, Hakon N. *Relational Religion: Fires as Confidants in Parsi Zoroastrianism*. Goettingen, Germany: Vandenhoeck & Ruprecht, 2019.

Trotman, David. *Crime in Trinidad: Conflict and Control in a Plantation Society, 1838– 1900*. Knoxville: University of Tennessee Press, 1986.

Trotman, David. "The Yoruba and Orisha Worship in Trinidad and British Guinea: 1838–1870." *African Studies Review* 19, no. 2 (September 1976): 1–17.

Tweed, Thomas. *Crossing and Dwelling: A Theory of Religion*. Cambridge, MA: Harvard University Press, 2006.

Vansina, Jan. *Paths in the Rainforests: Toward a History of Political Tradition in Equatorial Africa*. Madison: University of Wisconsin Press, 1990.

Warner-Lewis, Maureen. *Guinea's Other Suns: The African Dynamic in Trinidad Culture*. Fitchburg, MA: Majority Press, 1991.

Warner-Lewis, Maureen. *Trinidad Yoruba: From Mother-Tongue to Memory*. Tuscaloosa: University of Alabama Press, 2009.

Warner-Lewis, Maureen. *Yoruba Songs of Trinidad*. London: Karnak House, 1994.

Warren, Calvin L. *Ontological Terror: Blackness, Nihilism, and Emancipation*. Durham, NC: Duke University Press, 2018.

Watson, Alan. *Slave Laws in the Americas*. Athens: University of Georgia Press, 1990.

Watson, Tim. *Caribbean Culture and British Fiction in the Atlantic World, 1780–1870*. Cambridge: Cambridge University Press, 2008.

Watson, Tim. "Obeah and Empire: 'Humanitarian Intervention' and Religious Conversion in the Anglophone Caribbean, 1760–1800." John Carter Brown Library, Providence, RI, 2001.

Weheliye, Alexander G. *Habeas Viscus: Racializing Assemblages, Biopolitics, and Black Feminist Theories of the Human*. Durham, NC: Duke University Press, 2014.

Wilkins, Mrs. William Noy [Marcella Fanny Noy Wilkins]. *The Slave Son*. London: Chapman and Hall, 1854.

Williams, Cynric R. *Hamel, the Obeah Man*. Canada: Broadview Press, 2010.

Williams, Eric, ed. *Documents on British West Indian History, 1807–1833: Select Documents from the Public Record Office, London, England, relating to the Colonies of Barbados, British Guiana, Jamaica and Trinidad*. Port of Spain: Trinidad Publishing Company, 1952.

Williams, Eric, ed. *Historical Society of Trinidad and Tobago: Documents on British West Indian History, 1807–1833*. Port of Spain: Trinidad Publishing Company, 1952.

Williams, Eric. *History of the People of Trinidad and Tobago*. New York: Praeger, 1964.

Winer, Lisa, ed. *Adolphus, A Tale (Anonymous) and The Slave Son (Mrs. William Noy Wilkins)*. Kingston: University of the West Indies Press, 2003.

Wolf, Cynthia Griffin. "'Masculinity' in Uncle Tom's Cabin." In *Speaking the Other Self: American Women Writers*, edited by Jeanne Campbell Reesman, 3–26. Athens: University of Georgia Press, 1997.

Wood, Donald. *Trinidad in Transition: The Years after Slavery*. New York: Oxford University Press, 1986.

Wood, Peter H. *Black Majority: Negroes in Colonial South Carolina from 1670 through the Stono Rebellion*. New York: W. W. Norton, 1974.

Yellin, Jean Fagan. "Doing It Herself: Uncle Tom's Cabin and Woman's Role in the Slavery Crisis." In *New Essays on Uncle Tom's Cabin*, edited by Eric J. Sundquist, 85–106. New York: Cambridge University Press, 1986.

Young, Harvey. *Embodying Black Experience: Stillness, Critical Memory, and the Black Body*. Ann Arbor: University of Michigan Press, 2010.

Index

(obeah) and, 94–97, 119–20; promotion in post-emancipation Trinidad, 50–51; in *Uncle Tom's Cabin*, 117–18, 120–21. *See also* Living Gospel

Christian-Obea (obeah), 97; white man's Obiah, 123

Chrysostom, John of, 85

City of God (Augustine), 85

Clarke, Robert, 154–56

class structure in Trinidad, 63–64; Irish immigrants and, 106–7

Cobham, Rhonda, 108

Code Noir of 1789 (France), 96, 112–13

Cohen, Peter, 145

Collins, J. H., 153

colonialcraft, 53, 98

colonial cult of obeah fixation, xi, 54, 98, 179, 205

colonialism: Africana religious practices under, 150–54; British North American colonies, legal violence in, 90–94; contesting epistemologies of black bodies and, 87–94; Cooper case and history of, 168–81; erotic epistemology of black body and, 72–84; folk medicine and, 58–61, 89–90; free Africans and, 143–48; growth of Trinidadian slavery and, 23–28; inter-society pluralism in Trinidad and, 14–16, 25–28, 33–41; law on slavery in, 28–32; Obeah/obeah fixation and, xi, 2–3, 9, 52–55, 97–102, 195–202; Orisa and, 2–3; policing of slavery under, 55–61; Polydore trial and, 3–5; postslavery legislation on Obeah and, 148–54; promotion of Christianity and, 50–51; Spanish colonial rule in Trinidad, 16–23; tribal and nation typology and, 49–51; Trinidad diasporization and, 8–9; in Trinidadian literature, 104–40

colonial pornocracy, 81; pornotroping, 80. *See also* Spillers, Hortense

colonialscape, 55, 76

Company Villages of African American Baptists, 8–9, 43–44, 50; "Merikans," 43

confession, in colonial law, 170–71

Cooper, John (Hou Quervee), trial and acquittal of, 3, 10–12, 47–48, 103, 141–43, 150, 154, 164–81, 199–202, 203–4

Corps of Colonial Marines, 43–44

Council of Advice (Trinidad), 107

Court, Henry, 169, 187

Crown Colony system, in Trinidad, 34–35

Dâaga Rebellion, 70, 148, 223n128

David, Peter, 189

death-bound-subjects, xi, 15, 16, 212n14

Delany, Martin, 113–17

de Robles, Cristobal, 57, 70–71

De Verteuil, Louis Antoine, 78, 146, 159

diaspora*ed*, 8, 11, 206, 212n24, 235n78

diaspora studies: Caribbeaning diaspora and, 5–7; Obeah and, 15–16; orthography and terminology, 212n24; Trinidad diasporization phases, 7–12

"Diasporic African Sources of Enlightenment Knowledge" (Parrish), 58

dismemberment, colonial legal violence and practice of, 76–84, 89–90; in British North America, 90–94; Irish immigrant support for, 107; symbolism of, 111–17

document of legal violence: punishment records, 71–72, 74, 76–77, 89–90; remuneration for executions, 91–92

domestic feminism, literature on slavery and, 132–39

Douglass, Frederick, 108–10, 113–15, 117

Ears, used in punishment, 14, 71, 73–74, 79–80, 88–89, 91–93; (Stowe) severed black ear, 111–12

economic conditions in Trinidad, 63–64

Elliott, Ebenezer, 3

El Segundo Encuentro Internacional Yoruba, ix

entrapment of Obeah offenders, 183–86, 191

epidermalization: of blackness, 4, 72; of religion, 4–5. *See also* Young, Harvey

Epstein, James, 101

erotic epistemology of black bodies, legal violence against Trinidad slaves and, 72–84

European travel literature, free Africans in Trinidad discussed in, 147–48

Eusebius, 85

Evans, Chris, 68

Parrish, Susan Scott, 58, 60
paternity, in literature on slavery, 135–39
Paton, Diana: on colonial Obeah, 97–98,
142–43, 183–84, 198–202; on colonial
power relations, 67; on legal violence,
71, 89, 99, 101, 171, 176
Patterson, Orlando, 84
Patterson, Tiffany Ruby, 6–7
Payne, William, 73–74
peddler culture in Caribbean diaspora,
86–87
performativity of slave punishment,
83–84, 88–89, 91–94
Philippe, Jean Baptiste, 39
Phills, Sam, 2
Picton, Thomas (Sir): children of, 82;
criminal charges against, 98–102; criticism of, 65–66, 71–72; Crown Colony
system under, 34–36; intervention in
legal processes by, 87–88; Irish immigrants and, 107; oath of allegiance
imposed by, 65–66; personality of, 65;
punitive technologies used by, 73–74,
80–84, 90; slavery in Trinidad under,
29–30, 61–72; Smith as mistress of,
82–83; suppression of Obeah under,
54–58, 61–72, 95–97; torture practices
under, 78–80; as Trinidad governor, 10,
13–14, 41, 61–66, 122
Pierre, Philip, 169
Pierre Francois, trial and execution of,
76–77, 80–81
plantation estates: free colored alliance
with, 43–44; Trinidadian slavery and,
25–28, 33–41; in Uncle Tom's Cabin, 113;
women as owners of, 124–25
plant-based epistemology, Obeah linked
to, 15–16, 58–61, 89–90
Plato, 85
poisoning by slaves, colonial fear of,
67–72, 89–90, 92–94; in Wilkins's Slave
Son, 121–28
Polydore (Old Polydore), trial of, 3–5
Port of Spain Gazette, 161, 186, 196–98
power: obeah as display of, 52–55; punishment for slaves as display of, 67, 75,
78–84
prisons in Trinidad, conditions in, 64–65

Protestantism: black bodies and, 111–12;
in Uncle Tom's Cabin, 115–17
Protestant religion, religious education
for slaves and, 96–97
punishment of slaves: in British North
American colonies, 90–94; colonial
power relations and, 67; documentation of, 71–72, 74, 76–77, 89–90; erotic
epistemology of black body and, 72–84;
Irish immigrant support for, 107; in
literature on slavery, 129–31; for Obeah,
171; as performance, 83–84, 88–89,
91–94; public displays of bodies and
heads, 14, 71, 78, 88, 90, 93–94, 205;
records of, 71–72; souvenir penalties,
80–84

race: ambiguity in Trinidad of, 25–28,
32–41; black bodies in context of,
97–102; black masculinity and, 135–39;
flogging penalties and, 171; in literature
on slavery, 117–20; obeah representation and, 53–55; race pandemic in US
and, 204–7; theology of, 5
racecraft, xi, 5, 207
"A Rada Community in Trinidad" (Carr),
183
Rada tradition, emergence in Trinidad of,
49–51, 173–74, 177–78, 182–87
Rajkumar, Fiona, 42
rational management, colonial repression
of obeah framed as, 53–55
"Registry of Personal Slaves," 31
"Registry of Plantation Slaves," 31
religious identity: Asian immigration in
Caribbean and, 43–47; black bodies
and, 2, 4–5; colonial repression in
Trinidad of, 9. See also Africana reli-
gious studies
Return of Criminal Causes (1824), 102
A Review of the Colonial Slave Registrations
Acts in a Report of a Committee of the Board
of Directors of the African Institution,
26–27
Rimmer, Mary, 108
Rivera, Mayra, 53–54, 97–98
Robinson, Lisa Clayton, 32–33
Robinson, William, 151

Theodoret, 85

Thisbe, trial and execution of, 78–81, 86

Thomas, J. J., 49

Three Eyes for the Journey: African Dimensions of the Jamaican Religious Experience (Stewart), 55

torture, colonial legal violence and use of, 13–4, 53–54, 61, 62, 69, 71, 76–84, 89–91, 98–101; in British North American colonies, 90–94; Irish immigrant support for, 107; psycho-torture, 54; torture cells, 78

Travels in Trinidad during the Months of February, March, and April, 1803 (McCallum), 64–65

Treatise on Domestic Economy for the Use of Young Ladies at Home and at School (Beecher and Stowe), 132

Trinidad: African religion in literature of, 104–40; anti-obeah laws in, 55–61, 67–72; British seizure of, 33–34; Caribbean diaspora and, 5–12; Chinese immigrants in, 41–42; Christian-Obeah rivalry in, 94–97; colonial law in, 28–32; early African presence in, 19–23; folk medicine in, 59–61; free Africans in, 143–48; growth of slavery in, 23–28, 214n52; healing and healthcare in postslavery era, 156–64; illegal slave smuggling in, 30–32; Indian immigration into, 43–47; inter-society pluralism in, 14–16, 41–47; mixed-race population in, 25–28, 32–41; Obeah traditions in, 5; pan-colonial history in, 5; postemancipation African Americans in, 47–51, 213n35; post-Picton Obeah in, 97–102; postslavery legislation on Obeah in, 148–54; racial ambiguity in, 25–28, 32–41; Shango tradition in, ix–x; slave revolt in, 13–14, 37–41, 223n127; slave trials in, 67; Spanish colonial rule in, 16–23

Trinidad Association for the Propagation of the Gospel, 50–51

Trinidad Chronicle, 141–43, 147, 159, 174, 200

Trinidad Guardian newspaper, 186

Trinidad Infirmary and Marine Hospital, 59–60

Trinidad Medical Board, 160

Trotman, David, 49–51, 60–61, 147

Troubling Confessions: Speaking Guilt in Law and Literature (Brooks), 170

Tulsa Black massacre, 204–5

Turner, Nat, 80

The Uncivilized Nations of the World (Wood), 189–90

Uncle Tom's Cabin, or, Life among the Lowly (Stowe): black bodies in, 111–17, 128–31; children in, 137–39; Christianity in, 117–18, 120–21; critical analysis of, 113–17; domestic feminism and, 132–39; evocative potential of, 139–40; publication of, 10, 104, 106, 108; sanctioned violence in, 113; Wilkins's *Slave Son* compared with, 117–20

"Unfinished Migrations: Reflections on the African Diaspora and the Making of the Modern World" (Patterson and Kelley), 6–7

United States: racial violence in, 204–7; southern slave codes in, 112–13

University of Pennsylvania, 205–6

Ussher, Herbert Taylor, 182

unslaving religion, 199

Valentine, trial and execution of, 92

Vesey, Denmark, 204–5

vesseled Africans, 157, 235n82

Voyages: The Transatlantic Slave Trade Database, 25

Walker, Jayland, 205

Warner, Aucher, 188–98, 203

Warner, Charles William, 169, 178

Warner-Lewis, Maureen, 143

Warren, Calvin L., 89

Waterloo, John, 169, 172–73

"Ways and Customs of Trinidad" (Gray), 177

Weheliye, Alexander G., 84

West Indian Scenery, with Illustrations of Negro Character, the Process of Making Sugar, &c. from Sketches Taken to, and Residence of Seven Years in, the Island of Trinidad (Bridgens), 125–26

West India Regiment, 7, 9–10, 44, 70

Whe (Chinese numbers game), 184